Off-Centre

Cultural Studies Birmingham Series

This new series will publish work by postgraduates, undergraduates, staff members and associates of the Department of Cultural Studies at the University of Birmingham. The new department seeks to develop the interests of the former Centre for Contemporary Cultural Studies, which earned an international reputation for its empirical research and innovatory theory. It also hopes to develop research activities into the new concerns and areas through making connections with other groups and organizations.

Off-Centre

Feminism and cultural studies

Edited by

Sarah Franklin, Celia Lury & Jackie Stacey

Lancaster University

HarperCollins *Academic*
An imprint of HarperCollins *Publishers*

Published by **HarperCollins***Academic*
77-85 Fulham Palace Road,
Hammersmith, London W6 8JB UK

10 East 53rd Street,
New York, NY 10022
USA

First published in 1991

British Library Cataloguing in Publication Data

Off-centre: feminism and cultural studies.
  1. Great Britain. Feminism
  I. Stacey, J. II. Franklin, S. III. Lury, C. (Celia)
  305.42

  ISBN 0-04-445666-2
  ISBN 0-04-445667-0 pbk

Library of Congress Cataloging-in-Publication Data

Off-centre: feminism and cultural studies/edited by Sarah Franklin,
    Celia Lury, and Jackie Stacey.
        p.   cm.
    Includes bibliographic references and index.
    ISBN 0-04-445666-2. — ISBN 0-04-445667-0 (pbk.)
    1. Feminist theory. 2. Culture. I. Franklin, Sarah.
    II. Lury, Celia. III. Stacey, Jackie.
HQ1190.034 1991
305.42'01 — dc20
                                                90–27327
                                                    CIP

Typeset in 10 on 12 Bembo by Falcon Typographic Art Ltd.,
Edinburgh & London
and printed in Great Britain at the University Press, Cambridge

Contents

List of Plates

(between pages 178 and 179)

Preface

Off-Centre is the product of both a particular history and a particular tradition of work in cultural studies at Birmingham. Like its predecessor, *Women Take Issue*, this book has its roots in the collectively organized subgroups in which much of the work of the Centre for Contemporary Cultural Studies, now the Department of Cultural Studies, has continued to take place. This tradition of collective work, which has survived despite the pressures imposed on higher education, such as cuts in student grants and increasing work loads for staff, has been a definitive component in the formation of a distinct intellectual and political academic practice in cultural studies at Birmingham.

Since *Women Take Issue* was produced, the tradition of women working together in subgroups organized around feminist concerns has continued at Birmingham. If not an untroubled trajectory, it is at least an unbroken one, and one we hope this publication will both do justice to and perpetuate. As noted often in this volume, the relationship between feminism and cultural studies is not always an easy one, and this is as true of approaches to working practices as it is of approaches to intellectual and political concerns. However, this volume was itself conceived and produced out of a strong commitment to the usefulness of combining these approaches, and of continually refining and redefining them against and through one another.

Off-Centre grew out of the subgroup known as the Women Thesis Writers' Group, formerly known as the Women and Culture Group, in which feminist postgraduates, and other women affiliated with the Centre were able to exchange written work, provide and receive feedback, and discuss ideas. Meetings were also occasions where more general feminist issues were discussed.

In part, the impetus for *Off-Centre* was provided by the ten-year anniversary of *Women Take Issue*, the first feminist anthology to come out of the Birmingham Centre. This anniversary, imminent at the time of this book's conception, clearly indicated the need for a successor project, in which the continuing contribution of feminists to cultural studies at

Birmingham could be documented, and through which it might be made more widely available.

It was also significant, we felt, that this anniversary should occur at a time when the dialogue between feminism and cultural studies, the importance of cultural theory to feminism, and of feminism to cultural theory, were becoming more widely recognized. That this overlap was increasingly being seen as significant, and receiving more attention in terms of both research and teaching in many parts of Britain as well as abroad, suggested to us the need to provide a forum for feminists working in connection with the Birmingham department to contribute to wider debates.

Most importantly, the period during which the plans for this book were formulated was an active one in terms of the Women Thesis Writers' Group itself. Successful efforts had been made to create and sustain a momentum for this group, which, more than anything else, enabled the possibility of this project to, at first, become thinkable, and, then, to become realizable. It is for this reason that the book is dedicated to the group from which it emerged, and to the continuing tradition of collective feminist research at Birmingham.

To the members of the Women Thesis Writers' Group our appreciation is extended for much support, encouragement and for making this project possible. In particular, we would like to thank Janet Newman, who was unable to co-edit due to other commitments, but who gave invaluable help and support. Many people who were unable to contribute chapters to this volume were none the less important contributors to its emergence, most notably Mieke Bernink, Michelle Fuirer, Diane Hamer, Klaartje Schwarzer and Jayne Warburton. We are also grateful to Maureen McNeil and Richard Johnson of the Department of Cultural Studies at Birmingham who, despite hectic timetables, read and offered useful commentary on drafts of chapters in this collection as well as the introductions. In addition, we would like to thank the members of the Department of Sociology at Lancaster University for providing feedback on Introduction Two of this volume, and for providing support for the production of the book as a whole. Finally we owe our greatest debt of thanks to the contributors, many of whom struggled against considerable odds to produce the work contained in *Off-Centre*.

Part One:
Introduction

Introduction 1
Feminism and cultural studies: pasts, presents, futures

SARAH FRANKLIN,
CELIA LURY & JACKIE STACEY

This book is concerned with forms of knowledge, power and politics. In it we are bringing together feminism and cultural studies in a variety of contexts and at different stages of development.[1] Both feminism and cultural studies have complicated and contradictory histories, inside and outside the academy. It would be impossible to map out a comprehensive outline of these developments here, as well as perhaps undesirable to construct such an account, as if there were simply one single, linear or unified history. However, we feel it is important to highlight what we consider to be some of the key issues in these developments which relate both to the chapters in this collection and to the context of the production of this book. In the first section of this introduction we look at some parallels between feminism and cultural studies in terms of these histories. In the next section, we look at the lack of overlap, and explore some more general questions about the feminist analysis of culture. In the final section, we introduce the contents of the book in terms of three kinds of overlap between feminism and cultural studies.

Inside and outside the academy: contested territories

Both women's studies and cultural studies have in common a strong link to radical politics outside the academy, having their academic agendas informed by, or linked to the feminist movement and left politics respectively.[2] The interdisciplinary basis of each subject has produced consistent and important challenges to conventional academic boundaries and power structures. Thus, there has been a shared focus on the analysis of forms of power and oppression, and on the politics of the production of knowledge within the academy, as well as elsewhere in society. In addition, both subjects have attempted to challenge some of the conventions of academic practice, such as introducing collective, rather than individual work, encouraging greater student participation in syllabus construction and opening up spaces for connections to be made between personal experience and theoretical questions. These challenges have recently come under increasing pressure in the context of public spending cut-backs in Britain and the attempt to transform politically educational practice in the name of enterprise under the Thatcher governments.

Feminism and women's studies

Despite the commonalities mentioned above, women's studies and cultural studies have developed unevenly. Women's studies has offered feminism an institutional base in further and adult education over the last ten years; there are now a number of undergraduate and postgraduate courses in women's studies, and most major publishers now have women's studies or gender studies lists,[3] alongside the wide range of publications available from the feminist presses. Many of these achievements have been hard won, and feminists in all areas of education have struggled to get issues of gender inequality on to the syllabus and to keep them there. Struggling against tokenism, the 'add women and stir' approach, co-option and marginalization, feminists have managed to establish a space within educational institutions from which to document, analyze and theorize the position of women in society.

Early interventions by feminists in the academy often involved highlighting the absence of attention to gender within existing theories and debates. As well as challenging existing academic knowledges, feminists have also introduced new issues into the academic arena. Many of these emerged from the women's movement in the 1970s and 1980s, where consciousness raising groups, political campaigns and national and local conferences were important in raising issues based on women's experiences, which were unfamiliar in mainstream political and academic contexts. Concerns such as male violence, sexuality and reproduction were introduced on to academic agendas by feminists convinced that the 'personal was political'. These topics, amongst others, became subjects of study in their own right in sociology, anthropology, history and literature, as well as within women's studies.

Alongside the documenting of women's oppression which occurred across a broad range of disciplines, feminists began to develop generalized theories to explain how and why women are oppressed. These theories have taken very different starting points and produced a highly complex and often competing set of perspectives on the subject of women's subordination. Whilst it is problematic to summarize such a large area of scholarship, because of the dangers of reductionism and exclusion, a few examples are none the less illustrative of the developments in this area. Some feminists have drawn on already existing social theory to formulate generalized accounts of women's oppression; so, for example, feminists have extended existing Marxist theories of the exploitation of labour within capitalism to look at women's position in paid employment. These writers include Beechey (1987), Phizacklea (1983) and Dex (1985). Marxist theory has also been extended to examine areas conventionally outside its remit, such as the sexual division of labour within the household; so, for example, Benston (1970), Seccombe (1974), James and Dalla Costa (1973) all contributed to the domestic labour debate. Other feminists, such as Ferguson (1989), Walby (1986; 1990), Lerner (1986) and O'Brien (1981), believe the basis of women's subordination to be located outside class relations, and have developed theories of patriarchy as a relatively separate system of exploitation. Amongst those who have attempted to introduce entirely new frameworks and concepts to analyze patriarchal society are MacKinnon (1982; 1987; 1989), Daly (1978) and Rich (1977; 1980b). Finally, feminists who have emphasized the embeddedness of patriarchal social relations in a matrix of intersecting inequalities, such as racism, heterosexism, imperialism and class division, include Lorde (1984), Spelman (1990), Bunch (1988) and hooks (1984; 1989).

The usefulness of the term patriarchy in explanations of women's oppression has itself been debated within feminism (Rowbotham, 1981; Barrett, 1980; Beechey, 1987), and this in turn, has encouraged a greater specificity in its use. One of the key issues in this debate has been the extent to which women are universally subordinated. Feminists working within anthropology (Ortner, 1974; Rosaldo, 1974; MacCormack, 1980; Strathern, 1980) and history (Leacock, 1981; Lerner, 1986; Riley, 1988; Davidoff and Hall, 1987) have been particularly significant in this debate about the commonality of women's subordination cross-culturally and transhistorically. The analysis of precapitalist societies has been a particularly important source of insight into the question of the extent to which gender inequality can be understood as a product of colonization, imperialism and capital accumulation (Mies, 1986; Leacock, 1981; Ortner and Whitehead, 1981).

Early feminist theory tended to emphasize the commonalities of women's oppression, in order to establish that male domination was systematic and affected all areas of women's lives. Feminists offered analyses of women's subordination, exploitation and objectification at all levels of society. This emphasis on commonality, however, often resulted in the neglect of differences between women. Differences based on ethnic identity, nationality, class and sexuality have been increasingly important within feminist work, leading both to the documentation of experiences (Bryan, Dadzie and Scafe, 1985; Moraga and Anzaldua, 1981; Lorde, 1984; Walker, 1984), and to challenges to theories and concepts within feminism based on limited models of the category 'woman' (Carby, 1982; Parmar, 1982; Riley, 1988; Lugones and Spelman, 1983; Spelman, 1990; Ramazanoglu, 1989). These changes within feminist theory have been influenced by changes within the women's movement more generally, where differences between women have come to be seen as one of the strengths of the feminist movement, in terms of a diversity of both national and international politics (Cole, 1986; Bunch, 1988). These differences between women, however, have also been seen to call into question the collective 'we' of feminism (Ramazanoglu, 1989; hooks, 1984; 1989; Cliff, 1983). The challenge remains, at both a theoretical and political level, for feminists to be able to hold on to certain commonalities in women's position in relation to oppressive patriarchal social structures, without denying the very real differences between women and the resulting specificities in the forms of their oppression.

The questioning of the category 'woman' within feminist theory was not only a result of changes in the women's movement and challenges to the limits of its inclusions. It also drew its impetus from areas of academic theorizing which had a significant impact on feminist thought, namely, poststructuralism and postmodernism (Weedon, 1987; Fraser and Nicholson, 1988; Nicholson, 1990; Diamond and Quinby, 1988; Spivak, 1987). The general engagement with these theories of ideology, subjectivity, discourse and sexual difference was seen by many feminists to offer a more complex understanding of the operations of patriarchal power and the reproduction of inequality. Indeed, the scepticism about the unity of identities, characteristic of these perspectives, produced a questioning of the possibility of a unified and meaningful category 'woman', the subject of so much recent feminist analysis. The influence of psychoanalytic theory in particular, which asserted the disruptive nature of the unconscious to any coherent, unified identity, undermined some of the foundational assumptions of feminist analysis. However, these influences remain relatively marginal within many women's studies courses and research, as well as being theoretical perspectives which many see as incompatible with feminism (for a discussion of this issue, see Wilson (1981), Sayers (1986), Brennan (1989), Mitchell (1975), Gallop (1982) and Rose (1986)). These are contested areas within feminist research, but what remains important is that feminist debates continue to produce more complex understandings of the different forms of women's subordination, patriarchal society and the conditions of its existence and reproduction.

Marxist theory, left politics and cultural studies

Responding to changes in Marxist theory and left politics, cultural studies has been a major site of developments within theories of cultural production, and more recently, cultural consumption. Like women's studies, cultural studies is not a unified body of work, set of practices, or even an easily defined academic subject (Johnson, 1983; see also Chapter 6, this volume). Rather, it has offered a place within higher education, and elsewhere in adult and further education, for traditional disciplines to be challenged, for the kinds of knowledges produced to be questioned and for power relations in educational practices to be transformed.

Cultural studies has been a particularly important site of developments within Marxist theory which attempt to leave behind the limits of economic determinism, and an over-emphasis on the mode of production as the key contradiction within society. This shift has taken place in Marxist theory generally, but cultural studies has been central in the development of analyses which take the cultural dimensions of power and inequality seriously. This is, in part, because cultural studies itself emerged from critical perspectives within several disciplines, including history, literature and sociology. These perspectives challenged the terms of previous theoretical assumptions within those subjects. For example, in the study of literature, Marxist cultural theorists challenged bourgeois notions of the literary, and the limited understandings of 'culture' prevalent in that academic subject. The study of popular cultural forms was introduced on to the syllabus alongside a re-evaluation of the literary canon (indeed, the concept of the canon itself). Cultural studies has provided similar challenges to the academic analysis of history, the state, education and the media (CCCS, 1978, 1982a) and, in conjunction with Marxist theorists in these fields, produced a substantial body of alternative knowledges and approaches.

Recent developments within cultural studies can be attributed to various influences. One of the most important of these has been the impact of critical theory, particularly the Frankfurt School, poststructuralism, psychoanalysis and postmodernism. Discourse theory, deriving from the work of Foucault, has been a significant strand in poststructuralist theory, challenging traditional understandings of the relationship between knowledge, power and politics. The notion of discourse provided an alternative to the concept of ideology which had been developed within Marxist-influenced cultural studies to explore the cultural aspects of the reproduction of inequality. Through an understanding of discourse as power-knowledge, dispersed in a network of micro-relations, this work criticized monolithic and totalizing notions of causality and determination and challenged assumptions of a linear, progressive history. It also proposed an understanding of the subject produced through the discourses of 'self'-knowledge, developed through the construction of social categories such as madness, discipline and sexuality.

The critical elaboration of psychoanalysis under the influence of poststructuralism, most notably by Jacques Lacan, and the subsequent emergence of what has come to be known as sexual difference theory, associated with journals such as *m/f* and *Screen*, have been another source of important theoretical influences on cultural studies. In particular, a concern with the importance of the unconscious in the formation of identity led to an acknowledgement of both the fragmented nature of subjectivity and the difficulty of maintaining stable, unified identities. Taking the notion of the unconscious seriously meant that the previously unified subject of cultural analysis was called into question; instead, social identities were seen to be complex and heterogeneous. In addition, questions about the role of pleasure, desire and fantasy began to be analyzed more frequently as part of the process of cultural construction of subjects, identities and practices.

Most recently, the emergence of postmodernism as an influential critical perspective (Lyotard, 1984; Baudrillard, 1988; Jameson, 1984; Kroker and Cook, 1986) has challenged the so-called foundationalist underpinnings which had informed previous theory within cultural studies. Postmodernism is associated with a set of questions about the state of knowledge in contemporary society. It poses a challenge both to conventional understandings of the standpoint of the knowing subject (objectivity, neutrality, distance) and the traditional object of knowledge (a separate reality about which the truth can be discovered). These modernist, foundationalist, or post-Enlightenment assumptions are challenged by postmodernism, which argues that they are essentialist, falsely universalist and ultimately unsustainable. Unlike poststructuralism, which also raised these issues, postmodernism is associated both with actual contemporary phenomena, such as architectural styles and other representational practices, and with broad changes in the organization of Western consumer culture. These changes are seen to include the breakdown of the historical distinction between high and popular culture, the disappearance of what is variously called the depth, content, or referent of signification, and the increasing instability and complexity of contemporary cultural processes.

Another of the main influences transforming cultural studies through the 1980s has been the impact of feminism. *Women Take Issue* (Women's Studies Group, 1978) was an early example of feminist work within cultural studies, both using and attempting to transform Marxist theory. Looking at questions of cultural reproduction as well as production, *Women Take Issue* highlighted the need for cultural studies to engage with the 'personal' dimensions of culture in the political context of a feminist analysis. Since then, the impact of feminism on cultural studies has had an increasing significance. The shift, for example, from interest in issues concerning ideology and hegemony to those concerning identity and subjectivity can, in part, be attributed to feminist interventions, as well as to the influence of psychoanalysis and poststructuralism. Another area of increasing interest within some strands of cultural studies which can be seen as evidence of the impact of feminism is sexuality. However, while work on the construction of sexual identities (Mulvey, 1989; Heath, 1982), the analysis of narratives of romance (Modleski, 1982; Radway, 1987), cultural representations of

AIDS (Watney, 1987) and studies of state regulation of sexual 'deviancy' (Weeks, 1981; 1985), addresses sexuality as well as gender, the way in which sexuality has been taken up has been selective, and often has not been integrated with feminist analyses such as those of the patriarchal institution of heterosexuality. Similarly, lesbian and gay issues are only very gradually beginning to be taken seriously within cultural studies.

Theories of ethnicity and analyses of racism have also made an important contribution to shaping developments within cultural studies. *Policing the Crisis* (Hall *et al.*, 1978) stressed the role of racist representations of social problems such as crime in the emergence of a law and order society in Britain in the early 1970s. Following this and other work on the construction and representation of ethnicity and national identity, *The Empire Strikes Back* (1982) criticized the pathologization of race within race relations and sociology, and the racism of some white feminist analyses. It also explored the importance of racist ideologies in both shaping aspects of state regulation in Britain, such as immigration law, and the construction of notions of Britishness and citizenship informing contemporary definitions of national identity. Another area in cultural studies which has been influenced by the study of ethnicity has been the analysis of subcultural practices (Hebdige, 1979; Gilroy, 1987). Earlier models of subculture were challenged and transformed to include an acknowledgement of both the history of ethnic inequality and racism, and the struggles for collective self-representations by black people. However, the impact of debates about and struggles against racism on cultural studies continues to be rather uneven.

Changes within left politics have also had an effect on the kinds of political questions taken seriously within cultural studies. What has been seen as a crisis in left politics had led to a rethinking of political strategies, allegiances and agendas by some on the left. In some circles, this has contributed to a broadening of agendas and a desire for stronger political alliances with other radical forces such as the women's movement, black politics, the green movement and lesbian and gay liberation.

These, then, are some of the principal influences in the development of cultural studies and feminism in the last decade or so. As this account makes clear, there are a number of points of overlap between feminism and cultural studies. Theoretically both are concerned with analyzing the forms and operations of power and inequality, and take as an integral part of such operations the production of knowledge itself. To some extent, each has drawn on critical insights from discourse theory, poststructuralism, psychoanalysis, semiology and deconstructionism. Both have drawn on strands of critical theory which are seen to offer more sophisticated tools for analyzing the reproduction of social inequality, and relations of dominance and subordination at a cultural level. The analytic possibilities opened up by these approaches were seen to strengthen existing theories of power and resistance within both cultural studies and feminism. To some degree, then, overlaps in both areas have produced possible points of convergence between feminism and cultural studies.

The lack of overlap: feminism and cultural analysis

There are, however, also considerable divergences in interest which suggest a rather different ordering of priorities within feminism and cultural studies. Just as many feminists earlier posed critical questions about concepts such as ideology and hegemony, drawing attention to the ways in which they and the traditions of thought which produced them were gender-blind, there is now caution about the use of concepts such as discourse, deconstruction and difference. In addition, although feminism has influenced cultural studies, there are limits to this influence which are important for what they reveal about the uneven interaction between the two fields. Perhaps one of the clearest indicators of the limits to this influence is provided by the lack of interest within cultural studies in the developments in feminist theories of gender inequality discussed earlier; for example, the models of culture employed within cultural studies have remained largely uninformed by feminist theories of patriarchy. This has produced a number of problems for feminists working in cultural studies.

Many of the reasons why the influence of feminism on cultural studies has been limited can be traced back to some of the more general understandings of culture employed within cultural studies. These include the models of culture derived from certain strands of Marxist thought. As discussed earlier, cultural studies was itself both central to, and in some senses a product of, a major set of shifts within Marxist perspectives away from the assumption of a mechanistic economic determinism. Indeed, the influence of feminism has been particularly significant within cultural studies around this issue. On the one hand, for example, the Althusserian framework offered greater attention to the cultural within (or, relative to other) Marxist frameworks, and has informed some of the most influential feminist work in cultural studies (Williamson, 1978; Barrett, 1980; Winship, 1987; Women's Studies Group, 1978). Yet on the other hand, the appropriation and development of these models within cultural studies did little to counter the marginalization of issues of importance to feminism.

Indeed, these theoretical frameworks, which are largely unable to account for sexuality, reproduction and violence, are characterized by quite fundamental conceptual limitations from some feminist points of view. Within the Althusserian framework, for example, the social field is seen to be composed of economic, political and ideological levels. But, the economic level, conceptualized in terms of the forces and relations of production, is seen to determine all other levels in the last instance, and thus retains a privileged significance in the construction of inequality. This limited move away from economic determinism is inadequate for many understandings of gender inequality. Some feminists, for example, have disputed the Marxist conception of the economic, in so far as it is seen to be based on the industrial mode of production associated with capitalism, and to naturalize the sexual division of labour (Firestone, 1974; Delphy, 1984; Mies, 1986). Other feminists (Daly, 1978; MacKinnon, 1987, 1989) have suggested that not only is such an ordering of determination open to question, but that the division of levels is unhelpful for an analysis of gender inequality: how is sexuality, for example, to be understood in relation to these discrete levels of power?

Another powerful model of culture which has been developed in cultural studies has its origins in structuralism. This model has two principal strands, deriving from social anthropology and linguistics. The first of these was introduced into cultural studies through the work of Claude Lévi-Strauss. This version of structuralism takes the exchange of women as the original or founding cultural moment, thus creating an essentialist tautology from a feminist point of view, and providing little hope of ever changing patriarchal society. As has been pointed out (Rubin in Reiter, 1975), by constructing the sexual division of labour and sexual difference as *a priori* constants, structuralism reifies patriarchal dominance as a 'natural fact'. The problem for feminists, therefore, is that this model of culture takes for granted precisely what feminism is most concerned to explain.

The second broad strand of structuralist thought that has been influential within cultural studies is based on the work of Ferdinand de Saussure, who proposed a structural analysis of language as a system of signs. This has since been extended in semiotic, poststructuralist and sexual difference theories to the analysis of other cultural systems, including, for example, fine art (Parker and Pollock, 1981), advertising (Williamson, 1978) and film (Cowie, 1978). From this perspective, meaning is understood to be produced through the play of difference and is relational (produced in relation to other signs) rather than referential (produced by reference to objects existing in the world). The development of these interpretive techniques, in which the analogy of language as a system is extended to culture as a whole, marked a substantial break from the positivist and empirical traditions which had limited much previous cultural theory. However, while structuralism and poststructuralism have been important for feminists in so far as they provided important critiques of some kinds of reductionism and essentialism, and facilitated the analysis of contradictory meanings and identities, their use has often obscured the significance of power relations in the constitution of difference, such as patriarchal forms of domination and subordination.

However, one strand of poststructuralism, developed by feminists working within cultural studies, which has addressed the reproduction of such patriarchal relations, is that which draws upon psychoanalysis in order to provide an account of how difference is fixed as inequality through the acquisition of a gendered identity (Mitchell, 1975; Rose, 1986; Mulvey, 1989). This, in turn, has been challenged by others, who argue that sexual difference is so fundamental to the very terms of psychoanalytic thought (as in the strand of structuralism which derives from Lévi-Strauss), that its use invariably contributes to the naturalization of gender inequality (Rubin in Reiter, 1975).

The poststructuralist tendency in cultural studies outlined above has also been supplemented by the use of literary methods of analysis, such as deconstructionism (Derrida, 1981; Ricoeur, 1986; De Man, 1979), in which cultural processes are analyzed as texts. The advantages for feminists of the bridge between literary analysis and social science constructed in the wake of 'the structuralist challenge' are clearly apparent. The ability, for example, to locate the production, criticism and consumption of literary texts in the context of the non-literary 'texts' of patriarchal social relations opened up an obvious space for more politicized readings of both the literary canon and what had been excluded from it. Likewise, the emphasis on how meanings are encoded into practices of cultural production and consumption opened up a whole range of radical rereadings of traditional subjects in both the humanities and the social sciences.

Nevertheless, this understanding of cultural processes as texts obscures the specificity and significance of different kinds of practices and results in a reductionism which raises problems for feminist analysis. Central issues for feminists, such as the control of women through their bodies, present problems for this textual analogy; some feminists would suggest that the female body cannot be considered simply as a text. Furthermore, such a method may contribute to the problem of objectification, whereby the female body becomes an object of scrutiny and investigation, devoid of subjectivity or personhood. Analyzing gender within the model of culture 'as a language', then, presents specific problems for feminists who have highlighted the objectifying practices (or, the construction of woman as object) within language itself.

There have been other influential frameworks for the study of culture within cultural studies, including, for example, the understanding of culture as 'ways of life' and 'ways of struggle' as developed in the work of Williams (1961, 1965, 1981), Thompson (1968, 1978), Hoggart (1958) and Seabrook (1985, 1988). These have sought to construct new understandings of culture based on working-class experiences and positions. However, whilst they have offered alternative models of culture to the dominant versions, based on bourgeois life and values, they have often excluded the gendered dimensions and specificities of working-class experience (Steedman, 1986).

Ethnographic work within cultural studies, drawing on perspectives from anthropology, has provided one of the main sources of exploration of 'lived cultures'. Working-class culture has been a particular focus of this work within cultural studies, where ethnographic material has been used as evidence of the relationship between dominant culture and subordinate groups. In particular, forms of resistance (Willis, 1978) and the formations of subcultures (Hebdige, 1979; 1988) have been explored in this context. These have also been challenged by feminists within cultural studies, not only for their gender specificity, but also for their lack of acknowledgement of the patriarchal elements of these forms of resistance (Griffin, 1985; McRobbie, 1980).

In this section, then, some of the important models of culture employed within cultural studies have been discussed in terms of the limits, as well as the possibilities, they pose for feminist analysis. The aim has been to show the way in which the frameworks outlined above pose substantial problems for feminists concerned with *patriarchal* culture, and limit the potential influence of feminism upon cultural studies, as well as of cultural studies upon feminism. Thus, while feminists have turned to disciplines such as cultural studies for frameworks to analyze the cultural dimensions of gender inequality, and whilst the work of feminists has been influential in both challenging and reworking these frameworks, there remain substantial difficulties in defining what might be meant by specifically feminist under-standings of culture.

Ironically, this is true at a time when cultural issues are seen to be of growing importance to feminism. The power relations of pornography, abortion, male violence, technology and science have increasingly come to be seen not only in terms of social institutions and practices, but also of symbolic meanings, the formation of identities and deeply-rooted belief systems. Even in those areas that appear to be most easily understood in conventional social and economic terms, such as paid work, feminists have begun to uncover the ways in which the construction of gender-appropriate identities and subcultures helps to organize, for example, the hierarchies in internal labour markets and the nature of workplace activities (Cockburn, 1983, 1985; Game and Pringle, 1984; Beechey, 1988; Phillips and Taylor, 1980). Indeed, cultural issues are so central to a wide variety of analyses of women's subordination that it might seem surprising that feminists have not developed general frameworks within which the significance of cultural processes might be more fully realized.

However, to the extent that feminism has long relied on an eclectic combination of frameworks and methods, often extracted from traditional disciplines and reworked to take account of gender, this may require less explanation. Moreover, the fact that some feminists have explicitly resisted overarching models and 'grand' theories, which belong to what has been seen as a masculine tradition, in part explains the lack of attention to a clearer definition of the elements of specifically feminist analyses of culture. Nevertheless, this lack of clarity about what is meant by cultural analysis in the context of feminism has led to some confusion in recent debates.

This results both from the implicit or unacknowledged use of models of culture and the explicit naming of a disparate set of analyses as cultural.

One example of the confusion which results from the implicit use of different understandings of culture is provided by the current debate about pornography. Some feminists (Coward, in Betterton, 1987; Merck, in Betterton, 1987) see pornography as a process of signification or representation, ultimately irreducible to, and, to some extent, separate from, social and economic relations. They attempt to demonstrate the continuum between pornographic and other images of women circulating in contemporary culture, arguing for the impossibility of drawing a fixed line between offensive and acceptable images. Pornographic images of women, then, are understood as the extreme articulation of the objectification of women *at the representational level*. The model of culture being drawn upon here is one which assumes that representations have a relative autonomy and are a mediated articulation of social practices. Other feminists (Dworkin, 1981; Griffin, 1978; MacKinnon, 1979) propose an understanding of pornography not as a representational form of patriarchal culture, but as its exemplary moment of expression: pornography reveals to us the truth about what men really think about women. It is seen as an expression of male sexual violence and as an integral part of violent practices against women. Here, culture is seen to parallel directly the social, and is derivative of the misogyny deeply embedded in patriarchal society. Thus, an analysis of pornography forces us to face and to challenge the full extent of misogyny in this society. What is at stake, then, in discussions about whether it is possible to distinguish between pornography and erotica, or in disagreements about the role and relevance of censorship, are not only different understandings of pornography, but also implicit models of culture which are rarely addressed in these debates.

Another important example of feminist work where the models of culture have not been foregrounded is the analysis of gender and objectification. Feminists who have emphasized the objectification of women in terms of commodity fetishism and the circulation of objects within capitalist relations of exchange often draw heavily on Marxist models of culture (Gaines, 1982). Another perspective criticizes the voyeuristic and fetishistic construction of woman in visual images, and uses a psychoanalytic account of the cultural construction of gendered identities to explain and challenge the patriarchal pleasures offered by such processes of objectification (Mulvey, 1989). A third approach develops an analysis of the forms of female objectification through the construction of female sexuality in patriarchal culture, and points towards a feminist methodology which would challenge such objectification (MacKinnon, 1979, 1982, 1987, 1989).

As these debates make clear, attention to the cultural dimensions of gender inequality is not simply about arriving at a sharper understanding, or a more encompassing set of explanations. They are also about the strategies for change and transformation which are at the core of feminist politics. How one defines the power of pornography depends in large part on how one understands much more general processes involved in the cultural construction of meanings, images and identities. This, in turn, has direct implications for how to challenge pornography. Similarly, discussions about the question of whether the processes of objectification imply consent or coercion lead to very different strategies for change or resistance.

In addition to the problem of understandings of culture being present but submerged, as in the current debates over pornography or objectification, there is another set of questions which arises out of the explicit use of radically heterogeneous understandings of the cultural. Again, bespeaking the divergent roots and resources of feminist scholarship across a wide range of disciplines, cultural criticism has come to mean a very wide variety of things within feminism. The resulting confusion is perhaps most evident in the description of some American radical feminist work as cultural feminism.[4] The proliferation of understandings of the cultural further contributes to the need to define more clearly the assumptions underpinning frameworks in the analysis of culture, and raises the question of whether there are any commonalities that run through the various uses of 'cultural' as a modifier.

Some feminists working within women's studies have used more explicit models of culture drawn from the disciplines in which they are based. For example, feminist sociological theory tends to analyze the cultural as something distinct from the social, a differentiated sphere which is structured through specific institutions, such as the media, education and religion, and has drawn on a range of methods of analysis to conceptualize the specificity of the cultural in this sense. Alternatively, feminists working within anthropology, in which culture is the traditional object of study, have drawn upon a diverse set of frameworks and methods for cultural analysis. These include detailed ethnographic accounts, crosscultural comparisons, evolutionary and archaeological approaches, and linguistic studies. Culture is also studied within other disciplines, such as psychology, linguistics, literary criticism and history, through frameworks which are formulated in various ways in relation to the primary objective of study. Many of these approaches to the study of culture from the traditional disciplines have been borrowed by feminists in order to investigate the cultural dimensions of gender relations.

The importance of theories of culture to feminism, then, arises from many different sources and for many different reasons. Be it due to the limits of existing models within cultural studies and conventional disciplines, the increasing importance of cultural issues within feminist theory and politics, or the confusion arising out of the use of divergent models of culture within feminist analysis, the need to clarify what might be meant by feminist analyses of culture becomes increasingly important. This concern arises both from the recognition of these problems and the desire to provide a set of terms for an analysis of culture which addresses the specificity of patriarchal power and suggests ways in which to challenge it.

However, the question of what these terms might consist of is only just beginning to be asked. It might, for example, be possible to argue that a feminist cultural analysis would, given the intimate nature of women's subordination, be shaped by an interest in the construction of sexuality, the gendered body and the realm of subjectivity. Yet there are acknowledged problems with reinforcing links between the personal and the feminine which would require the issue of essentialism to be addressed. Debates about the implications of the conceptual distinctions between lived experience, the subjective and subjection, lie at the heart of many current debates within feminism, not the least of which is that concerning the strategic value of the category 'woman', and all of which are concerned to transform the significance of what it is to be a woman.

One of the primary aims of this book, in bringing together feminism and cultural studies, is to consider the significance within feminist theory and politics of questions concerning the cultural dimensions of gender inequality and patriarchal power. This introduction has suggested that there are two ways of exploring this significance: to investigate the role of culture in the reproduction of gender inequality; and to ask how an analysis of gender can contribute to an understanding of culture. However, it seems that whilst feminists have gradually built up a complex picture of the operations of patriarchal culture, there has been less of an attempt to systematize generalized theories of these power relations. We have tried to suggest some of the reasons for this, including both the limits to feminist influence within cultural studies and the difficulties of asking what a specifically feminist cultural analysis would look like.

However, the diversity and heterogeneity of contemporary feminist analyses of culture would suggest that such a project, while focused on a common set of themes, is not, and is unlikely ever to be, unified. This is itself indicative of the strength and diversity of contemporary academic and political feminism. This anthology does not represent a definitive or comprehensive set of approaches to this question. Rather, in three different sections, addressing three different kinds of overlap between feminism and cultural studies, it provides a range of contributions towards the aim outlined above. It is to these forms of overlap that we will now turn.

Three kinds of overlap

The contributions to this book have been divided into three sections: 'Representation and Identity', 'Science and Technology', and 'Thatcherism and Enterprise Culture'. At one level, these subdivisions are the product of the interests of the contributors, most of whom were connected with the Department of Cultural Studies at Birmingham University at the time this collection was conceived. At another level, however, each section is significant for what it indicates about the different kinds of interaction between feminism and cultural studies in different areas of analysis.

The chapters in Part I, 'Representation and Identity', contribute to an area of study in which both feminism and cultural studies have been well represented. This section thus includes work in which the overlap between the two different sets of approaches is well established, due to the history of their shared focus on issues related to popular culture and the analysis of representation and identity. The shift in recent years towards questions of cultural consumption in both fields, for example, is evident in several chapters in this section. It is the increasing emphasis within feminism on recognizing differences between women and challenging the notion of *the* female spectator, coupled with the increasing impact of the cultural studies emphasis on context in media analysis, which has produced this overlapping interest in the practices of consumption and reception.

Angela Partington focuses on the importance of an analysis of the historical relations of consumption for an understanding of the role of genre in the construction of gendered identities. The specificity of women's position in relation to the processes of consumption is explored through a detailed study of the social and cultural conditions of viewing for the audience of melodrama in the 1950s. This, in turn, leads to a discussion of the class-specific forms of pleasure enjoyed by women at that time.

Helen Pleasance also considers the role of the gendered dimensions of the relations of consumption in her study of the teenage music magazines *Smash Hits* and *Just Seventeen*. Contrasting two very different perspectives within cultural studies, one which emphasizes the power of dominant culture to shape our lives, and the other which focuses on our power to resist and transgress, this chapter looks at the complexity of changes in youth culture, gender and pop music in the late 1980s.

In addition to that by Angela Partington, two other chapters in this section focus on the relationship between genre and the construction of identity, drawing on feminist theory and cultural studies to explore the links between representation, politics and pleasure. While both Yvonne Tasker and Celia Lury are concerned to assess critically the notion of the progressive or feminine text, in order to take account of the post-structuralist and post-modernist challenge to this notion, they come to different conclusions concerning its implications for a feminist cultural politics. Yvonne Tasker suggests that the equation of the feminine with an open or plural text has led to an essentialist equation between feminine textual positions and women as a social group. This equation, Tasker suggests, denies the complexity of the relationship between gender and genre, which, she suggests, may be so contingent that it is impossible to fix through the relationship of identification. In contrast, Celia Lury argues that it is precisely through an exploration of the diverse politics of this relationship of identification as it is constructed in, for example, the social relations of reading and writing autobiography, that feminists can challenge the rigidity of the category 'woman'.

In the final chapter of this section, Joyce Canaan offers an analysis of gender and subculture. Based on ethnographic interviews with young English working-class males this chapter investigates the activity of male versus male fighting and its centrality to constructions of masculinity. Whilst cultural studies has in many senses pioneered the ethnographic study of youth subcultures, it has done so with little or no regard to gender, and has been very largely focused on the class-related significance of the activities of men. Similarly, whilst feminism has done much to raise awareness and concern about the extent of male violence against women in society, it has yet to provide a more textured account of the ways in which male violence is socially and culturally mediated. By combining approaches, Canaan argues, it is possible to move beyond the previous limits of both feminism and cultural studies.

Part II, 'Science and Technology', represents a very different form of overlap between feminism and cultural studies than do the contributions to Part I. Here, rather than shared interests and approaches, there is little common ground between feminism and cultural studies. Whereas the analysis of science has become one of the most significant trajectories within contemporary feminist scholarship and politics, it has rarely been the focus of sustained or critical investigation within cultural studies.

Some of the reasons for this lack of overlap are explored in the opening chapter of Part II, co-authored by Maureen McNeil and Sarah Franklin. Following a comparison of approaches to science and technology in cultural studies and feminist theory, this chapter moves on to consider how, despite their lack of a shared tradition, these approaches can be usefully brought together. In particular, it examines the work of recent feminist analyses of science (including the work of Haraway (1985), Martin (1987) and Harding (1986)) and suggests ways in which approaches from cultural studies could extend and contribute to feminist research and politics in this increasingly important area.

The results of a collective project by the Science and Technology Subgroup, working in the Department of Cultural Studies at Birmingham University since 1986, comprises the remainder of this part. This collective project presents an analysis of the implications of the Alton Bill (a recent anti-abortion initiative) for the position of women through an explication of the role of medical expertise, scientific knowledge and the capacity of medical technology in the cultural construction of reproduction. Motivated by a concern that reliance upon medical, technological and scientific definitions of pregnancy is increasingly being used to erode and replace more woman-centred frameworks for reproductive decision-making, this project was designed to explore the cultural role of science in the Alton debate from a variety of perspectives. Hence, framed by a collectively authored introduction and conclusion, Chapter 7 contains five subsections, each principally authored by an individual member of the subgroup, but formulated in co-ordination with the group as a whole. Beginning with an overview by Maureen McNeil, establishing the context of the Alton debate, Chapter 7 continues with a history of abortion legislation in Great Britain by Wendy Fyfe; an analysis of the terms employed in the parliamentary debate over the Alton Bill by Deborah Lynn Steinberg; a critique of the medical construction of foetal personhood by Sarah Franklin; and an account of the media representation of the Alton debate by Tess Randles. Throughout this chapter, an attempt is made to establish the usefulness of bringing together approaches from feminism and cultural studies, particularly in the analysis of the role of science and technology in setting the terms through which the abortion question is publicly debated.

Whilst the contributions to Part II attempt to introduce cultural studies approaches into a set of debates which have been central to feminist research, Part III tries to do the reverse, that is, to introduce feminist approaches into an area which has been central to debates within cultural studies – 'Thatcherism and the Enterprise Culture'. Whereas the lack of overlap in Part II results from a somewhat curious silence within cultural studies with regard to issues of science and technology, the discrepancy in Part III results from an equally noteworthy lack of attention to the gendered dimensions of Thatcherism and enterprise culture, two of the most significant sources of political and cultural change in contemporary British society.

Within cultural studies there has been considerable debate evaluating the significance and novelty of Thatcherism. Attention has been focused, for example, on its relationship to other forms of conservatism, and the role of the left in providing, or failing to provide, a sufficiently popular alternative to the Thatcherite ethos. These debates about Thatcherism within cultural studies are part of a more general debate within left politics and Marxist theory about how dominant culture reproduces itself and, in particular, about the role of ideology in this process. Meanwhile, there has been limited feminist analysis of the gendered dimensions of Thatcherism or of the forms of patriarchal culture which have emerged during the Thatcher governments. 'Introduction 2: Feminism, Marxism and Thatcherism', explores the possible reasons for this lack of attention by feminists to the question of Thatcherism in more detail. In it we aim to explore some of the theoretical issues addressed in this first introduction in a specific cultural and political context. Our discussion of Thatcherism is thus a case study of the particular gaps and overlaps between feminism and cultural studies in one specific instance. We end the second introduction with a brief elaboration of some possible directions for the analysis of its gendered dimensions as a cultural phenomenon.

This project is developed in more detail by the contributors to Part III of this anthology. Whilst maintaining a scepticism about the use of the concept of Thatcherism, and the left's concern with this phenomenon, Maureen McNeil discusses some of the aspects of these debates which deserve particular attention from feminists. These include a discussion of Thatcher's image and rhetoric, the politics of work, the family and sexuality, as well as what McNeil refers to as the 'new oppressed' of the Thatcher decade. She concludes by discussing the contested relationship between feminism and Thatcherism, arguing that feminism has made both more and less of a difference to the gender politics of the decade than is usually acknowledged.

Janet Newman and Estella Tincknell both explore aspects of the contemporary reworking of enterprise, and outline its contradictions for women through explications of current popular representations of the relation between femininity and individualism. *A Woman of Substance*, Barbara Taylor Bradford's best-selling novel, published in the same year as Thatcher's election as Prime Minister, is the subject of Estella Tincknell's analysis, while Janet Newman focuses on the recent wave of 'how-to-succeed at work' manuals aimed at women. Both of these chapters explore the textual construction of patriarchal femininity in the context of enterprise capitalism. Again, the theme of how many of the tenets of feminism have been recuperated into the new language of competitive individualism central to the dominant enterprise ethos of the Thatcher governments is remarked upon by both authors. Similarly, the popular currency of the image of the successful entrepreneurial woman is examined in the light of how these texts represent women as successful competitive individuals without transgressing the norms of acceptable and appropriate femininity.

During the last decade the Thatcher government has attempted to redefine notions of nationhood, 'Britishness', acceptable forms of active citizenship and the relationship between individualism and familialism. At the heart of many of these reformulations has been the construction of threats to the new British respectability. Both Evelyn Reid's and Jackie Stacey's chapters look at these recent forms of oppression in Britain and discuss strategies and effective forms of resistance to them. Evelyn Reid addresses shifts in black cultural politics which have occurred in response to both the cultural racism of the new right and the political need to represent the diversity of black cultures, intersected by the multiple discourses of ethnicity, class, gender and sexuality. The chapter by Jackie Stacey on the successful introduction of Section 28 (a government-sponsored anti-gay/lesbian initiative) traces a similar process of struggle for self-representation on the part of lesbians and gay men against dominant definitions of homosexuality and lesbianism. The notion of Section 28 as a simple backlash against feminism is challenged in favour of the analysis of it as a response to the successful feminist redefinitions of sexuality as socially, not biologically, determined. Using discourse analysis to investigate the recent public debate over Section 28, and sources from the popular media to examine the cultural construction of sexuality, this chapter addresses an area which continues to be marginalized within most cultural studies courses.

In bringing together feminism and cultural studies in different ways in these three sections of the book, we have tried to illustrate three various kinds of overlap between them. These in turn provide a number of ways to approach the question of how to develop feminist cultural analysis. This important project can draw much that is of value from work within cultural studies. Yet, it must also take account of the shortcomings and limitations of the models of cultural analysis on offer within cultural studies. In turn, as it has already done, feminist analysis will likely serve as both a resource and a stimulus to cultural studies, in their continuing shared project to challenge the existing conventions of producing and sharing knowledge, and to combine theoretical debate with strategies for change.

Notes

We would like to thank Maureen McNeil for her detailed comments on an earlier version of this Introduction.

1 Whilst 'women's studies' and 'cultural studies' might seem to be more obviously analagous terms, we have chosen to use 'feminism' and 'cultural studies' in order to include developments in feminist theory and politics which have occurred outside the institutional boundaries of women's studies.
2 However, women's studies and cultural studies have rather different relationships to radical politics, given that women's studies emerged as a direct result of the women's movement. Cultural studies, on the other hand, has had a more tenuous and uneven relationship to left politics.
3 The recent shift from women's studies to gender studies has produced considerable debate and controversy. Mary Evans offered a sceptical analysis of the political significance of this shift in her keynote paper at the Women's Studies Network Conference, Coventry Polytechnic, 18 March 1989.
4 The range of American radical feminist work labelled 'cultural feminist' is very broad and thus the term is often confusing. It includes work which attempts to reclaim a 'woman-centred' culture, exemplified in the films of Barbara Hammer, as well as critiques of patriarchal culture and knowledge, such as those developed by Mary Daly.

Introduction 2
Feminism, Marxism and Thatcherism

SARAH FRANKLIN,
CELIA LURY & JACKIE STACEY

Originally given cultural currency by Stuart Hall, the term Thatcherism signified the disturbing popularity of a deeply authoritarian right-wing government and the problems and challenges it presented for the left. It is now over ten years since the publication of Hall's influential article, 'The Great Moving Right Show' (1979), where the term was first used as an 'ism'. Since then the term has taken on a wide range of meanings.

As a term Thatcherism has been culturally constructed in a variety of different contexts, signifying different things in different places and frequently functioning as a vehicle for extending already existing debates about broader political and cultural issues. The attention to Thatcher, in the media particularly, fixed the term as an 'ism' of everyday life in the late 1980s and early 1990s. In the plethora of media investigations marking the anniversary of the tenth year of Thatcher's office as Prime Minister her tenure was variously dubbed 'The Thatcher Years', 'The Thatcher Factor', 'Thatcher's Decade', 'Thatcher's Reign' and 'Thatcher's Rule'. The effect of this was not only to give the term a certain stability, but to naturalize and stabilize it as a political phenomenon in a way that reinforced its own self-definition as an inevitable, permanent fixture of our political future.

In contrast, we are using the term Thatcherism here with the intention of problematizing it, emphasizing its constructedness, and its relative meanings according to context. We are keen not to reproduce its implicit power and stability, not to assume a unified coherent set of political ideas and practices, and not to overestimate its success. Indeed, we aim to analyze its construction in relation to different academic and political contexts.

In this introduction we offer an analysis of the debates about Thatcherism within cultural studies, drawing attention to their lack of concern with gender. We then go on to look at the feminist literature on Thatcherism and its specific implications in terms of gender politics. This work questions the validity of referring to the last decade of Conservative governments with a specific term such as Thatcherism. Finally, we investigate the question of whether a combination of feminist and cultural studies approaches might lead us to conclude that Thatcherism could indeed be held together as an 'ism' in relation to an analysis of gender.

Cultural studies, Marxism and Thatcherism

The debates on the left in which the term Thatcherism (Hall, 1988a; Jessop *et al.*, 1988; Gamble, 1988) has become significant are extremely diverse. These range from analyses of the crisis in world capitalism, the restructuring of the international division of labour, the emergence of 'enterprise culture' in the postwar period, the political development of the new right in Europe and in the USA, to specific analyses of the meaning of Thatcherism in the British context.

These debates pivoted around several concerns. One was a periodization of postwar British political history, particularly in terms of the question of whether Thatcherism was a new or distinct project, or whether it was merely a regrouping of traditional Tory ideas in a new configuration. In other words, there has been a debate about whether there was something so distinctive to Thatcherism that it required the development of new analytical approaches. A second concern was the extent to which Thatcherism could be considered in terms of a failure of the left, and in particular whether this might be conceptualized in terms of a failure to take people's 'needs' and 'desires' seriously. Finally, there was a debate about the importance of the role of ideology, and the extent of the achievement of hegemony within this period, both in terms of defining the specificity of Thatcherism in particular and in its significance within political analyses in general.

Within each of these debates there were complex disagreements about what Thatcherism meant, how to define its specificity and how 'successful' it was. We do not intend to offer a thorough review of these different aspects of the debate about Thatcherism here. Instead, we intend to address one of the most significant approaches developed in cultural studies to date, which is that initiated by Stuart Hall. The reason for this focus is the extent to which Hall's work was widely taken up within the debate about Thatcher on the left. Given its significance in this context, Thatcherism presents an appropriate case study in which to explore the relationship between cultural studies and feminism in an area where there was a considerable gap between them in terms of their theoretical concerns and political conclusions.

Following on from previous work in *Policing the Crisis* (Hall *et al.*, 1978),

Hall's analysis attempts to explain the rise of Thatcherism in relation to the failure of the left, the breakdown of postwar social democratic consensus, and the aim of the right to construct a new hegemonic force in British society. Hall sees Thatcherism as a combination of neo-liberalism in terms of *laissez-faire* economy and authoritarian conservatism in terms of law and order and the power of the state in everyday life.

In particular, Hall emphasizes the role of image and ideology in the achievements of the right. He argues for the importance of moving beyond traditional, class-based analyses to understand the appeal of Thatcherism. Rejecting the economism of many existing Marxist approaches, Hall urges the left to examine Thatcherism at a cultural level. Rather than simply evaluating the Thatcher governments on the grounds of whether their policies benefit voters, Hall argues that the success of Thatcherism must be seen as operating at the level of the power to define the terms of the debate, the power to constitute identities which people recognize (national, familial and individual), and the power to set boundaries around insiders (patriots, entrepreneurs, competitive individualists, homeowners) and outsiders (Argentinians, miners, black communities, socialists, gays and lesbians). Hall therefore rejects the rather mechanistic, functional model of the production of subjects by ideology, characteristic of previous Marxist theory, which failed to take account of such processes.

Hall thus challenges the left to produce more complex understandings of the work of ideology in this context. He emphasizes the need to take account of the several possible positions of identification, several sets of desires and several possible forms of recognition offered by the ideological discourses of Thatcherism. In short, he argues, there were a multiplicity of ways to be included in the 'us' and not the 'them' within Thatcher's Britain. Moreover, these may be contradictory and only partial, never fully unifying one coherent set of interests.

This understanding of the work of ideology has obvious implications for an analysis of subjectivity. Hall argues for a more complex model of subjectivity which allows for simultaneously contradictory identifications, lack of closure or linearity in the stories told and of our positioning as subjects (or objects) within them. Indeed, he suggests that one of the strengths of Thatcherism was precisely its ability to offer multiple, diverse and contradictory identifications, thus successfully including within its discourse and narratives many different, even opposed, sets of interests.

As well as analyzing the distinctive strands of Thatcher's hegemonic project, Hall's analysis can be seen as a more general reconceptualization of politics and ideology. Speaking at London's Institute for Contemporary Arts in 1989, for example, Hall declared that:

> Nothing has pushed me so rapidly away from the last vestige of a
> rationalist conception of ideology than trying to work on Thatcherism

for the last five years. The one thing that seems to me so manifestly, patently clear is that *that* way of attempting to understand what's going on politically simply has practically no purchase anymore. It shoots from under one any notion of ideology functioning in a rational way, of its interpellating subjects to a rational calculus . . . all of that seems to me to be shot to bits (Hall, ICA, February 1989).

This kind of argument is an indication of the way in which the debates about Thatcherism have been inextricably bound up with debates on the left generally about hegemony, ideology and the possibilities of resistance. Many of Hall's claims may have been brought out more clearly as a result of his study of Thatcherism, but they also could be, and have been, made independently of it. It is for this concern with rethinking ideology that Hall is so strongly criticized by Jessop and his colleagues (1988), amongst others, who accuse him of idealism. Interestingly, much feminist analysis of gender has also been criticized for this same reason. Indeed, we would argue that much of the emphasis of Hall's analysis both parallels and draws upon developments within feminist theory.

Some feminists, for example, have challenged the overemphasis on the mode of production in Marxist analyses, arguing that women are not exclusively defined by their position in relation to it. Feminists then, have challenged many Marxist class-based analyses which Hall is also trying to transform. Other feminists have also emphasized the importance of representation as a site of the construction of cultural identities. The power of the image and of ideology have been central to feminist work on patriarchal culture. Indeed, much work on media and popular culture has been generated by feminist questions in the last ten years. Feminist cultural critics[1] have produced some of the most influential work in the field of media and cultural studies, setting the agendas around sexual difference, desire, subjectivity and cultural consumption, issues which are increasingly present in Hall's analyses of contemporary British politics.

The concept of subjectivity which Hall advocates is immediately recognizable to those feminists whose work has foregrounded the fragmentary and contradictory construction of feminine identity in patriarchal culture. Feminists from many different perspectives have long argued that since women are largely excluded from power within patriarchy, the whole notion of the unified subject is a masculine privilege. Be it French feminist theorists who argue that women can never be speaking subjects within a patriarchal symbolic order,[2] or American cultural feminists who argue that a condition of femininity in this culture is living simultaneously contradictory truths,[3] or feminist theorists who illustrate the processes of exclusion of women from political and legal definitions of citizenship,[4] feminists have been theorizing the contradictions of feminine subjectivity within a patriarchal society for quite some time.

Thus, the main point to be made here about cultural studies approaches to Thatcherism is that there is an implicit relationship to gender analysis in these overlaps with feminist theory. Many feminist interventions have made similar challenges to more traditional Marxist analyses, and have shifted the debates in similar directions to those advocated by Hall.[5] Perhaps the similarities between Hall's arguments and much feminist work demonstrate the impact of feminist theory on cultural studies.

Yet despite this rather hidden overlap between cultural studies and feminism, there are clear limits to the influence of feminism on cultural studies discussed in the first introduction (see pp. 8–14). Certainly, any attempt to theorize Thatcherism in more explicitly gendered terms was largely absent from Hall's work, as it was from the responses to it. Despite attempting to revise traditional economistic understandings of political and ideological processes in favour of an understanding of Thatcherism as a hegemonic project, and despite drawing implicitly on feminist insights and theoretical developments, this approach to Thatcherism did not go as far as to include even a preliminary analysis of its implications in terms of gender.

While it attempted to revise traditional reductionist understandings of political and ideological processes in favour of an understanding of Thatcherism as a hegemonic project, it withdrew from a systematic analysis of the implications of this for gender relations. As a result, from a feminist perspective, Hall can be criticized for not extending his revised materialist analysis to social groups other than those explained solely by reference to class relations.

In order to investigate the question of whether Thatcherism could be held together as an 'ism' in relation to gender, we turned to recent feminist work on Thatcherism. Significantly, there is very little feminist work in this area. The analyses which have been offered by feminists fall into two distinct areas: first, the political effects of particular policies on women in Britain, and, second, an exploration of the phenomenon of right-wing women.

Feminist approaches to Thatcherism

The effects of the policies of Thatcher's governments on women

There are several perspectives from which feminists have discussed the implications for women of the policies of the Thatcher governments. Although there is not a coherent body of feminist argument about the effects of Thatcherism *per se* on women, feminists have offered analyses of changes in various aspects of women's social positioning. We have grouped these issues under two headings: the decline of the welfare state, and employment and enterprise. In both of these areas, feminists identified distinct consequences for women of Thatcher's policies.

From a feminist point of view, the development of the welfare state had contradictory implications for women. Premissed as it was upon the need minimally to compensate women's unpaid work of social reproduction through a variety of tax and benefit measures, it did nothing to challenge the underlying sexual division of labour, and ensured that women's identities and interests were overwhelmingly linked with those of their children. Despite this fact, the severe cut-backs in welfare benefits and services that have been a definitive and consistent component of the policies of the Thatcher governments had a profoundly negative effect on women overall, particularly in their long-established roles as carers, nurturers and homemakers. The increased responsibility of caring for children, the elderly, the sick and the disabled produced by the withdrawal of public funds from these services has been felt predominantly by women, who have, in essence, been asked to compensate for the reductions in public provision.

In terms of the National Health Service, cuts in services have produced a necessity for greater patient care to be provided in the home, or by voluntary carers, most of whom are women. As homemakers, women have been forced by cut-backs, such as the end to single payments, to stretch resources further and struggle harder to make ends meet in order to feed, clothe, house and care for their families. Single mothers were particularly hard hit in Britain under Thatcher, as they were in the USA under Reagan, where they constituted the fastest-growing and largest population group living beneath the poverty line. Cut-backs in maternity benefit, child benefit, housing benefit and unemployment benefit combined to hit single mothers with young children hardest, as they are most excluded from paid employment, and thus most dependent upon the state for their basic subsistence needs. Repeated indications that child benefit might be abolished entirely (it has been frozen at £7.25 per week per child since 1987) indicated that the Thatcher government did not feel it had succeeded in its attempts to rid society once and for all of the so-called 'dependency culture' it so deplored.

The cut-backs in state provision of healthcare, education, housing and welfare benefits and services also affected women independently of their role as carers, nurturers, mothers and homemakers (Finch and Groves, 1983). In each of these areas, women incurred specific losses. In terms of healthcare, for example, the closing of maternity and women's hospitals, of family planning centres and well-women clinics as a consequence of general cut-backs in the NHS (where women's health was never a priority) had negative implications for women's health. In the education sector, where women have traditionally made up a greater proportion of further, adult and continuing education students, the disproportionately heavy cut-backs in precisely these areas will have the greatest costs for women. Finally, women make up a greater proportion of the elderly, for whom cut-backs in services were also particularly severe and dependence upon benefit makes them an especially vulnerable group. Ruth Lister, former director of the Child Poverty Action Group, described the situation concisely when she said that Thatcher's 'social and fiscal policies spell increased insecurity and increased dependency for women' (Lister, 1987, p. 9).

Together, these and many other consequences of the decline of the welfare state for women in Thatcher's Britain indicate that what has been described as the 'feminization of poverty' in the USA has become a similar fact of life in Britain. It is, however, important to situate the effects of the decline of the welfare state for women in the context of changed patterns of women's employment, increased privatization and the rise of enterprise culture.

Women's participation in the labour force today nearly equals that of men. It is well known that a large proportion of women workers are in part-time, low-paid, non-unionized forms of employment, and this situation did not change under Thatcher. Indeed, it is the rise in the numbers of women in part-time employment that largely accounts for their greater participation in the paid workforce. Thus, the necessity of women working a 'double' day (as waged worker, housewife and mother) continued under Thatcher. As Elizabeth Wilson writes:

> The decline of the manufacturing sector, the increase in part time work in the service sector, and changes in technology and consumption patterns . . . have combined with changing family structure, and particularly with the rise in divorce rates to create a situation in which more and more women become wage workers, *yet as an increasingly vulnerable section of the workforce.* (Wilson, 1987, p. 208; emphasis added).

The typical situation of a woman part-time worker, enjoying minimal employment benefits or job security, facing limited opportunities for training or advancement, and earning low-pay, has become more typical of the workforce generally. In other words, more work is organized around decentralized, short-term, part-time, single-contract based or piecework terms of employment, which has extended what were previously largely female forms of labour to a much larger proportion of the workforce in general. Angela Coyle identifies the implications of this shift in no uncertain terms:

> what is happening is that the most vulnerable sections of the workforce are at the *forefront* of a general dismantling of the regulation and control of employment. Women are being used to pave the way for a significant deterioration in the terms and conditions of employment (Coyle, 1985, p. 17).

The changing position of women in the labour market is clearly due to broader transformations in work patterns which extend beyond the direct effects of the Thatcher government's economic policies, and indeed require an analysis of international divisions of labour (Mies, 1986; Mitter, 1986). Nevertheless, particular aspects of these policies, especially those associated with enterprise, have reinforced these broader transformations. The impact of an enterprise ethos on the labour force in Britain can best be summed up as a greater emphasis on the need for market forces to determine the forms and conditions of work, manifested by attacks on trade unions, equal opportunities schemes and workers' rights generally. For women, as the most vulnerable section of the workforce, this had very negative consequences.

Women's relationship to enterprise has, however, been contradictory. The extent to which women are addressed as individuals by the discourses of enterprise culture may be seen as progressive as well as restrictive for women. Enterprise culture has encouraged the development of women's training schemes and the participation of women in particular areas of work, especially self-employment and management, for example. Thus, on the one hand, certain spaces have been opened up for women, in terms of employment and training, but one must also ask, as Janet Newman does (see Chapter 9 below), what these spaces are offering and who is being asked to fill them. Obviously, not all women are equally positioned to take up the benefits on offer in the new climate of enterprise.

One final aspect of the way Thatcherism affected women in terms of employment is the decline in status, if not direct scapegoating, of many of the professions in which women have the greatest presence. Thus, teaching and nursing, for example, have been among the hardest hit of all of the professions as a result of the combined effects of cut-backs in public expenditure, privatization and the move towards enterprise culture. Professions such as that of social work have been the subject of much public blame in recent scandals. Moreover, as Maureen McNeil has argued, Thatcherism, also saw a scapegoating of women professionals as 'the enemy within', such as Marietta Higgs for her interventionist approach to the hitherto taboo subject of child sexual abuse and Wendy Savage for her stand against the male medical establishment's ethos of interference in childbirth (see McNeil, Chapter 8).

In this context, it is also important to add that it is in many ways illusory to speak of the effects of Thatcherism on women, as 'women' have been very differently positioned by it. For the general population, Thatcherism increased the gap between women in different segments of society, to the benefit of some and the detriment of others. Women well positioned to take advantage of the benefits for successful entrepreneurs had the most to gain from Thatcherism and enterprise culture, while those not in such positions lost out in proportion to the ever-widening gap between rich and poor. In addition, Thatcherism exacerbated the forms of inequality which divide women, including ethnicity, nationality, disability and sexual preference. Thatcherism did little to even things out. As Elizabeth Wilson points out:

> The group of women most penalised by Tory policies are black and ethnic minority women. Not only are they found in disproportionate numbers in the worst paid sectors and in the most exploitative work, but in some cases their immigrant status makes them even more vulnerable, while even if they are British nationals, racism still operates to prevent their gaining access to better jobs. (Wilson, 1987, p. 210).

Like Reaganism, the effect of the Thatcherite promotion of competitive individual success and minimum state provision of a safety net has been disproportionately to benefit those individuals already well placed in terms of employment and financial security, and to disproportionately penalize those in a more vulnerable position.

In sum, there are many ways in which it is possible to use feminist perspectives to trace the gender-specific implications of the social and economic policies of the Thatcher governments, taking into account the contradictions in women's positioning and the differences between women. However, these do not make up a coherent set of 'gender policies' on the part of the Thatcher governments. Processes such as the feminization of poverty or the changes in the sexual division of the labour force are in no way specific to Thatcherism, and should instead be seen as part of a much larger, international set of shifts. Indeed, many of the contradictions raised for women in relation to the rise of enterprise culture under Thatcher in Britain have direct parallels with the relation of Third World women to the development process and its effects on women's lives.

Thatcher's policies can thus be seen as largely consistent with those of previous governments, who have exploited women's labour market position and their unpaid work of social reproduction. In other words, from the point of view of gender relations, Thatcherism did not represent a discontinuity with the past. On the contrary, it appeared to be a continuation of policies that were neither novel nor unique. Feminist work further suggests that the period covered by the term Thatcherism is not appropriate for an understanding of social change which foregrounds the position of women. Thus, Gardiner (1983) locates her analysis of the Thatcher government in the context of the general economic recession, and Segal (1983) examines Thatcherism in the context of broader changes in women's lives in the last two decades. Both analysts therefore develop different histories of postwar Britain, as well as different analyses of welfare capitalism and social democracy, in order to explore the implications of the Thatcher governments for women. But in both accounts, the Thatcher governments are seen in terms of an intensification of existing inequalities between men and women rather than as a particularly novel or distinctive form of patriarchal exploitation. Hence, feminists working within the area of social policy have not found the term Thatcherism useful, since it does not seem to hold together as a concept in relation to gender.

Women and right-wing politics

The other area of feminist analysis relevant to the debates about the significance of Thatcherism for women is the work on right-wing women. This work does not so much address the social policies of specific governments, as the meaning of the emergence of the new right for women at a broader social, political and cultural level. Such analyses have been developed by Dworkin (1983) and Campbell (1987).[6] Although Dworkin looks at the USA and Campbell focuses on the UK, both address a common question: how does conservatism enable women to make sense of themselves and their world? Neither author is willing to accept the commonsense belief that women are inherently conservative, and both seek to understand the conditions which produce a distinctively feminine fatalism about the possibility of any challenge to patriarchal power and lead to this conservatism among women.

Dworkin's analysis starts from the premiss that women's lives are shaped by a fear of male violence, which is experienced as uncontrollable, unpredictable and threatening. She then proceeds to outline the ways in which the political right 'makes certain metaphysical and material promises to women that both exploit and quiet some of women's deepest fears' (Dworkin, 1983, p. 21). The moral ideology of the right, she argues, offers women a fixed, predetermined social and sexual order which in turn offers a secure and stable context for familial and marital relationships. Further, it promises to put enforceable restraints on male violence and claims to protect the home, family life and women's place within it. It is a politics, Dworkin argues, in which fear plays a central role. From this perspective, the support of some women for the right is understood as part of a struggle to avoid the 'something worse' that can happen if they transgress the rigid boundaries of appropriate feminine behaviour. Their support is thus to be explained in terms of a belief that the system of sex hierarchy is immovable, unbreachable and inevitable. This fatalism about existing sexual divisions is bolstered by the exclusion of women from the terms of participation in traditional party politics across the spectrum.

Turning to Britain, Campbell also argues that women have largely been excluded from most party politics – both in terms of their exclusion from organized politics, and thus from access to political power, and in terms of a failure to address them as political subjects. In contrast, she suggests that historically women have, to some extent, been addressed as political subjects within Tory politics. This address is made to women in terms of their traditional roles within the family and the private sphere. Thus, for example, the right-wing ideology that women are naturally maternal and domestic can appear as an expression of respect for women's domestic labour, in comparison with the silence about women's roles expressed by other parties. In short, Campbell suggests that in Tory discourse women as housewives, wives and mothers are ascribed a privileged status denied by other parties. Thus, as Campbell argues, even if women are addressed in the conventional terms of their maternal and domestic roles, at least women are recognized and included as socially significant.

This political analysis provides the context in which Campbell is able to argue that Thatcherism's support for authoritarian forms of legal and moral intervention drew on the fears of many women about male violence and power, which were legitimated in the idea of public retribution. Similarly, the rhetoric of the family is also seen in terms of a public support and recognition for women's domestic power in ways which build on the traditional feminine role as inscribed in Tory politics.

However, she also recognizes that under Thatcher support for the family was framed in terms of attacks on the welfare state, organized labour, single mothers and the 'pretended families' of lesbians and gay men. The 'fight against crime, lawlessness and intimidation', as Campbell notes, was focused on industrial action and terrorism, rather than the issues specifically related to women's fears. Moreover, Thatcherism did not address women's specific roles within or contributions to the family, uniting instead, for example, the housewife, the taxpayer and the elderly in their need for stable prices. Thus, the policies of the Thatcher government towards women and the family departed somewhat from those associated with the traditional views of Tory women. Significantly, Thatcher herself did not call for women to return to the home, but instead emphasized the compatibility of women's paid work with their roles in the home.

Indeed, Campbell further suggests that significant social changes in the position of women have meant that the traditional appeal of right-wing moral authoritarianism is being undermined. Through an analysis of voting patterns, she goes on to claim not only that Thatcher's initial electoral success was the result of a swing to the right by skilled working-class men, but that women have been moving away from the right. She explains this in terms of the success of feminism, and the increasing participation of women in paid work, the experience of which left them unhappy with Thatcher's break with postwar notions of equality. Thus, Campbell argues that women are increasingly offered identities and identifications which cut across any singular form of femininity and which undermine the right-wing tendency to define women by the domestic and the biological. In this respect, the feminist literature on right-wing women does not suggest that the Thatcher governments had either a traditional or a novel appeal to women.

The hesitation feminists displayed in taking up the term Thatcherism may, in part, be explained by a feminist disenchantment with totalizing theories, which have traditionally neglected or played down the subordination of women. However, it can also be understood as a consequence of doubt as to the usefulness of the term Thatcherism and the 'authoritarian populism' thesis for an analysis of gender inequality. The analyses of social policy and of right-wing women discussed above suggest that Thatcherism as a concept does not have the same significance in relation to feminist politics as it does for the left. In general, then, if gender relations are taken as the focus of investigation, the set of practices and ideologies known as Thatcherism is seen to be much less coherent and much more contradictory in effect. Thus, for example, Jean Gardiner writes that:

> the Tories' position on women is not [as] explicit or united as their approach to some other issues, e.g. trade unions . . . The Tory government is neither explicit about its attacks on women nor even probably aware that its policies have this effect. (Gardiner, 1983, pp. 195–6).

However, the feminist work we have looked at comes to these conclusions largely by examining social and political changes for women during the Thatcher era; in the following section, we ask what happens if we start looking at cultural changes. In other words, is it possible to distinguish certain unique or novel aspects of Thatcherism by providing a cultural analysis from a feminist perspective? The aim here is to consider whether, in bringing together approaches from feminism and cultural studies, we might find something more specific to Thatcherism than was established within the feminist approaches discussed so far. Looking first at Thatcher's image and moving on to address the significance of discourses of familialism within Thatcherism, we conclude with a discussion of the relationship of feminism to Thatcherism.

Feminist cultural analysis and the question of Thatcherism

Thatcher's image

One image which has been consistently defined as undoubtedly masculine has been that of public political power, on all three counts. What happens, then, when a woman takes up such a position of power? In taking up a conventionally masculine position, is her femininity called into question? Does a female leader necessarily have to negotiate the contradictions between the masculinity of the culturally defined position she occupies, and her own femininity? If so, how did Margaret Thatcher negotiate this contradiction? Or does the power of the position in some way move its occupant beyond gendered identity, giving other factors overriding significance? Furthermore, given that two of the characteristics of the self-presentation of Thatcher's national leadership were those of strength and conviction, how can this be reconciled with the fact that it was a woman who occupied this position?

The question of Thatcher's image has been addressed by a number of feminist cultural theorists. Brunt (1987), Warner (1985) and Rose (1988) have all commented upon the interplay of power and femininity in Thatcher's image. Each offers a different analysis of the means by which these two, seemingly contradictory identities are successfully combined.

Brunt contrasts Thatcher's image with that of other right-wing women. She characterizes these according to two traditional female Tory types. The first of these is exemplified by politicians such as Jill Knight, who is described as 'drawing on reactionary populist religion and appealing to petit bourgeois anxieties and women's fears about violence' (Brunt, 1987, p. 23). The second, 'more flamboyant type', who advocates women as the moral guardians of the nation, is exemplified by Barbara Cartland. In contrast to these two established types, Thatcher seemed able to combine an image of power with one of femininity in a new way. Brunt argues that 'Thatcher's success in the realm of patriarchal politics is precisely to do with her effectiveness as a woman, and the way she inhabits particular feminine roles, while appearing to disavow femininity' (1987, p. 23).

In popular political analysis, Thatcher's authority within her Cabinet was constantly reaffirmed through descriptions of her male opposition as 'Tory wets', and of Thatcher herself as 'the best man in the Cabinet', thus making her doubly superior. The epithet 'The Iron Lady', and her own 'This lady's not for turning', combined femininity with strength and determination in ways which both drew attention to her gender and undermined its conventional signification. Brunt argues that Thatcher managed to mediate the contradiction posed between her femininity and her leadership position in public, political life. Rather than seeming ill at ease with this contradiction, Brunt argues, Thatcher appeared to thrive in her role as a powerful woman politician.

In *Monuments and Maidens: The Allegory of the Female Form* (1985) Warner argues similarly that Thatcher managed to exploit her powerful role and image as a woman leader to her advantage:

> Margaret Thatcher has never repudiated as alien or undesirable the image of strength that clothes her, rather she interiorizes it with almost grateful eagerness, for it provides her personality with a dimension that traditional definitions of female nature exclude. (Warner, 1985, p. 40).

Indeed, far from presenting difficulties for Thatcher as the first British female Prime Minister, the characteristics of power and strength came to be central signifiers in Thatcher's image. One of the ways this was achieved, Warner argues, was through the association of Thatcher with Britishness itself, in particular a new form of British strength displacing several decades of fading colonial and economic power. Following the resolution of the Falklands War this conflation of Thatcher and Britishness worked particularly in her favour: 'after the Task Force victories, Mrs Thatcher welcomed the echo of the Iron Duke, conquering hero, and said on American television: "I have the reputation as the Iron Lady. I am of great resolve. This resolve is matched by the British people"' (Thatcher 1982, quoted in Warner, 1985, p. 41).

Warner investigates Thatcher's successful negotiation of this contradiction between femininity and power by situating her analysis in the context of historical representations of female British power, which, she argues, were reworked in Thatcher's image:

> The identification of the Prime Minister with the renewed military grandeur of Great Britain was accomplished in part through a language of female representation; it was natural, as it were, to see Mrs Thatcher as the embodiment of the spirit of Britain in travail and then in triumph, because of the way that spirit of Britain has been characterized, through its famous great queens on the one hand, and the convention of Britannia on the other. The first female premier did not rebel against the assimilation of the nation and herself; what Prime Minister would? (Warner, 1985, p. 41).

In a typically queenly manner, Warner argues, Mrs Thatcher managed to represent herself as 'near the heart of things' in Britain (1985, p. 43). Representing traditionalism, national pride and authoritative leadership, Thatcher came to replace the Queen as the 'symbolic centre of power' in Britain (1985, p. 43). Warner notes that many British children failed to recognize the difference between the Queen and the Prime Minister to illustrate this shift in the female figurehead of national identity.

Warner's analysis investigates the presence of conventional feminine roles as well as the construction of Thatcher's image through powerful women warriors/leaders from British history:

> In Margaret Thatcher . . . Britannia has been brought to life. But she achieved this singular hypostasis not because she is a battle-axe like Boadecia, but because she is so womanly, combining Britannia's resoluteness, Boadecia's courage with a proper housewifely demeanour. She is known after all by two cosy names as well: 'Mrs. T.' and 'Maggie'. (Warner, 1985, p. 51).

Thatcher herself contributed to the presence of femininity in her image through an inclusion of the traditional domestic feminine roles in her self-presentation. Despite her 'masculine' characteristics, then, Thatcher managed to preserve her status as a 'proper woman' through her fulfilment of the roles of wife and mother. For example, the press regularly drew attention to her domestic activities: she was known to have cooked for her Cabinet, she expressed interest in the kitchen, and on a visit to a factory she discussed the difficulties of making marzipan with women workers. Her inner Cabinet was referred to as the 'kitchen cabinet', and she not uncommonly drew analogies with housework to describe her Prime-Ministerial responsibilities, as in her descriptions of the national economy as if it were a domestic budget. Thatcher's image thus succeeded in holding together representations of powerful women from British history with the conventional feminine identities of wife and mother.

This 'softer', more 'womanly', component of Thatcher's image has generally been identified by feminists as one of the means through which some of the harsher policies of her government, such as the repression of the miners' strike, denials of trade union and civil rights, stricter immigration laws and the dismantling of the welfare state, were rendered more acceptable. Moreover, the disproportionate burden imposed on women by the cut-backs in public provision which formed a central component of government policy under Thatcher, including the freezing of child benefit and reductions in health services, to name but a few, was seen to be offset by Thatcher's cultivation of a domestic, feminine image. At the same time, Thatcher's association with a 'language of conflict and intolerance . . . in domestic affairs' (Warner, 1985, p. 42), and her authoritarian leadership style led, in later periods, to a 'softening' of her personal image which was seen as a political imperative.

Yet another pre-existing repertoire of familiar cultural idioms of British womanhood noted by Warner in her analysis of Thatcher's image was that which was reminiscent of the nanny or governess:

> Nanny, matron, governess . . . these are not Mrs Thatcher's personal role models. But they are perceived to be in character because they are women of discipline. Margaret Thatcher has tapped an enormous source of female power: the right of prohibition. She exercises over unruly elements, near and far, the kind of censure children receive from a strict mother. It is a very familiar form of female authority; it just looks novel applied by a prime minister. It is also an authority many are used to obeying (Warner, 1985, p. 52).

Significantly, these roles establish female power through discipline, authority and prohibition.

The relationship between femininity and forms of power and control, in particular those expressed through discipline and prohibition, is also explored by Rose (1988). Rose combines psychoanalytic and feminist theories to analyze the significance of Thatcher's gender identity in the collective imaginary of British culture. For Rose, it is not simply a question of shifting from a more mechanistic, rationalistic model of ideology to a model of hegemony which explains how consent is won and struggled over (see the discussion of Hall's argument above), but rather of extending this further to look at the non-rational dimensions of popular consent to political authority.

Although feminism has opened up the space for sexuality to be seen as political, Rose argues, this has not led to an analysis of the psychosexual aspects of political power. In addition, it has been questions of sexuality and desire, rather than violence, which have successfully crossed the boundary from the feminist to the cultural studies agenda. But for Rose the centrality of violence and terror to the psychosexual aspects of political power is particularly important for an understanding of the appeal of Thatcherism.

This is Rose's starting point for analyzing the repudiation of violence (such phenomena as terrorism, football hooliganism, rioting and the Hungerford massacre, for example) and the fascination with, or desire for, violence (the Falklands War, capital punishment, military strength, harsher law and order) which were simultaneously evident in Thatcher's Britain. She thus explores the significance of the fact that Thatcher is a woman for her ability to legitimate these forms of increased state violence.

Drawing upon the work of Kristeva, Rose argues that femininity sets the boundaries of the social, being defined in opposition to it as excess, chaos and irrationality. However, Thatcher's image as the politician of conviction, her rhetoric of consistency, persistence and sameness, and the apparent lack of a gap between her government's intent and achievement, all produced a super-rational image. Thus Thatcher, as a female leader, held together the contradictions of rationality and femininity, whilst embodying the fragility of that boundary. This produces the fascinating and yet terrifying powerful female executioner who legitimated extreme forms of state violence in the name of law and order. In this way Thatcher's gender identity held together the contradictory images of anti-violence and anti-statism on the one hand, and aggressive nationalism, militarism and a law-and-order state on the other. Seen from this perspective, Thatcherism could be characterized as a politics of violence and terror, mobilizing both people's fears and anxieties about excess and chaos and their desire for total control and order.

What is evident from all three perspectives provided by these accounts of Thatcher's image is the diversity of established cultural formations through which public political power and femininity can be reconciled. From Brunt's identification of the means by which this has been achieved by simultaneously drawing upon femininity and disavowing its significance, to Warner's analysis of monumental, domestic and disciplinarian idioms of British womanhood, to Rose's invocation of psychoanalytic accounts of the repressed association of the maternal with prohibition and violence, Thatcher's image can be seen, from a feminist cultural perspective, to have had a highly gendered significance. This in turn suggests means by which her identity as a woman may have served to mediate certain aspects of her government's policies, and secure popular consent for her leadership. Moreover, it suggests the ways in which her femininity could be both present and absent in her image, its selective invocation and denial facilitated by the combination of being a woman in a traditionally masculine role.

Discourses of familialism

A second area in which it may be possible to combine feminist and cultural studies approaches to consider the specificity of Thatcherism in terms of gender is the analysis of discourses of familialism. These discourses, because they held together so many of the key strands of the Thatcherite project, can be seen as one of its definitive features, particularly from a feminist point of view. However, it is important to note that discourses of familialism were produced in complex and contradictory ways, and emerged in different ways at different periods in the Thatcher governments. On the one hand, the family was the explicit target of political reform and was a key site for social engineering. On the other hand, the Thatcherite rhetoric of *laissez-faire*, the celebration of the autonomy of individuals and the sanctity of the private sphere, apparently left the family outside politics and reaffirmed it as a natural and necessary unit. Indeed, challenging many of the feminist arguments of the 1970s and 1980s, Thatcherite discourses of familialism attempted to depoliticize the institution of the family and the power relations within it. Thus, while the family was reclaimed as an apolitical sphere within the context of Thatcherite rhetoric of 'freedom' and 'choice', this very process has ironically demonstrated a high degree of political intervention.

In addition, discourses of familialism operated very differently within the neo-conservative or social-authoritarian aspects of Thatcherism on the one hand, and within the neo-liberal dimensions of Thatcherism, which emphasized the market as the mechanism for the establishment of individual rights and duties, on the other. The former strand of conservative thought has always made explicit and extensive references to the importance of the family as the social basis of moral and political stability. These references were further extended in the Thatcher period, although, as we shall go on to discuss, the traditional acknowledgement of women's role within the family was submerged rather than developed. In contrast, the family has traditionally only had an implicit presence in the neo-liberal traditions of conservative thought. Significantly, however, particular representations of the family were often used by members of Thatcher's governments to promote the rise of enterprise culture and compensate for the decline of the welfare state.

Thus, true to the ethos of her early speech-writer and family policy advisor, Ferdinand Mount, author of *The Subversive Family* (1982), Thatcher herself promoted the family as the source of freedom, liberty and dignity; of national pride; of moral values; and, most importantly, of consumption. There is nothing more natural, she claimed, than for an individual to want to better his family. Indeed, Thatcher claimed 'The desire to do better for your family is the strongest driving force in human nature' (Thatcher, 1986, The Conservative Women's Conference). Naturally, therefore, enterprise culture was rooted in the family unit and in its acquisitive drive for an ever more materially enriched future.

Another area where discourses of familialism were mobilized is in relation to the crisis in representative democracy. They provided a framework within which citizens were encouraged to realize their aspirations, not in their social being, not through parliamentary politics or collective action, but through active citizenship, consumerism and the assertion of familial rights and responsibilities. In addition, the family was seen as the locus of increased choice, in opposition to the prescriptive and interventionist bureaucracy of the welfare state. Being able to choose for yourself what is best for you and your children became a rallying cry in terms of education, healthcare, and pension schemes.

A new kinship universe was also proposed, in which 'there is no such thing as society, there are only individuals and families'. Rooted in the nuclear family in its own home, the kinship ethos of the Thatcher governments defined itself in opposition to the social; whether it was trade unionism, intruding social workers, unfashionably liberal teachers, or the nanny state. Persons were defined through consumerism, nationalism, parenthood and professional success rather than through any form of radical collective affiliation, which was rendered suspect. Passing on the wealth, and the moral values of right and wrong, from parent to child became the exclusive route of intergenerational transmission in the prescribed descent routes of social reproduction. The family *is* society, Thatcher argued, encompassing all of its institutions: 'It is a nursery, a school, a hospital, a leisure centre, a place of refuge and a place of rest. It encompasses the whole of society. It fashions our beliefs. It is the preparation for the rest of our life. And women run it,' she argued to the Conservative Women's Conference in 1988.

The implications of this conflation of family and society were particularly problematic for black people as their rhetorical inclusion in the categories of the individual, the consumer and the family was at the cost of a denial of the anti-racist community or political action as a source of social identities. In this way, the Thatcherite reconstitution of black identities, through the attempt to include black people as individual citizens within a future Britain which consisted of competitive individuals with enterprise values, was directly opposed to the radical black politics of the last two decades.

Despite its exclusion of so many people, the image of *the* ideal nuclear family has continued to hold an important place in cultural representations and in people's imaginations and fantasies. Given that most people in Britain no longer live in such a situation, it is striking that such an image not only still pertained, but held such a central place in the political discourses of the Thatcher governments. It is a version of family life in Britain which, ironically, denied the extent to which Thatcher's policies were actually destroying many families, as a result of unemployment, immigration laws, cut-backs in welfare provision and lack of childcare facilities. Its appeal remained firmly at the level of imaginary identification, and necessitated a displacement of not only other versions of family life, and in particular of women's experiences, but also of the effects of state policies on many families in Britain. It was an appealing fantasy, incapable of achievement by most of the population, but one that still wielded enough emotional power to evoke stability, safety and security, the desirability of which is, to some extent, understandable, given the rapid disappearance of their guarantee elsewhere in society.

We have suggested, more particularly, that discourses of familialism mobilized to legitimate certain key aspects of the Thatcherite project, including the promotion of both enterprise culture and active citizenship, and the denial of 'society'. What is interesting here, for our argument, is that this rhetoric of the family rarely had an explicitly gendered address. Indeed, in contrast to other right-wing ideologies which have explicitlyed called for women to be returned to the home, Thatcherism, as noted earlier, assumed the compatibility of women's private and public roles: 'The home should be the centre but not the boundary of a woman's life' (Thatcher 1982, quoted in Campbell, 1987, p. 235). Thus, there were very particular contradictions operating here in terms of gender, which can be read through the absences as well as the presences of the discourse.

The explicit mobilization of discourses of familialism during the Thatcher governments was a public valorization of the sphere in which women are paramount, by a woman who defined herself, in part, as a mother and a housewife. Women's presence was implied by the construction of the family which was being advocated, and indeed, as noted earlier, was necessary for the future vision of a reformed Britain. However, in contrast to those elements of right-wing thought which have traditionally celebrated women's contribution in the home, representations of women's position in the family were been noticeably absent. Indeed, the family, just as other institutions under the Thatcher governments, appeared to consist of genderless individuals. The sexual division of labour, women's unpaid work, processes involving reproduction, not to mention domestic and sexual violence, indeed all the aspects of the family politicized by feminists over the last twenty years, were made invisible or individualized within this discourse. This silence about the conditions of mothers and housewives was necessary for the idealization of the family within the Thatcherite populist project. In sum, whilst the family seemed to be a central institution in this vision of Britain, it was curiously exempt from close political analysis, and remained at the level of distant fantasy in order to avoid an exposure of the gendered inequalities within it.

Indeed, in many ways there has been a tension between discourses of familialism and those of enterprise culture: the homemaker and the entrepreneur could scarcely connote more divergent sets of values and practices. The ethos of professional individualism governing enterprise, despite attempts to root it in the family, has posed a potential threat to the notions of self-sacrifice, altruism and nurturing supposedly characteristic of a 'haven in a heartless world'. The entrepreneur in this heartless world has had to take risks, overcome adversities and out-manoeuvre competitors. The adventurer in the market place could be seen as the quintessential symbol of Thatcherite individualism in contrast to any notion of family life which presented an opposing set of values. Yet the entrepreneur depends upon some kind of domestic base, for without one the adventurer would have nowhere to go for physical and psychological replenishment; if this was not a domestic kinship base provided by unpaid female labour, then women in the service sectors would be needed to provide the necessary domestic and sexual back-up (restaurants, laundries and prostitution, for example). Thus, there has been an implicit dependency upon some form of 'feminine support'. Yet this was generally an invisible aspect of the constructions of market adventurers in enterprise culture.

It seems, then, that it is both the absence of a specifically gendered address and the simultaneous presence of women in terms of their assumed role which characterized the distinctive cultural significance of discourses of familialism under the Thatcher governments. Given the importance of the discourses of familialism to many of the policies of this period, it may also be that this cultural analysis may offer a way of understanding the specificity of Thatcherism as a distinctively gendered phenomenon.

Thatcherism and feminism

In examining the means by which Thatcher held together the contradictions of being a woman in a position of power traditionally defined as masculine, and the ways in which gender was both present and absent within Thatcherite discourses of familialism, we have highlighted two examples of the possible significance of a feminist cultural analysis to an understanding of Thatcherism. This brings us to our third and final question, which concerns the place of feminism in the emergence and character of what has been described as Thatcherism. This is a crucial question not only for contextualizing Thatcherism, and in particular the 'success' of Britain's first woman Prime Minister, but also for assessing the impact of feminism on gender relations in Britain over the last two decades.

Several issues emerge concerning the relationship between feminism and Thatcherism. To the extent that feminism aimed to force open barriers to women's equal participation in public professional life, to what extent was Thatcher's own success an ironic consequence of the 'successes' of feminism? What relation do the policies of her governments bear to feminism? If Thatcherism posed problems for the left, in the form of a necessity to rethink certain political strategies and principles, is this also true for feminism? Clearly, the ascendency of a woman to the nation's highest political office, and her subsequent stamping of an entire era with her name, in the midst of a substantial feminist challenge to male dominance and male privilege in public political life, raise questions which, however discomforting, deserve to be addressed. The question of how it became possible for a woman to become and to survive as Prime Minister, and the meaning of this for feminism, is part of the focus in this final section.

Constituted, among other things, against the spectre of the 'permissive society', the politics of the Thatcher governments invoked a particular construction of the 1960s and the 1970s as an era of loss and decline. Not only in relation to the 'decline' of the British nation and economy, but in terms of a perceived unravelling of the moral fabric of society, the demonization of the 'permissive era' and the return of 'Victorian values' were twin poles in the Thatcherite project to redefine British society. The women's movement was a central component of 'the permissive era', and indeed has at times come to exemplify its ills in the rhetoric of social conservative and new right campaigners. Feminism put forward a significant challenge to dominant definitions of the family, sexuality, reproduction and women's traditional roles in the home and in the workplace. The legacy of feminism – its gains, its losses and its contradictions – thus pose important questions in the analysis of both the emergence and the character of Thatcherism.

There is no doubt that Thatcher assumed a position of political leadership on very patriarchal terms, however much she may have played upon her identity as a mother, homemaker and housewife in her professional life. She has herself been unequivocal about feminism: in her mind the battle had been won. Moreover, women benefited little, if at all, under her leadership, as the analysis of the effects of the Thatcher governments on women demonstrates. The gender politics of Thatcherism in this respect, in terms of its impact on women, denotes nothing about her leadership which would distinguish it from those of men before her. As summarized in the poster showing Thatcher beneath the slogan 'My message to women of the Nation', her reply was 'Tough'.

Nevertheless, there are some who would still claim that Thatcher's success was indeed a success for feminism. Among these are women whose definition of feminism is access to male power, on its own terms. Hence, the 300 Group, a campaign organized by women to increase the number of women in Parliament, claims Thatcher's success was a gain for feminism. Such a position denies the extent to which many feminists do not simply want power on patriarchal terms, but want to transform the terms upon which it is defined. Claiming Thatcher as a sign of success of feminism is thus seen as a contradiction in terms. Other feminists, such as Brunt (1987), may not claim her as a 'success' for feminism, but do at least argue that she did not let the team down, as it were. While she was clearly not at all sympathetic to feminism, and her policies did not benefit women, she actively disproved the sexist assumption that women are incapable of holding high political office.

A much more common interpretation is that Thatcherism was part of a general backlash against feminism. Along with the rise of the new right, social conservative values, religious fundamentalism and a general bemoaning of progressive political movements, from 'loony lefties' to 'bra-burning Greenham militants', Thatcherism has been seen by many as part of a retrenchment of traditional conservative attitudes. According to this view, the privileges of substantial interest groups threatened by the demands for greater equality put forward by feminism, anti-racist movements, socialists and lesbian and gay liberation movements formed the basis for a general attack on progressivism.

While there has certainly been a backlash of sorts occurring, through which the language of rights, individualism and citizenship has been dramatically redefined, there are problems with this model of social and cultural change. It is important to acknowledge the complex reworking of many strands of feminism within the Thatcherite project; thus we would argue for a more complex model of power than the notion of a 'backlash' would suggest. Hence, while the emergence of a 'new oppressed' under Thatcherism, to use Maureen McNeil's phrase (see McNeil, Chapter 8), such as men's rights groups and fetal rights advocates, *does* represent an attack on gains made by feminism, it also represents an engagement with the terms set out by feminism. Importantly, this has not represented an engagement with feminism in the sense of furthering its aims. To the contrary, it has often been motivated by a desire to reject them. However, the idea that the influence of feminism has simply been displaced by the introduction of a reworking of the terms through which it successfully politicized a number of issues denies the extent to which those terms continue to define a number of political domains.

There are several points of overlap where Thatcherism not only engaged with the terms of feminism, but also with the language of feminism. For example, the language of rights, individualism and of equal opportunities, particularly in terms of the Thatcherite promotion of the enterprise culture as an arena in which women were invited to take up equal citizenship with men, is an important point of overlap. Thatcher's appeal to women to join in the new culture of enterprise denoted an important feature of her leadership which distinguished her from many conservative women campaigners; as did the lack of an explicit 'demonization' of feminism by the Prime Minister herself. Thatcher neither advocated a 'return to the home' for women, nor did she attribute to feminism *per se* the lion's share of blame for the perceived social disintegration following on from the 'permissive era'. Thatcher was a 'post-feminist' careerist, and was well known for her opinion that feminism was unnecessary: 'After all, I don't think there's been a great deal of discrimination against women for years', she asserted (Thatcher (1981) quoted in ten Tusscher (1986, p. 77)). Thatcher argued that women can have *both* meaningful lives as housewives and mothers *and* make a significant contribution to their families and society by entering paid labour or public, professional life, as she had done. It was in the name of furthering women's options in the paid labour force, for example, that Thatcher incorporated some of the language of feminism into her government's policies, such as the promotion of women's training schemes and her limited support for 'equal opportunities' programmes.

However, the double-standard in Thatcher's vision of women's 'equality' was clearly evident in her claim that:

> It is possible, in my view, for a woman to run a home and continue with her career *provided that two conditions are fulfilled.* First, her husband must be in sympathy with her wish to do another job. Secondly, where there is a young family, the joint incomes of husband and wife must be sufficient to employ a first class nanny-housekeeper to look after things in the wife's absence. *The second is the key to the whole plan.* (Thatcher (1960) quoted in ten Tusscher (1986, p. 79); emphasis added).

Women's 'choice' to enter the labour market is thus only open to a particular set of women: 'career' women who can pay to have other women perform 'their' domestic labour for them. Even for these women, it is contingent upon their husband's approval ('sympathy') and upon their earning a suffi-ciently high wage to ensure their children's well-being and the replacement of their household services. In the context of the cut-backs to welfare state provision of services for care of the elderly, the infirm and 'the community', which women have been expected to provide, the invitation to women to choose to take up their place in the enterprise culture has been severely limited indeed.

This 'presence' of 'feminism' within the policies of successive Thatcher administrations also corresponded, as Wilson (1987) has pointed out, to

Thatcher's desire to be seen as a leader with modern, forward-looking, up-to-date ideas which contrast with the out-dated, dependency culture ethos of her opponents. Necessary to this 'presence' of 'feminism' in the policies of the Thatcher governments, however, then, were significant absences. Her promotion of 'equal opportunities' training schemes for women and minorities was decollectivized and de-politicized through the language of 'greater individual choice' and the staunch opposition of her administration to any state role in the legal enforcement of greater equality of access. 'Greater choice' in this context did not mean 'equal opportunities' for women, but simply 'greater access' to the same lower rungs of the employment sector, in which women overwhelmingly perform low-paid, part-time, deskilled forms of work.

As there were both presences and absences in Thatcher's selective incorporation of the language of 'feminism' into her government's policies, so there was an equally selective taking-up of the moral conservative agenda proposed by women campaigners such as Mary Whitehouse. It is significant, for example, that the Thatcher governments avoided taking a clear stand on many of the issues of concern to moral conservatives, including abortion, pornography and sex education. While such absences may be seen as politically motivated, in the sense of minimizing opposition to the government, they were also evidence of a reluctance to invoke the powers of the state to intervene in 'moral' issues (a concern that is exercised selectively), a stance which clearly differentiated the Thatcher governments from moral campaigners who seek far more stringent measures. On the other hand, the concerns of moral conservative women were very clearly *present* in Thatcher's own rhetoric and policies, as well as those of other government officials, around the issue of the family. It was in her consistent and outspoken advocacy of a strong traditional family, discussed in the previous section, that the moral agenda of conservative women (and men) was incorporated into the Thatcherite project.

Conclusion

At the outset of this introduction, we examined cultural studies approaches to Thatcherism, highlighting an implicit overlap between Hall's work and developments within feminist theory generally. We also suggested that Hall's distinctive conceptualization of Thatcherism should be seen within the broader context of debates on the left about the place and significance of ideology in social and cultural analysis. We then looked at areas of feminist work in which one might expect to find an analysis of Thatcherism. However, we found that in feminist work that has been done on right-wing women and the effects of Thatcher's social policy on women, the relevance of the concept of Thatcherism as a distinctive phenomenon in terms of gender relations was problematic. This raised the question of whether Thatcherism can indeed be constituted as an 'ism' in relation to gender.

In an attempt to explore this question further, we outlined some of the ways in which approaches from feminism and cultural studies might be brought together in such a way as to identify the gendered dimensions of Thatcherism as a cultural phenomenon. Through an analysis of Thatcher's image and discourses of familialism, we indicated how the management of the presence and absence of gender, the denial of its significance and yet its implicit centrality, may have been linked to the management of key contradictions or tensions within Thatcherism more generally. We then analyzed some of the ways in which Thatcherism, rather than returning us to a pre-feminist context, actually reworked and responded to some key cultural shifts resulting from the impact of feminism.

Finally, we are suggesting in this introduction, as we do in this volume as a whole, that the combination of feminism and cultural studies can provide a significant set of analytical and conceptual frameworks within which to analyze both the gendered dimensions of culture and the cultural dimensions of gender. In the following chapters in this volume, approaches are applied to a range of cultural phenomena including popular culture, subcultures, and science and technology. In the final section of the book, we return again to the question of Thatcherism, where many of the issues raised in this introduction are explored further.

Notes

This introduction is based on a paper given to the Department of Cultural Studies, University of Birmingham, and the Department of Sociology, University of Lancaster, in June 1989. We would like to thank all those who contributed to the discussions which inspired us to rewrite and add to the original paper. We would like to thank Richard Johnson for his detailed commentary on the arguments presented here and Janet Newman for her comments upon, and encouragement with, the development of the ideas for this introduction.

1 These include Mulvey (1989), Kuhn (1982), Williamson (1986a) and Coward (1984).
2 See, for example, the writings of Hélène Cixous, Luce Irigaray and Julia Kristeva in Marks and de Courtivron (1981).
3 See, for example, Rich (1980b).
4 See, for example, Smart (1989) and Pateman (1988).
5 It would be interesting, for example, to analyze the contradictory discourses of Thatcherism in terms of how they might inscribe women specifically. The identities of wife/mother/waged worker/sexually attractive woman/female

consumer, for example, are contradictory ones, and are often constructed as mutually exclusive to a greater extent than their masculine equivalents. Thus, if the appeal of Thatcherism has been its ability to offer contradictory identifications, as Hall (1988a) argues, then there may be a gendered particularity to this appeal.

6   Other feminist work on right-wing women includes Koonz (1987).

Part Two:
Representation and identity

1

Melodrama's gendered audience

ANGELA PARTINGTON

Cultural studies has concerned itself with the relationships between 'real' differences, such as gender and class, and differences as represented through the leisure market, namely, differences in taste. Instead of dismissing differences in taste as superficial or immaterial, cultural studies has emphasized their meaningfulness. But the assumption that differences in taste are not 'real' has persisted, most recently in the notion that the mass-market system for the production and distribution of cultural commodities, such as films, has resulted in a 'waning of affect' (Jameson, 1984, p. 61), because real differences have been absorbed and made arbitrary by becoming 'pure differentiality'. In my view, such conclusions are the consequence of attempting to understand mass culture through textual analysis alone. If we study the *relationships* between audiences and commodities, and the *conditions* of meaning-making, it can be argued that consumer skills, and the development of tastes and preferences, are the very means by which differences survive and intensify in mass culture. By looking at some of the reasons why British working-class women may have found pleasures in watching film melodrama in the 1950s, I hope to show how class and gender-specific knowledges may have been invested in the films, as part of meaning-making processes which ensure the reproduction of class-gender differences.

In this chapter, I will attempt to place the audience for film melodrama in its historical context, instead of simply conducting a textual analysis of films. Rather than attempting to discover *the* meaning of the films, I will suggest some of the ways in which they may have been invested with particular meanings by a specific audience. I will argue that a mass-market culture does not simply 'express' extra-textual differences, such as class and gender, but provides the conditions for the 'simulation' (reproductive transformation) of differences, which is carried out by consumers when they invest goods with meaning. My contention will be that women's use of goods, including film viewing, is a ritual celebration of feminine identity – 'masquerade' (see p. 50), an opportunity to express exclusive knowledges, and therefore provides the conditions for struggle between classed and gendered groups. I will argue that any textual unity which exists 'does so primarily as discursive relations, creating objects rather than referring to them' (Hustwitt, 1984, p. 94).

By drawing attention to the way in which working-class women's skills proliferated around commodities in the 1950s, I want to suggest some of the ways in which these skills may have been used in meaning-production, through the consumption of Hollywood melodrama. It is often assumed that in melodrama 'the address is from one bourgeois to another bourgeois' (Nowell-Smith, 1977, p. 114). But by emphasizing the specificity of the knowledges and competences of working-class women at that time, I hope to show how melodrama's combination of the display of goods with the invitation to engage emotionally offered opportunities for the investment of this audience's knowledges, and for producing meanings and pleasures for which the text's manipulation of cinematic form, and its construction of an ideological subject, cannot account. I will try to show how the mass-market system itself facilitated this proliferation of consumer skills, enabling women to use commodities, such as films, to satisfy needs which were not anticipated by the producers and distributors, or recognized or endorsed by those professionals who were trying to educate working-class women as consumers at the time.[1] In short, I will argue that working-class women's consumption of film melodrama was a form of appropriation, and that their enjoyment of melodrama was in terms of 'masquerade', an acting out of the repertoire of femininities produced within consumer culture, and therefore a form of resistance against those who were attempting to socialize them into housewives.

I am not assuming an essentially antagonistic relationship between the pleasures of consumption and the needs of capitalism, but drawing attention to the contradictions of hegemony. A mass-market system cannot simply translate class and gender differences into commodity aesthetics in a contradiction-free way; neither can it fix the use-values of commodities (see Slater, 1987). Women's narcissistic pleasures cannot be dismissed as fulfilling the needs of capitalism, because the relations of 'looking' are historically constituted and therefore open to contestation. I will argue that the mass-market system, which gendered relations of looking support, provides consumers with a means of articulating 'real' difference. I will emphasize those conditions of melodrama's class and gender-specific meanings which derive from its being re-merchandized in the 1950s for a working-class female market. This re-merchandizing involved a particular presentation of stars, clothes, interiors and 'emotions' on which I will focus as a possible basis for a reading of film melodrama, which contradicts the 'ideologies' implicit in the construction of a housewife identity.

Reading melodrama

Film studies has understood melodrama to refer to social reality through a process of abstraction and/or symbolization/allegory:

> The persistence of melodrama might indicate the ways in which popular culture has . . . made note of social crises . . . but has also resolutely refused to understand social change in other than *private contexts and emotional terms* . . . it has also meant a lamentable ignorance of *the properly social and political* dimensions of these changes and their causality, and consequently it has encouraged increasingly *escapist* forms of mass entertainment. (Elsaesser, 1973, p. 4; my emphasis).

Melodrama's 'unreality', then, is a consequence of the critic's class and gender-specific notions of 'reality', or of specific comprehensions of conflict and change. The experiences of working-class women, in which conflict and change are inevitably 'private and emotional', are relegated to the realms of 'escape', rather than reconciled with the 'properly social and political'.

Film studies has also carried out a rehabilitation of melodrama, rendering it 'film as film', and appropriating it in order to consecrate the pleasures of form while devaluing the pleasures of consumption. This has involved a reassessment of the literary theories and methodologies used in the criticism of bourgeois drama, and the development of anti-realist or modernist criteria according to which melodramatic meaning can be seen to be generated at a symbolic and/or metaphorical level within the text itself. Although it is assumed to share the 'ideology' of bourgeois drama, its tendency towards non-naturalism and unrealism has allowed criticism to focus on its ability to serve the modernist pleasures of 'pure form'. The presentation of cinematic events 'for their own sake' suggests to the critic a break between signifier and signified, in which 'the play of meaning' can occur, unrestricted by references to the 'extra textual' (see Feuer, 1984, p. 5).

Feminist criticism has contributed substantially to the development of this textual analysis, by arguing that not only is the extra-textual the province of realism and therefore bourgeois, but that it also serves to obscure patriarchal ideologies at work in the text. For example, it has been argued that 'The shape of these films' texts consists of intra- and intertextual relations at work in any given film, a network within which the ideologies (e.g. a form of patriarchal ideology) are produced' (Johnstone, 1975, p. 123).

But feminists have also concerned themselves with the contextual aspects of film's production and consumption, in order to stress that meanings are a product of the relationship between viewers and texts, rather than of the text itself (see Gledhill, 1987). However, there remains an emphasis on textual unity, and an insistence on the text as a representation of the extra-textual, which is decoded by the viewer. Contextual studies tend to share the assumption that the meaning of melodrama is constituted in what-it-does-to-the-audience, and therefore the assumption that films can be categorized into the 'ideological' on the one hand and the radical or feminist on the other, according to the meanings it enables the audience to construct (see Tasker in this volume). In contrast, I am interested in what the audience does to the film, and in how films might be *read* as feminist, or made to embody women's interests by reading them in particular ways. To this end, I would put the emphasis on the discursive relations which the audience provide, and of which textual unity is an effect.

I want to question distinctions between the intra-textual and extra-textual, by arguing that meaning-production is a consequence of their interdepend- ence and inseparability. The persistence of such distinctions explains why so much of film studies appears as a search for the 'hidden meanings' (Biskind, 1983, p. 3) or the 'real meanings' of a film, as if they are buried deep in its textual layers and are only accessible to the skilled digging of the formalist critic. My contention is that the meanings of melodrama (or any cultural form) are produced in its relationship with audiences, and are therefore not 'fixable' in this way.

Rather than reading melodrama as an expressive or representational form, as film studies is inclined to do, I would argue that melodrama is meaningful by virtue of its relationship with a historically specific, gendered audience. This means that not only is the meaning of the film dependent on a gendered viewer, but that a particular reading of the film requires membership of a group which is simultaneously being addressed as the consumer of other goods. It has been pointed out that melodrama is determined

> by an ideology of the spectacle and the spectacular . . . the creation or re-enactment of situations which the spectator can identify with and recognize . . . depends to a large extent on the aptness of the iconog- raphy (the 'visualization') . . . In other words, the aesthetic qualities of this type of cinema depend on the ways 'melos' is given to 'drama' by means of lighting, montage, visual rhythm, decor, style of acting, music. (Elsaesser, 1973, p. 8).

Melodrama is a formula, a particular configuration of elements or 'ingre- dients' whose popular meanings depend on its repeatability. Its meanings for a popular audience reside not in the expressive/symbolic/metaphorical use of these elements, but in the consumption of melodrama as a social act. The particular elements mentioned here (interiors, clothes, emotional confrontation, swelling music) draw on knowledges and competences which are both specifically feminine and specifically consumerist. In the 1950s it was working-class women who were being actively constructed as consumers by the marketing industries. What Elsaesser calls 'visualisation' could equally well be called *styling*, and compared to the use of design as a marketing tool in manufacturing and retailing. This is the basis on which I shall suggest readings for the film melodrama of the 1950s.

Some feminists have argued that melodrama demands 'the traditionally feminine competences associated with the responsibility for "managing" the sphere of the emotional life' (Brunsdon, 1981, p. 36). These competences must be historicised, however, and located in their material circumstances (rather than in the psyche), if they are to explain how melodrama is *used* by a specific audience (rather than reflecting already formed desires). These competences were combined with new consumer skills for working-class women in the 1950s, so that melodrama's setting/decor is no longer primarily expressive of the characters' fixations, but an opportunity for this audience to exercise exclusive competences.

Gendered consumption

The notion of the expressive/representational text has created a problem for critical practice about how to theorize the gendered viewer. Differences between audiences ultimately have to be attributed to psychic determinations of the viewers' relationships with the text, to explain their different decoding processes. The female spectator is presumed to oscillate between feminine (narcissistic) and masculine (masochistic for women) positions (invoking a transvestite metaphor), in order to read the image (see Mulvey, 1975). A spurious distinction between 'the social act of consuming' and 'engage[ment] in the processes and pleasures of meaning-making' (Kuhn, 1984, p. 23) has been erected. The female gaze has been described as an 'inability to fetishize' (Doane, 1982, p. 80) and an 'over-identification' with the image. While these theories differ in some respects, they share a tendency to take reading positions 'produced' in the text, combined with psychoanalytic theory, as a substitute for a view of the audience in its historical context.

But 'unease and the personal experience of contradiction' (Gamman and Marshment, 1988, p. 5), has contributed to a controversy surrounding the use of psychoanalytic theory in cultural analysis. Such a theory of the gaze is tautological; if a woman looks, she is masculinized, if a man is the object of the gaze, he is feminized, because both are 'trapped' within a logic which aligns sexual difference within a subject/object dichotomy. But an analysis of the historical and economic determinants, which have positioned women as narcissistic consumer-displayers, provides an alternative to accounts which pathologize the female spectator.

It can be argued that narcissistic identification with objects does not preclude the ability to objectify/fetishize, as most theories of looking assume. Associations between masculinity and voyeurism, and between femininity and exhibitionism (on which psychoanalytic theories of the gaze draw), have been *historically* constructed.[2] Kaja Silverman has challenged the simple subject/object dichotomy on which the above theories of the gaze depend. Instead, she emphasizes the 'inside-out structure of the gaze' (Silverman, 1986, p. 143), and argues that exhibitionism and voyeurism are not mutually exclusive, but are interdependent for both men and women, though in different ways. Therefore objectification is an aspect of the-one-who-looks as well as the-one-who-is-looked-at.

If we consider the implications of this collapse of the subject/object dichotomy for feminine subjectivity, it becomes apparent that voyeurism and exhibitionism are also interdependent. Again historically, in order for women to become skilled in inviting the look, they have had to acquire knowledges and competences enabling them to discriminate between other objects, and to use them to adorn themselves and their surroundings. In order to exercise such skills, in the expression of preferences and tastes, women have had to become subjects of a (female) voyeuristic, fetishizing gaze, while at the same time identifying narcissistically with objects (goods), since they were constituted themselves as objects of the male gaze.

The accounts of women's consumption of 1950s film melodrama which I will offer below are intended as evidence that women's narcissism is not a consequence of their inability to fetishize, but on the contrary, of their insistence on using objects in meaning-making. Objects become accoutrements of femininity not just because they invite a voyeuristic male gaze, but because *looking at them* is the basis of women's shared knowledges and pleasures. Female subjectivity is acquired through learning-to-look as well as learning-to-be-looked-at. Indeed, the latter is made possible by the former. As an alternative to psychoanalytic accounts, I suggest that the female consumer reads images by using them in the processes of 'masquerade', a kind of subjectivity which evokes the specifically feminine, and historically specific, fusion of exhibitionism and fetishism.[3] The details revealed in set design and costume, close-ups and deep focusing, lighting and choreography, are the same ones emphasized in women's magazines – about hair and make-up, interior decoration, the preparation of food, the cut of a suit, etc. They are not mere 'setting' or 'metaphor' but the material conditions of a feminine culture. This suggests that there is a female gaze which is neither masochistic nor passively narcissistic.

Although I will use my own readings of melodramas to support this view, I do not want to suggest that women's investment in this cultural form can be read off the films. My readings are deliberately contrary to those provided by textual analysis, because I am concerned to show how any unity/coherence they may have is a consequence of the discursive practices brought to bear on them. My attention to the text will be subordinated to a concern with how the gendered subject may have 'recognize[d] her . . . needs' (Koch, 1985, p. 114). I would argue that my readings help to explain melodrama's particular popularity in the 1950s, because they emphasize the historical and cultural *conditions of meaning-making*, of which textual coherence is an effect. My objective is not to discover *the* meaning of the 1950s melodramas, but to explore how working-class women may have used them in the recognition and articulation of needs which brought them into conflict with male and/or middle-class audiences. My interest in films is restricted to intertextual relationships through which different needs may have been recognized, not as already formed needs (as in psychoanalytic approaches), but as needs which depend on cultural products for their existence and articulation in the first place.

The historically constructed 'hegemony of looking' which I have outlined above is unstable and conditional, in that it provides the conditions for women to resist the roles which patriarchal ideologies assign to them, at the same time as supporting the construction of women as consumers. This is because late capitalism requires a multiplicity of cultural codes (each specific to a consumer group) in order to support mass markets, and it is this multiplicity which provides conditions for difference, conflict and resistance. Consumption reaffirms differences, since consumers reproduce or 'simulate' differences by making choices and expressing preferences. The identification and targeting of working-class markets for films confirms the existence of a class-specific feminine cultural code, according to which films might have meaning. Melodrama was a Hollywood product targetted at working-class women in the 1950s, and while, on the one hand, it can be seen as promoting goods in its display of clothes and interiors (part of the construction of markets), on the other, it can be seen as providing conditions for women's articulation of 'improper' desires. The film industry was using fashionable clothes and elaborate interiors as a way of packaging the melodrama, in order to target working-class women, but I will argue that the audience would have been in a position to use their knowledge of these clothes and interiors to construct readings of the film which were incompatible with the producers' 'ideological' intentions.

The attempt to construct new working-class markets for goods was made in a number of ways by various professionals in the 1950s. The aestheticization of the working-class home, for example, took place through the introduction of the discipline of home-management and the mechanization of domestic labour, establishing a need for new manufactured and designed goods. There was an attempt to manage scientifically and supervise consumption and reproduction, to regulate the sphere of exchange and to socialize domestic labour, in the context of late capitalism. The 1950s witnessed an acceleration in these developments (see Winship, 1983; Bland *et al.*, 1978), and their application with regard to working-class women in particular. Welfare provision was largely about setting up new norms of family life for the working-class housewife (see Wilson, 1977, p. 77). Women's magazines became manuals/trade press for consumer-labour

(Winship, 1983, p. 34), and a means of educating working-class women in home management (Forty, 1986, pp. 216–17); they also promoted modern design and 'labour saving' equipment. The efficiency of the working-class housewife was defined increasingly in terms of proper consumption (to satisfy endorsed needs) of approved commodities. Advertising continued in its wartime attempts at the management and regulation of consumption patterns, to join the ranks of the 'planners' (see Myers, 1986, pp. 30–9). New consumer skills became an essential part of the repertoire of knowledges for working-class women.

According to experts in the 1950s, housewifely duties were to be carried out through the consumption of the products of reorganized production through the exercise of restraint, and the repression of desires for the useless and frivolous, that is, the acquisition of precisely defined, highly specific, but finite and limited consumer competences. These developments contributed to the changes in the circumstances under which films were produced and distributed.

None of these developments was a threat to the film industry, indeed they created an interdependence between different industries (e.g. television became another outlet for films and provided a new way of publicizing them, as well as a source of new talent), but they explain the need for the film product to be *remerchandized* for working-class female audiences. British television was no 'competition' for Hollywood (see Lewis, 1978, p. 208), but it did eventually provide a replacement for the low-budget women's picture in the form of soap opera, so that the new 'women's genre' for the cinema had to be differentiated from this, hence the appearance of the full-blooded melodrama in the 1950s. It was Hollywood's solution to the problem of finding an audience amongst working-class women whose repertoire of consumer competences was rapidly expanding.

The Hollywood product and working-class markets

Unlike many of the other commodities being mass-marketed in the 1950s, films already had working-class markets, since cinema-going had been popular with women before and during the Second World War. But, as with any other industry in the postwar period, the priority was to *segment and identify market sections through product differentiation*, rather than to produce a 'mass market' product, in order to remain competitive (see Balio, 1976, pp. 315–31). This was because commodified leisure, and the proliferation of other goods for working-class markets, meant that cinema-going would not remain a primary instance of consumer spending, and a change in strategy was necessary for the film industry to remain profitable. As a consequence of the successful deployment of new merchandizing strategies, to target class- and gender-specific markets, people went to the cinema less often in the 1950s than they had before the war, but paid more to see 'bigger' films chosen for different reasons. Eventually, television also stimulated this demand for a new kind of film. The decrease in the number of cinemas was a deliberately deployed strategy of the film industry, not a direct result of competition from television.

Changes in the conditions of production (with more profit at the point of distribution rather than exhibition) resulted in a transformation of the kind of films being made. The trend towards fewer, more expensive 'custom tailored' (Whitney, 1982, p. 196) films which had begun during the war years, when cinema-going was at the height of its popularity, now became the main preoccupation of the industry. Since customized films ran longer to fuller houses a reduction in the numbers of films produced was possible. So while the costs of film production increased during this period, this was easily compensated for by a dramatic rise in profits. Although there was a decline in profits between 1947 and 1950, the rise of the customized 'big picture' (musical extravaganza, biblical epic, star vehicles, melodrama) succeeded in restoring wartime profits.

Anti-trust legislation proved to be a way of regulating and rationalizing the industry, rather than of inhibiting monopolistic practices (its ostensible function), since they benefited monopoly capital in the long term by enabling major companies to adjust to changing markets (see Glomery, 1982, pp. 206–9). Investment in distribution (including promotion and advertising) became the key to the maintenance of monopoly power (see Gordon, 1976, p. 467), so that by the 1950s it was not even necessary to own a studio in order to be a 'major' (e.g. United Artists). The same studios which had enjoyed oligopolistic powers in the earlier integrated (studio) system became constituents of huge multifaceted conglomerates.

Although the product became more expensive to produce in the 1950s, it was more 'designed', in the sense that a greater proportion of the budget was spent on its appearance-in-the-market place, and on merchandizing. In other words, the industry was now able to target audiences, as market segments, as well as control the quality of its product. The film melodrama, as one of a range of Hollywood products, can be compared with certain fashion and domestic goods which were being produced within a mass-market system for the first time, in that the target was the newly defined working-class housewife. Changes in the conditions of production and distribution of goods in general, including films, demonstrate that the mass-market system depends not on 'democratization', the diffusion of cultural practices across classes or the erosion of differences between groups, as is often assumed, but on segmentation and the multiplication of class and gender differences.

In the late 1940s, the British film industry finally conceded to American dominance in the international market, following the disruptions of war and the accumulation of a huge quantity of Hollywood products ready to be released in Britain and the rest of Europe. The home-grown product had not completely died out, and British 'weepies' such as *Brief Encounter* (1945) continued to address the middle-class housewife who may have been offended by the 'vulgarity' of American films. For British working-class women, however, Hollywood films could be used to articulate desires for the 'superfluous' and the 'trivial' which were directly opposed to 'good' (middle-class) taste. British experts defined good taste in terms of restraint and efficiency, and were opposed to the use of styling in the production of designed goods. Since the Hollywood melodrama was made according to an aesthetic which deliberately gave priority to glamour and fashion, in order to reach a specific market, it represented an antithesis to the aesthetic of disinterest which was being promoted by the British cultural leadership.[4] This irresolvable contradiction, between the planners of the national economy, for whom consumption had to be regulated, and the international capitalists, for whom consumption had to be 'libidinised' (Hall, quoted in Moore (1988)), contributed to the conditions of meaning-making brought to melodrama by working-class women.

Shopping and cinema-going

In a mass-market system, the 'buyer' is at least as, if not more, important than the designer/stylist, because s/he is responsible for understanding popular taste and 'what the consumer wants', rather than what she 'should' want (see Blumer, 1973, p. 331). The consumer has specific expectations which are very different from those of the traditional customer (see Clarke and Critcher, 1985, p. 96) and it is the buyer who is responsible for assessing and translating these into specific demands. The increased emphasis on distribution in the film industry suggests that audiences were being seen more and more as consumer groups. For example, the run a theatre had became a crucial factor in product differentiation (see Huettig, 1976, p. 246), which can be compared to the identity which shops confer on other goods. The distribution and exhibition of 'big' pictures can be compared with the merchandizing of new products in the context of the diversification which took place in the fashion and retailing industries in the 1950s, specifically to pursue new working-class markets. For example, the 'chain store' strategy enabled a standardized product and decreasing costs, based on the recognition that this included the 'movie-going experience' and not just the film. This can be compared with the development of retailing chains for fashion goods in Britain in the 1950s, which suggests the recognition of a proliferation of consumer competences and expectations (see Gardener, 1986). The larger chains invested in heating systems, spectacular design, auxiliary services and ultra-helpful staff, so films could be expected to draw audiences on the basis of the cinema in which they were screened.

Cinema-going patterns were affected by postwar reconstruction (housing, town planning, etc.), and longer runs and costlier seats were possible as a result. Postwar reconstruction, the resulting demographic and geographic changes and the promotion of the home as the site of consumption and leisure became the basis on which the film industry repositioned its 'women's' product. The quantity of films for women audiences shrank, while the 'quality' (in terms of more lavish sets, bigger stars, etc.) increased. It can be argued that these characteristics are a source of pleasure for a (working-class) audience who 'notice . . . the material world' (Press, 1989, p. 229) which the film depicts, while they offend the sensibilities of (middle-class) audiences who are looking for characters with whom to identify.[5] Working-class women could read melodrama as conforming to 'realism's ever-shifting criteria of relevance and credibility, for it has power only on the premiss of a recognizable, socially constructed world' (Gledhill, 1987, p. 37). Melodrama's display of material goods could be used by an audience of working-class women to forge this recognizability. For working-class women, cinema-going became just one of a whole range of leisure practices, which now included shopping.

My analysis of *Ruby Gentry* (1952) is meant to demonstrate some of the possible consequences of this use of melodrama. There is a dramatic change in the kinds of clothes worn by the central character of *Ruby Gentry*, which takes place when she marries a wealthy man. The early scenes show her in denim jeans, while she wears Parisian style haute-couture later in the film. It is possible to read the clothes symbolically, representing her humble origins which contrast with her privileged married status. For instance, in an early scene Ruby is seen looking at the expensive clothes worn by her socially superior rival for the affections of Boake, her childhood sweetheart. In such a reading the clothes are seen as signifiers within a text which is understood primarily as the mediation of a narrative, helping to express in visual terms why and how the Ruby character becomes so ambitious.

But if we attend differently to the clothes, and the way they are worn and photographed as material things, it is possible to see how more meanings, which are not entirely compatible with the 'message' of the narrative, might proliferate around them. For instance, in the first few minutes of the film, there are several lingering shots of Ruby, played by Jennifer Jones, in her jeans (which are tight at the waist, cropped to reveal the ankles, and worn with a clinging sweater), in which she stands in a doorway so that the light from the interior throws the shape of her body into silhouette. Since the film is in black and white, the effect is particularly striking. (This image was also used as a publicity still.) These shots, together with many others which show this and other outfits from a variety of angles, can be compared with photographic fashion imagery from women's magazines at the time, through which casual clothes such as denim jeans were beginning to acquire status as fashion items. So, far from looking poor and scruffy, Ruby looks glamorous and fashionable. This reading contradicts that which attention to the narrative would construct, in which the jeans are simply a sign of Ruby's class position.

Ruby's fashionableness has particular resonance for a working-class audience, since she manages to achieve it despite her poverty. In comparison with her, Tracy (her rival) looks prim and housewifely: attention is drawn to the white gloves she wears, which match the white collar on her dress, by a close-up shot of her hand on the driving wheel of her car which has no narrative function whatsoever. In a later scene, we see Ruby sporting dark glasses and a smouldering cigarette as driving accessories, which again emphasize her assertive and glamorous femininity, which contrasts with Tracy's passive and demure image. When Ruby becomes wealthy, her outfits are not only expensive like Tracy's but the very height of fashion, unlike Tracy's. In a scene where all the characters are in evening dress, Ruby wears a strapless gown with a boned bodice and a chiffon stole, undoubtedly inspired by Christian Dior's controversial postwar designs, while Tracy wears a white organza dress with puffed sleeves, not unlike Joan Crawford's 'Letty Lynton' dresses. Women viewers would have known that this style had been around since the 1930s (see Herzog and Gaines, 1985), and therefore out of fashion. While middle-class women may have read these differences as expressions of 'character', working-class women could have used them as a means of exercising new consumer skills while at the same time celebrating class identity.

These readings contradict those which foreground the narrative and the plot of poor-girl-craves-wealth-and-power-to-take-revenge-for-being-jilted, because the jeans do not simply connote poverty. Readings which foreground the clothes as referents to other images, rather than as simple expressions of the story, also have consequences for the film's characterizations, because the question of who deserves to get Boake is answered differently if we see Ruby as strong and resourceful rather than as someone who does not know her place. The clothes denote the contrasting characters of Ruby and Tracy, but because the 'bad girl' is fashionably dressed throughout, it makes it difficult to rely on 'identification' as a means of judging their actions. For a working-class viewer familiar with contemporary fashions, the response to the revenge Ruby takes on Boake when he marries Tracy would be of sympathetic anger and admiration rather than disapproval, and sits uncomfortably with the sad and pitiful character with which the narrative resolution presents us.

The star system and fashion

In the 1950s, stars were used increasingly by the film industry as a means of product differentiation (it had been long understood that different stars appealed to different audiences). Melodrama's presentation of the interior motivation of individual characters is often deemed unrealistic, partly because the star's presence never disappears beneath the illusion of the narrative. Indeed 'the powerfully, inescapably present, always-already-signifying nature of the star images more often than not creates problems in the construction of character' (Dyer, 1981, p. 265). In so far as the middle-class viewer is looking for character portrayals in the pursuit of the pleasures of identification, as I have already suggested, the melodrama offers little satisfaction. But for a working-class viewer the star's function as clotheshorse and model offers particular pleasures, and an opportunity to exercise exclusive consumer skills.

Audience interest in stars' private lives is largely an interest in their personal tastes and preferences. Annuals such as *Preview* included picture articles like 'Cars of the Stars' (1956), and photographs of their homes and gardens. Pin-ups are illustrations of hairstyles and make-up as well as publicity for an actress or actor. The consumer skills of the working-class woman, acquired partly through the consumption of other films but also through other media products and designed goods, enables her to decode the melodrama in terms which are irreducible to a narrative logic. Her appreciation of the star's image, in terms of a look or a style achieved through the use of cosmetics, clothes and other accoutrements, enables the film to be read as a 'vehicle' (e.g. close-ups need not have a narrative function) and not necessarily a privileged instance of the star's image.

The ability to read a film as a star vehicle provides the possibility of 'an excess of effect' which depends both on specifically feminine reading skills and on a capacity for emotional investment in the relationships presented in the film. For example, to read *Ruby Gentry* as a vehicle for Jennifer Jones (a 'Fury' rather than a 'Sex Goddess' or a 'Vamp') enables a sympathetic engagement with the contradictions and frustrations of her situation, and draws out the lack of resolution to the problems raised in the narrative. This kind of engagement is much more nuanced than the moralistic stance encouraged by the narrative closure (according to which she is either a transgressor who has brought her own punishment on herself, or a victim of the class system). Her 'spectacularization', achieved through the combination of costume and lighting, enables 'introjection', a mode of identification in which 'stereotypes of the feminine character . . . contain the promise of gratification to women' (Koch, 1985, p. 118).

The characters in Hollywood melodrama are created through clothes, cars and houses, but at the same time these things elaborate on the 'always already signifying' star images. In *Written on the Wind* (1956) there are four main characters played by stars of varying degrees of fame. Each character has a very different style, suggested by the kinds of clothes they wear. Their clothes can be read as part of the characterizations, which help to support a narrative reading of the film, but equally they can be read as elaborations of the stars' images, which are not reducible to the sense of the narrative. Indeed, reading the clothes constructs more 'sense' than the narrative does, making the plot structure somewhat redundant. This is because the way the clothes contribute to the stars' personae completely changes the problem posed by the narrative, and the audience's relation to it, from the one assumed by textual analysis. The question of what might ensue as a result of the characters' interactions would not have been relevant for working-class female viewers, because this audience's knowledges about stars and about clothes enabled them to know the answer to this at this outset. The only pleasure the narrative could have offered this audience was in showing how the ending is arrived at.

For instance, Rock Hudson, who plays Mitch, wears casual 'outdoorsy' clothes for many of his scenes. These contrast with the playboy-style outfits worn by Robert Stack, who drives around in a yellow sports car as Kyle. Rock Hudson, a much bigger star than Stack, cultivated something of a 'new man' image, in that it was rugged and traditionally masculine but sensitive, honest and gentle rather than brutal – 'tough but tender' (Segal, 1988, p. 71). Thus, the rural connotations of his appearance (also visible in *All That Heaven Allows* of the previous year, pp. 65–6) are part of his general image-management. This look exemplified the new, slightly softer, more casual style which was beginning to influence men's fashion. But, this preferability of the character played by Hudson as against that by Stack is contradicted by the narrative, in that Lucy, played by Lauren Bacall, chooses to marry Kyle instead of Mitch. It is only when this marriage fails that Lucy realizes Mitch would have been a better choice, but an audience who were becoming skilled consumers of men's clothes (working-class women) could have told her this right at the beginning, just by looking at what the stars were wearing.

Similarly, the audience's knowledge of the clothes worn by the female stars, Lauren Bacall and Dorothy Malone, generates more meanings than the narrative can support. As Marylee, Malone wears tight, brightly coloured dresses and trousers, stiletto heels and shirt-style blouses with the collar turned up, ostentatious jewellery and glamourizing accessories such as chiffon scarves worn as neckerchiefs. There are several scenes, most notably where she dances in front of a photograph of Mitch, where she 'poses' in front of the camera so that the image resembles a pin-up. The obvious contrast with Lucy (Bacall), who is restrained and tasteful, signals to an audience who is attending to the characters and the narrative that there is no way Marylee is going to achieve happiness (i.e. win Mitch's affections). But for a viewer who is interested in the clothes for their own sake, they do more than simply characterize. Dorothy Malone, while not as big a star as Bacall, was building an image of assertive sexuality, beautiful but tough and indomitable, striking rather than conventionally pretty. So, although her function in the narrative is to represent a weak, neurotic woman who does not deserve to be loved, this is contradicted by the suggestion, which the clothes make to viewers with specific consumer skills, that she does not need a man at all but is independent and self-sufficient.

At the end of the film it is Marylee who inherits the oil business, rather than either Kyle or Mitch. This resolution can be read as a satisfactorily Freudian closure to the narrative, in that the business (symbolized by the phallic model oil-rig which she caresses in the penultimate scene) is presented as a substitute for fulfilment through a man (Mitch). But, if we have been paying attention to the way Malone's clothes assert a positive female sexuality, we can respond to her fate with a sense of triumph rather than condescending pity. Instead of seeing the inheritance as a consolation prize, we can see it as the real object of her desire (for which Mitch had been a substitute, not the other way round). It is not such a surprise that she has beaten both men in their competition to prove their worthiness as heirs, to an audience familiar with contemporary fashions. Like Jennifer Jones/Ruby Gentry, the conflation of Malone/Marylee produces a force which 'challenges ideological assumptions about women's place in the family' (Budge, 1988, p. 107), since she destroys the family instead of holding it together. Not only does she get away with it but she is rewarded with power and wealth.

While providing a means of product differentiation, then, the star system also exemplifies the limits of attempts to control consumption. It enables the viewer to construct meanings beyond the confines of the individual commodity-text, precisely because of stars' values as signs of difference. As an example of a mechanism for product differentiation and target marketing, the star system exemplifies both the need for a mass-market system for the expansion of capital, and the consequence of such a system in that it enables the rearticulation of class difference and provides new conditions for class–gender struggle. The melodrama, like the clothes and interiors its stars display so well, becomes the conditions for the articulation of a specifically feminine subordinate culture.

Melodrama's styling

A mass-market fashion system relies on an injection of design into manu-facturing, in order to create differences between otherwise similar objects. A mass-market film system also relies on an injection of styling, which is a combination of the work of designers, costumiers, lighting camera-men, technicians and actors/actresses, as well as writers and directors, to determine the look of the product. I would argue that the reason the Hollywood melodrama reached its peak in the 1950s was precisely because of the more accurate targeting of working-class women as an audience, through the tailoring of the melodrama to meet this audience's expecta-tions. It was at this time that consumption was becoming 'an emotional trip' (Schwartz–Cowan, 1976, p. 16) for working-class women in Britain. The melodrama addresses specifically working-class women in that, unlike the prewar 'women's picture', both 'domestic' and 'emotional', it provides opportunities for the exercise of a particular combination of skills specific to that audience, that is, newly acquired consumer skills.

Both the virtual disappearance of the 'women's picture' and the differences between it and the new melodrama are effects of mass-marketing and commodification. The women's picture has been identified as a genre, in that its themes, preoccupations, formal structure and visual style have been used to describe it as such (see Haskell, 1973). While melodramas are often 'weepies', they differ from the women's picture in terms of styling. For instance, *Brief Encounter*, with its chintzy interiors and classic clothes, is a post Second World War version of a women's film rather than a melodrama, since it does not offer any opportunities for the exercise of newly acquired consumer skills. In the women's film, emotional investment by the audience is an essential part of the process of identifying with the central character (see Haskell, 1973). But in melodrama, extreme emotion from ecstasy to agony, 'panic and latent hysteria' (Elsaesser, 1973, p. 13), becomes a feature for its own sake, detached from strictly narrative necessities, as if the audience is expected to be already familiar with the range of emotional responses a film can arouse, and to be able to experience them without necessarily 'identifying' with a character or being convinced by the fictional situation.

Although 'the pleasure of being touched and giving way to tears' (Neale, 1986, p. 6) has been identified as specific to melodrama, the particular appeal this has for women audiences has not been examined:

> melodrama involves extremes of polarised emotion: love and hate, joy and despair, and so on. These extremes mark and are marked by the vicissitudes of desire: its coming into existence, its realization (brief or lasting) or its failure, and in particular the blockages to its fulfilment . . . The tears, in their function as demand, inscribe a position of narcissistic *power* in implying an Other who will respond . . . The words 'if only' mark both the fact of loss, that it is too late, yet simultaneously the possibility that things might have been different. (Neale, 1986, pp. 12, 22).

If instead of evoking the loss of the mother in the Oedipal drama, which is usually used to explain the pleasures of melodrama for an undifferentiated audience, we attend to the specifically feminine subject positions created culturally and historically, from which desire and narcissistic power can be articulated, we begin to see how the melodrama draws on women's competences and offers opportunities for meaning-production to a specifically working-class female audience. Women's desires are articulated through the knowledges and pleasures of consumption, where both the emotional and the domestic have been redefined through the construction of working-class markets.

Melodrama's particular use of sound, lighting, montage and decor, or what I have referred to as styling, has been noted. But the meanings ascribed to these elements tend to echo the themes in the story, and become simply a visual language for the expression of ideas which could have been mediated in a literary form. The meaningfulness of contrasting materials and textures, subtleties of surface or shape, differences in colour or tone, is attributed to the 'vivid eye' of the director rather than to the consumer skills of the audience. The social significance of decor and clothing is reduced to the 'symbolization of objects', that is, given a literary value which denies the pleasures of an audience whose desire for consumer goods is already being addressed elsewhere. For example, it has been argued that 'the critique of culture posed by *All That Heaven Allows* is hardly very profound . . . Although the film presents a clash of two sets of values, the conflict between them often boils down to *no more than* a choice of different lifestyles' (Biskind, 1983, p. 332; my emphasis).

For a male critic in the 1980s the differences are insignificant, for a working-class housewife who is expected to be able to tell the difference between a 'well-designed' kitchen and an 'inefficient' one, these differences would not only carry connotations of class, gender and age, but represent notions of style about which it is precisely women's task to know. The 'two dimensionality' (Haskell, 1973, p. 272) of 'perfectly coiffed' housewives refers to their unreality for the critic, but for this audience their resemblance to magazine images gives them resonance, and makes it possible to construct meanings beyond the confines of the narrative. The resemblance of the images in *All That Heaven Allows* (1955) to the pages of a glossy women's magazine, enables the production of meanings which counter the ideological 'message' of the film, or the values which the director has attempted to express through it.

The orthodox reading of the film is as a critique of middle-class suburbia which it compares unfavourably, through the narrative structure and the characterizations, with a kind of pre-hippy rural utopia. Cary, a widow played by Jane Wyman (known for her 'weepies'), meets with horrified snobbery when she falls in love with her gardener, Ron, played by Rock Hudson. Her own milieu is represented by her pseudo colonial-style home, which is luxuriously furnished and decorated, by the television set she receives from her children at Christmas, and by the country club where she socializes with the local bourgeoisie. The alternative way of life is represented as a rural idyll, Ron's converted mill with stone fireplace and exposed beams, and by his friends' informal wine parties. The prejudices of small-town people are contrasted with the openness and tolerance of country folk. It is necessary for the audience to judge the style of

Ron's home as superior to that of Cary's, to read it as 'disinterested' good taste rather than conspicuous consumption, in order to support the narrative resolution (in which Cary leaves suburbia). In one scene, Cary mentions that she is 'getting rid of some of the clutter' in her house, and the narrative significance of this statement depends on an analogy between the simplicity of contemporary style and enlightened attitudes.

However, another look at the interiors, and the way they are photographed, generates other meanings which are incompatible with this message. Cary's house is just as beautifully lit and framed as the interior of the old mill. We are shown the drawing room, shot from different angles in different scenes to reveal more features, such as the white grand piano, the mirrored wall tiles, and the 'through' dining room. We are shown the kitchen, with fitted cupboards, electric cooker and fridge, and Cary's bedroom, with its thick carpet, full-length drapes, triple-mirror dressing table and silky counterpane. We are even shown the patio, with its potted plants, awnings and garden furniture. There is no narrative requirement to use so many different rooms shot in so many different ways. Ron's friends' house is carefully photographed, with a shot of an empty room before the characters enter, and an 'unnecessary' shot of Cary bringing a stool from the kitchen into the dining area in order to show off the dramatic, conservatory-style sky-light above the sink units. The interior of the converted mill looks spectacular when photographed by a long-shot which displays the open-plan arrangement and the high ceilings. The lighting reduces the colours to a tasteful range of warm sepia tones emphasized by the glow from the open log fire.

So, although the styles of the interiors are very different, and this difference is not insignificant (as Biskind claims, see p. 65), the visual styling of the film enables the viewer to use them as options from a repertoire of looks, rather than examples of inferior and superior taste. Certainly, it is difficult to see how working-class women of the 1950s could have rejected the suburban life style, since it is photographed so lusciously. They would have been familiar with the contrast between contemporary and traditional styles, since women's magazines used similar contrasts. But, as I have argued elsewhere (see Partington, 1989), working-class women 'sampled' and mixed together elements from contrasting images and styles, in the processes of masquerade. The film's resemblance to colour magazine photographs, through styling of the image, makes possible a reading which contradicts the 'ideological message' of the film. The tears which may have been shed over *All That Heaven Allows* need not have been a consequence of character-identification, given the inseparability of the emotional and the material within consumer culture.

Conclusion

This chapter argues that for working-class women in the 1950s the meaning of the melodrama is in its 'surface discontinuity', rather than its 'expressive depth'. In other words, I have shown how the film melodrama acquired meaning predominantly in relation to other images and visual objects which also addressed these women through a whole range of media, and was therefore dependent on the reading of a gendered, class-specific audience, rather than as a consequence of narrative structure and/or character development. I have approached consumption as the gendered subject's articulation of needs, not as an expression of already formed (in the psyche) desires, but as a reproduction of feminine subjectivity – masquerade. Needs and desires are derived from the very place – the market – where professionals aspire to deny them, and they are defined precisely in terms of their *difference* from the needs of the male and/or middle-class subject. Women's familiarity with, and particular understanding of, commodity aesthetics, the appearance of goods in the market place, enables them to use goods in a non-disinterested way. Because mass markets ensure that consumer skills are class- and gender-specific, they provide subordinate groups with the knowledges with which to contest meanings.

It is often assumed that consumerism erodes or absorbs 'real' differences, but my analysis of melodrama is intended to show that different consumer groups are always identified in terms of exclusive knowledges and expectations. It is also intended to argue therefore that resistance, or the articulation of conflict, depends on consumption, rather than on a refusal of the role of the consumer. By arguing that the British working-class female consumer of Hollywood melodrama in the 1950s read films not only in terms of narrative and characters, but simultaneously in terms of extratextual and intertextual determinations, I hope to have shown how the working-class audience may have negotiated and resisted the 'housewife' identity (as defined by experts and professionals) they were supposed to adopt, by making it part of the repertoire of femininities which is masquerade. My own readings of the films are not being put forward as *the* meanings of these melodramas in the 1950s, but only as possible consequences of their consumption under specific conditions of meaning-making.

My interest is in the survival of difference in mass culture, and I have tried to argue that class–gender differences have multiplied through the 'simulation' of femininity in the exercise of consumer skills. The loss of origins (extratextual reality), or the unfixability of meanings, is not the end of politics, but the very thing which enables politics in a mass-market system. Women's consumption of goods is a form of appropriation which can bring them into conflict with the intentions of producers and distributors, by conferring on goods 'the sacred aura denied [them] by the conditions and mode under which [they were] produced' (Hebdige, 1987a, p. 72).

This is not a 'waning of affect' but an intensification and amplification of it. Women's relationships with goods transform them into objects which can serve many ritual and symbolic functions, meet many diverse and contradictory needs and elicit 'an excess of feeling, an undecidable mix of . . . emotions' (Hebdige, 1987a, p.72) which takes them beyond the reach of textual analysis.

Notes

1 I have argued elsewhere (see Partington, 1989) that working-class women's appropriation of designed goods brought them into conflict with the design establishment who presumed to 'improve' their tastes, and that the 'gap' between 'good taste' and popular taste cannot be dismissed as simply the result of industry's failure to promote contemporary design sufficiently to 'educate' the consumer.

2 What the fashion historian J.C. Flugel termed 'The Great Masculine Renunciation' refers to an historical process, coinciding with industrialization, through which men were obliged to sacrifice their narcissistic/exhibitionistic tendencies by adopting a more sombre form of dress which would reflect their concern with professional work and business (see Silverman, 1986).

3 'Masquerade' implies an acting out of the images of femininity, for which is required an active, desiring gaze to decode and utilize those images, while at the same time constructing a self-image which is dependent on the gaze of the other. In this sense womanliness, or femininity, is a 'simulation', a demonstration of the representations of women, performed by the female viewer. Simulation is not an imitation of the 'real' (which would exist independently of representations), or a false version of it, but an image which refers to another in the production of 'reality', or 'that which is always already reproduced. The hyperreal . . .' (Baudrillard, 1983, p. 146).

4 Dick Hebdige has documented the postwar preservation of English middle-class taste through anti-Americanism (see Hebdige, 1981). Reyner Banham wrote of the survival of the 'throw-away aesthetic' in the post Second World War period, made possible partly by the import of American goods to satisfy popular tastes, despite the design profession's systematic devaluation, and attempted eradication of it (see Banham, 1981). Pierre Bourdieu has commented on how 'disinterestedness' is used to naturalize the superiority of middle-class taste above the popular (see Bourdieu, 1980).

5 Andrea Press has shown that 'working-class women are more likely to notice the . . . material world which television depicts . . . Middle-class women, in contrast, are more likely to identify personally with television characters and their problems' (see Press, 1989).

2

Open or closed: popular magazines and dominant culture

HELEN PLEASANCE

Problems

> According to some authorities, both narrative and metaphor work by
> bringing together things that at first seem separate and distant, but
> which then, moved towards each other through logical space, make a
> new and pertinent sense. But this shift through space depends on our
> ability as listeners and readers to accept the new ordering of events and
> entities which has been made by the plot of the story, or by the use of
> the metaphor. Where there is not the vision that permits understanding
> of these new connections, then a story cannot be told (Steedman, 1986,
> p. 138).

All processes of making sense involve an ability to make connections
between disparate and even contradictory material. The questions and
assumptions with which we begin will determine how objects are connected, the order in which material is placed, and the final sense that is
made. The same social and cultural information can be recruited in quite
different ways, to provide conflicting and even oppositional versions of
the sense that the social world makes.

In this chapter I shall take particular examples of cultural material and
order them through two distinct theoretical frameworks within cultural
studies to produce opposing accounts of how social relations work. It is
the status ascribed to dominant culture which characterizes the difference
between the two frameworks. In the first, dominant culture is the site where
dominant power relations are both successfully extended and reinforced;
any form of resistance is recouped into dominant culture itself. In the
second, dominant culture is seen as a site of conflict and struggle, a place
where power is never fully or permanently secured; it is thus a site where
dominant power relations can be pulled apart and challenged.

These theories, like other strands of cultural theory, can be considered in terms of the different cultural narratives they themselves employ. I will describe the two different theoretical approaches to dominant culture outlined above as narratives in order to draw attention to the ways in which the narrative dimensions of cultural theory contribute to their differing analyses of cultural production. I am using the term narrative here very loosely to refer to patterns and conventions of making sense. I have named the first set of approaches 'closures' to refer to their emphasis on the successful establishment of power relations within dominant culture, and the second set of approaches 'openings' to highlight their focus on the constant processes of struggle and negotiation in dominant culture.

These two frameworks characterize, rather schematically, approaches to the analysis of power within both cultural and feminist studies. In the fields of both cultural studies and feminism these frameworks have been set *against* each other, the one supposedly refuting or undercutting the other. In this chapter, I want to see if anything can be gained by holding the contradictions between the two frameworks together, since within my own work their polarization has left me with an impossible choice between two apparently contradictory models of how culture works.

Four photographs (Plates 3–6) will be used to frame my analysis.[1] The photographs either come from or refer to *Smash Hits* and *Just Seventeen*, the two best-selling teenage magazines of the 1980s. *Smash Hits* is a pop music magazine and *Just Seventeen* is a more general girls' magazine. Both are produced by a relatively new, entrepreneurial company: EMAP Metro. Hence, they can be theorized as examples of dominant culture. They are produced in order to make as healthy a profit as possible for the company, an aim which is achieved by convincing as many people as possible to become consumers of the product. The questions I want to address here are: what social and cultural exchanges are possible within these parameters, and what can be gleaned about people's relationships to these dominant cultural forms?

Closures

The whole drive of our society is toward displaying as much difference as possible within it while eliminating where at all possible what is different from it: the supreme trick of bourgeois ideology is to produce its opposite out of its own hat . . . the ideology of difference is not, in fact, different from the ideologies that imprison us all. (Williamson, 1986b, pp. 100, 106).

The theoretical approaches used in this section, typified by Judith Williamson's claim above, stress how dominant power relations work and are reproduced in popular cultural forms. Cultural products are typically used to construct a closed and fixed story of social cohesion. Within this theoretical framework, then, popular forms are seen as one of the means by which dominant social meanings are maintained.

Pop music, consumption, youth and gender can be connected to tell a story of how particular groups of people are securely tied into dominant social relations. The particular notion of difference, employed by Williamson above, enables this story to be told through a narrative of closure. One might initially hypothesize that by producing images, ideas and narrative techniques which look different from those produced in the context of school, work and family structures, *Smash Hits* and *Just Seventeen* offer teenagers alternative ways of making sense of the social world. However, as Williamson suggests, the abundance of difference can be seen to add to their efficacy; in this way, difference becomes imprisonment.

Williamson's use of the term imprisonment can be seen as a metaphor of closure and containment; indeed, there could be few greater indictments of a cultural system and its effectivity. Within this framework the choices offered by a popular cultural form are nothing more than illusions as long as the underlying structures remain the same. It is their ideological significance which determines the meaning of cultural forms: cultural forms become the narrative devices which make sense of, and tie us into, the real, material story. The proliferation of differences covers the tracks of the real story, by, if you like, laying red herrings in our path. They are most successful when they seem to have the least to do with material social relations.

In applying this framework to *Smash Hits* and *Just Seventeen* I will indicate why this emphasis on closure is an important aspect of cultural analysis. I will place the fragmentary, nonsensical information of the 'Bitz' (Plate 3), into the dynamic, linear story of *Smash Hits* as an entrepreneurial success. I will examine in greater detail the Midland *Livecash* and the NatWest *On Line* advertisements (Plates 4 and 5), to show how 'resistant' cultural forms might be used to secure closure and containment. Finally, I will use Simon Frith's analysis of pop music and romance (1983) as a further example of the move to narrative closure, and to see what sense can be made of pop music, consumption and girls' lives.

Significantly, the quotation from Williamson which begins this section is taken from an analysis of advertising. She argues that dominant market forces, in the shape of advertising, offer images and ideals of difference to individuals, in ways which disguise the social inequality between classes. In addition to the metaphor of imprisonment, which I have used to illustrate the emphasis placed on closure in this theoretical narrative, she also uses the notion of colonization to suggest how our social imprisonment is achieved: 'How can new markets be opened up once the rest of the world has already been colonized? By creating new uses, new needs, new definitions . . .' (Williamson, 1986b, p. 102). From this perspective, the construction of difference is seen as a marketing strategy which always works to benefit producers. They are the ones with the power to define the terms through which meaning can be made. While difference-as-choice is offered in order to draw in as many people as possible as consumers, these processes work to preclude an awareness of difference-as-conflict.

The 'Bitz' page (Plate 3), a regular feature in *Smash Hits*, presents an array of different pop musical pleasures. The whole look of the page seems to signify enjoyment, as quirky graphics surround photographs and small pieces of writing. The writing itself is in a style particular to *Smash Hits* – a gossipy, ironic language which is used to express the pleasures of pop music. Every genre of pop music is discussed in these terms by *Smash Hits*: 'Who the Juggins are the Funky Worm?!', 'Seven Astonishing Facts About Siouxsie'. The style proffers a seemingly endless choice of pop musical pleasures, in the form of songs, stars and genres. Yet, diversity and difference can be read as fulfilling part of the publishing company's aim, that is, they maximize the forms and possibilities of consumption.

Indeed, an EMAP Metro company representative had explicitly recognized the importance of diversity for successful sales:

> *Smash Hits* is continuing to break all records, selling more than all other music titles put together, with a circulation four times the size of our nearest rival.
>
> 1,361,000 of our loyal readers *don't* read *any* other music magazines. We've captured a captive audience. Our readers are as diverse as the music you market. (advertisement in *Music Week*, 10 September 1988).

The use of terms such as 'diverse' and 'captive' in such close proximity suggest that the logic of *Smash Hits*' business narrative might support Williamson's notion of colonization. EMAP Metro are certainly eager to produce statistics to prove their success at constructing consumers: 'The Most Powerful Way to Reach Teenagers' is the slogan brandished across the glossy package of graphs which their publicity department produces to map its success against other magazines and within particular age groups. In short, it can be argued that the journalistic style, of refusing to pin pop music down, and playing with its meanings, is the difference needed for the colonization of teenagers as readers and consumers.

These two different articulations, one produced on the pages of *Smash Hits*, the other on the pages of company reports and biographies, are both concerned with the production of consumers. The example of *The Great Smash Hits Pop Caper* helps further to explain this process. This was a board game given away free with the magazine in the summer of 1988. The aim of the game was to 'take a trip through the topsy turvy world of pop and become the most rich 'n' famous 'n' good looking pop star ever!!!'. However, the phrase *The Great Smash Hits Pop Caper* can also be seen to have a wider meaning, as it hints at both the journalistic assumptions within the magazine, and the relationship between the journalistic and marketing strategies of EMAP Metro. These strategies seem to assume that the world of pop music works like a market, with the logic of competition, meeting demand with supply. The notion of pop music escaping the market place is ludicrous within this framework, because it cannot function outside market forces. Hence, *Smash Hits* readers are encouraged to relate creatively to pop music *as consumers*. The display of difference-as-choice on the pages of *Smash Hits* enables consumers to engage creatively with the pop market.

It is this 'topsy turvy world' which is presented on the 'Bitz' page. The ironic and knowing style gives a sense of fun to finding out about new artists, new records and new musical genres. So the plethora of differences displayed, and the apparent chaos of imagery, lead to greater and greater market control for EMAP Metro, as more and more pop styles are represented on the market and more and more pop fans are addressed through the market. In this way, the magazine contributes directly to further consumption of the records and other pop related products which are promoted within its pages.

An analysis of EMAP Metro's relationship with the advertising industry pushes this story a little further, and enables it to make a little more sense. Advertising, more than any other form of cultural endeavour perhaps, represents the logic of colonization. Cultural material is taken from a plethora of sources, and is reorganized for the purposes of selling products. The original, or previous, meanings are recruited for a specific purpose: the buying (and consumption) of a product. If the advertisement works then the purchase of its product becomes the resolution of cultural desire. The NatWest advertisement will help to explain this: here reference is made to a particular dress style, which has its origins in hip-hop, a black music form. The combination of this street scene, shot out of focus, a second figure only just in the frame, with the coloured arrows and the slogan 'Readies when you are', is able to represent youthful independence and empowerment by drawing on the context of assumed knowledge of youth subcultures.

Youth cultures are commonly seen to have enabled young people to subvert and resist dominant culture. Subcultural theory[2] has seen youth subcultures to be constituted outside and against school, work and family cultures, and to facilitate the expression of unease and dissatisfaction with them. The figure in the NatWest advertisement is an exemplary figure of this view: he is on the street, empowered by his look, his youthful independence. So what is he doing in a banking advertisement?

Subcultures, it has been argued, allow young people to resist dominant meanings by providing a context in which they can rework material away from its original, mainstream context. In this advertisement, the process seems to be working in reverse; subcultural material is introduced in the service of dominant culture. The marketing strategy is to make ownership of an *On Line* cashcard part of a stylish youthful identity. In this way, subcultural resistance is incorporated within dominant relations of financial exchange.

The knowledge which enabled this advertisement to be produced involves a subtle understanding of the codes by which pop music makes sense to its consumers. The fragmented way in which the visual narrative is constructed, drawing material together in a relationship, but not spelling that relationship out, trusting the reader's ability to make sense of it, owes a lot to *Smash Hits'* visual style. The relationship of seaside drawings to pop gossip only makes sense if the 'fun' of liking pop music is part of a reader's cognitive skills. What is important here is that the same skills are required to read the advertisement as are required to read the journalistic text. The mode for consuming pop music which is set up in the 'editorial' text of the magazine, is continued in the text of the advertisement, which is a page of the magazine. In short, the relationship between the magazine and the advertising industry is vital in more ways than one. The textual strategies are similar *and* they depend upon each other materially:

> Our business is directly related to the health of the UK advertising industry. Fortunately for us this industry has grown faster than almost any other sector of the UK economy during the last decade, and all the forecasts indicate that a steadily higher proportion of gross national product will be put into advertising expenditure. (EMAP Company Report, 1988, p. 25).

Within marketing there is the knowledge that teenagers want rebellious identities, and instead of fighting that impulse it has been harnessed, so that rebellion now takes place on the terms of the market with the help of its products. The market has realized the potential of its products to tell the story of youthful rebellion. In this way, resistance, difference and rebellion can be recouped within dominant relations.

The techniques of the Midland advertisement are less figurative than those of the NatWest's, and so spell out the relationship between youth culture and consumption in a more direct way. All the products represented in the advertisement have rebellious meanings, and signify independence: wearing make-up as a sign of not being a little girl any more, cinema tickets suggesting being out in the evening, and, of course, pop music. But even here, the significance of these objects is not spelled out, it is assumed that the relationship can be grasped, the sense secured by the readers. Again, I think the advertisement owes much to *Smash Hits* style: for example, on one of the advertisement's appearances I turned from it to a page of the 'editorial' text to find the same Madonna record photographed in exactly the same way. Similarly, the phrases 'kicks at the flicks', 'Wicked war paint' and 'vital vinyl' offer a (pale) imitation of *Smash Hits* ironic style.

Banking advertisements, particularly, have used these devices to tell stories of youth rebellion and empowerment. Banking, the organization of finances, cannot avoid being about our incorporation into dominant social relations. To represent that moment as an act of rebellion is to colonize, to incorporate, not only those who might want 'first car, marriage, kids',[3] but also those who expressly reject that version, who want something *different*. The invitation to openness becomes a tighter closure, as consumer capitalism promises to meet our every desire.

What is important here is that banking, which could use ideas of saving and security to sell itself in these magazines, makes use of images of consumption. All of the banking advertisements in the magazines analyzed,[4] bar that for the Trustees Savings Bank, made the idea of using banking services pleasurable in terms of an immediate, exciting and empowering lifestyle:

Smarter than a pocketful of cash . . . get at your money whenever you like.

(*Barclays Bank*)

Saturday night was better than you'd expected. And more expensive. You haven't even enough cash for a pint of milk and the Sunday papers. But nothing is going to ruin your morning . . . Halifax cardcash. The smart way to bring your money to life.

(*Halifax Building Society*)

You start working for money. Money starts working for you.

(*Abbey National Building Society*)

Suddenly I landed a job and needed a place to stash my cash. FAST.

(*Royal Bank of Scotland*)

Records and tapes from HMV. Make-up from Boots 17. Tickets from the back row. Livecash from Midland.

(*Midland Bank*)

Readies when you are. Press for action.

(*National Westminster Bank*)

Teenage magazines are a good place for banks to advertise because their readers are making a transition from familial dependence into adult independence. The NatWest advertisement is a typical expression of such independence, defined in terms of the power of consumption. To be on the street, with the empowerment of cash, is *not* to be tied to the home, and a familial identity, but to be self-determining.

Femininity as closure

The subject of girls' lives in relation to pop music has been taken up by Simon Frith (1983). However, it is noticeable that his analysis of 'Girls and Youth Culture' is dealt with in a discrete section, while the analysis of boys' relation to music is dealt with in the main body of the text. This is in part because he argues that boys' lives make meaningful sense independent of pop music and, as a result, music can function as 'pure' music: 'It is boys, as we have seen, who are interested in rock as music, want to be musicians, technicians, experts' (Frith, 1983, p. 228). Girls, on the other hand, get tied into pop music quite differently, a consequence of the restrictive future Frith outlines for them: 'Marriage is still *the* female career, and it is only in cases where it is not *the* career choice for a woman that other leisure possibilities open up for her' (Frith, 1983, p. 223). Frith argues that he has structured the story of feminine development through pop music thus, because of the harshness of 'the material basis of women's lives' (Frith, 1983, pp. 233–4). In this way, he suggests that popular culture is both a site of reconciliation of the powerless to their position, and a means of making that condition desirable: 'Girls grow out of the fantasy sexuality of teeny-bop as they begin to date and dance and go out more seriously, but the relationship between music and the bedroom continues' (Frith, 1983, pp. 226–7).

The gendered dimension which Frith introduces into his analysis of pop music is helpful in the study of the processes of consumption represented in *Smash Hits* and *Just Seventeen*. Making use of Frith's argument, in conjunction with that of Williamson, it is possible to show how feminine identity is fixed in these magazines through particular representations of consumption.

Pop music is explicitly used to tell romantic stories in the pages of *Just Seventeen*. Pop stars are discussed in terms of their looks and their love lives, even in terms of their sexual capabilities; girls are invited to fantasize about their desirability as romantic partners. But alongside this, and I think including it, everything is examined as consumable. The format of the magazine is organized around buying: the first few pages, visually organized in a very similar way to the 'Bitz' page in *Smash Hits*, are taken up with information about new products: new videos, new fashions, new cosmetics, new accessories, new anything in fact. Fashion and beauty features follow, with either clothes or cosmetics to be bought. In these articles readers are often 'transformed', with ordinary 'before' photographs and unrecognizable 'after' photographs: a new hairstyle, a new wardrobe, or a new make-up routine has produced a new identity. Sometimes there are short stories, but not always. But there is always lots of pop music.

The advertisement in the photograph (Fig. 2.4) was addressed to the music industry, and was produced at the time when the magazine introduced a 'four-page pop pull out' as a new feature. From this advertisement it seems that the conclusion of their market research was that teenage girls identify with pop music; it is a selling point. Even though there is much in the magazine which is not directly about pop music, I think it is pop music which holds the fragmentary strands of information together. It is able to do this because of the use of techniques first formulated on the pages of *Smash Hits*, in which the incorporation into consuming practices is made through pop music. Pop music, in the shape of its stars and trends, is continually promoted in *Just Seventeen*: stars' consumption habits are investigated, their records publicized, and fashion features suggest how to dress like particular kinds of pop fans. There is an assumption that readers make sense of themselves through identification with particular musical genres or stars.

Let me take an example. In the 10 August 1988 issue, *Just Seventeen* presented the finalists in a competition to find a model. The finalists' 'personalities' were represented by a list of their likes and dislikes. Here are two illustrations: 'likes: James Brown, fast cars and Levi's 501 ads' and 'likes: Rob Lowe, Coca Cola ads, chocolate cake and old American cars'. Both the young women's lives are presented as having meaning through relationship to objects of consumption. The finalists, who are fulfilling a popular feminine fantasy, are made desirable by allusions to 'classy' forms of consumption. In a further twist, some of that 'classiness' is articulated through advertisements which depend entirely upon pop music for their meaning. For example, the song *First Time*, used in the Coca Cola advertisement, was so popular that it was released as a single, and the Levi's advertisements were the first to cull the history of pop to find songs that would represent the authenticity of their jeans. These examples reinforce my argument about the effectivity of pop music to make sense of consumption, and the effectivity of consumption to make sense of girls' lives.

Arguably, then, the emphasis on pop music which is carried over from *Smash Hits* characterizes a gendered narrative of consumption as opposed to the process suggested by Frith. What is interesting here is that consumption, unlike romance, does not proffer only one social route for girls, the road to marriage. Rather, it offers the pleasures of continual transformation and change. *Just Seventeen* displays the experience of consumption through gendered modes of address as it gives meaning to femininity. Feminine identity is presented as an endless series of choices, through which girls can differentiate themselves, both as a group and from each other. These choices appear to be about self-definition and personal freedom. But, as in Frith's analysis of romance, within the narrative of closure put forward by Williamson, the choices and freedoms apparently offered by consumption hide the lack of material choice for women. Indeed, the unending logic of consumption secures an even tighter closure than romance, because dissatisfactions can be assuaged more easily; consumable products are meant to have limited appeal, romantic partners are not. The endless production of new and different femininities through increasing possibilities of consumption can thus be read as a particularly powerful form of closure.

This reading of *Just Seventeen* has emphasized the mechanisms of popular culture to fix and contain identities. It has made use of the narrative of closure, which presents the social world as structured by dominant power relations in which we are all incorporated. I have constructed a reading of *Smash Hits* and *Just Seventeen* within such a narrative of closure to illustrate an approach to the study of culture which shows how dominant power relations forever draw us in, and which suggests they do so systematically, reworking our very dissatisfactions with those relations. But this is only one possible narrative. It is also possible to rework this material and tell a different story.

Openings

> The market is not an institution with rigidly defined (if consistently subverted) hierarchies, structures, orders and conventions . . . The machine is never intrinsically monstrous; it is both manipulated, controlled and controlling. (Carter, 1984, pp. 188–9).

The problem with the types of cultural analysis offered above is that the story is already told, social processes are complete, and meaning is fixed. They tend to lead to a pessimistic understanding of popular culture which sees it as constantly reproducing new forms of domination and control to keep us in our place. In contrast to these readings of popular culture, other theoretical perspectives have offered a rather different set of conclusions. In this section I shall use the theoretical devices of postmodernism and psychoanalysis to construct a narrative of cultural processes as open, incomplete and constantly moving.

Postmodernism's stress on surfaces[5] encourages an analysis of consumption which does not for ever return it to the material relations of capitalist production or the patriarchal institution of marriage. Psychoanalysis provides ways of looking at individual psychic patterns and strategies for making sense, which do not necessarily correlate with the external social form of dominant power relations. Both these frameworks of cultural analysis emphasize the possibilities of escaping or resisting dominant culture in different ways. While we might all be placed within a dominant order, we might also be refusing and challenging that order as part of the same process.

So far, the reproduction of dominant power relations through cultural forms has been seen to work effectively, but now I want to look at cultural processes as a continual push and pull between contrary and even oppositional forces. This push and pull will be explored in the processes of both production and consumption. By not assuming a static power relationship between practices of production and those of consumption, 'colonization' can be theorized as a more dynamic process.

The model of culture suggested in the quotation from Carter's work contrasts with Williamson's model discussed earlier. In particular, it implies a different conceptual framework through which to view the notion of difference. It suggests that cultural differences, produced in a dominant site, such as the market, can be made to yield openings, as well as closures, in the workings of those dominant relations. 'Difference' has quite a different status in such a narrative than in the narrative of closure discussed previously.

Carter's challenge to a monolithic model of culture is part of her analysis of young women's practices of consumption, and of ways in which they offer a possible site for feminine resistance. In contrast to Williamson's view of social and cultural relations, power is not set up here as an achieved position, but as a constant struggle between various groups. From this perspective, the 'Bitz' page and *The Great Smash Hits Pop Caper* can be re-examined and pulled into a different shape, to present a Carteresque version of social and cultural relations in which 'the machine is never intrinsically monstrous; it is both manipulated, controlled and controlling' (Carter, 1984, p. 189).

Taking *The Great Smash Hits Pop Caper* as a metaphor for the relations of marketing and consumption in which the magazine is caught up, the game can be reread as one of struggle. Earlier, the game was seen as an exercise in defining the ground and limits of cultural activity by dominant forces. The machine was monstrous, as it developed an unchallengeable logic of its own, which brought all meaning under its control. But now I can break into the 'system', tame the monster: the *Caper*, this time, will be played by competing groups, all of whom attempt to create meanings and have different stakes in the game.

There are all sorts of people involved in making meaning out of *Smash Hits* and *Just Seventeen*. Even within the company of EMAP Metro there are different kinds of producers, different kinds of power, which might not sit easily together, and are, at best, in contingent alliance. Financial and creative producers want to produce quite different things – financial worth and cultural worth do not necessarily correlate – but need each other to produce anything at all in an entrepreneurial market. The relationship depends upon a continual working out of their differences. Theirs is only one of the many relationships which are played out across the magazine's pages: journalists, photographers, advertisers, the music industry (with all its own groupings and differences), and for *Just Seventeen* the fashion and beauty industries all contribute to the final product. And this is before we even get to the consumers as a group or collection of groups with particular stakes in the game who complicate the picture further. This is not to argue that there is a harmonious and equal plurality of producers, but to conceptualize their power as a contingent process, always dependent upon the various groups caught up in its field.

These struggles both indicate how power might be changed, and also how power is fragmented in its very construction. The 'Bitz' page (Plate 3) can take on a new metaphorical meaning, as the fragments of information are fought over: 'Who the Juggins Are The Funky Worm?' They are a pop group who have just had their photograph taken for *Smash Hits*. Their record company has high hopes for them, they could fill a nice little gap in the market, enhance the company profile. The writer of the piece thought there was a quirky angle to be taken, a bit of fun to be had. The record buying public was not convinced though, the first single did all right, but that name is a bit stupid isn't it? You're hardly likely to say your favourite group is The Funky Worm, even if you do have some good memories of that party where the single was played to death. The photographer thought they seemed like quite nice people, a bit taken in by all the company hype, but at least they weren't Kylie Minogue. I thought they might make a good example of the different meanings that a pop group can have. I'm playing *The Great Smash Hits Pop Caper* as well.

Without explicit reference, Carter's work points to a postmodern conceptualization of social and cultural relations. In its most radical forms postmodern theory offers a challenge to traditional definitions of politics, and asks new questions about how to read 'the cultural' politically. E. Ann Kaplan and Angela McRobbie have both theorized postmodern culture in helpful terms. Kaplan in her work on the MTV (Music Television) cable network in the USA suggests that:

> MTV arguably addresses the desires, fantasies and anxieties of young people growing up in a world in which all traditional categories are being blurred and all institutions questioned – a characteristic of postmodernism (Kaplan, 1987, p. 5).

McRobbie, in a general tour of popular culture focusing on youth culture, argues that:

> Unlike the various strands of structuralist criticism, postmodernism deflects attention away from the singular scrutinizing gaze of the semi-ologist, and asks that this be replaced by a multiplicity of fragmented and frequently interrupted 'looks'. (McRobbie, 1987, p. 63).

Smash Hits and *Just Seventeen* can be situated within this framework of postmodernism. The banking advertisements, for example, can be seen to address 'the desires, fantasies and anxieties of young people' within a structure of 'fragmented and frequently interrupted "looks"'. Looking at magazines is always a fragmented and frequently interrupted process for the reader. The content of the magazines is fragmented in itself, and is further disjointed by the plurality of other cultural and social activities and processes with which it co-exists. To put forward this reading of the magazines undermines any notion of a straightforward incorporation of the reader into dominant culture.

The advertisements brought together for analysis here are read as pages of a magazine, not one after the other, but chanced upon haphazardly. There is no direct relationship between the reading of an advertisement and physically taking action, 'pressing for action'. Reading between pages of pop is very different to literally walking down the street to the NatWest bank and gaining access to money. Within a narrative of closure, the fantastic nature of the advertisements acted to ensure a tying in of youth rebellion to dominant closure. Through postmodernism, fantasy can have a logic which does not return it to such material relationships quite so easily. One of postmodernism's most radical priorities has been the importance which is given to the status of fantasy in the everyday workings of culture. Pop music and its place within youth cultures have been central to postmodern theory for this reason. They have been theorized as a key example of how such fantasies invade and inform the social. Banking, as part of a youth cultural fantasy about life within dominant relations, can have a much more radical meaning than that already given. As fantasies about lifestyles and money these advertisements are as much about people's lack of real attainment of these things as they are about easy incorporation into their processes.

Femininity as openness

Psychoanalytic theory contributes further to this narrative of cultural openness, in its conceptualization of the psychic strategies of making meaning. This will be argued here through the example of the construction of femininity as one of the key forms of adolescent identity in transition acknowledged in the magazines. So, finally, in this section, I want to re-examine the narrative of gendered consumption I set up by drawing on Frith's work, but this time I will look at it through the light of psychoanalytic theory, particularly as it is used by Jacqueline Rose. She argues that:

> What distinguishes psychoanalysis from sociological accounts of gender . . . is that whereas for the latter, the internalization of norms is assumed roughly to work, the basic premise and indeed starting point of psychoanalysis is that it does not. The unconscious constantly reveals the 'failure' of identity. Because there is no continuity of psychic life, so there is no stability of sexual identity, no position for women (or for men)

which is ever simply achieved . . . Failure is not a moment to be regretted in a process of adaptation, or development into normality which ideally takes its course . . . Instead failure is something endlessly repeated and relived moment by moment throughout our individual histories. (Rose, 1986, p. 184).

This claim undermines many of the assumptions which are made in Frith's account of the processes of achieving a fixed feminine identity through romantic involvement in pop music. His account focuses on the production of the meaning of pop music and its function in relation to the gendered structures and institutions in society. Underneath the superficial certainties, this second narrative suggests lie contradictory impulses and personal refusals. This turn to individual, and diverse psychic strategies has particular consequences. What is revealed is not the successful role of pop music in the reproduction of dominant relations of gender inequality, which is revealed by Frith's approach, but rather possibilities of incoherence and lack of fixity.

As pop music is played across a girl's face in the *Just Seventeen* advertisement, she expresses a yearning look of desire. But how many desires can pop music fulfil, how many visions can it encompass? In the previous section I delineated some of the differences between romance and consumption, and some of the diverse ways in which pop music was used within the pages of *Just Seventeen*. If the logic of consumption is taken with the plethora of pop musical senses which the magazine employs, then, in a similar way to that indicated in the previous analysis of the banking advertisements, this image can be used to open up the story. The continual search for meaning through the pages of a magazine can be made to yield the continual, inevitable failure of personal identity in the real material world.

If teenagers seek to resolve their identities and find self-recognition through forms of consumption, then here is a possible clue to the idea that they are dissatisfied with social life as it is. That their dissatisfaction is played out, week in, week out, with the buying of magazines, then, can be used as evidence that the social system is quite patently *not* working, since there is always the desire for something *different*. The solutions that are offered in *Smash Hits* and *Just Seventeen* are structured in a particular way, in a particular context, but that does not necessarily mean that there is a final closure.

In relation to the question of the gendering of identity this would suggest that the intention is not necessarily an achieved resolution, but that popular forms might create new sets of problems and dissatisfactions. The fragmentary, dispersed nature of femininity, as it is constructed in *Just Seventeen* can, within these psychoanalytic terms, be read as an opening, rather than as a closure.

Frith's story of girls' relationships to pop music culminates in an achieved moment of coherent identity as a wife and mother in marriage. In terms of Rose's concept of failure this closure becomes both arbitrary and misleading. Marriage does not necessarily satisfy the desires which led to it in the first place; it does not adequately contain sexual identity. In relation to consumption, I argued earlier that the closure was paradoxically tighter because of the greater choices offered, but consumption can also be read differently within Rose's framework. The example of the girls in the model competition, who represented themselves through particular cultural commodities, can be read as an expression of the desire for something different. Instead of being a closure, difference can be read as an opening, because it indicates dissatisfaction with and refusal of that which is offered in dominant social relations. This is perhaps nowhere more apparent than in the processes of achieving a feminine identity.

In this section, then, I have used theoretical frameworks which stress the incompleteness and illogical ways in which cultural and social relations develop in order to read those relations in an open way. The refusal to place them in a closed narrative order is an attempt to indicate how change might occur, indeed to say that it can occur. In the narrative of openness, our relationships with pleasurable, dominant cultural forms does not sentence us to a social imprisonment, but can indicate our continuous refusals of, anxieties about and disassociations from those relations.

(Ir)resolutions

I feel I have reached a difficult moment. I find it impossible to bring together the two versions of social relations I have constructed in the two narratives in this chapter. I have, in fact, wilfully made them irreconcilable. Closure and openness will always contradict each other. Of course, I could argue that these relations are in some senses closed, in others open. This is part of the story. By my problem is that it is the very points of closure in the first version which became openings in the second.

Both versions are important, both have effects. The first narrative, that of closure, is important because it gives a sense of the broad sweep of entrepreneurial capitalism and patriarchal social relations. This sweep has had effects not only in the public sphere, but also at the level of personal desires. Indeed, it is through the shaping of such personal desires that the larger social shape is formed. Consumption is a form through which dominant power relations have been articulated and maintained. For feminists, the particular incorporation of women and construction of femininity through these relations of power becomes an important point of closure.

However, the second narrative presents an attempt to get beneath the monolithic dimension of power; it proposes a view which sees dominance as contingently constructed, and suggests that dominant culture is a site of struggle. Consumption as a dominant cultural form is seen to contain these openings. There are points at which these two versions can be held together, need not contradict each other. It can be argued that there are ways in which the relations of consumption are closed, others in which they are open. At different times and for different reasons, it would be imperative to argue closure, at others openness. But I want to suggest that there is always duality and contradiction between the two. It is through that duality and contradiction that relations of dominance are lived, and changed.

Competing notions of difference are central to this duality. On the one hand, difference is the coinage needed for our construction within dominant power relations, while on the other hand, it is a continual sign of our disaffection with those relations and the slippages which they themselves produce. The narratives I have constructed here through the analysis of *Smash Hits* and *Just Seventeen* are only examples, but I think that the notion of duality has relevance for an understanding of power relations more generally. It is a contradiction which I want to be recognized before we go on to tell other stories.

Notes

1   Plates 3 and 4 are taken from *Smash Hits*, 10–23 August 1988; Plate 5 from *Smash Hits*, 9–22 March 1988; and Plate 6 from *Music Week*, 10 September 1988. The other two banking advertisements appeared in other issues of both *Smash Hits* and *Just Seventeen* during 1988.
2   Dick Hebdige's *Subculture: The Meaning of Style* (1979) is central to the critical debates which have discussed youth in terms of subcultures. Angela McRobbie's 'Settling accounts with sub-cultures' (1980) and Gary Clarke's 'Defending ski-jumpers: a critique of theories of youth sub-cultures' (1982) are useful continuations of this debate.
3   The Trustees Savings Bank was the only one to advertise by reference to ideas of future security. They did this by invoking a traditional lifestyle, where the future holds 'first car, marriage, kids'.
4   All these advertisements appeared in both *Smash Hits* and *Just Seventeen* through the summer of 1988.
5   Postmodernism is strikingly different from previous theoretical positions because of its refusal to make hierarchical distinctions in popular culture.

3

Having it all: feminism and the pleasures of the popular

YVONNE TASKER

Before I studied English Literature . . . I read romantic fiction indiscrimi-
nately. I didn't properly appreciate the distinction between *Jane Eyre* and
Regency Buck . . . I thought that being able to tell the difference meant
success in life . . . Now, as a feminist I believe I was sold a pup when
I gave up books and started reading Literature. I have returned to the
books of my teens, which is also the bulk of the reading of thousands
and thousands of women of all ages, to ask: why is all this powerful
and why does it matter? (Batsleer, 1981, p. 52).

Feminist cultural criticism, fresh from its colonization of melodramatic
territory, turned its attention in the late 1970s and early 1980s to re-
evaluations of forms such as romance fiction and soap opera. The re-
evaluation of forms which, within a feminist 'common sense', form part
of the representational conspiracy to keep women in their place has been
problematic. Yet the terms of this tentative process of examining these
forms 'for' women anew adopted/adapted a familiar stance. Established
through the recovery of such practices as embroidery, knitting and women's
writing, this process drew on feminism's history of reclaiming those cultural
products and practices with a low cultural esteem seen to derive from an
association with women and/or femininity. Thus Janet Batsleer's comments
(above) carry both reminders of a presumed shared past in reading romance
at odds with an acquired feminism, and a suggestion that the rejection of
such works as 'pap' was itself bound up with male and classbound notions
which it is our duty as feminists to move beyond. Batsleer manages to
convey a sense in which critical work can tap into a cultural practice (not
just a form) in which 'thousands and thousands' of women are engaged. At
the same time, since the shift is one from questions of value to a discourse
of power, this intervention retains a clear feminist emphasis. Such moves
represent a convergence of, on the one hand, resistance to a perceived
critical double standard, and on the other, a fear of rejecting women who

enjoyed such forms, indeed a fear that feminists were rejecting their own past pleasures in an attempt to be equal to male cultural standards.

Moves to reassess what is at stake for women in such popular pastimes fit nicely, then, with an emergent stress on pleasure and use in the study of cultural forms more generally. Feminism's rediscovery of the popular, this 'looking again', appears within the wider context of critical work on popular cultural forms, drawing on both traditions of analysis developed in cultural studies and on a more specifically feminist set of imperatives. The emergence of new theories of and attitudes to the audience, to readings and readers, has led to a more general re-evaluation of popular pleasures in which ideology becomes a lived relation and meaning a contested arena, so that audiences gained the power to negotiate ideologically with the text. Such interventions shifted the ground from an implicit assumption that ideology simply 'happened to other people' and not to 'us': that those engaged in critical work were somehow outside of the equations of experience, of the production of knowledge and of ideology. These developments have also perhaps allowed the left and feminism to move away from the avant-gardism of the late 1960s and 1970s and into the embrace of the popular. From a critical focus on the ideological power of the text emerged a cultural politics concerned with the construction of new kinds of texts, capable of positioning an audience in new and radical ways. However, since popular culture had become a site of negotiation/contestation, it was not only acceptable to engage with it, but politically correct. And, for feminism, this engagement was also deeply rooted in the desire to reclaim a women's culture. That is, popular culture had been re-named and in the process became a different object.

The fact that popular culture could no longer be conceived of as simply a site for the transmission of ideology has, however, served to further problematize the notion, important for feminist analyses, of the progressive text. A tension can be perceived between feminist imperatives and other critical traditions so that feminist criticism has often found itself uncomfortably situated within and between critical traditions: between structuralism and poststructuralism, modernism and postmodernism. While critical developments have shifted emphasis away from the production of good and bad textual objects, there is a sense in which the project of feminist analysis itself emerges precariously from this process.

It is within such a context that I want to explore the deployment within feminist cultural criticism of another term, 'gendered genre'. In part, recent uses of this formulation address a specific local interest, for example in relation to television soap opera, a form which has been the site of an explosion of critical work over the last ten years – work which has attempted to explore the significance of this particular form for a female audience. This term and the area that it delineates also serves to open up a wider set of questions around what is at stake in feminist analysis of popular culture. This chapter seeks to address such recent (and not so recent) work, situating it within a critical context and raising some further questions for the study of such popular fictions.

A special relationship

The 1980s have seen a proliferation of references to genres, forms and fantasies as gendered. While this process of naming has been mainly concerned with textual processes (the narratives typically discussed), it has also drawn on the significance of a sexed audience (a female readership) for, and sexed authorship of, particular cultural forms. Ken Worpole, for example, points to a body of writings for and often by women, noting that, 'historically, novel reading and writing has been predominantly, but not exclusively, a "feminine" activity' (1984, p. 31). The assertion of this activity as feminine is positioned within an ambiguous space, an uncertainty signalled by the use of inverted commas. This textual marking is retained alongside the claim that 'the "femininity" of reading and writing has a *material* basis,' that of 'an activity that can be engaged in domestically . . . and without threatening the dislocation of woman's role at home' (Worpole, 1984, p. 32; emphasis added). In the implied equation (set of associations) between a 'feminine' activity, an activity located in the domestic sphere and an activity for women, Worpole is drawing on an already existing context provided by feminist criticism. This is recognised in his assertion that while the very pre-eminence of women in the production and consumption of popular fiction demands some form of attention within the parameters of his survey, 'there are clearly very real problems of perspective and empathy when such a study is written by a man'. Worpole recognizes the importance of these questions but accepts that it is not his place to comment, pointing the reader to 'studies by women who take all these questions further and obviously have a more direct relationship with this reading and writing' (Worpole, 1984, p. 31). What then characterizes this mysterious 'direct relationship' and what makes it so 'obvious'?

This reluctance to comment on the 'feminine' together with a willingness to comment on the 'masculine' (see Worpole's (1983) account of crime fiction) points to an academic division of territory – male critics excluded, excluding themselves from speaking about certain issues, most particularly gender (and most particularly not class). I am not claiming that Worpole has set up these boundaries, nor that he is prevented from commenting on the basis of biology or sensibility, but rather indicating that these boundaries do exist and manifest themselves at the points when writers signal the position from which they speak. Crossing the boundary in this fought over terrain seems to constitute a taboo act.

At the confluence of critical reconceptualizations, of the audience, of the popular and therefore of the progressive, lies the emergence of 'gendered genre' as one way of speaking about sets of texts. 'Gendered genre' may be invoked in studies which prioritize the analysis of texts, or by those which seek to read the audience. Not surprisingly since it derives from many sources, the notion of gendered genre has been diversely invoked. In summarizing recent work on melodrama and soap opera Annette Kuhn (1984) discusses texts which are enjoyed by a mass female audience; which primarily address themselves to women; which inscribe female desire, female point-of-view or a woman-centred view in their narratives; and texts which either address or construct a feminine subject/spectator. Such diverse points of reference have produced 'gendered genre' as a dense formulation, creating in turn a pool of terms loaded with significance for feminist cultural criticism.

The general assumption that the audience for forms such as the soap opera, romantic fiction and the melodrama is female constitutes a starting point for much critical work which takes up the question of, for example, the specific appeal to women of such forms. These forms are seen to be primarily directed at women readers, addressing and/or constructing a feminine subject (position) through targeting, features in women's magazines and a textual stress on the world within which women are assumed to be constituted. This takes the form of an address to concerns of the family, the personal and the domestic: arenas which speak to a particular construction of femininity and to a 'cultural capital' which women are most likely to possess (Brunsdon, 1982).

However, both the assumed fact of a female audience and the notion of a textual address to women have also been critically extended into a more general argument to do with the reading practice of a social group, women. For example, Tania Modleski (1982) in an early work on day-time soap opera in the USA, evocatively refers to the 'rhythms of reception'. Here women's work in the home is directly related to viewing patterns, and through this to the narrative patterns of the form, with the endless structure of soap opera offered up as a parallel to the position of women – caught up in a constant state of expectation. The soap opera, Modleski argues, with the multiple identifications that it offers and the portrayal of endless family dilemmas, 'constitutes the subject/spectator as a sort of ideal mother' (1982, p. 92). Women in the home, engaged in housework and in watching (day-time) soap opera do not form an extensive category of viewers, however, but a highly specific one. The concerns elaborated here are not with one possible subject position or context of reading, but with the imposition of a reading position: *the* position from which we can understand the narrative of soap opera and into which the text structures us. This is the 'spectator' as an effect of the text. An initial problem emerges when a discussion of the spectator and of spectating positions is routed through a notion of the social audience (the women at home referred to by both Modleski and Worpole), since a collapse of terminology and a loss of specificity is invited. This can result in the conflation of categories which can prove almost impossible to differentiate: women, women watching soap opera, the feminine. In the consideration of a textual address to or construction of a feminine subject position, do we end up with a discourse of femininity which speaks women? One feminine text reading another? The possibilities and problems of such a slippage pervade recent work on gendered form.

The identification of the linked aspects of female desire, point of view and woman-centred narratives in forms such as the melodrama raises a related set of questions. Where is the specificity to a discussion of female desire, for example? Literally, what does this *mean*, or *how* does it mean here? In part this language draws on models developed in relation to the typical narrative structure of the (classic) Hollywood film in which male characters drive the narrative onwards while the female is conceived of as fetishized object of the 'male look'. This particular critical strand is concerned with the textual inscription of desire, and within this the search for the textual inscription of *female* desire (usually read as the desire of the female protagonist) has proven almost as obsessive as the search for 'positive images' that it in part served to displace. In melodramatic narratives women play central roles, and it is their desires which are therefore seen to drive the narrative onwards. Thus, there is more room than usual for same-sex identification on the part of female members of the audience. In the same way, Lovell (1981) comments favourably on the possibilities which the soap opera opens up for the female viewer: the pleasures of seeing credibility given to the sexual desires of middle-aged women, for example.

Here, though, I want to relate such discussions of female desire, female point-of-view and woman-centred narratives to the framework provided by gendered genre; that is, notions of the 'feminine' or 'masculine' text in which male desires are correspondingly characterized as 'goal-centred', closed and female desires as 'process-centred', open (see, for example, Fiske (1987)). As an instance we could cite the critical language which surrounds the soap opera, which is constructed in opposition to the genre that it has ousted from the spotlight, the crime series (or the 'male crime series'). The crime series with its 'closed' narrative structure (resolution), is concerned with the 'public' realm (law and order), with action and violence and is centred on the individual male hero. In contrast, the soap opera is 'open' (lacks resolution), concerned with the private world of interpersonal relationships, with the texture of gossip, and centres on the family and the community. Crime series address themselves to men and represent a 'masculine form', while the soap opera addresses itself to women and represents a 'feminine form'. Thus a fit is established between the narrative patterns, the thematic content of these shows, particular qualities associated with masculinity/femininity and, finally, male and female viewers.

Constructions of gendered genre, then, crucially draw both on femaleness (the audience, the protagonists) and femininity (as subject position or set of cultural competencies), so that the soap opera is a 'feminine form' and/or one component of a wider set of 'women's genres'. Perhaps as a consequence accounts of gendered genre function problematically within the painful critical orthodoxy of defining and maintaining a distinction between sex and gender. Within feminist discourse reference to the 'feminine' brings with it so much baggage that it seems a confusion or slippage between meanings is inevitable, and yet it is the crucial lack of fit which precisely makes the sex/gender distinction both so problematic and so useful.

A complex network of associations converges as the soap opera pulls together a female audience, a focus on female characters and those formal features which can be equated with a certain subversive femininity. The absence of male viewers in critical accounts of the form presents us with a new set of problems. Placing women in a privileged position for study is an imperative for feminism, not a problem (given an awareness of the operations of power), and yet this can tend to produce a circular argument through which the feminine is fixed with women. The operation by which the feminine is displaced on to the female body is crucial and returns us to Worpole's difficulty in speaking 'as a man'. In his hesitation, in his reluctance to speak, we can see sex (his maleness) becoming a problem in speaking about women's writings, that is, when the object of his study (publishing, contemporary literature) enters a terrain dominated by feminist discourses which are often articulated precisely 'as a woman'.

A radical culture

Retained as a tantalizing illusion, an imaginary construct always beyond reach, the 'progressive text' or the transgressive moment, with its proffered possibility of positioning the audience in new and radical ways, inevitably returns us once more to the controlling power of the text. Yet to abandon the progressive, to move from a notion of ideological work to semiotic play, has also implied the abandonment of evaluation which, within feminist criticism, has been crucial to the establishment of a cultural politics. A discussion of radical culture helps to contextualize both the 'special relationship' between women and the feminine that is worked over and through in commentary on the soap opera, and the significance of textual evaluation more generally. To some extent feminist cultural politics has necessarily relied on the designation of some texts, some forms as better than others, as open, or as progressive. The desire for a radical culture or at the very least an alternative culture is deeply and necessarily marked within feminism, but it is the definition of the radical and its relationship to a political project that is significant here. While it is not possible simply to produce new critical and cultural traditions on demand, it is none the less important to consider the significance of those elements that are retained (and those that are not). The cocktail of popular pleasure and radical culture that emerged in the feminist cultural criticism of the 1980s provides a significant context for understanding 'gendered genre' as an analytical framework.

The continuing importance within feminist discourses, however articulated, of the progressive indicates an ambivalence towards, even suspicion of, readers. A typical critical strand here considers transgressive readings of the melodramatic text, or the possibility of them, which arise due to the existence of 'cracks' or 'fissures' in the smooth ideological surface typical of the narrative of that genre. In such accounts we are pulled between the rejection of a version in which only some ('us') know how to read texts 'properly' (spotting the subversive subtext), and the search for progressive potential in a specific set of texts – defined against all others. The conflict that can emerge between these two impulses helps to situate the particular ways in which feminist criticism has sought to move in new directions. Jane Feuer, in her analysis of the prime time melodramatic serial of the 1980s, suggests that the form represents a '*radical* response to and expression of cultural contradictions' but that the question of interpretation, 'whether that response is interpreted to the Right or to the Left is not a question the texts themselves can answer' (Feuer, 1984, p. 16; emphasis in original). While the text cannot reveal its own 'interpretation', it is significant that the terms in which audiences are given the freedom to respond – 'to the Right or to the Left' – are strictly delineated. That is, the assertion of the 'radical' as a non-specific property of the text is qualified by its insertion within a traditional political discourse.

Here it seems that the status of the text presents itself as a more central problem for feminist analysis, with the intrusion of an unspoken notion that, within this model, *every* text opens up the potential for subversive readings. Indeed, the text that we have critically produced through feminist analysis, isolated as it is from other histories, cannot define the political potential that is at stake for a feminist analysis of culture. However, as feminist analysis has seen the need to go beyond the autonomous text, the associated problems have to an extent been relocated within the fixed convergence of text, spectator and setting. Thus a certain group (women) reading certain texts within a specific setting (say, the domestic) can make manifest (draw up through the cracks and excesses of the surface) a subversive latent content, the meanings of which are essentially already there.

Within this framework, Kuhn contrasts the woman's picture, marked by its 'construction of narratives motivated by female desire and processes of spectator identification governed by female point of view', with the soap opera which 'constructs woman-centred narratives and identifications'. The difference emerges in soap opera's refusal of the 'enigma-retardation-resolution structure which marks the classic narrative' (Kuhn, 1984, p. 18). Feminist approaches to soap opera developed through the 1980s seem to shift emphasis away from the textual processes of narrative resolution – how it sorts out its ideological problematics into some kind of order – as the source of meaning, turning instead to what is offered within the text and the range of meanings and pleasures made available. However, it is precisely soap opera's *refusal of resolution* (its 'endless narrative structure') which has been the site of so much critical comment and interest. Why should this be the case? Is there a link between the persistence of this tradition and the ways in which new critical developments have been taken on board by feminist critics? After all, it is soap opera which seems to offer itself as both popular (mass entertainment) culture and as an 'open' text, without resolution and therefore in line with the requirements of a radical culture.

The femaleness (of the audience and the text) of soap opera and its potential for providing the space for a woman's discourse has been a central point of concern for feminist writings. Significantly, this space can be and has been conceived of as radical. It is the progressive, if not the politically correct, that provides a specificity for the non-specific invocation of a 'radical' value. While stressing availability (popular culture had, at least in theory, become a site of negotiation, contestation, ambivalence) feminism's political project needs to retain the fixed ground of evaluation. These formulations operate within a space which allows a return to the *terra firma* of ideology, firmly sited within the text. While the fixity of meaning is not necessarily stressed, there remains within feminist analyses a significance attached to the importance for a radical project of popular forms which fail to (textually) resolve/cope with the contradictions they raise. If, however, *all* texts are (inevitably) marked by contradiction, then the implication is that the focus of these critical writings lies with those texts which are marked in highly specific ways.

Feminist criticism through the 1980s encompasses both moves away from a notion of fixed textual meanings, identifying the ambiguity and availability of texts, and a characteristic search precisely for fixed, radical ('progressive') meanings within specific texts or sets of texts. These two impulses, inextricably bound together, emerge from the specific history of the development of cultural studies, of the analysis of popular culture and diverse attempts to establish a feminist cultural politics. The history of the analysis of popular culture is itself a history of contested, polemical positions, operating as it does within an arena in which critical work needs to be justified, made legitimate not only academically but politically. Judith Williamson once described a left enjoyment of mass culture (however critical) as a 'perverse contradiction': in doing so she echoes the history of suspicion which has greeted the study of popular/mass culture, suspicions which precisely articulate an uncertainty about what is at stake in a re-evaluation of the popular.

In this context a Gramscian legacy has been crucial for British cultural studies and for the kinds of analysis produced around the soap opera. Offered here is a language of resistance and crisis which implicitly guarantees the political effectivity that is required. Thus, soap operas do not just lack narrative resolution, they 'refuse' it: implicitly the reader/viewer is carried along by this active refusal on the part of the text. Indeed, while suspicious commentaries provide a context in which popular cultural analysis needs to demonstrate its political effectivity, it is also the case that it is precisely the suggestion of the radical in the popular (along traditional lines) which leaves the project so open to such criticism. If the shift to the popular attempts to retain a language which speaks of the need for a radical, open progressive culture (and simply relocates it), it is not altogether surprising that radical critics would reject that shift. It is precisely at the points of such hesitation that concerns arise that the left and feminism are treading on dangerous ground in their desire to embrace the popular.

The 'feminine' text

I have brought together here writings which hold in common a concept of gendered form, but which consider diverse objects through diverse methodologies: melodramas of the 1950s and soap operas of the 1980s; reference to the feminine as open and the masculine as closed; femininity and masculinity as cultural competencies and positions for the viewer; forms enjoyed by women, and forms that focus on female characters. Earlier, in an attempt to untangle the broad categories designated by gendered genre, I pointed to an implied critical opposition between the soap opera and the crime series, oppositions that are made explicit in John Fiske's *Television Culture* (1987) in which he devotes two chapters to 'gendered television', one to 'femininity' and one to 'masculinity'. The essential criteria of Fiske's argument articulate an understanding of feminine television as resisting resolution (soap), focusing on women (soap, *Cagney and Lacey*) and as watched by women. Masculine television, in a complementary way, is characterized by an action-based drive towards narrative closure, a focus on men and an assumed male audience (*The A-Team*). Fiske takes the division between masculine and feminine television to its logical extreme, and what is significant here is that these divisions can seem at once so obvious and so ludicrous, workable and unworkable. Two key areas which deserve to be highlighted in this context are the status of the text and the question of identification. Fiske discusses the soap opera in terms of plenitude and polysemy, referring not to the condition of all texts but rather to the form's despised counterpart, the closed masculine action series. If, however, we want to stress a notion of plenitude, then the distinction between soap opera and other forms must surely be drawn in other ways. Just as there is a fundamental need to displace the operation whereby the women at home are brought together with the women on the screen in an investigation of the pleasures of same-sex identification (and such a stress is not limited by any means to feminist work on the soap opera). Identification is not necessarily unambivalent, not necessarily same-sex, or stable.

If, when applied to television, reference to certain 'feminine genres' acts as a convenient shorthand for a type of programme, then do these programmes represent something new or at least something distinctive? When Lidia Curti points out that 'pure mono-gendered narratives do not seem to exist' (1988, p. 156), it is no surprise that she follows up with reference to the (now defunct) American police series, *Hill Street Blues*, much noted for its use of devices associated with the soap opera. Fiske follows suit suggesting that 'shows like *Cagney and Lacey* and *Hill Street Blues* are interesting mixtures of masculine and feminine form' (1987, p. 216). Of course, the distinctive features so much discussed in relation to the soap opera (parallel plotting, emphasis on the spoken and the interpersonal) are found elsewhere and not only in forms aimed primarily at women. That this relates in part to the conditions of production of television (but also of formulaic material in a wider sense) is a basic point which has not gone unnoticed in other contexts, but the implications of which are too easily glossed over. The particular resonance achieved through reference to closed and open texts allows the endlessness of soap opera to suggest a refusal of resolution which can be read as a radical textual transgression. In part, an understanding of the resonance that these terms hold relates to the conventions of (textual) analysis that have developed in film studies (single events, attempts to construct a canon to gain respectability) and those that dominate in the study of television (undifferentiated mass of product). While the sheer quantity of television material has tended to highlight the limitations of an analysis based on the interpretation of single texts, such a strategy is consistently mobilized. In one sense, then, the ahistorical feminine text can be seen as a function of the generalized application to soap opera of notions of the open text derived from film studies with little or no reference to the production context from which that form has arisen and in which it evolves.

The talk-show and the chat-show along with the up-market serial, indicate a more widespread emphasis on the spoken and the interpersonal as well as action-based visuals within contemporary television. Analysis of the soap opera needs to take account of trends within contemporary television, both more generally (not just in programmes aimed at or about women), and more specifically. In turn, this system and what it offers can itself be contextualized by the rise of the video market and situated within a critical emphasis on television as a social technology.

While certain forms are aimed at women by production and marketing teams, this can only offer a generalized starting point. We need to ask whether a simplified and sanitized version of 'his 'n' hers TV' is really useful. An appeal for specificity at this level involves a recognition of television as institution and system. If the notion of gendered form can bring disparate work and ideas together, it is perhaps because soap opera as a case study can be read as offering a promise of completeness, can fulfil the desire to have it all. That is, the soap opera as a form seems to offer a match (a coherent fit) not only between the aims of the producers and the female audience (targetting), but between textual patterns (the structure of the narrative) and the audience: both function as open, feminine texts within a basic binary system. Within the vagaries of a reference to gendered genre (mobilized with both extreme generality and extreme specificity at different points) feminine positions and female viewers can be seen neatly to merge. The particular focus on those forms defined as feminine in one way or another and investigated by feminist criticism has tended to imply that only forms aimed at and focusing on women can be useful/interesting to women and/or feminism. In contrast, with some exceptions, sustained work has yet to be undertaken on women's use of forms which have been defined as male, such as the action or horror film (or forms seen to have an absolutely exclusive address to men, such as pornography). An exploration of the production of meaning, of use and pleasure, is not well served by reference to generalized figures of consumption such as the twentieth-century woman-at-home-watching-television or the nineteenth-century woman-at-home-reading-novels.

Popular pleasures: some conclusions

It seems that the imperative to 'take popular culture seriously', to ask as Batsleer, 'why is all this so powerful and why does it matter?' can all too easily reduce into an attempt to establish a fit between these forms and a pre-existing agenda, a set of political criteria deeply bound into modes of evaluation rooted with notions of the progressive *text* and of what a feminist aesthetics might be. It can be suggested that feminist writings on forms such as the soap opera operate within a wider concern to inscribe the radical within the popular in terms of a *textual* openness. In this sense, the invocation of a feminine form achieves its resonance at the expense of a conflation of text and audience expressed in terms of the feminine as a set of values and as a position inhabited by women as an homogeneous group. From a position of opposition a question is often posed, 'what, then, would a feminist cultural politics look like?' – what shape would it take and how might it be possible to produce a feminist analysis of texts? Of course, it is still possible to produce a feminist analysis of texts – the question which remains, however, is the status that might be claimed for such an analysis within a critically transformed field. Yet the very form of such questions retraces the same ground, taking us back to the text as significant object. It is important to stress that the production of a feminist analysis does not necessarily involve a search for the recognizably radical or lie in the construction of oppositions between those texts that reproduce and those that resist (those readers who reproduce and those who resist). While it might be desirable (though I remain unconvinced) to make popular cultural forms aimed at women articulate feminist struggle, that is not a feasible project.

The status of the texts discussed here needs to be seen in relationship to the status of *all* texts. Otherwise the figure of the 'open' text or the 'feminine' text is not a function of availability, of a stress on use in the study of popular cultural forms, but a function of that on which it is premised, the 'closed' or the 'masculine' text. It is in this sense that we might understand the position of feminist analysis so precariously caught between structuralist objects and poststructuralist processes, between a modernist agenda premised on the distinction between good and bad objects (radical/reactionary) and a postmodern free-for-all.

My intention here has been neither to criticize nor celebrate the move to the popular within feminist cultural criticism, but to point to a real ambivalence around the ways in which this move has occurred. It seems to be precisely the theorizations that have led to a stress on the *use* of popular cultural forms that contradict the ways in which *feminists* have sought to use those same forms. While meaning is destabilized, as it slips out of the control of the text and into the hands of the reader, popular forms are textually rewritten as radical within the parameters of cultural criticism. The invocation of the 'feminine' text in which 'feminine' can be read as 'open' or as hinting at a subversive incoherence stabilizes meaning once more. If, as I suggested earlier, all texts are marked by contradiction, then the concerns of recent feminist cultural criticism have been directed towards those texts (or sets of texts) which are marked in highly specific ways, those that can be seen to offer something distinctive, recognizably radical. This is, however, only the appearance of something radical, and feminist cultural criticism needs to look beyond the terrain of this debate. I began with a stress on the significance of the romance as cultural *practice*. To end, I would suggest that actually to shift from a discourse of textual value, whether of greatness or political correctness, would be a positive step.

4

Reading the self: autobiography, gender and the institution of the literary

CELIA LURY

In this chapter I want to address the vexed question of the use of the autobiographical form and the first person narrator in women's fiction. The intention is not only to contribute to the continuing debate within feminism about the significance of autobiographical writing, but also to use this debate as a means of analyzing the critical status of women's writing in general, and its problematic relation to 'the literary' as an institution.

The chapter starts from the assumption that autobiographical or confessional writing has come to occupy a central position in the continuing debates around the status of women's writing because it can be seen to provide one of the limiting cases for the definition of 'the literary' as an institution. That is, as a genre, through the use of the first person it appears to call into question some of the principal defining characteristics of post-romantic literature – in particular, its fictional character, and its ability to transcend the purely personal – and, moreover, to do so in a way which highlights its gendered constitution. Thus, it has conventionally been argued that the literary character of autobiographical writing is dependent on the success with which the use of the 'I' transforms the issue of fictionality (whether something is fact or fiction) into one of aesthetics through a transcendence of the personal. More generally, even Roland Barthes, a renowned opponent of the doxa of Literature, claims that if a writer 'says "I" (which happens often) this pronoun' should not have 'anything to do with an indexical symbol'. Indeed, for writing to be seen as literary, this 'I' should be 'nothing but a "he" to the second degree, a reversed "he"'. He writes that the move from 'I' to 'he' is the

> operation the writer requires in order to utter himself . . . so that to write, far from referring to an 'expression' of subjectivity, is on the contrary the very act which converts the indexical symbol into a pure

sign. The third person is therefore not a ruse of literature, it is *its act of institution previous to every other*: to write is to decide to say 'he' (and the power to do so). (Barthes, 1975, p. 114; my emphasis).

In this comment, Barthes elegantly provides both an astute definition of the partriarchal nature of the institution of literature and (in parentheses) an indication of the contradiction which upholds it: the 'pure' sign of the third person, which is held to be necessary for the very existence of the institution of literature, is upheld by power relations which construct it as masculine.

Historically, women have not had the power, and perhaps not the inclination, to decide to say 'he' in the sense that Barthes outlines. As Andreas Huyssen writes,

> Given the fundamentally differing social and psychological constitution and validation of male and female subjectivity in modern bourgeois society, the difficulty of saying 'I' must of necessity be different for a woman writer, who may not find 'impassibilite' and the concomitant reification of self in the aesthetic product quite as attractive and compelling an ideal as the male writer. The male, after all, can easily deny his own subjectivity for the benefit of a higher aesthetic goal, as long as he can take it for granted on an experiential level in everyday life. (Huyssen, in Modleski, 1986, p. 190).

The 'difficulty of saying "I"' which Huyssen introduces can be seen to be responsible for the current ambiguities associated with the definition of writing by women as women's writing.

On the one hand, the fact that women have been denied access to literature's act of institution, has meant that the use of the first person, because it cannot achieve the status of a reversed 'he', becomes something that is limiting. This is clearly evident in the relatively frequent characterization of women's writing as obsessively concerned with questions of personal relationships and the emotional or sexual spheres, as self-indulgent, moralistic and of interest only to women. On the other hand, it has simultaneously been seen as a site from which to construct an alternative 'feminine' third person position – possibly even a 'she' which would be more than a ruse of women's writing, but would stand as its act of institution equivalent to that ascribed to the use of 'he' by Barthes.

Arguably, it is for this second reason that the autobiographical mode has been so significant for women writers and more particularly for contemporary feminist cultural politics. From this perspective, the use of the first person is the most appropriate form in which to claim and convey a new-found voice, a new-found authority. For example, Elizabeth Wilson has written that, 'If there is a typical literary form of contemporary feminism it is the fragmented, intimate form of the confessional, personal testimony and the diary – "telling it like it was"' (Wilson, 1982, p. 153). Similarly, Elizabeth Cowie and others have claimed that, 'The last decade has seen a revival of the women's novel as a first person realistic narrative, a form which is ideologically appropriate to feminism; authors see it as a way of telling women's story for the first time in an undisguised voice' (Cowie *et al.* 1981, p. 242). As a process of self-definition, the use of the first person has thus been seen to imply a degree of political self-consciousness in so far as it confers an authoritative right to speak on the level of 'personal experience'.

However, this use of 'I' – whether fictionalized or not – and the associated use and understanding of the term 'personal experience' have been strongly criticized from both within and outside the women's movement, most determinedly by those who subscribe to the self-denying ordinances of poststructuralism and postmodernism. This view suggests that although the use of the first person – in the semi-autobiographical or confessional novel – allows women writers the right to present their heroines as active, speaking subjects, it still leaves them closely tied to conventional forms and values, such as the use of a linear narrative, and the emphasis on female sexuality as the key to women's identity. In the journey of self-discovery, it is argued, there is an essentialist identification of the author with the protagonist, and of both with all women, a conflation which is made explicit when women's writing is marketed as the autobiography of a gender (Coward, 1980).

Through the celebration of woman as a full-speaking subject, it is argued, both the act of writing and the common theme of sexual fulfilment are presented as the problem of the individual woman trying to find and express her 'authentic self'. The focus on women's sexual activities in these writings functions, therefore, not as a radical critique of a patriarchal society that has no place for women's desire, but, more often, as a confirmation of women's position as 'personal, ahistorical, sexual and non-political'. Cowie and colleagues, for example, argue that

> the rejection of woman as, simply, the object of desire in the text, and her transformation into the subject of her sexuality ignores the whole problem of her position as the subject of her own discourse; it assumes that the first resolves the second. The heroine gets what she thinks she wants, her man or woman or orgasm, and the author is assumed to have her unspoken demand for a voice fulfilled by writing about it. (Cowie *et al.* 1981, p. 242).

This double triumph, so the critique goes, is equated with liberation: yet neither writing nor sexual pleasure as individual satisfactions are seen to have been questioned in their relation to aesthetic, social, or political demands.

It is argued, then, that the naive appropriation of the autobiographical mode denies the aesthetic nature of writing, since the effect of the (assumed) identification between author, text and reader is to obscure the displacement present in all forms of writing in the distance between the subject and representation. In this way, it is suggested that the privileging of the first person in women's writing relies on an extreme reflectionism, in which 'reality' and 'experience' are presented as the highest goals of literature, the essential truths that must be rendered by all forms of fiction. It is further argued that, in so far as such an aim is used as a more general criterion of evaluation, it undermines the literary status of all women's writing. In short, it is claimed that the feminist 'demand for authenticity . . . reduces all literature to rather simplistic forms of autobiography' (Moi, 1985, p. 46).

This critique has been presented more generally in feminist academic circles in terms of a theoretical debate over the status and use of the concepts of 'image' and 'representation'. As such, it is part of wider arguments about the status of realism, modernism, the nature of the self and the relationships of gender and genre (see Tasker, Chapter 3). Within the framework of these debates, it is argued that most feminist 'commonsense' criticisms of high and popular culture – such as attacks on sexism and demands for more positive images of women in fiction – make use of an (unsophisticated) approach which views representations of women as phenomena that reflect, or are determined in some way, by the position of women in the real world. In opposition to this, it is suggested that a more satisfactory approach involves a notion of representation as an autonomous process of signification that does not necessarily directly relate to the real world.

At best, the 'commonsense' approach is seen as a stage in the development of a feminist literary criticism, necessary to establish a common sense of identity, but ultimately restrictive: for example, Kaplan writes that

> This 'common sense' approach to the literary, which did not have a theory of representation or of the specificity of imaginative writing . . . was soon seen to be of somewhat limited use in understanding how sexual ideologies are constructed and circulated so that they assume 'natural' meaning for both men and women as writers and readers. Feminist critics began to look around for more adequate explanations of ideology, writing and sexual differences . . . (Kaplan, 1985, p. 14).

In this way, some academic feminist cultural criticism, drawing on the theoretical developments which have fuelled this second approach, has come to dismiss the type of women's writing which gives primacy to representing the experience of personal change.

This critique has been helpful in challenging both the prescriptive and exclusive implications of a politics of solidarity and the simplicities of a naive aesthetics of authenticity. An emphasis on the validity of lived experience, particularly when understood as in some sense a privileged but unspecified inwardness, can undoubtedly lead to a kind of reifying of experience. This can result in a limited aesthetics which assumes that the direct expression of a woman's immediate experiences, emotions and feelings is necessarily of aesthetic value. I would suggest, however, that the strength of this tendency in feminist cultural politics has been overemphasized. Moreover, it can be argued that the critique outlined above has mistaken its ability to deconstruct the formal techniques of autobiographical writing for an analysis of that practice's effects in a specific historical conjuncture. What the criticism does not take into account – because it is pitched at the level of formal generality, that is, the individual reader confronting the individual text – is the possibility of a different relation between reader, writer and text altogether. In other words, it ignores the practical and political context in which such writing is actually produced and consumed, and thus does not consider the possibility of different meaning-effects being produced for and producing the subject through processes of identification and recognition. In short, what is left out of these accounts is the possibility of other subject processes obtaining in that relation of representation.

This approach, then, lacks a sense of the wider contexts in which women read and talk about writing, particularly those women outside and independent of any academic structure. It may be, then, that the debate about the status of autobiographical writing should be seen as a further indication of the gap, identified by Grizelda Pollock (1977) over ten years ago, between a popular, experientially based interest in cultural politics by women and the kind of cultural analyses elaborated by a number of professionally involved women who have attempted to deconstruct the category of 'experience'. Yet this is precisely the gap from which new analyses can be developed. Not only do the cultural texts which make up the corpus of women's writing offer serious critiques of dominant patriarchal representations of women (and men), they also came into being in new ways and are heard, seen, or read differently by their audiences. Much of this work has been explicitly concerned with the democratization of hierarchical relations of cultural production and exchange, and women have worked together collectively, either outside, or in a deliberately problematized relation to, the traditional individualist ethos of artistic work. Indeed, it is something of a cliché to note that the informal groups which have emerged indicate that women's writing is read by women in networks rather than as individual, isolated consumers. Yet little attempt has been made to look at what these changes in the conditions of production and reception actually imply for either the *aesthetics* of a feminist literary culture, or for the mainstream institutions of the literary.

In order to begin such an analysis, I will look here at one particular example of these changes: the network of women's reading, writing and study groups scattered throughout the country.[1] To do this, I will employ a method of literary analysis, which, in its most general form, requires that the unit of analysis is neither the text, nor the writer, nor even the reader, but the social relations of representation to which the actions of individuals are articulated and which gives them form, determination and meaning. In this view, to write is to enter into a relationship with a community of readers, and various forms of writing are seen to involve and imply, at any particular time, various forms of relationship. This web of social relations is seen to be embodied not just in the organizational structures of production and distribution, but also in the very conventions of writing and reading (see Sharratt, 1982). This framework of analysis means that in so far as a text is clearly written/read within a particular genre, it can be seen to rest upon a more or less specific set of social relations. It also means that 'textual relations' – that is, formal techniques, reading strategies and so on – are not held separate from 'non-textual relations' – such as methods of cultural production and modes of distribution – and that the latter can be seen to help construct 'literary value'.

The women's writing groups focused on here have much in common with a wide network of adult education and literacy classes, community publishing projects, working-class and black writers' groups and local history projects. They are often low-key, improvised, haphazard and ephemeral; they work with the resources of a particular place and time. Nevertheless, they are in themselves an important indication of the fact that higher education does not monopolize the area of women's writing. They vary in size, structure and make-up, but usually make use of the small group or workshop as their method of working and organizing. This does not necessarily mean writing during group meetings (though it may do), but it does indicate a commitment to using the group as the first readership or audience for the work, and as the body that decides about editing, shaping, public reading, or publication. This use of the workshop implies and helps to construct a particular view of both writing and authorship, and what it means to be a writer. It also indicates a concern with the process of writing as a means of self-expression rather than with the finished product; an emphasis on writing as a collaborative activity through the involvement of others in the reading back of first drafts and practical discussions; and a willingness to see writing as a skill, which can be taught, rather than a gift whose origin is unknown.

Within these groups there is often a privileging of the use of the first person and an emotional investment in the value of writing as revenge, seduction, compensation, or therapy. One understanding of the way in which these groups work is that, just as personal recognitions and identifications can be generalized through the processes of collective self-reflection and analysis which have come to be known as consciousness-raising (Brunsdon, 1978), so individual life-stories may be given the aesthetic values of authenticity and representativeness in the context of their production through an awareness that women have many experiences in common. Thus, for example, the common critical vocabulary of 'honesty' and 'telling it like it is' which is used in such groups can usefully be seen to be embedded in a process of speaking from and to personal experience in a way which displaces the individual (whether writer or reader) as the originating or unique source of this experience by pointing to its social and cultural constraints and by challenging the 'naturalness' of the feelings through which women experience their sense of self.

In this context, texts are seen to be representative, significant and of aesthetic value, not because they express a general, abstract notion of 'woman', or a particular, unique subjectivity, but because they are the product of a collective process of a specific group of social individuals. The understanding or pleasure produced in this way is valued not because it is 'the truth' or 'true to life' in an empiricist sense, but because it is 'authentic' or 'honest' in a social sense: 'By better we mean more honest, more true to our experiences, more understandable to others' (Bilgorrie *et al.*, 1984, p. 16). From this perspective, 'experience' need not be understood in terms of the privileged certainties of liberal humanism, nor need it refer to an individualistic, idiosyncratic sense of something belonging to one, but as a mediating relation between authorship, textual properties, contemporary social reality and historically formed readers; in other words, as a process of self-representation which en-genders the subject in language through relations with others.

In introducing this analysis of women's writing groups to question the terms of the continuing theoretical debate over the issue of representation, I am not suggesting that recent work in feminist cultural analysis should be dismissed because it is not immediately applicable to practice. Rather, I am suggesting that it is necessary to look at the underlying implications of some of the positions into which this work has become locked. Too often the effects that have been attributed to different practices have been understood on the basis of their formal properties alone, resulting in a forced choice between abstract and polarized options, posed with little regard to the possibility that different strategies might be appropriate in different contexts, or in relation to different social relations of reading and writing. This is not to argue for a completely open or pluralist approach to feminist literary criticism, but, at the very least, to point to the need to contextualize each strategy through an analysis of the ways in which their understandings are played out in the actual socially organized relations of cultural production and consumption (including textual practices) that bring them into being.

It may be that one solution to the perceived problem of the individualism and reflectionism of the traditional autobiographical narrative is to be found at the formal level – in a disruption of narrative, a deconstruction of the subject position of the author and an exploration of the form of autobiography as the creative distance between experience and self-representation. However, the approach outlined above suggests there are also other solutions – for example, to develop further a collective politics of reading and writing. It also points out that these solutions are not necessarily either/or alternatives, and may, indeed, both suffer from their mutual isolation. For example, it is worth noting that those strategies which draw on 'more adequate' explanations of representation, and in particular the notion of sexual difference in language, have recently been criticized for the way in which they have facilitated the adoption of an 'imaginary male femininity' by partriarchal critical theory (Lauretis, 1989) as a result of their abstraction from any social context.

In addition, however, an approach which focuses on the social relations of reading and writing stands to gain from a critical exploration of the relationship between 'I' and 'she', and what it has meant for women readers and writers. In part, this involves the reinterpretation of texts by women writers as part of a project to construct for themselves, and for other women, their own relation between 'I' and 'she'. One explicitly self-conscious example of this would be Christa Wolf's *The Quest for Christa T* which begins 'The quest for her: in the thought of her. And of the attempt to be oneself' (Wolf, 1982, p. 3). It would also be possible to consider the work of Monique Wittig in this way, particularly since she herself has said that, '"as far as she could tell as the author, the subject of all of her books . . . was personal pronouns. Each book was the reconstitution and reappropriation of a pronoun"' (quoted in Kricorian, 1984, p. 12). From this perspective, even the title of H.D.'s *Her* (H.D., 1984) suggests a range of possibilities.

However, as a supplement to such formal interpretations, it would also be useful to provide other analyses of the ways in which, historically, the relation between 'I' and 'she' has been constituted. This might include, for instance, an analysis of the way in which women writers have used and adapted autobiography itself as a base from which to make 'she' speak for more than herself by first learning to speak for and of herself. Feminist literary critics have shown that historically, when women writers have used 'I', they have been forced to engage with traditional representations of women in fiction, and the conventional (social) role and (textual) identity of the woman author, in short, with a masculine 'you'. As a result, for women writers the power to assert 'I' has had to be fought for before they have been allowed to say 'she'.

Thus, for example, Elizabeth Winston (in Jelinek, 1980) has charted the way in which the historical change in the female autobiographer's relation to her readers is related to changes in her self-image. She argues that the commitment to formal autobiography, in the sense of a story of self written with the intention of distribution, implies a claim of significance which has troubled women. For this reason, women whose autobiographies were published before 1920 'tended to establish a conciliatory relationship to their reader, by this means attempting to justify their untraditional ways of living and writing so as to gain the audience's sympathy and acceptance' (p. 93). She suggests, in contrast, that women who published autobiographies after 1920 did not apologize for their careers and successes, although a few still showed signs of uneasiness at having violated cultural expectations for women: 'These more recently published writers openly asserted their intellectual and aesthetic gifts and their serious commitment to literary life' (p. 93).

Sometimes, however, the aim of moving from 'I' to 'she', in a manner which is not forced into concessions by a masculine 'you', is (as I suggested earlier through the example of women's writing groups), approached through the use of 'we', a collective subjectivity: 'The testimony of consciousness-raising and of those women's literary forms of diary, autobiography and confession . . . has made possible the identification of points of similarity which have formed the basis for collective politics' (Wilson, 1982, p. 153). The use of 'we' is not meant to be understood literally here, but in terms of a particular set of social relations of reading and writing that work to construct a collectivity. The sense of a 'we' can be constructed in the practices of recognition and identification during the process of reading, a mode of interpretation which is often applied against the grain of traditional criteria.

One illustration of this is clear in Juhasz's discussion (in Jelinek, 1980) of the critical response to Kate Millett's autobiographical novels, *Flying* (1974) and *Sita* (1977). Many reviews were dismissive: *Flying* was described as 'an endless outpouring of shallow, witless comment' or as nothing more than confession which 'is not disciplined autobiography'. Reviewers seem to have disliked the books because they were so personal: 'She conveys absolutely everything, including her (well-founded) doubts about how good a job she's doing. Breakfast, lunch, dinner; it seems that Kate can't bear to leave out a single meaningful detail.' Critics tended to argue, in particular, that Millett failed to fulfil two of the criteria essential for a good autobiography – distance or objectivity and significance. '*Flying*'s detailed all-inclusiveness' is objected to as 'inchoate when it is not incoherent'; 'free-association is seen to have supplanted thought'; 'the assemblage of raw materials' which comprises the book 'might have been transmuted to literature' only if Millett had been capable of 'that particular detachment esteemed by Henry James' (all quotations from Juhasz, 1980, pp. 164–6).

As Juhasz notes, this is a prescriptive suggestion that comes not only from Henry James, but is supported by the accepted canon of autobiographical writing. What feminist critics have argued, however, is that in so far as the genre of autobiography can be seen by writers, readers and critics to embody, as an established set of conventions, a way of writing that operates within a certain set of problems and purposes and uses a known and cumulative set of solutions defined by (a certain class and race of) men, women writers and readers are systematically disadvantaged. Juhasz argues that both *Flying* and *Sita* challenged that canon, refuting the criteria of transcendence and impersonality established through the construction of autobiography as a literary genre. When the books were received positively, readers connected their own lives with Millett's through the processes of recognition and identification which have been much criticized within poststructuralist theory:

> In the Millett of *Sita*, for example, I recognise myself, and it is an uncomfortable lesson, for it is a self I would not wish to be . . . Certainly Millett's feeling transcends self-indulgence, as her personal experience confronts and illuminates my personal experience. There are no doubt many more readers who also share that particular 'personal'. In the process, the process of sharing the personal by means of a book, she is altering our definitions of the personal by giving it a public dimension. (Juhasz, in Jelinek, 1980, pp. 229–30).

In other words, Juhasz notes, some women readers made use of new means of arriving at 'transcendence' within an alternative set of writing/reading relations. This meant that the collective experience of an individual text could be freed from the constraints of restrictive literary criteria: 'we must restore and reiterate the fact that our experience of the text [*Flying*] is not an experience of any kind of totality, as a genre definition would imply, but, instead, a series of feelings, emotions, expectations, responses, questions, revelations' (Kolodny, in Jelenek, 1980, pp. 257–8).

Despite such challenges, and although women's fiction has a range, a power and a public political presence today that it has rarely had before, it is nevertheless true to say that 'she' still continues to be read as an indexical symbol rather a pure sign by the literary establishment. How should this be understood? While the poststructuralist critique of the privileging of the autobiographical form in feminist cultural politics outlined above suggests that the continuing emphasis on personal experience reinforces the interpretation of 'I'/'she' as an expression of subjectivity, this analysis has suggested that it is inappropriate to blame an aesthetics of experience for this continuing reduction. Instead, my analysis implies that the strategic use of the category 'experience' (Spivak, 1985) – as one of the primary mediating relations between authorship, text and reading in contemporary feminist politics – will remain important in so far as it bears on issues which still retain their urgency for the women's movement as a whole: sexuality, subjectivity, self- and group-representation and political practice. Moreover, it suggests that recognition and identification are, at some level, vital, for they are the experiential terms in which the social articulation of difference is mediated through the relations between object and subject. From this perspective, the strategic use of the category 'experience' is one way of maintaining that productive tension between the act of representation and a sense of that-to-which-the-act-of-representation refers which has been useful for a feminist aesthetics. More than this, it suggests that this tension is precisely productive, and not simply a question of reflection or constraint, and, further, that it should not be understood in purely formalist terms.

Women's writing has always been problematic for traditional literary criticism in that it questions the irreducibility of the transcendental imperatives of the literary institution; the critic cannot authenticate a piece of writing as literature within this system of representation when the author is sexed and her truth partial rather than universal. Women's autobiographical writing, because it necessarily takes what it is to be a woman as its subject, is central in this confusion. Women writers have fought within and against the literary institution in a variety of more or less successful ways. Within feminist criticism it has been seen as a fight which is resolvable at the level of de-sexing the author, or of claiming a whole, centred subjectivity for the author (which may come to the same thing). It has been seen as a problem of 'images of women' and how to change them. It has led to calls for the need for a variety of formal(ist) experiments. What this analysis has argued is, first, that it is necessary to see all these suggestions in the wider context of the social relations of reading and writing, not in isolation from each other, and to consider their part in the political project of the (self-)assertion of women. Further, it has suggested that the relation between 'I' and 'she' is not directly analagous to that between 'I' and 'he' – that is, it is not simply one of inversion, and does not result in a pure sign – because of the gendered power relations which structure the institution of literature (although this is not to suggest that certain women writers have not written works of 'great' literary merit, but that their achievement has been precisely on an exceptional basis).

Following on from this, it seems that in so far as literature, through its act of institution, denies its dependence on structured relations of domination and subordination, there are a number of problems with claiming the status of 'the literary' for women's writing. The question then arises, do we want 'she' to stand as a pure sign, as a 'reversed he'? As noted above, de Lauretis (1989) argues that the adoption of hypothetical feminine reading positions by male writers and critics – the use of 'she' as a pure sign – relocates female subjectivity in the male subject, and contributes to the reproduction of patriarchal power. Similarly, Huyssen argues that

it has . . . become clear that the imaginary femininity of male authors, which often grounds their oppositional stance vis-à-vis bourgeois society, can easily go hand in hand with the exclusion of real women from the literary enterprise and with the misogyny of bourgeois patriarchy itself.

Against the paradigmatic 'Madame Bovary, c'est moi', we therefore have to insist that there is a difference. (Huyssen, 1986, p. 189).

Such a view would suggest that the questions about the status of auto-biographical writing as literature should be reformulated. Rather than asking how women's writing could acquire the status of literature, the debate should address the issue of whether, if any notion of the literary is necessarily dependent on the denial of difference, the cost of literariness is worth paying?

Notes

I am grateful to the members of the Women's Thesis Writing Group for comments on earlier drafts of this chapter, especially Sarah Franklin, Janet Newman and Jackie Stacey.

1 This account is based on some research I carried out on community writing groups in the West Midlands. Thanks to Viv Wylie and Geoff Hurd at Wolverhampton Polytechnic.

5

Is 'Doing Nothing' just boys' play? Integrating feminist and cultural studies perspectives on working-class young men's masculinity[1]

JOYCE E. CANAAN

Nearly fifteen years ago (1976), Paul Corrigan wrote a paper entitled 'Doing Nothing', in which he explored how some working-class young men spent their informal time together on the streets on Saturday nights. As he described it, 'doing nothing' meant talking, developing 'weird ideas' such as smashing milk bottles and, for some, fighting. These activities structured both time and social relations; the former was filled and the latter were solidified by 'doing nothing' collectively.

As my title suggests, this chapter questions some of these assumptions in Corrigan's work, and in the youth subculture perspective that has developed in cultural studies more generally. I do so by exploring how some white working-class young men among whom I conducted ethnographic research use the activity of fighting in the construction of masculine subjectivity and subculture. I will argue that although the youth subcultures perspective rightly explores how working-class young men's fighting rests on and expresses their subordinate class position, it does not consider how fighting also elaborates their dominant position in terms of gender relations.

To do this, I want to extend recent feminist analyses of male violence. These analyses stress both the formal and informal means by which male violence against women is perpetrated. They suggest that male socialization presumes and encourages violence; violence against women is therefore seen as part of a more pervasive and determining system of male values through which patriarchal social relations are organized.

These analyses explore how male violence against women is part of a social value system which extols male strength, control and competition and reinforces these values in social institutions and through the media. But they do not explore in depth how class and race also shape male violence. While these analyses emphasize the centrality of socialization to male identity, their focus on the effects of this socialization on women prevents them from considering the contradictory ways in which men themselves experience this socialization. Nor do these analyses examine the relationship between male violence against women, other men and themselves[2] (Bart, 1989; Hanmer and Saunders, 1984; Russell, 1984; Walby, 1990).

This chapter explores how the young men among whom I conducted research conjoin gender and sexuality in their constructions of masculinity, and shows the links between male violence against women and violence against men.[3] The next section, which provides the background for the central ethnographic section, describes the research method and setting and provides a brief review of the relevant literature. The ethnographic section explores how the young men with whom I talked construct and interpret drinking and fighting in contradictory ways. I conclude by showing how bringing together feminist and cultural studies perspectives enables a more nuanced understanding of masculinity to be developed than that which either perspective alone provides.

Background information

Data for this chapter were collected at two youth clubs which I visited four times each. I told youth club leaders that I wanted to talk to white young men between 16 and 24, so they selected groups willing to talk to me. I told these young men that I wanted us to talk about their spare time activities. The initial interview was structured; I asked them what they did from morning until night during the week and on weekends. Since most of them began talking about fighting as their most esteemed leisure activity, I directed my questions to this activity so that they could discuss it in detail. Interviews were taped. I then listened to these interviews and wrote down questions which they raised. I used these questions as the basis for my next interview with subjects.[4]

Most data for this chapter were collected from young men in two communities in Wolverhampton.[5] One community, Wilton Manor, has a youth unemployment rate of 11.9 per cent; the other, Carr Lake, has a youth unemployment rate of 21.8 per cent.[6] My qualitative findings substantiate these statistics; most of the young men to whom I spoke at Wilton Manor were semi-skilled or unskilled labourers who performed jobs such as mechanic, painter and decorator and dustman. Most at Carr Lake were unskilled and unemployed. The employed young men at Wilton Manor, in their mid to late teens, claimed to fight frequently, while the mostly unemployed young men from Carr Lake, in their early twenties, claimed to fight less than before.

Some comments by the older young men suggest some reasons for these differences. They state that they are beginning to find fighting frightening as weapons replace fists and as they face legal repercussions if caught because they are over 16. Those who are unemployed claim that they have less money and drink and go out less than previously. They therefore have fewer opportunities to fight. Finally, these older young men have already developed a notion of masculinity and therefore have less need to test it. For these reasons at least, the mostly unemployed young men with whom I spoke from Carr Lane fight less than their more often employed and somewhat younger counterparts from Wilton Manor. While these findings are not definitive, they suggest that fighting is not a key activity of many unemployed young men; only their wealthier counterparts can afford to drink enough to achieve the mental state necessary for fighting.

This research is informed by three bodies of literature: cultural studies analyses of youth, feminist analyses of male violence and recent studies of men and masculinity. The youth subcultures perspective of cultural studies rests on earlier sociological research on working-class young people. While these studies are ostensibly about both genders, they actually focus on young men. Although Chicago sociologists in the 1920s and 1930s explicitly explored how poor youths (as well as poor people of other ages) meaningfully responded to social disorganization in their neighbourhoods, these studies' focus on male 'gangs' indicates that for them 'youth' meant young men (Canaan, 1990). Similarly, Miller's study of the so-called 'delinquent' values of working-class young people (1978) characteristically was male-oriented. He stressed that these young people have certain 'focal concerns' which include: getting into trouble by breaking the law, demonstrating 'toughness' by being strong and brave when physically threatened, and 'search[ing] for excitement' during weekly 'nights on the town' when they drink, listen to music, have sexual adventures and where young men fight over young women. This short burst of excitement is followed by a longer period of boredom when they are 'hanging out' and doing 'nothing' (Miller, 1978, p. 145). Clearly, this list of focal concerns and activities indicates that the 'young people' being studied are male. There is no attempt to explore how young women make sense of and are affected by these male-oriented focal concerns or whether they have focal concerns of their own.

Much of the work on youth subcultures within cultural studies similarly ignores gender in developing an explicitly class-based analysis of working-class male youths' focal concerns. For example, Cohen notes that working-class young people who lack the monetary resources to participate in leisure consumption as fully as their middle-class counterparts 'manufacture excitement' of their own, based on their focal concerns, to affirm their class position (Cohen, 1978, p. 269). He claims that the components of these concerns rest on those which Miller delineated (e.g. 'trouble', 'toughness' and 'excitement' (1978, p. 270)), which again indicates that he focuses on working-class young men alone. Most of the later cultural studies projects maintain this exclusive focus.[7] Some explore how (male) youths most marginalized from middle-class institutions elaborate class-based identities in and through leisure consumption (Hall and Jefferson, 1976; Hebdige 1979). Others, such as Corrigan (1976) and Willis (1977), examine these (male) youths' activities in middle-class institutions, thereby suggesting how marginalization in these institutions provides the basis for these young men's leisure consumption. Willis also notes that his subjects view fighting as a key means of articulating their focal concerns of masculinity, 'dramatic display, [and] the solidarity of the group' (Willis, 1977, p. 34). It enables them to distinguish themselves from their more conformist working-class counterparts and to resist dominant middle-class cultural values more generally.

While these mostly white male researchers claim to be elaborating an understanding of working-class 'youths' in general, later researchers show that this understanding rests on data collected from, and the elaboration of analyses applicable to, white working-class male youths (Amos and Parmar, 1981; Clarke, 1982; McRobbie, 1980; McRobbie and Garber, 1974; Mac an Ghail, 1988). These later researchers explore how other subordinate young people (e.g. working-class young women and black youths) are affected by the activities of their more powerful white male counterparts.

This chapter focuses on male fighting because the young men to whom I spoke, just as those spoken to by other researchers, view fighting as 'the moment when you are fully tested in the alternative culture' (Willis, 1977; p. 35). As I shall show, at this moment they elaborate and affirm some key components of what masculinity means to them.

While this analysis, like those of the new mens' studies (e.g. Brod, 1987; Kimmel, 1987), examines men and masculinity from the perspective of the men who are experiencing it, it differs from men's studies in that it considers the consequences of male experience for women. Indeed, as Griffin and I argue elsewhere (Canaan and Griffin, 1990), it is difficult, if not impossible, for a dominant group such as men to explore how their power affects subordinate groups and to develop strategies through which they voluntarily give up their power. Feminists, it can be argued, must therefore continue to study men and masculinity, and must continue to make men feel uncomfortable, because feminist work offers insights into how male power works and affects us. It might also help us develop more effective strategies that challenge male power.

Ethnographic evidence

The mostly white working-class young men with whom I spoke did not suddenly start fighting during adolescence. As Andrew, from Wilton

Manor, notes, he learnt about fighting by seeing others do it when he was a boy:

> A: When there has been fights, there's been little six- or seven-year-olds there, like. Not that them doing [it], they just come for the excitement of it. But I think that also puts it [fighting] into their heads cos them going when them six or seven. They ay gonna get hit, but I think that puts the idea what you gotta do when you'm older.

Andrew suggests that boys obtain a glorified picture of fighting by standing on the outskirts and seeing only its 'excitement' while experiencing none of its pains or terrors. Realizing its importance for their elders, they learn early about the centrality of fighting to masculinity.

According to Andrew, fighting becomes increasingly important as little boys start growing up:

> A: Once you get to school, I mean, little five-year-old, he don't give a shit about who's hard or not . . . But once you start growing up, you get people who start coming up and fighting you and you have to defend yourself. And it just starts from there, its sommat you can't avoid.

Andrew's comments suggest that the need to fight is not something which males acquire 'naturally'; they do so in and through the social contexts in which they act.[8]

Perhaps not surprisingly, given its prominence in primary school, fighting is also central to the construction of the male peer group system during secondary school. As Andrew and his friend Keith, also from Wilton Manor, maintain:

> K: Its like, when you'm at school, you've always got a cock of the school. Or a few people who are harder than the rest. They have to fight to see who's the hardest in school . . .
> A: The strongest, who can lamp everybody.
> K: You only get about 15 guys in the whole school that are the hardest.
> A: . . . [T]hey'll hang around together in a gang. Then you have the next hardest lot go round in a gang and then you get the bottoms. The ones who just ay there! . . .

Those who are hardest, or strongest, and most capable of 'lamping' or beating up their opponent form the top peer group.[9] Group members fight each other to determine who is the 'cock', or the most powerful male. This term refers to both a male animal known for its aggressiveness and to the male genitals. The male genitals are also explicitly acknowledged in the term for the least masculine young man, 'wanker'. This suggests that hardness is embodied and symbolized through the male genitals, which are considered most formidable when hard.

During secondary school young women are also thought to affirm this male criterion. Andrew notes that they find hard young men most desirable:

> A: You find the girls go out with the harder ones. They set a reputation when they go out with the girls, no matter how they look. Like you'll find a girl will go out with them . . . [T]he girls go with them to look good being seen with them. They think its good to be seen with a hard person.

The relationship between hardness and sexual attractiveness to young women suggests that these young men are developing forms of masculinity that are constituted and affirmed in and through their relations with young women. Andrew's comments suggest that he views these relationships with some ambivalence. On the one hand, he acknowledges that young women have a certain power because they prefer the hardest males. On the other hand, he denigrates them precisely because they exercise power in this way. His comment that young women choose such males because they 'think its good to be seen with a hard person' suggest that they exercise power merely to raise their own status. Yet his discussion of drinking and fighting, and, indeed, that of the other young men with whom I spoke, suggests that they too use hardness to build up their status. This suggests that young men denigrate young women for using the criterion in the same way as they do themselves. Evidently young men maintain that hardness is something which only young men should recognize in each other.

As Andrew and his friend Jonathan note, hardness is also exhibited spatially. These young men note that their 'territory', like them, is assessed according to its hardness:

> JC: So about territory, when did you first start thinking about this as your territory? . . .
> J: But you don't sort of say one day, 'This is Wilton Manor territory', like but as you grow up, you see other people who belong to the estate like fighting 'cos of the territory. Then you think, 'We should do that.'
> A: Not just that, you don't want other kids coming over here, starting to cause trouble and thinking they can get away with things, and before you know it, the area's got a name. 'Oh, you can go up there and do what you want.' . . . Its got a reputation, like.

Just as boys come to value fighting by seeing their elders doing it, so they come to esteem their territory by watching their elders fight to defend it. The fact that a territory is defined by its degree of hardness suggests that it functions symbolically as the materialization of their collective bodily strength.

The working-class young men with whom I spoke view the *notion* of hardness as central to the *activity* of fighting. This can be seen in the following conversation between myself and several young men from Wilton Manor, Andrew, Keith and David:

JC: What makes someone really hard?
K: Fighting. If he's got the ability to fight and he can beat other guys, he's hard.
A: You fight someone, like, say if he [K] had a fight with him [D], right, and he lamped him, right, and say me, we had a bit of argument or sommat. I'd be scared of him [K] and then people just don't want to fight.
K: See, if I really smashed his face in . . .
A: bashed him to a pulp . . .
K: then they'd have seen it, they'd have thought, 'Oh, don't mess with him, 'cos he can fight.'
A: Even though you might be able to beat him.
D: Its intimidation . . .
A: Its an attitude.
K: Its being better than the rest. Knowing that they know that you are the best.

These comments suggest that the fight is the ultimate demarcator of hardness. It is the means by which the 'best' is selected from the 'rest'. But fighting need not occur frequently. Indeed, those who fight on any occasion are less esteemed than those who only fight occasionally. As Andrew notes, when young men see, or hear about, other young men's hardness, they are unlikely to start a fight when tensions arise between them. A hard young man may merely 'intimidate' rather than fight another. By displaying an 'attitude' that he is harder than they, he implicitly imposes his power on them, which is usually enough for them to acquiesce to his point of view. Thus, this is considered superior to fighting.

Categories of masculinity and the concept of hardness

The concept of hardness contains at least two components, *acting* and *being* hard, as Jonathan and Andrew observe:[10]

J: I mean, how hard you act and how hard you am are two different things. Like there's some people who act really hard but they just ay at all. Put down in one punch. Whereas other people keep themselves to themselves and you go up to them, you have a fight with them, and they tek your punch, no trouble, and when they throw a punch at you, you know about it.

A: You can be hard and act hard, and you can not act hard and be hard, or you can act hard and not be hard. I think the best of them is to be hard and not act hard.

These remarks suggest several things. They suggest that being and acting hard rank social contexts as well as people. How hard one *is* refers to what happens in a fight, where a young man's supposedly 'true nature' is revealed. How hard one *acts* refers to one's actions in other contexts. Because one's nature as revealed in the fighting situation is thought to shed light on one's activity in other contexts, the fighting context is separated from and ranked above all other contexts. The fight is the 'last move in and final validation of' the components of hardness that are displayed in other contexts (Willis, 1977, p. 35).

The components of acting and being hard explicitly rank three forms of masculinity: those who do not act but are hard; those who act and are hard; and those who act hard but are not. These young men's comments and those of two young men from Carr Lake, Steve and Neil, show that the preferred form is being but not acting hard:

JC: Don't people think you're a wanker if you don't fight?
S: Nay.
N: A mate'll respect you if you walk away from drunkenness.
S: If anyone comes up to you and says, 'Do you want a fight?', you say, 'Fuck off'. If they doe, you just beat them up. You give them a chance to walk away. Say, 'I don't want to fight, alright? I doe want no trouble, just gu away like'. You'm still standing your ground, you'm standing there saying, 'Gu away'.

The fact that being but not acting hard is the preferred form of masculinity substantiates the point made in the last section that fighting does not occur frequently. One who is 'standing the ground', even when drunk, is most respected. He only fights when there is no way not to do so. The expression 'standing his ground' suggests that while such a young man does not fight, he also does not walk away. By preventing a fight he shows that he can 'manfully' control himself without flying off the handle when the first spark of tension arises. He thereby displays his masculinity in another way. While the other initially proposes a fight, the protagonist's decision to reject this proposal enables him to redefine the situation. If the other accepts this redefinition, the protagonist effectively demonstrates that he is the more powerful of the two. In so doing, he shows that he is not only powerful when fighting, but that he, more than others, determines when he will and will not fight.

As this suggests, there is a simultaneous valorization of fighting and of not fighting as signs of hardness. This same mentality is evident in the nuclear deterrent strategy which constructs the fantasy of omnipotence as the last defensive strategy in a war which, it is hoped, will never reach the point where this omnipotence is demonstrated.

One who 'stands his ground' is, as this trope suggests, able to occupy space because he successfully makes his might known to others. Because he can keep the other at a distance and thereby defines the situation, he is able to operate on and control this other. He has a particular kind of male power; his presence and literal staying power imply the threat of violence.

This exercise of force and skill requires what Seidler defines as 'self-control'. One must be able to hide his inner fears and vulnerabilities from himself and others. In speaking of his own experience, Seidler observes that he was

brought up to denounce whatever fear I was feeling . . . I learnt not to show my fear to others as I learnt to hide it from myself. But also I discovered that in hiding my fear I hid my vulnerability . . . We fear that if we allow our softer feelings to surface we shall never be able to regain control of ourselves. (1985, pp. 150, 159).

Seidler's usage of the term 'soft' indicates that the 'hardness' of thought central to masculinity requires that vulnerabilities and feelings be stifled.[11]

One who is but does not act hard exercises force, skill and self-control in several ways. In the fighting situation, he may physically fight, which, if successful, means that he uses his strength so skilfully that he can beat his opponent. While fighting, he also controls the pain that he feels from the blows he receives. If he decides not to fight, he aims to control how the situation proceeds mentally, thereby demonstrating that his force and skill extend beyond physical to mental action. He may also exercise mental control in other situations by displaying an attitude of hardness and the implied threat of violence that makes others submit to him. He thereby shows that he is harder than others outside as well as inside the fighting situation.

The second kind of masculinity is evident in the young man who acts and is hard. Just as with the first kind, he exercises force and skill as well as control in a fight, although he is more likely to fight than not to fight in a tense situation than the first kind. Unlike the first kind, he exercises these abilities in other contexts. This suggests that he does not temper his force and skill by control outside the fighting situation. That is, he is viewed as being somewhat out of control in non-fighting contexts. On the other hand, because such a young man *does* exhibit hardness in a fight he is viewed as being hard. Because he does display this key male attribute in the most important context in which it can be displayed, his form of masculinity is esteemed. Although less esteemed than one who does not act hard, he is preferred over the third type.

The third type of young man acts but is not hard. He displays his hardness in all contexts *except* the fight. In the crucial fighting context he is defeated and, consequently, his 'true nature' (which in this case is shown to be false because he misrepresents himself) is revealed. As Keith notes, 'If you keep yourself to yourself, nothing will happen, but if you start going 'round acting hard or something, when you ay, people are going to come down on you.'

One who acts hard everywhere but in the fighting context is not only *not* considered hard, he is considered a sham. This suggests that hardness is not acceptable as a pose; it must be grounded in male identity. Otherwise the way a young man acts outside the fighting context is not substantiated in it. Probably because such a young man misuses the notion of hardness, he finds himself rejected by peers who 'come down on' him. This indicates that the peer group provides evaluative criteria of masculinity which it then publicly imposes on those who do not comply with its dictates. This imposition, in turn, both consolidates and reaffirms these criteria.

But these three kinds of masculinity are not the only ones that these young men elaborate. Elsewhere some of them discuss a more ambiguous, fourth kind of masculinity, that of the 'wanker', which they construct in relation to a fifth, non-'wanker' kind. Neither of these two kinds of male fight: they neither act nor are hard. They are evaluated differently from the other kinds and from each other, as Andrew and Keith note:

A: You got some kids like Tom, he woe fight, but it doe make him a wanker or nothing like that.
K: No, cos we know he doe want to fight . . . You know he wouldn't fight, but you know he's your mate. That's because that's his way, he woe fight.
A: Someone ay got to be hard to be your mate. If someone's a complete wanker, we doe want him. If you doe fight, it doe mean you'm soft . . . He's got more sense than some people.

Andrew suggests that the difference between these two kinds of masculinities is the difference between young men who are 'hard' and those who are 'soft'. He notes that softness is associated with one who is a 'wanker'. Such a young man *never* demonstrates hardness, in or outside of the fighting context. Since hardness is central to masculinity, a wanker seems to be the least preferred form of masculinity.[12]

It is significant that the term wanker quite literally means one who engages in masturbatory sex. This indicates that those who have sex without a woman and without penetration (the importance of which the requisite hardness of 'cocks' suggests) are not 'real men'. This also suggests that only those who have sex with women are 'real men'. The young men with whom I spoke link hardness with heterosexuality in other ways. Steve claims that he is more likely to have a fight when he is out with a young woman than at other times because it is a means by which he can 'show off in front of a wench'. Andrew and Jonathan elaborate this point:

A: [B]oys want to fight in a way to look good to girls. Its a manly thing, ay it?
J: Its macho . . .
JC: Do you ever get to fight when you're with a girl?
A: Yeah. 'Cos you can cause some trouble then. That's even more reason, ay it? The girl's there, someone's causing trouble, you ain't just gonna laugh it off. They [girls] think, 'What's he doing? He's a bit of a wanker, ay he?' Whereas if you stand up and have a go . . . you try and impress them, don't you?
J: Thing is, you've got more of a chance of getting into a fight when there's a girl there, 'cos there's a lot of fights happen caused over girls, like. Like you'm going out with someone, someone tries to get off with her, that's it.
A: That's why territory fights can start, 'cos you've been out with a girl from that area. You start going down and people from that area won't like it, 'cos she's going out with someone from another area. Before you know it, they'll have a go at you and then the whole area's having a fight, ay they?

These young men suggest that fighting is 'manly' and thereby enables them to demonstrate their hardness to young women. But they claim that they are motivated to fight in this situation not just because they want to show off, but because they fear that their female partner might consider them 'a bit of a wanker' if they do not fight. This suggests that they feel somewhat uncertain around and need to demonstrate their masculinity to young women.

However, the fact that these young men maintain that other young men may try 'to get off with her' indicates that they consider young women to be pawns in a competitive game that is played by and for males only. But young women are not mere tokens in this game; they are considered the cause of such competition between young men, which can become very violent, as Andrew and Jonathan note:

A: Girls can cause trouble between mates easily. They can split two best mates apart.
J: Easily.
A: To hating each other. To want to kill each other.

Young women are blamed for the consequences of actions between the victors. And Andrew's comment that young men get so angry at each other when young women ostensibly cause fights raises the question of how young men feel about and act towards the supposed female perpetrator of divisiveness between men. If they can hate and 'want to kill' the other whom they view as an equal, how might they feel about and act towards a subordinate antagonist?

Some idea of the ways young women experience their role as tokens in a male game can be seen by considering how Hilary, a 16-year-old white working-class young woman at a college outside Wolverhampton, interprets her relationships with young men:

> H: Like, what you got to do when you're out with somebody, right, they always try it on with you . . . A bloke will go off with a slag, right, but when its time to get married, they'll look for the quiet, well, not quiet, but decent girl . . . So when a bloke tries it on you, you kick him in the donkeys and tell him to get lost . . . When I was going out with this bloke, right, he tried it on with me and I thumped him and everything. And after he said to me, 'Well, at least I know you'm decent now,' you know what I mean. So sometimes its a test.

Hilary's comments indicate that young men's aim to demonstrate hardness in their heterosexual relationships has serious ramifications on their relationships with young women. They make these relationships into competitive 'test[s]' similar to those in which they compete against male peers. If young women fail the 'test', they will be labelled 'slags' and thus considered sex objects to be used instrumentally by males. If they pass the 'test', at this point in their lives their male partners are likely to drop them for a 'slag', or 'sexually easy' young woman. Young men thereby make heterosexual relationships a context in which they struggle against young women in a contest that the latter cannot win. Clearly, young men view young women as even more subordinate than the softest young men because they do not compete against the former.

This subordination of young women to young men is further suggested by the fact that going out with young women from another territory is thought to cause territorial fights. Such an action is considered a violation of *territory*. Young men give no thought to whether such a violation also includes a violation of young women, which Hilary's comments suggest. This indicates that young men view young women as part of their territory, of their collective materialization of bodily strength.

The construction of masculinity around hardness thus has direct consequences for young women. Young women cannot choose their partners;

the young men in their territory seek to control this themselves. Even more ominously, once they enter into relationships with young men, they may be seen as objects through which their partner's masculinity is displayed to other young men.

It is not just heterosexuality that is central to these young men's preferred forms of masculinity, but a heterosexuality that is literally and figuratively substantiated in and through the male genitals. As I have suggested, during secondary school Andrew and his mates viewed the hardest or most powerful young men as 'cocks' and now view the softest young men as 'wankers'. This indicates that the male genitals play a central role in these young men's constructions of masculinity. They constitute masculinity through two opposing sexual orientations of the male genitals: penetrative sex with a young woman and non-penetrative, masturbatory sex (where such 'hardness' is unnecessary and 'softness' prevails).[13] The former is preferred and the latter is denigrated. This indicates even more starkly how the preferred form of masculinity of the young men with whom I spoke does not just denigrate young women but constructs the latter only as subordinate objects of sexual desire.

While the fifth kind of masculinity, like that of the wanker, involves not fighting, it has more positive connotations. If it is a young man's 'way' not to fight, and if, simultaneously, he is not 'soft', then he is considered to have force and skill and to exercise mental control because he *chooses* not to fight. Andrew makes this point when talking about his friend Jonathan:

> A: [H]e [Jonathan] doe go to any of the fights. That don't make him a wanker. I think that makes [him] pretty good . . . I think he's standing out from the rest and I think that's better . . . That shows he's got it up here [points to his head]. He knows what he's on about.

Andrew approves of Jonathan's conduct because it indicates that Jonathan exercises mental self-control – he 'has it up here'. This indicates that there is a mental equivalent to bodily hardness. Like bodily hardness, mental hardness assumes that one has a kind of self-control. Like one who is but does not act hard, such a young man thinks before he acts; he relies on mental capacities to avoid a fight. Unlike the former, however, such a young man never fights. He therefore is in a different category to the former and, indeed, to most other young men. For he chooses not to construct his masculinity with the criteria that they use. Partly because the masculinity which he develops relies upon a notion of self-control, and partly because this masculinity calls upon the strategy of mental self-control used by the most esteemed young men, this form of masculinity is acceptable to and even admired by other young men. Thus Jonathan is respected because he thinks before he acts.

While this form of masculinity, which stresses mental capacities, is admired, it is not the preferred form. My male subjects view their bodies as the main source of their power and esteem. This is not surprising since those of them who work do skilled or unskilled manual labour; they at least partly affirm their male identities in and through this labour and the wage packet it provides. This differs from middle-class young men, who view their minds as their source of power and control at work, and strive to sharpen their mental control in leisure (Canaan, 1990).

All five types of masculinity which these working-class young men develop rest on the bipolar opposition of hardness and softness. Cocks are hard, wankers are soft, and all other kinds of young men exhibit hardness, its mental analogue, or softness to a greater or lesser degree.

This ethnographic analysis of these forms of masculinity adds to the feminist understanding of male violence in several ways. It demonstrates that the category of hardness provides the idiom with which masculinity is articulated. It further suggests that this masculinity is located in and symbolized by the hard state and heterosexual orientation of their genitals. Relationships with young women thereby presume and are affirmed by penetrative sex. Because this constitutes young women as mere signifiers of male power, young women hold a subordinate position in the male world. Because this world is the more encompassing one, and because young men strive to control young women in their spatial territory as well as in relationships, this suggests that in both public and private contexts young women's movements are limited and monitored by young men. Finally, if these young men construct forms of masculinity that so centrally focus on demonstrating the potential of physical might over male subordinates, might they not also extend this demonstration into their relationships with young women, the gender they consider subordinate to their own?

It is significant that young men construct several distinct forms of masculinity even within a relatively homogeneous population of mostly white, heterosexual working-class young men. This has implications for both feminism and cultural studies. For feminism, it suggests that the social construction of male violence must be understood as mediated by complex and contradictory notions of masculinity, class identity and subculture. For cultural studies, it suggests that analyses of working-class male fighting cannot simply be considered as the expression of their class position.

Conclusion

This chapter has aimed to show how some working-class young men's construction of masculinity is highly contradictory and multifaceted. The fact that masculinity can take several forms, even among a small fragment of white working-class heterosexual male youths, suggests that masculinity is not a unified entity. It can mean different things to different young men in different contexts. Not all of these forms rest on and affirm violence, which suggests that violence against women is not something that is central to all forms of masculinity. Working-class male violence is not something that singularly expresses working-class identity or masculine identity; it is a particular conjunction of these two, and other, factors. In addition, this analysis suggests that male violence is constructed as much through gender as class; it is central to masculinity in general and takes particular forms among distinct groups of working-class young men, which reveals much about their class and gender as well as their sexual orientation and age.

By integrating cultural studies analyses of males fighting other males, which stress class relations, and feminist analyses of male violence against females, which stress gender relations, I have sought to contribute to a more complex, textured and multivocal perspective on masculinity. Both class and gender must be seen in a more encompassing framework, one which considers how people organize these, and other components, into their identities.

Notes

Earlier versions of this chapter were given as papers at the Department of Cultural Studies, University of Birmingham and at the University of Exeter School of Education. I would like to thank participants at those seminars for their comments. I would also like to thank Debbie Steinberg and the Women's Thesis Writers' Group (especially Sarah Franklin) for their insightful and encouraging comments on earlier drafts of this chapter.

1   The research on which this chapter is based was funded by the Gulbenkian Foundation for their project on cultural provisions for young people between the ages of 16 and 24 directed by Paul Willis. This chapter uses a small yet problematic part of the data which I collected as the ethnographer on this project during four months of participant–observer research at a college outside Wolverhampton. I also spent one month at youth clubs in two other communities outside Wolverhampton.
2   Michael Kaufman (1987) calls this 'the triad of men's violence'.
3   I do not meant to suggest that fighting is exclusively male; during my research among upper middle-class American teenagers (Canaan, 1990) I heard about fights between young women, which other studies explore in more detail (e.g. Campbell, 1984). Nor do I mean to suggest that violence is limited to working-class males. My data on American upper middle-class young men in the longer version of this chapter suggest that they develop forms of verbal violence that are much more insidious than those of working-class British young men.
4   The research which I conducted can only loosely be termed ethnographic. Unlike the more traditional anthropological ethnography on American

suburban upper middle-class teenagers (Canaan, 1990) which I wrote, this research was neither long-term nor very extensive. Yet just as an anthropological ethnography, it was qualitative and aimed to tease out the terms and strategies with which working-class young men constructed some aspects of their identities.

5   From the earliest days of the Industrial Revolution until recently, Wolverhampton has been a central site for the manufacturing and distribution sectors of the British economy. However, these sectors are currently diminishing in importance as the service sector of the economy expands. The manufacturing that remains is moving away from old industrial cities such as Wolverhampton. That which is left relies on a smaller workforce. The level of unemployment in Wolverhampton has been relatively higher than elsewhere in the country and this is especially true for young people. In the early 1980s one-third of all young people were unemployed (Willis *et al.*, 1988).

6   Names of communities and of the young people to whom I talked are pseudonyms.

7   Exceptions include: Griffin (1985), McRobbie (1981), McRobbie and Garber (1976) and McRobbie and Nava (1984).

8   Other data for this study and my prior study of white middle-class suburban American young people (Canaan, 1990) suggest that young people have contradictory ideas about the 'natural' and 'cultural' components of their conduct. Sometimes they emphasize one component, at other times the other, and sometimes they acknowledge both. Further research is needed to clarify in what circumstances they emphasize these factors.

9   The criterion of hardness does not simply constitute the most powerful group of young men in school. Other male groups are also ranked by hardness. The next hardest group occupies the middle rung. Those at the bottom rung who 'just ay there' probably seem invisible because they do not fight and therefore do not demonstrate hardness.

10 When I gave this chapter as a paper at the University of Exeter, Jeff Meiners noted that his students use a third criterion, 'looking hard', that is, dressing in a way which conveys hardness.

11 If these 'soft' qualities are not contained, males may feel very threatened. Interestingly, Holloway's (1984) male subjects use the term 'soft' as a verb to describe how they feel when attracted to a woman. This suggests that such attraction is fundamentally threatening to masculinity because it requires that one reveal the qualities that one previously attempted to conceal:

> Wendy: But I think that there's a question about . . . how much you show yourself to be vulnerable.
> Martin: But you do, just by showing that you're soft on somebody. It seems to me that when you've revealed that need, you put yourself in an incredibly insecure state. You've before managed by not showing anyone what you're like. By showing them only what is publicly acceptable. And as soon as you've shown that there is this terrible hole in you – that you want somebody else – then you're in an absolute state of insecurity. (Holloway, 1984, p. 246).

Martin's description of the display of vulnerabilities as that which makes him feel so incomplete that he has a 'terrible hole' inside, suggests how fundamental the containment of vulnerabilities is to the construction of masculinity.

12 Chris Griffin at the University of Birmingham pointed out that this was a distinct type of masculinity.
13 The upper middle-class American teenagers I worked with use a slang term, 'weaponhead'. They gloss this as a male who is controlled by his genitals rather than his brain, which suggests that the male genitals can function as a kind of lethal weapon. The implications of this term for male violence against women are dangerously suggestive (Canaan, 1990).

Part Three:
Science and technology

6

Science and technology: questions for cultural studies and feminism

MAUREEN McNEIL & SARAH FRANKLIN

Introduction

As mentioned in the general introduction to this volume, this section on science and technology represents a particular kind of overlap, or rather, lack of overlap, between feminism and cultural studies. When *Women Take Issue* was produced at the (then) Centre for Contemporary Cultural Studies at the University of Birmingham (hereafter CCCS), the feminist analysis of science was only just beginning to emerge. Since then, it has become one of the most challenging dimensions of feminist theory and politics, raising questions relevant to a wide range of inquiry and research. With its trenchant epistemological critique of existing (patriarchal) frameworks for understanding, it anticipated many of the concerns later associated with poststructuralism and postmodernism, such as the role of bipolar constructions of difference (nature/culture; reason/emotion; mind/body, etc.) and the modernist conceptual heritage of the Enlightenment (the ideals of progress, objectivity, realism, etc.). Yet, while these general questions were taken up within cultural studies, very little attention was paid to their roots in science, or the privileged place accorded science and technology, in the authentication of 'true knowledge'. Hence, this section explores an area where feminist concerns have been the basis for a new trajectory within cultural studies, the cultural analysis of science and technology.

This chapter is written out of the intersection between feminism and cultural studies where we have begun to develop a feminist cultural account of science. This effort is not without precedent, the formative work of many feminist interpreters of science being the basis for much of our discussion below. It is, however, a particular vantage point, which we feel has significant implications in terms of reviewing what we have in the way of a feminist cultural account of science, what it includes, what it leaves out and where it might be heading.

The inclusion of a section on science in a volume of recent feminist work within cultural studies was facilitated by the formation of a subgroup on science and technology at CCCS in 1986. This group was composed mainly of women involved in the feminist analysis of science, and its activities have culminated in a project highlighting the importance of science (scientific expertise, scientific discourses, scientific progress, etc.) to recent debates about abortion in Britain (included below). To us, this evolution speaks of a certain analytical affinity between feminism and cultural studies in terms of approaches to science. Yet, this affinity is accompanied by certain discordances (as are many of the encounters between feminism and cultural studies chronicled in this volume). It is to these affinities and discordances, and the question of what they can tell us about both the feminist analysis of science and cultural studies, that we have directed our comments here.

Our chapter is divided into several sections. We begin by looking both ways from our interdisciplinary crossroads: at the analysis of science within cultural studies, and within feminism. Next we have organized our discussion around what we consider to be key features in the feminist analysis of science. This is done through a review of three important contributions to the feminist debate about science. In turning to the writings of Sandra Harding, Emily Martin and Donna Haraway, we are able to show the diversity and strength of what feminists have achieved in this sphere. In so doing, we are also trying to establish a kind of dialogue between these projects and some of the insights of cultural studies. It is our hope that we may thereby explore some directions for development of this important facet of feminist work, and it is with some reflections on these projects for the future that we conclude.

Some of the questions which have circulated within debates about postmodernism hold together both the works we have considered and our own thinking in this area. These include questions about the category 'woman', the standpoint of the analyst, the demise of certain privileged 'Enlightenment', 'modernist' or 'foundational' assumptions, and the diversified sites of the cultural production of scientific meanings in contemporary Western society. The latter is a concern which also leads us to explore aspects of the 'body politics' which have played a central role in the feminist analysis of science, and within feminist politics generally.

Cultural studies and science

While a science question clearly emerged within feminism, there was no such question within cultural studies until quite recently. The carving out of a cultural studies project in Britain in the 1960s and 1970s precluded this possibility for a number of reasons. The emerging British form of cultural studies was deliberately severed from its potential progenitor – the Frankfurt School. For many British researchers, the pathologization of forms of popular culture was the hallmark of the Frankfurt School and this was at odds with their more positive evaluation of popular cultural forms. However, in turning their backs on this school, English speaking students of cultural studies were also abandoning one of the most powerful set of political analyses of scientific thinking, Enlightenment traditions, and instrumental reason within Western culture. It was only much later, as suggested below, in what could be seen as the return of the repressed, in the new guise of postmodernism, that many of the concerns of the Frankfurt School (regarding progress, authoritarian meta-theories, etc.) would be addressed within cultural studies.

Additionally, the critiques of the foundations of disciplines, most notably sociology, literary studies and history, that characterized some of the initial work within British cultural studies (often referred to as 'mapping the field') did not extend to the natural sciences (see Hall *et al.* (1980), Johnson (1983)). This was in part due to the Althusserian basis of much work within cultural studies in the 1970s. Althusser (1969) insisted upon a clear epistemological break with Marx's own work (both his pre-scientific and scientific work, before and after *Capital*), thereby establishing the aspiration to scientificity as a goal of much Marxist social theory. Most work within cultural studies during the 1970s and early 1980s adapted to this Althusserian mandate. Indeed, early feminist work at CCCS drew heavily on Althusser, extending his categories in various ways, but never questioning his scienticism (see *Women Take Issue*).

The main challenge to Althusserian hegemony within British cultural studies came instead from Edward Thompson. Thompson opposed Althusserian theory and its influence through an impassioned defence of English empiricism – hardly a vantage point which would yield many questions about science or scienticism. In both 'The peculiarities of the English' (1965) and *The Poverty of Theory* (1978) Thompson sang the praises of good, old-fashioned English empiricism, and in his 1965 essay, of its most famous exponent – the hero of English bourgeois intellectual culture – Charles Darwin.

Indeed, the only founding father of cultural studies who questioned the role of science and technology within Western culture was Raymond Williams. Williams was highly ambiguous in his treatment of science and technology. His short essay on 'Ideas of Nature', first published in 1972 (Williams, 1980), remains a valuable investigation of this pervasive cultural category. However, Williams totally failed to notice the negotiation of gender relations in and through this category (Ortner, 1974; Merchant, 1980; Brown and Jordanova, 1981; Griffin, 1985). Nor did he specifically interrogate this category in relation to the idea of natural science. Yet, in *The Country and the City* (1973) and *Keywords* (1976), Williams continued this investigation of the social investment in the category 'nature' specifically within British culture.

More generally, Williams often suggested the importance of technological aspects of contemporary British culture. His book *Television: Technology and Cultural Form* (1974) and some of his essays in *The Year 2000* (1983) were indicative of this sensitivity. Yet, he was often disappointing on this topic. In 'Culture and Technology' (1983), Williams restricts himself to a discussion of the 'cultural conservatism' and technological determinism associated with much technological innovation. He has some interesting comments on the history of the development of mass-communications technologies, such as radio and cable television. Quite rightly, he insists that 'it is not good enough to oppose this or that technology' (Williams, 1983, p. 139). Nevertheless, he has little sense that opposition to new communications technologies can be anything but conservative. 'The moment of new technology is a moment of choice', he concludes (Williams, 1983, p. 146), thereby invoking a use–abuse model of technology. This is disappointing from someone who has been so thorough in his demonstrations of the creation, coding and layering of other cultural products, be they words, literature, or concepts (see Williams, 1983).

In general, the founding fathers and frameworks of cultural studies did little to encourage the examination of science or its parameters. The institutional and methodological foundations of cultural studies, which drew heavily on literary studies, contributed to this exclusion. CCCS originated as a unit affiliated to the English Department at Birmingham University. As Richard Johnson has argued (1983), work in this field, from its earliest days to the present, has relied heavily on the tools of literary analysis. To be in a literary camp in England, as C. P. Snow's (1959) analysis of Britain's 'two cultures' and Perry Anderson's (1969) study of the contours of English intellectual life suggest, is clearly to be outside the remit of the natural sciences. For this reason also, science was not seen as a force with which to engage.

Finally, cultural studies took as its object of study 'whole ways of life' or 'whole ways of struggle' (Williams, 1965; Thompson, 1961a, 1961b). The creation of meaning on an everyday basis, particularly by socially subordinated groups, was the main concern of the cultural studies researcher. Hence, many saw this domain as far removed from the lofty formulations of science, which were associated with established knowledge and authoritative statements.

In the 1980s, the science question, or more accurately, questions about science have been seeping into cultural studies. In part, this reflects a shift in theoretical frameworks. The high theoreticism of certain forms of Marxism, particularly Althusserianism, has given way to frameworks that question many earlier scientific premises. At the core of Michel Foucault's work, for example, is a set of concerns about knowledge which undermine the presumptions of a liberationist Marxist science, such as the knowledge–power relationship, and the roles of disciplines and of intellectuals. Deconstructionism and postmodernism have been unevenly influential within cultural studies, but they have also questioned presumptions of progress, the role of grand theory and empiricist notions of representation.

The constituency with which cultural studies researchers identify has also shifted. In its Marxist heyday, class struggle was the paramount concern of those working within the field. Today, the range of political identifications amongst cultural studies researchers is more diversified. Minimally, sexism and racism have come to share the spotlight with class oppression. Moreover, the 'new social movements' of the late 1970s and 1980s in Europe, North America and Australia have had some impact on the priorities of cultural studies. In particular, the ecology (or green) and anti-nuclear movements (in addition to feminism and anti-racism) have influenced the political and intellectual agendas of cultural studies.

Both the theoretical shifts within cultural studies and its altered constituency have led to a greater emphasis upon science. For those committed to struggles against sexism, racism and homophobia, scientific arguments are formidable and ubiquitous obstacles. Recourse to biology is frequently a more important ploy by those defending gender, racial and sexual inequalities than it is for those maintaining class barriers. The 'whole ways of struggle' for those involved in challenging racism, sexism and heterosexism are frequently forged in and against biology and the pronouncements of 'natural science'. Moreover, at the core of the anti-nuclear and ecology movements has been the issue of the relationship between the 'natural world' and scientific innovation or technological 'progress'.

Beyond this, high technology increasingly pervades daily life in the Western world. It was always a striking omission that cultural studies has for so long ignored the technological dimensions of the mass media. With video, cable, television, personal computers and other developments in mass communications and information technology, this omission has become a more obvious shortcoming. Meanwhile, with new reproductive technologies, genetic engineering and biotechnology, and their potential dramatically to transform agriculture, healthcare, procreation and much else, it is clear that 'everyday life' is increasingly inseparable from the influence of science and technology. Though it may have been slow to awake to the significance of this dimension of contemporary culture, it is clearly apparent that within cultural studies science and technology are likely to be of increasing importance.

Feminist approaches to science

Whereas the analysis of science within cultural studies has remained something of a neglected area, it has emerged as one of the most powerful trajectories within contemporary feminist scholarship. In part, this is the result of feminist challenges to science as a form of patriarchal epistemology, thus addressing the very nature of knowledge and what it is to know. In this respect, the feminist analysis of science has much in common with the postmodernist critique of the 'legitimating metanarratives' of Western industrialized society, through which knowledge has been defined and authenticated through particular constructions of truth and progress, which have more recently come to be seen as 'in crisis' (see Lyotard, 1984). However, the feminist critique of scientific epistemology was not primarily motivated – as was much of the 'postmodernist' movement – by largely philosophical or theoretical concerns. To the contrary, the feminist critique of scientific epistemology has deep roots in the social and political concerns of the women's movement, which, from its inception in the early 1970s, identified scientific and medical power-knowledges as key sources of patriarchal control over women.

The evolution of the pioneering and influential anthology *Our Bodies, Ourselves,* published in 1973 by the Boston Women's Health Collective, serves as a useful microcosm for the general emergence within feminism of a practical and theoretical critique of science. This project began in 1969 as a discussion group on 'women and their bodies'. It was also called 'the doctors group' because of shared anger at the medical profession resulting from women's experiences of medical 'male-practice'. The evolution of the project from a discussion group concerning 'women and their bodies', to a course entitled 'Woman and Our Bodies', to an internationally circulated book entitled *Our Bodies, Ourselves,* represents well the historical process of increasing feminist recognition of the centrality of 'expert' knowledges about women's bodies in the maintenance of women's oppression.

It was an extension of this recognition of the power of scientific ideas to define women's sense of bodily awareness, sense of self and sense of reality that propelled the feminist analysis of science to investigate the historical emergence of particular constructions of women and the natural within scientific discourse (Merchant, 1980; Easlea, 1980, 1981); the entrenched misogyny of the male 'conquest' of women's reproductive capacity in particular (Oakley, 1984; Ehrenreich and English, 1979; O'Brien, 1981; Donnison, 1988); the masculine forms of identity and self predominant within the production of scientific knowledge and the scientific worldview (Bleier, 1986; Keller, 1983, 1985); the relationship between biological determinism as a form of sexism and its links to forms of race and class oppression (Fausto-Sterling, 1985; Bleier, 1984; Lowe and Hubbard, 1983; Hubbard, Henifin and Fried, 1982; Rose and Rose, 1976);

and more recently, the emergence of a considerable feminist literature on new reproductive technologies (Arditti, Duelli-Klein and Minden, 1984; Corea, 1985, 1986; Klein, 1988; Spallone and Steinberg, 1987; Stanworth, 1987; Rothman, 1986, 1989).

In sum, the feminist analysis of science had early roots in the political challenge to patriarchal science and medicine launched by the women's movement in the early days of its most recent phase. This challenge subsequently came to be a central organizing focus of feminist scholarship and activism, through which a highly developed critique of science as a key locus of patriarchal power and patriarchal culture was developed. As is discussed further below (vis. Harding), this challenge culminated in a thoroughgoing critique of patriarchal scientific epistemology as epitomizing the patriarchal power to define reality. In the next three sections of our analysis, we will indicate some of the different directions in which feminists have pursued and developed analyses of science.

The feminist critique of scientific epistemology

Sandra Harding's *The Science Question in Feminism*, published in 1986, marked an important turning point in the feminist analysis of science. It provided a comprehensive review of this new field of inquiry, thereby marking something of a coming of age for this strand of feminist research. Harding surveyed the field comprehensively. She was both thorough and sharp. She begins with some philosophical reflections on the nature of both of her key variables – 'science' and 'gender'. From there, she organizes her presentation around what she calls 'the five research programs' that have been developed by feminist critics of science. These include: equity studies, or studies of women's participation in and exclusion from the world of science; analyses of sexist biological constructions of 'woman's nature' and of sex differences; accounts of sexual imagery within science and 'feminist standpoint positions', or attempts to construct a feminist science. In later chapters of the book she draws on the history and sociology of science and feminist insights to expose the mythical dimensions of the established version of the origins of science and of the scientific method.

The Science Question in Feminism was refreshing in that it acknowledged weaknesses and limitations, whilst remaining positive and assertive about what feminists had achieved. In fact some of the inconsistencies in this work were turned on their head, as Harding pronounced that 'feminist analytical categories *should* be unstable at this point in history' (Harding, 1986, p. 244; emphasis in original). It is Harding's aversion to 'totalizing theory' which facilitated this optimistic conversion. This aversion also marked the intersection of her feminism with her endorsement of postmodernism. Her postmodernism was a particularly attractive version. She was gentle and accessible in tone, hence avoiding the rather ironic, but symptomatic tendency among some advocates of postmodernism to declare the death of totalizing theory in an authoritarian, totalizing voice. Perhaps more importantly, the orientation of her analysis encouraged the establishment of priorities. Her bold claim that it had been 'movements for social liberation, not the norms of science' (Harding, 1986, p. 25) which have most increased the objectivity of science was perhaps the most overturning element in her assessment. It undercut the methodological basis of scientific legitimacy, while constituting a brilliant denial of any inherent progressivism within the methodology of science. (The latter is crucial as it has been the source of much of the attraction of science in left, alternative and some feminist quarters.) But perhaps it is even more significant that Harding's clarification of the source of progressive developments challenged presumptions about the role of the analyst or theorist: social and political movements, rather than scientists or theorists, were identified as the agents of progressive change.

The main limitation of Harding's analysis is that it represented a feminist sorting out only at the level of theory and, in some ways, of method. This is true in several different respects. The book is, itself, an overview: 'The Science Question'. The fact is that only theorists encounter science in this way. Most people's daily lives are made up of a plethora of *questions* about *sciences*, framed in terms of nature, medicine, expertise, knowledge, and so on. These are precise and specific questions and are not usually posed in the generalist and abstract way in which Harding approaches them. This is not to say that they do not relate to Harding's important feminist question, but merely to suggest that it is only those who approach science theoretically who would see it in this way.

In the end, Harding's resolution is an epistemological one: social and political movements increase objectivity. It is the epistemological potential that is taken as the standard of evaluation. Even feminist instability and uncertainty are legitimated by reference to postmodernist theory. There are likely to be disagreements among feminists on this resolution: some who feel that the epistemological difficulties have to be tackled and that Harding does this well; others who feel that this is not a priority. The problem is that there is a contradiction at the heart of Harding's project, in that she is questioning the primacy given to conceptual resolutions and theoretical adjudications within science and within feminism while she is herself engaged in this very same project.

The practical dimensions of this resolution are more elusive. The only concrete issues Harding considers in her conclusion are potential strategies in relationship to affirmative action programmes within science (Harding, 1986, pp. 247–8). Here she is equivocal: 'these strategies alone cannot create equity for women within science'; 'the natural sciences remain a male preserve'; 'the personal price for making it is often very high'; *but* 'such changes [do] bring small advances', 'changes a few minds', 'make a little more space for future generations of women', etc. Such equivocation is understandable, but it is often only theorists who can opt for *and* against a particular strategy. In concrete encounters with science *questions*, such equivocation is often neither possible nor desirable.

For those of us familiar with the history and philosophy of science, Harding's book represented a moment of feminist pride: feminists could out-philosophize the masters! The flaws in the epistemological project of modern science were clearly illustrated, and their historical origins convincingly documented. We could beat them at their own game! But it is now some five years since Harding's book first appeared. The feminist critique of science is now widely circulated, but there is very little sign that institutional science is being deconstructed in light of it (or of the outstanding body of feminist scholarship it examines). Positivism has not lost its credibility because it is epistemologically inconsistent!

It does not, of course, detract from Harding's accomplishment that the scientific establishment did not reply 'Eureka!' to the feminist assessment of its limitations. Indeed, it is unlikely that either Harding or the many feminist critics of science she surveys would ever have expected them to do so. However, this fact most certainly underlines the critical turning point represented by Harding's work, highlighting as it does the need to move away from the assessment of science as an epistemological system, and towards an assessment of it as a cultural belief system, as indeed a faith. This is precisely the response of scientists themselves, such as Eric Glashow, who unabashedly declared in response to Harding (at the Twenty-fifth Annual Nobel Conference on 'The End of Science?' in 1989) that her philosophical arguments were irrelevant to those who wished to continue to 'affirm that there are external, objective, extra-historical, socially neutral, external and universal truths' because this is their 'faith' (Glashow, 1989).

Both inside and outside the scientific community, it is clear that science is not only powerful because it is rational, coherent or logical, because proving that it lacks these qualities does very little to undermine its authority. Even scientists themselves recognize that science can be irrational, internally contradictory and illogical. The point is that despite these facts (or perhaps even because of them) science is simply 'good to think with'. It is tied to deeply rooted, and virtually sacred ways of thinking about the world, about masculinity and femininity, about nature and culture, about knowledge and ignorance. It is, moreover, not only good to think with, but good to act with, releasing particular forms of agency and initiative which enable certain forms of power, influence and status to be acquired. It offers the reassuring certainty of all universalistic and authoritarian belief systems, and it is a uniquely powerful means of both imagining the world and the place of the individual within it.

Harding's turning point is particularly important from the perspective of cultural studies, where science as a 'whole way of life' becomes a viable subject of inquiry. The investigation of the cultural (or subcultural) dimensions of science has been initiated to a certain extent through ethnographic studies. Supplementing these approaches with insights from cultural studies, such as the emphasis on the formations of gendered forms of identity, the cultural narratives which inform specific forms of work or professionalism, and the meaning of science at a more popular level (eg. science fiction, scientific autobiography, science docu-dramas, etc.), opens up a number of new avenues of inquiry. These have the potential to move the feminist analysis of science beyond the epistemological realm, which, though an important and necessary project, has to a certain extent exhausted itself as a theoretical and political strategy. Indeed, as we shall now see, some feminists have been exploring the cultural constructions that pervade and shape women's lives.

The feminist analysis of science as culture

Emily Martin's recent volume, *The Woman in the Body: A Cultural Analysis of Reproduction* (1987), is an ambitious study which attempts to extend the feminist analysis of science. Whereas it is the voices of feminist theorists that predominate within Harding's text, it is the voices of women encountering science at a more concrete, specific and 'everyday' level that are the predominant voices in Martin's text. Hers is a project very much in line with the earliest feminist initiatives in this area, such as the *Our Bodies, Ourselves* project. Indeed, it is specifically addressed to the very same question of the relationship between women's body images and women's identities, in the context of the dominant bio-medical constructions of 'female biology'. Yet, it is also informed by much of the feminist work which has emerged in the intervening years since *Our Bodies, Ourselves* was first published, and is explicitly concerned to draw attention to the problem posed by the category 'woman' as a monolithic concept. It draws its impetus from feminist anthropology, in which debates concerning the category of the 'natural', the cultural construction of gender, sexuality and reproduction, and the importance of the body to definitions of personhood have been developed.

Martin's analysis could best be described as an ethnography of women's body images, in which the central cultural system of meaning at issue is that of science. It is a project in which a critical reading of the construction of reproduction within current medical literature has been brought together with ethnographic accounts of women's reproductive experience in order to investigate the extent to which women internalize dominant definitions of menstruation, the menopause and pregnancy. Through interviews with a range of women in a large American city, varying in age, race and class, Martin has sought to investigate empirically the power of dominant scientific representations of reproduction in the formation of 'ordinary' women's commonsense assumptions about their bodies and their selves.

Setting out a historical evolution of scientific constructions of women's reproductive capacity in the opening chapters, Martin highlights the shifts within these dominant constructions over time. Drawing on the work of historian Thomas Laqueur, she argues that 'it was an accepted notion in medical literature from the ancient Greeks until the late eighteenth century that male and female bodies were structurally similar' (Martin, 1987, p. 27). This changed in the eighteenth century as a result of the emergence of liberal democratic notions of individual equality, which 'led to the loss of certainty that the social order could be grounded in the natural order' and the consequent need for the social and biological sciences 'to be brought to the rescue of male supremacy' (Martin, 1987, p. 32). A second major shift identified by Martin was the emergence of new metaphors of bodily processes based on the imagery of the industrial era. Hence, market forces, factory processes, manufacturing, communication systems and industrial production became the sources of analogy and metaphor in the medical literature.

With these developments, women's bodies, and in particular their reproductive capacity, were radically differentiated from those of men and viewed negatively. This became further evident in the metaphors of industrial production through which they eventually came to be represented in the medical literature. Still today, Martin demonstrates, menopause is described in terms of a breakdown of the production system, evoking 'horror of idle workers or machines'. Menstruation is described as 'failed production', or as 'production gone awry, making products of no use, not to specification, unsaleable, wasted, scrap' (Martin, 1987, p. 46). Contrasting the exuberant medical assessment of spermatogenesis, in which 'the normal human male may manufacture several hundred million sperm per day' (Martin, 1987, p. 48) with the unhappy descriptions of women's ova, which, Martin writes, 'seem merely to sit on the shelf, as it were, slowly degenerating and aging like overstocked inventory' (Martin, 1987, p. 49), she demonstrates the ways in which metaphors of production construct negative images of women's reproductive capacity.

Drawing on the work of David Noble, Martin extends the analysis of metaphors from factory production in relation to the medical representation of birth. Here, the labour process is also defined in terms of industrial language, such as the doctor being described as the mechanic, who guides the workings of the 'woman-laborer whose uterus-machine produces the baby' (1987, p. 63). The implications of this construction of birth for the 'management' of 'fetal outcome' during delivery are described by Martin as the alienation of women's reproductive labour.

In subsequent chapters on the menopause, menstruation and pregnancy,

Martin turns her attention to the ways in which women have responded to dominant medical constructions of reproductive processes. The separation of the self from the body is a central organizing finding throughout these discussions, consistent with the sense of alienation from and fragmentation of their bodies which many women feel. In discussions of menstruation at work, premenstrual syndrome and women's anger and the birth process, Martin demonstrates that alongside passive acceptance of these organizing metaphors there is resistance, alongside confusion and discontent are clarity and agency, and alongside feelings of alienation and fragmentation are feelings of wholeness and of gaining control. Martin also claims that the differences among women in terms of race and class are significant, with women 'at the bottom' of the social hierarchy having the greatest ability to be critical of the dominant definitions, and to resist them.

In 'The Embodiment of Oppositions', Martin concludes that because 'women's bodily processes go with them everywhere, forcing them to juxtapose biology and culture' women literally embody the possibility of 'glimps[ing] every day a conception of another social order' (1987, p. 200). She also addresses the forms of practical self-consciousness which emerge from the experience of inhabiting a female body and performing female work, which, she argues, have much in common, especially for black and working-class women who are responsible for the 'housekeeping of the whole "social body" in addition to the housekeeping of their own bodies and families' (p. 206). Women's reproductive bodies and women's productive and reproductive work are seen as the basis for women's oppression and resistance, the basis both of women's consciousness and an alternative woman-defined world-view.

Martin considers it important not to romanticize women's relationship to their bodies, or to postulate some 'back to nature' argument regarding women's reproduction, and her conclusion does not advocate a position of this sort, although it does invoke a suggestion of a return to 'wholeness'. However, in her attempt to address the cultural construction of science not only in terms of epistemology, but also at the level of commonsense, Martin's analysis is the key to an important new trajectory within the feminist analysis of science. Equally, in its attempt to hold together the differences between women in terms of age, race and class, with what they have in common in terms of their bodily experiences and identities, Martin has negotiated a critical problematic within contemporary feminist debates. However, and perhaps in the nature of a pioneering attempt such as this, there remain significant shortcomings in respect to what she describes, in the subtitle of her book, as 'a cultural account of reproduction'.

As is mentioned in the general introduction to this volume, the modifier 'cultural' has come to mean many things within contemporary feminist theory and politics. In providing 'a cultural account of reproduction', Martin relies upon several different types of cultural analysis. The first is a textual strategy, which, in the early chapters of the book, takes the form of interpretation of medical texts. Here, attention to metaphor, analogy and textual imagery are used to extrapolate from the language of medical texts to the circulation of dominant cultural meanings. In the later chapters, a set of analogies to Marxist frameworks is used to correlate the medical 'management' of reproduction with the forms of control of the labour force. This comparison first establishes a parallel between paid, public, productive work and unpaid, private, reproductive work. Second, it draws attention to the ways in which dominant medical representations of women's reproductive capacity function in a manner similar to that of dominant ideologies. Additionally, an anthropological model of culture is apparent in the ethnographic dimension of Martin's project, and in her justification of this approach in relation to her previous anthropological fieldwork in non-Western cultures. It is through this method that the key cultural categories through which women construct their reproductive identities are identified. Lastly, there are in Martin's analysis several components which might be identified as belonging to a more feminist model of culture, such as that discussed in the introduction. The emphasis upon simultaneously contradictory versions of self, the proximity of subjection and resistance, and obviously the primary focus on gender and reproduction are significant in this respect.

While this ecclecticism is both characteristic of and a necessity for feminist analysis in general, there are significant shortcomings in Martin's approach to the analysis of culture and of science. The textual approach to scientific discourse, for example, locates 'the cultural' at a specific level, and it is not clear to what extent medical practices correspond to textual representations. This reductionism may in turn lead to oversimplified accounts of the history of science as a trajectory of increasingly mechanistic analogies, for example. Likewise, there is a more familiar problem of reductionism evident in the more Marxist approaches used by Martin to establish an analogy between productive and reproductive exploitation. Martin presumes the appropriateness of simply transferring the model of control within productive labour to her analysis of the management of reproductive labour. It could be argued that this does not account for the specificities of women's oppression. Finally, while there are clear advantages for feminists, for whom the priority of women's lived experience has long been central to both theory and politics, in the use of ethnography, there remain many qualifications that need to be made around the 'authenticity' of the 'voices' this method has a tendency to suggest. In other words, ethnography as a method leaves several questions still unanswered at the level of theoretical or political interpretation.

Martin is not unaware of these problems, and is careful to anticipate difficulties, such as the danger of reifying women's experience, constructing science as a monolithic force, or of relying on productivist frameworks.

Yet her basic model of cultural production and consumption raises many important questions for future feminist initiatives. Her basic model of culture is still one of 'dominant ideas' (i.e. medical texts) which are 'internalized' by the oppressed ('ordinary women') through their incorporation into commonsense beliefs about themselves and their world, their bodies and their selves. Moreover, she is still working very much within the Marxist models of culture developed in the context of a class analysis. From a feminist point of view, notions such as 'alienation' are not entirely adequate to describe what is at stake for women in terms of their bodies or identities. More importantly, they leave open the question of how models of culture can be reworked to take better account of its specifically gendered dimensions.

Feminism, science and postmodern culture

The foregoing observations about Martin's work take on a further significance when we contrast her account with the work of Donna Haraway, in which a radically different approach to the cultural analysis of science is developed. Whereas Martin ultimately returns us to the foundationalist premises of Marxism, Haraway takes these as her satiric foil in a thorough overturning of the assumptions which have underpinned much leftist and feminist cultural analysis of the past decade.

Perhaps more than any other figure, Donna Haraway has been consistently attentive to the question of the relationship between science and the production of culture. From early interrogations of scientific knowledge (primatology) as a critical discourse of patriarchal capitalism, both shaped by it and essential to its maintenance and reproduction, Haraway has moved simultaneously towards a more anthropological account of the place of science in refiguring such basic distinctions as that between nature and culture, human and animal, or organisms and machines (Haraway, 1985) and towards a more quotidian focus on the place of science in the formation of a semiology of commonsense, for example in the conceptualization of the immune system (Haraway, 1988b).

The questions raised by postmodernism are at the centre of Haraway's recent work, as they are in Harding's. Most recently she has been concerned with the changes in the production of meaning, of identity and of bodies in the 'postmodern scientific culture of the United States in the 1980s' (Haraway, 1988b, p. 40). The very form of her writing expresses her dilemmas in recognizing that there is no escaping patriarchal culture, and that we are engendered in a culture in which we constantly live with, in and through science and technology. She thereby tackles many of the dimensions of science Harding's epistemological orientation leaves untouched – its corporate, subjective and visual dimensions, for example.

Haraway's style and wit make her an attractive spokesperson for those facing similar dilemmas. She denies that women *qua* women have a unified political (oppositional) status and insists that there are no easy resolutions of postmodern dilemmas. For her, there are no quick escapes to 'nature' or ultimate refusals or rejections possible in a culture which is as saturated in science and technology as is that of the Western post-industrial world. Haraway sees hope only in the acknowledgement and acceptance of these contradictions. The general spirit of her writings encourages celebration of these aspects of 'postmodern culture'. This is seen as a revenge on the old gods and goddesses, and, like all rites of passage, a series of openings and new possiblities.

Haraway's most recent volume, *Primate Visions: Gender, Race and Nature in the World of Modern Science* (Haraway, 1989), represents a culmination of many of her earlier projects. In this volume she extends Harding's argument about 'standpoint' epistemologies to develop the idea of 'situated knowledges' (this is also the title of a recent article replying to Harding's work (Haraway, 1988a)). At one level, *Primate Visions* is a history of primatology, charting its emergence in the interwar period and tracing its development up to the present. At another level, it works as a cultural analysis of science, examining its embeddedness in a matrix of social inequality and how this is mapped on to the primate body and the 'field' of primatology. Here, the primate is presented as a palimpsest of shifting cultural constructions, of nature, culture and humanity, of knowledge and power. At yet another level, it is a series of stories, generously seasoned with overdetermined episodes drawn from the history of our relationship to 'our closest evolutionary relatives'. As such, this study is also a kinship analysis, a veritable soap opera of monkey business, saturated with the requisite dilemmas of money, sex and fame. In sum, *Primate Visions* is a multi-layered text – its postmodern plot concerned with questions of power, knowledge and pleasure in late twentieth-century Western capitalist society.

Haraway states in Chapter 1 that

> Biology and primatology are inherently political discourses whose chief objects of knowledge, such as organisms and ecosystems, are icons (condensations) of the whole of the history and the politics of a culture that constructed them for contemplation and manipulation. (Haraway, 1989, p. 10).

It is this theme that Haraway pursues through the sixteen chapters of *Primate Visions*, tracing the icons of primatology from the African Hall of the American Museum of Natural History in New York, to the early primate laboratories of would-be social engineers, and exploring their enunciation through the primate in nature, the primate in outer space, the primate as movie star and the primate as feminist heroine. This exhaustive iconography of primate knowledges is held together by a strong theoretical emphasis not only on the social construction of the primate as object of (popular, scientific, military, taxidermic) scrutiny, but on the embodiment of the various standpoints from which this object is viewed. *Primate Visions* thus has a double meaning: the field of primatology viewed as cultural landscape, and the primatologist's gaze as situated and embodied viewpoint. Hence, it is not only the primate as 'natural-technical object' of knowledge with which Haraway is concerned, but the primatologist as the (culturally constructed, historically and politically located) knowing subject.

What is most significant about *Primate Visions* for the feminist analysis of science as a cultural phenomenon is Haraway's method. In each of the chapters, as in the many influential articles published by Haraway in the decade during which this volume was produced, a hallmark of her approach has been the particular way in which she draws together the history of science and cultural theory. The success of this combination derives both from the range of interpretive approaches it can knit together, and the breadth of evidence which can be fed into the resulting analytical framework. The result is a distinctive hermeneutical practice that is both impressive and compelling. It is this method which enables Haraway to work at several different levels: from analysis of popular culture (advertising, 'Tarzan' films, the *National Geographic*), to 'real science' (molecular phylogeny, ergonomics, paleo-anthropology), to monopoly capitalism (Gulf, Kodak, the Rockefeller Foundation). It is also this multi-layered technique which makes her prose extremely dense, and eminently rereadable. Most significantly, it is by this means that her history of primatology becomes a study of cultural production in the fullest sense: of science as both a process and a location through which we negotiate the classification and the boundaries of human diversity.

For this reason Haraway's volume is also open to a variety of readings and mis-readings. This openness is intentional – an extension of its own exhaustive intertextuality, and emphasis on situated readings. It can, however, be mistaken for a radical exercise in cultural relativity – a depoliticized postmodern dispersion of standpoints from which to tell stories about ourselves and our origins. This is not Haraway's argument. She makes her own situated standpoint, her 'investment' in primatology, clear in the conclusion:

> *Primate Visions* does not work by prohibiting origin stories, or biological explanations of what some would insist must be exclusively cultural matters . . . I am not interested in policing the boundaries between nature and culture – quite the opposite, I am edified by the traffic. (p. 377).

Haraway is interested in new ways of thinking about this traffic, not merely in deconstructing this cultural boundary. Her invitation 'to remap the borderlands between nature and culture' (p. 25), to embrace the permeability of this distinction, is a pleasurable one. There are, however, also some disquieting aspects to Haraway's approach. Haraway herself is always reaching out of her own postmodernist, deconstructive texts to concrete changes in the world. Yet, despite her questioning of 'foundationalist' categories and assumptions, she hangs on to the 'socialist feminist' label and refers to the plight of various subordinated groups as the *raison d'être* of her politics. But, in less committed hands, both postmodernism and poststructuralism can become ends in themselves and, even for Haraway, the connections between deconstructionist projects and specific concrete political goals are often difficult to fathom.

The attractions of poststructuralism and postmodernism are that they tackle the epistemological dimensions of science not only as abstract logical systems, but as specific cultural forms, dispersed over many sites in contemporary Western society. Nevertheless, there remains a danger that in pursuing these forms of cultural theory, feminists will be heading down a path well trodden by other cultural critics. In its most extreme version, textual analysis becomes synonymous with both culture and politics, and the reader (however subversive) becomes the only political agent. In this respect, cultural studies could teach feminists much about the limitations of deconstructionist and textual strategies (see, for example, Johnson, (1983)).

Conclusion: feminism, science and culture

In this chapter, we have addressed several approaches to the feminist cultural analysis of science, specifically considering three recent attempts to combine feminist and cultural theory. In doing so, we have attempted both to identify the different models of science and the different models of culture which characterize these approaches. In arguing for new ways in which these approaches can be combined, we have attempted to identify both the shortcomings and the usefulness of existing analytical frameworks: locating their emergence in the context of theoretical and political developments within feminism and cultural studies, and suggesting future directions they may help to develop.

As argued in the first introduction to this volume, feminism has benefited considerably from its engagement with the interpretive frameworks offered by cultural theory such as poststructuralism and postmodernism. These tools have enabled the development of more sophisticated and insightful accounts of both cultural production and consumption, and have thus provided a greater understanding of possibilities for resistance. As we have also argued, the feminist attention to the power of science as a dominant cultural belief system has also contributed substantially to cultural studies, where this domain of cultural meanings and practices had been neglected. In turn, as argued in the final section, cultural studies may have a significant contribution to make to feminism, in warning against the dangers of a reductive, and depoliticized mode of cultural theory. The balancing exercise which becomes clear in this assessment, between the attractions and the shortcomings of contemporary cultural theory, is a familiar one for feminism, which has continually challenged the terms through which knowledge is produced, whilst simultaneously attempting to claim a space within that process. The questions addressed by Harding, Martin and Haraway are consistent in their focus upon both the embodiment of knowledge and the context-specificity of its production. These connections will continue to inform the feminist cultural analysis of science, in its attempt to hold together local, situated knowledges with broader, overarching concerns about the sources of social inequality which are the object of feminist resistance.

7

In the wake of the Alton Bill: science, technology and reproductive politics

THE SCIENCE AND TECHNOLOGY SUBGROUP

Introduction: Why the Alton Bill?

This chapter is concerned with recent abortion legislation in Britain, in particular the Alton Bill, which was introduced into Parliament in the autumn of 1987, and was aimed at reducing the upper time limit of legal abortion to 18 weeks. This project brought together two sets of activities for the five of us who were involved in producing it. For two years we have been working collectively as a group examining the place of science and technology within cultural studies. During this period we also became involved (in different ways) in the feminist campaign to defeat the Alton Bill, the most recent and the most nearly successful of a string of challenges to existing abortion legislation in Britain[1]. Part of the inspiration for this project came from the recognition that these two activities were closely linked: that the Alton Bill debates were centrally about the role of medical experts, scientific knowledge and technological innovation in contemporary British culture.

By the time we began working on this project the Bill had been defeated. Nevertheless, our sense of the importance of the project did not diminish. Indeed, the chapter that follows was undertaken because of our conviction that, although feminists have won short-term gains, we fear we may be losing the larger struggle over commonsense assumptions about abortion. The following analysis is intended to examine critically the legacy of the Alton Bill debate and what it revealed about popular perceptions of abortion, motherhood, scientific medicine and new reproductive technologies.

Since 1967, there have been regular parliamentary challenges to abortion rights in Britain. More recently, we have witnessed the imposition of severe restrictions on those rights elsewhere, particularly in the USA. Likewise, there continue to be efforts in Britain to introduce legislation 'in the spirit of the Alton Bill'. In short, feminists in Britain and in much of the Western world have had to be on the defensive in relation to abortion for over twenty years. These campaigns have been important, both in gaining allies, such as trade unions and representatives of political parties, and in uniting many parts of the women's movement. Nevertheless, it is clear that neither defending existing rights nor reacting in moments of crisis are sufficient strategies. Hence, our analysis derives from our conviction that we must not only struggle to defeat parliamentary bills, but also to gain popular support. This involves understanding more about the many ways in which Alton did succeed, particularly in setting new terms of the debate, despite his ultimate failure.

This chapter is divided into five sections, each written in close collaboration with the group as a whole, but primarily researched and authored by one member of the group. We begin by situating the Alton Bill in its immediate context, move on to examine the Bill historically in relation to preceding legislation and the emergence of abortion as a legal question, look in more detail at the abortion question as it was constructed within parliamentary debate, explore the medico-scientific discourses which continue to structure public debate over abortion and, lastly, consider how it was presented in the media and the formation of public consensus. In each section, we have attempted to combine approaches developed within cultural studies with the perspectives which have informed the feminist analysis of abortion. For us, the Alton Bill presented a situation where the combination of approaches from feminist and cultural studies was especially useful, as the abortion debate is clearly being waged at the level of deeply held cultural assumptions about parenthood, the sexual division of labour, technological and scientific progress, and so forth. It is in addressing the cultural dimensions of current public debate about abortion that we see the potential for stronger and more effective forms of collective feminist politics, which in turn can inform our analysis of the intersection between reproduction, science and technology more generally.

Note

1   Since this chapter was completed in early 1990, the upper time limit for abortion has been reduced from 28 to 24 weeks via an amendment to the Human Fertilisation and Embryology Act.

Section 1

Putting the Alton Bill in context

MAUREEN McNEIL

The debate about the Alton Bill occurred in a very particular context. In what follows, some of the most salient features of its setting are outlined. In so doing, the aim is to suggest some of the continuities and contradictions which shaped the discussion of proposed changes to the availability of abortion in Britain. The analysis looks in turn at the state of the National Health Service (hereafter referred to as the NHS); the elaboration of women's responsibilities for childcare and development; cuts in maternity rights and benefits; new concerns about fatherhood; the rapid spread of new technologies in healthcare; and the changing moral climate in Britain.

The NHS

The debate about the Alton Bill took place against a background of increasing protest at the significant cuts in public funding of the NHS imposed by the government. Numerous demonstrations, including industrial action by nurses and professional protests by doctors, characterized the time during which the Bill was under debate. It typified the period to have coverage of the debate over the Bill juxtaposed with a headline such as 'Children's Cancer Wards Closing' (Ferriman, 1988). It was precisely during this period that a number of high-profile cases of individual children denied access to high-technology medicine (particularly for heart operations) captured both media and parliamentary attention. These cases were taken by many as evidence that Thatcher and her government were 'uncaring', inconsistent and insincere in their policies. While public outrage over the cutbacks in NHS spending and the dismantling of the welfare state in general continued to grow, many questions about what kind of healthcare service was desirable, and particularly the role of high-technology medicine, were left unanswered. Instead, lack of high-technology facilities became a symbol of the government's lack of commitment to adequate public healthcare provision, particularly the needs of children.

However, the cuts in the NHS were linked even more directly to the abortion issue. In abortion, as in all other NHS services, cuts have meant delays. One fifth of all abortions performed after 20 weeks of pregnancy (in 1986) had been referred before the end of the twelfth week of pregnancy. This evidence, together with the well-known difficulty of securing prompt appointments with GPs, long queues, delays in pregnancy testing, amniocentesis and other antenatal procedures, are bound to have affected the abortion profile in Britain. In addition, they provide an important background to a debate which was largely focused on 'late' abortions.

The regional unevenness of NHS provision also figured in this situation. Of course, this is a feature in all NHS provision, but it is accentuated in the case of abortion where the 'conscience clause' is an added factor. This allows those in the medical professions who are antipathetic to abortion on moral grounds to opt out of the provision of this NHS service. The result is delays, as women must search for sympathetic doctors. It also introduces further inequalities of provision, since the more well-informed a woman is about how to contact sympathetic doctors, where to go to get support, and so on, the greater her chances of securing a quick abortion. Obviously, this tends to work to the advantage of women who are less isolated, better off financially, or who have greater access to resources, such as transportation.

The debate about the Alton Bill also highlighted the fact that abortion is one of the main fields of NHS provision where British women have consistently opted for private medicine. Having reviewed abortion services available within the NHS, the Lane Committee observed in their 1977 report: 'Too many women have been forced to pay for abortions when they have legitimate grounds for termination of pregnancy under the [1967] Act' (cited in Savage, 1987). Wendy Savage claims, for example, that 'half of all women have to pay for their abortions because local gynaecologists do not do them or long delays force GPs to advise women to go to one of the two non-profit making abortion charities, or privately' (Savage, 1988).

Thus, the debate about the Alton Bill must be situated against the backdrop of a deficient and depleted NHS. In abortion, as in many other spheres, women's needs are not being met by the service and the Bill's focus, late abortions, was, at least to some extent, a problem created by the system itself. Significantly, the solution embodied in the Alton Bill involved policing women, not the NHS, more closely.

Children and fetal rights

A second key constituent of the background to the Alton debate was the growing concern for fetal rights. Here, I would argue, there are both long- and short-term developments which must be understood. In the long-term, the industrialized Western world has witnessed the progressive expansion and elaboration of the mother's responsibilities for childcare. Since the Romantic movement in the nineteenth century, childhood has increasingly come to be seen as an important period. The sphere of maternal responsibility was further widened by Freud and his followers, who saw infant and early childhood as key developmental stages. Within this framework, women were not only responsible for physical care, but for securing a reasonable passage for their children along the treacherous path of psychic growth. Of course, there have been countless subsequent delineations and expansions of maternal duties including, most notably in Britain, those of John Bowlby.

In terms of the conceptualization of maternal responsibilities, we seem to have entered into a new phase. This involves the elaboration of maternal responsibility for the fetus. In the last few years in both America and Europe there has been a number of manifestations of this new phase. Court cases brought on grounds of maternal neglect are but one facet of this shift. These involve women either losing child custody prior to birth or being charged with neglect in relation to a fetus they are carrying or have carried. Yet another strand in the elaboration of maternal responsibility has been the increasing emphasis on their responsibilities for fetal health of women who are either pregnant or trying to conceive. Both of these trends are characterized by a redefinition of child development to include not only the growth of the fetus, but also the period prior to conception. They have been accompanied by an elaboration of notions of fetal personhood and a proliferation of fetal imagery which are discussed later in this chapter (see below under Fetal Fascinations). Alton drew on this awareness in referring to a 'revolution in our awareness of the humanity of the developing child' (cited in Grice, 1988b). In so doing he was pointing to a palpable change – the extension of the social expectations of women's responsibilities for childcare to, at least, nine months prior to birth.

Certain press panics during the period of debate over the Bill reinforced this enhanced status of the fetus. On 8 February 1988, the popular press featured headlines of 'Abortion baby took three hours to die' *(Daily Mail)* and 'Aborted baby's "3 hours to die"' *(Daily Mirror)*. These articles involved the reports of a nurse about an abortion that had occurred the previous September (1987). Whatever the accuracy of the reporting and the significance of the timing of the press attention, the story served to conjure sympathy for an independent fetus, constructed as a suffering baby. The responsibility for such suffering was clearly laid at the feet of the mother who sought the abortion.

It is interesting to contrast the emergence of an extended scope of maternal responsibility for fetal development with another controversy in Britain contemporaneous with the Alton debate, that concerning child abuse. It is well known that in most cases of child abuse the perpetrators are the fathers.

Yet it is interesting to note that despite the fact that these cases often involve undisputed incidents of direct violence of adult men against young girls, there has been considerable *controversy* over *who* is responsible for male violence against children. This reveals a rather strong contrast between the extension of maternal responsibilities and seemingly diminishing paternal responsibilities. It also reveals the extent of the double-standard applied to men and women in relation to parental responsibility, whereby women are held accountable for abortion as a form of violence, yet the degree of men's responsibility is held in doubt, even in the face of explicit acts of violence against children under their care.

As I have suggested elsewhere in this volume (see McNeil, Chapter 8), Thatcherism has generated an agenda of provision for the 'new oppressed'. One of the ways it has mobilized support is by conjuring sympathy and concern for the rights of those who have not generally been considered to be oppressed. This has included fathers, tax-payers, parents, children and most relevant here – fetuses. This is, of course, a way of diverting concern from groups that have been the targets of left attention. But, perhaps most significantly, within this agenda there has been little concern for the oppressions of women. Thus, it is no coincidence that it is often *women's* rights that are seen as blocking these neglected groups. As one commentator put it, starkly referring to a shift which is key to the strategies of the new right: 'after two decades of a woman's right to choose, the emphasis in debate has slid with a minimum of fuss towards the child's right to life' (Grice, 1988b).

Maternity rights

The trend towards the extension and elaboration of maternal responsibilities, and the elongation of the period of 'child development' to include that of fetal development, must also be considered in relation to the high cost of motherhood in Britain today. Thus, while the 'job description' has been enlarged, the 'pay for the job' and the resources available to women have been significantly reduced.

Somewhat ironically, a report that appeared in December 1987, amidst the furore over Alton's Bill, made it clear that women in Britain today pay an extremely high price for motherhood. In the report, entitled *The Cash Opportunity Costs of Childbearing*, Heather Joshi, a researcher from the Centre for Economic Policy Research, calculated that a typical mother who gives up work for several years to rear two children forgoes £122,000 of income. Another figure which she mentions is £30,500, the estimated average cost of childrearing for the first sixteen years (Joshi, 1987).

The Conservative government of the late 1980s and early 1990s would seem to be uninterested in this high economic burden borne by mothers.

Maternity rights have been noticeably curtailed under its period in office: there have been drastic cuts in the availability of nursery places; a freeze in child benefit payments; the elimination of maternity payments and reduced maternity rights in the workplace. In short, while the Alton Bill sought to limit the circumstances in which women could opt out of childbirth, government measures were actually increasing the burden of childrearing. In this sense British government policies stand in stark contrast to those of other countries, such as Scandinavia, where substantial maternal rights have gone hand-in-hand with liberal abortion laws. In these circumstances, the Alton Bill seemed a particularly punitive, coercive way of making women opt for motherhood.

Growth of concern for fathers

Unlike mothers in Britain, to date, fathers have not been subject to policing under the present government to fulfil their paternal responsibilities (although this may be changing according to more recent reports). To the contrary, it is not the responsibilities but the *rights* of fathers that have emerged as a new social issue, championed by the new right in Britain and the United States. There has been much discussion of paternal rights, and pressure groups concerned to protect these have made their appearance in Britain in recent years. The courts are a good barometer of social trends in this respect and controversial custody cases involving challenges to the assumption that children are generally best off with their mothers have gained considerable attention.

Since the screening of *Kramer vs Kramer* (dir. Robert Benton, 1979) there has been a number of Hollywood films addressing the supposed threats to paternal rights posed by feminism and changing patterns of employment and domestic arrangements. Some of these films have focused on men's relationship to children and their rights (particularly, against those of mothers) in such relationships (cf *Three Men and a Baby* (dir. Leonard Nimoy, 1988). The hugely successful *Fatal Attraction* (dir. Adrian Lyne, 1988) can likewise be considered to share in this theme, in that it presents the dilemma of a man faced with the prospect of becoming the father of a child he does not want, while losing access to the child he does. In this film, women's reproductive capacity is portrayed as threatening both to men and to the established nuclear family. Though none of these films is explicitly anti-abortion, they suggest a mobilization of popular fears about loss of patriarchal control and, in particular, a reassertion of fathers' claims to children.

The two issues of legal battles over custody and the extension of female duties to the fetus came together dramatically in 1986, when an Oxford postgraduate, Robert Carver, unsuccessfully took High Court proceedings against his girlfriend to try to prevent her from having an abortion.

Although Carver was blocked in the courts, he did win an injunction to stop her having an abortion. Both his pursuit of the case, and the media attention to it, indicate that in the current climate it might be possible to force a woman to carry an unwanted child. Certainly, in taking the case to court, Carver managed to focus public attention on his girlfriend and, despite losing his legal battle, in the end, he had his way, for she did not have a termination. Indeed, the case was a forerunner of the Alton Bill, anticipating the new terrain on which challenges to abortion rights would be mounted, the terrain of days, weeks, months upon which the legal battle over time limits for abortion is now fought.

This case was resurrected in January 1988 when the Sunday papers gave coverage to the revelation that Carver was bringing the baby up. According to an *Observer* account, Carver's girlfriend had had 'a last-minute change of heart' (Fitzsimons, 1988). These reports pulled on the popular heart-strings that had already been worked upon by films of the *Kramer vs Kramer* genre. Here were the caring new fathers, and the implication that the courts should protect them and their offspring.

But, Carver's was not just a personal crusade, his was an attack against abortion rights *per se*. He had launched his campaign by attempting to prove that abortion after 18 weeks was illegal under the 1929 Infant Life (Preservation) Act. The news that he eventually assumed care of the baby was used by David Alton to bolster his own campaign: 'Robert Carver has shown that abortion is not only an issue for women and that men are prepared to shoulder the responsibility' (Fitzsimons, 1988). Alton jumped from an extraordinary instance to the generalization (certainly, by no means justified by the evidence of patterns of financial support or childcare) that men are willing to take responsibility for children. He neglected the specific situation in which Carver had done so, and the fact that considerable public pressure (including court proceedings) had been exerted on the mother to have the child – against her stated desires. One, extraordinary instance of male behaviour was thus used to justify the denial of the right to all women to make decisions to have abortions.

It is worth looking at how one newspaper, the *Observer* presented the Carver 'revelation' since its reportage epitomized some of the contradictions surrounding paternal rights and the abortion debate. The Carver story was given front-page coverage by the *Observer* (17 January 1988) with the head-line: 'Abortion Case Father Raises Campus Baby' (Fitzsimons, 1988). Of course, such coverage was effectively a gift to the Alton Bill campaigners. Above this article was a photograph which constituted the paper's only reference to demonstrations that had been held throughout the country the previous day by those fighting the Alton Bill. The picture was of a very glum child holding a placard with the slogan: 'A Women's Right to Choose'. The boxing off of this picture with the report of the Carver case completely undermined the protests against Alton's proposed legislation.

It also effectively suggested that women's rights are pitted against those of children and babies. The structure of the front page encouraged the reader to view the child as literally carrying the burden of women's claims to 'a right to choose'.

The new concern with fatherhood and the defences of the rights of fathers were an important element in the setting of the Alton Bill debate. Alton himself, although single and not a father at the time, made much of his own experience working with handicapped children. Once again, 'caring men' were juxtaposed with 'hard, uncaring' women (particularly those who seek abortion). Much was made of a few extraordinary situations and only occasionally did the other side of the picture – women's independent, caring labour – emerge.

The era of technological advance

Perhaps what most distinguished the context of the debate about the Alton Act from that in which other proposed amendments to the 1967 Abortion Act had been considered was the growing awareness of the role of technology in the field of reproductive medicine. Writing in the *Sunday Times*, journalist Elizabeth Grice claimed that 'what has happened to alter David Alton's chances of abortion reform where at least 12 others have failed is that life in the womb is not nearly so shadowy as it was 20 years ago' (Grice, 1988b). In this account, the reference to fetal life having become less 'shadowy' is not merely metaphorical, as in arguments about the sanctity of life, but quite literal, referring to the role of imaging technologies, which have given rise to an ever widening circulation of fetal imagery. For not only has medical research into embryo and fetal development exploded during recent years, but its development has also been given an extraordinary amount of media attention. We have grown accustomed to the narratives of unhappy couples given 'hope' by medical science and the promise and realization of test-tube babies.

The specific touchstone for many of those advocating time limits on abortion has been the existence of technological interventions to support premature babies. Indeed, that new technology can improve the chances of survival for such babies has become the main argument for many supporters of a 22 or 24 week limit on abortions. These developments have undoubtedly captured the popular imagination: 'Both sides acknowledge that public opinion is affected by the films, photographs, and articles on the work being done keeping alive very tiny babies born from 23 weeks on' (Kennedy, 1988). The emphases in all these reports are on the extraordinary achievements of medical science and the miraculous achievement of the 'gift of life'. While the argument stems from medical achievement, the emotional dimensions are clearly played on. Elizabeth Grice refers to 'an acute sense of paradox that today in the same hospital one 24-week-old baby could be cherished in an intensive-care unit, with a reasonable chance of survival, while another – invariably labelled foetus to protect sensibilities – could be consigned to the sluice room' (Grice, 1988b).

A number of issues are side stepped in such reports including the failure rate of such interventions, their aftermath and their cost. It is the success stories that are news, and there is not much information available about the failures. Moreover, relatively little attention has been given to the unknown territory of the after-effects of such procedures: the quality of life for the 'saved' infant and its family. Finally, in terms of resources, such medical initiatives are very costly in a very straitened NHS. So, while many marvel at such wonderful accomplishments with premature babies, the expenditure in this area is not generally juxtaposed with the closing of cancer wards for children or the queues for heart operations. In other words, there are real questions about economic priorities and resources which are fudged here.

Against this background, 'technical viability' has become a key phrase in recent debates about abortion. It was given emotional resonance when, for example, in a *Panorama* programme (16 December 1987), the former Bishop of Birmingham, Hugh Montefiore, was shown holding a premature baby 'saved by modern medicine'. This has been locked into the existing legal framework, in particular to provide a new interpretation of the 1929 Infant Life (Preservation) Act. The argument in such appeals is that if, in technical terms, medical science can keep a baby alive at 22 or 24 weeks, this should determine the deadline for abortion. This shifts the focus of decision-making away from women who, in opting for or against abortion, make complex evaluations of their particular circumstances and of the social sustainability of new life. Such decisions have little to do with what medical science can sustain technologically. Saying that it is theoretically possible to plug a 24-week-old fetus into life support apparatuses is very different from saying that you personally will take primary responsibility for supporting – in every sense – a child through to adulthood.

What was interesting about the Alton campaign was its ability to draw on both the aspirations for, and fears of, high technology medicine. In April 1988, shortly after the Alton Bill came up for debate on its third reading, a story broke about the use of fetal tissue in transplants into the brains of victims of Parkinson's disease by a medical team in a West Midlands hospital (see Hodgkinson, 1988; Phillips, 1988). There was a considerable furore surrounding this revelation, as it raised the spectre of deliberate conception and abortion to produce such tissue. Although there might be countless reservations about such initiatives and reasons (including economic ones) for objecting to the practice, it easily fed into an anti-abortion mentality, or at least the feeling that tight restrictions should be placed on abortions to prevent abuses related to such interventions.

So complete was the technicization of the framework in which the

Alton Bill was debated that it was hardly surprising to find a story about a technological fix which would eliminate the need for abortion altogether. In the *Observer*, under the headline 'Doctors plan to weed out sick embryos', Robin McKie reported that 'Scientists are preparing plans to remove embryos from mothers, screen them for genetic illnesses in the laboratory and then re-implant only the healthy ones' (McKie, 1988). Indeed, one of the members of the Warnock Committee commented on this development: 'This new technique means that once a pregnancy is started, it can be completed in the knowledge that there will be no prospect of abortion because of the genetic complaint' (McLaren, quoted in McKie, 1988). Such an argument presupposes that the major reason for abortion is a genetic disorder. It effectively by-passes the woman and her decisions about when an abortion is appropriate. As is argued in the subsequent sections of this chapter, the technicization of the right to abortion may be the most significant and long-lasting legacy of the debates over the Alton Bill.

The 'new moral climate'

In an editorial prior to the first reading of the Alton Bill in Parliament, the *Guardian* referred to the Bill as marking a change in the 'moral climate' (21 January 1988). The references were not clear, although there were vague allusions to the 'certainties of 1967' giving way to 'more complex questioning'. In a sense what I have been describing – including cuts in the NHS, changing expectations surrounding motherhood, the tightening of maternity rights, a growing concern about the roles of fathers and increased deference for technological achievements in medicine – are all elements in that change of 'moral climate'. However, the editors of the *Guardian* were probably more circumspect in their separation of 'moral' from 'economic' (or, indeed technological) change. They were referring to a range of narrowly defined 'moral issues' current in contemporary Britain. Some of these are dealt with elsewhere in this book (see Stacey and McNeil's contributions) and it is to a particular dimension of them that I will now turn.

Fears of sexuality

While the late 1960s and early 1970s witnessed experimentation around sexual identities and some breaks with established conventions around sexuality in the industrialized West, the current era has been preoccupied with the dangers of such adventures. The scares about AIDS have conveyed the clear message that sex (particularly non-heterosexual, and/or sex outside of monogamous heterosexual relationships) is dangerous. Such thinking formed an important and persistent part of the background to the Alton Bill.

In her complex and brilliant examination of abortion in the USA, Rosalind Petchesky (1984) makes it clear that the control and restriction of access to abortion is always, in part, an attempt to control female sexuality. In the wake of the moral panic about AIDS we have become sensitive to charges that non-reproductive sexual activity is dangerous. The Alton Bill campaign was able to draw out this sensitivity by highlighting both personal and social dangers inherent in relatively unrestricted access to abortion.

Drawing attention to the personal price paid for abortion was a favourite strategy of David Alton and his supporters. In a characteristic warning, he cautioned: 'Rarely are women warned of the psychological and physical consequences that follow abortion' (Alton, 1988). Once again, the agenda was medicalized and a new medical term integrated into the vocabulary: 'post-abortion trauma'. The term originated in the USA where it had been adopted and used by some as a label for a medical condition. This label is one in a series which, throughout the history of medicine, has provided the medical profession with the tools (material and ideological) for regulating female behaviour (see Ehrenreich and English, 1979). In debates about abortion, this provides medical certification for the message to individual women: 'you must pay a price for abortion – it will make you ill'; 'if you try to separate female heterosexuality from reproduction this is the price you must pay'.

The flurry this new medical condition created in the Alton Bill controversy was somewhat dissipated by some doctors (including Wendy Savage) who challenged the category with their own evidence that abortion need not be traumatic for women: 'Post-abortion trauma is another condition dreamt up in the US and flown over here to add weight to the argument. Studies of women (including one I did myself) do not show that long-term regret after legal abortion is at all common' (Savage, 1988; Kennedy, 1988).

It is not only the price for individual women, but the social price of abortion which was highlighted. References to societies which do not value life, and to 'more authentic human values' (Alton, 1988) suggested that moral decline results from the separation of female heterosexuality from reproduction. This dislodging was portrayed as undermining the moral fibre of the nation. Once again, innovations in vocabulary were indicative of the ambiance surrounding the recent controversies. Alton himself used the term 'abortionism', implying presumably an unquestioning and irresponsible reliance on abortion. He linked it to those undesirables – 'big business', 'utility' and 'defeatism' – which he considered to undermine morality (Alton, 1988).

To claim that there is a moral climate in which sexuality has been overwhelmingly equated with danger, and in which there has been a clear if spurious delineation of the dangers of abortion, is not to deny individual women's uncertainties in making specific decisions about abortions. Legal access to abortion does not guarantee women's freedom in the area of sexuality. The fact that some women find the decision for or against abortion a difficult one or that, in ideal circumstances, some would choose not to have abortions should not be taken as a fundamental 'ambivalence and doubt' about the right to abortion. The problem is that the current context has definitively encouraged women to connect the two (see the *Guardian* leader referred to above as a clear example of this (21 January 1988)). In other words, we have been led to view our hesitations to seek abortion (whether they have to do with the conditions under which we would have one, the limited options and resources for childrearing, or the specific personal and interpersonal context of our decision-making etc.) as indicative that the personal and social price for abortion is too high.

This feeling of too high a price resonates with spurious arguments that are conducted with those who are against abortion. They sometimes try to back women into a corner by asking them to declare categorically whether they would have an abortion now if they became pregnant. Such a question is, of course, completely abstract and hypothetical. Women's decision-making on abortion is richly and complexly concrete. Posing the question in this way denies this concreteness and tries to flatten any specific ambivalence into a definitive stand for or against the right to abortion.

During the debate over the Alton Bill in Britain, this requirement for an abstract 'yes' or 'no' occurred on a broad social scale. Even those who did not support Alton have been cautious about abortion. The 'changed moral climate' and the panic about moving outside the sphere of 'safe' sexual contacts made it possible to channel *any* ambivalence about abortion into a sense of the need for further social regulation. In both the personal and the social sense, women have been made to feel that the cost of abortion is too high. In a time of economic belt-tightening and fear of sexuality, we are being urged to be sexually conservative.

Conclusion

The foregoing discussion has been designed to examine some key elements of the immediate social context of the debate surrounding the Alton Bill. The state of the NHS, the elaboration of child development responsibilities for women, cuts in maternity support, new concerns about fatherhood, technological developments and what has been labelled 'a changed moral climate' were the main features examined. Seen in this light, the Alton Bill appears not as anomalous, but as contiguous with much broader social trends. To secure women's reproductive freedoms, these developments, and not only specific initiatives such as the Alton Bill, must be tackled.

Section 2

Abortion Acts: 1803 to 1967

WENDY FYFE

Introduction

In order to appreciate more fully the significance of recent public debates around abortion in Britain represented by the Alton Bill, it is necessary to locate this initiative in the context of previous abortion legislation in Britain. This section offers an analysis of the Acts pertaining to abortion from 1803 to 1967. It will focus in particular on the influence of the medical profession in shaping the terms of the law. It will examine how this influence has defined the abortion issue through two processes of separation represented by the Acts. First, the separation from women of definition and control over pregnancy will be examined in relation to abortion legislation. Here, the focus will centre on the shift from what were initially religious/moral grounds to the medico/moral grounds of more recent debates. Second, the explicit separation of the fetus from the woman, the emergence of the notion of 'viability', and the subsequent licensing of increased medical/state intervention will be investigated.

In framing these arguments, there are several qualifications which need to be noted at the outset. First, these separations were part of a 'progression' of a particular way of thinking and living within unequal power relations. They were defined in relation to 'common senses' and daily experiences as well as the Acts themselves. While the medical (and legal) professions have gained the power to define, this is not independent from popular consent (see below, The Alton Bill and the media's 'consensual' position). While acknowledging the preoccupation with self-interest, power and status at stake for the medical profession, it is important not to view the definition of abortion in terms of separation as purely conspiratorial, which would disregard the complexities within wider historical and social relations.

Second, rather than being seen as having fixed meanings, the Acts will be seen as sites of struggle. A critical source of tension, for example, is the struggle between the medical and legal professions over the control of abortion. Hence, I will examine the convergence and conflict between the legal and medical professions in a negotiation of the right to define and control reproduction. This can only be understood by looking at historical, cultural and political forces outside of the Acts which both informed and were influenced by them.

Third, it must be stressed that this section is a partial history, both in terms of its limits, and in terms of the standpoint taken. I am looking at the way in which abortion has been framed within the law by excluding women, in ways that act to control women. I am also addressing the ways in which women live outside of the law, while also being subject to it. Since this is a process, and is not monolithic, understanding the ways in which women's position has been constructed is necessary in order to develop ways of 'breaking out'. I aim to explore these two facets, this duality of inclusion and exclusion of women in the Acts, in a broader historical context.

Finally, this section is part of a process of thinking and questioning from an overly subjective point of view, by a woman who sees and feels she is outside the law, while also being subject to it, and who also believes that the law is not something in and of itself but symptomatic of wider male dominance and power of definition. It must also be noted that laws have often been ignored and/or broken, and therefore that the law itself does not necessarily reflect public opinion or daily behaviour. There is a much more complex and contradictory interplay between them which needs to be recognized. That this section is not a neatly fixed, conclusive study is precisely the point I want to make about the abortion debate itself. It is not a complete process of legitimation, but one which is contradictory and multifaceted. That the abortion debate is far from closed is a positive aspect for women and feminist resistance. Women have had real effects on the debate, and the analysis offered here is part of this continuing effort.

This section is narrated through three chronologies to show the multi-layered processes involved in the definition and control of reproduction. The first chronology concerns the shifting definitions in the Acts. It is followed by a chronology concerning wider cultural shifts around the Acts. The third chronology addresses the ways in which the Acts are often unclear, how the meanings change and are often carried through with ambiguity. Throughout these three chronologies the growing influence and power of the medical profession, medical knowledge and the authority of patriarchal expertise will be a consistent focus.

Chart 1: The Abortion Acts from 1803 to 1967

TITLE: An Act for the further prevention of malicious shooting, and attempting to discharge loaded fire-arms, stabbing, cutting, wounding, poisoning, and the malicious using of means to procure the miscarriage of women; and also the malicious setting fire to buildings; and also for repealing a certain Act, made in *England* in the twenty-first year of the late King *James* the First, entitled *An Act to prevent the destroying and murdering of bastard children;* and also an Act made in *Ireland* in the sixth year of the reign of the late Queen *Anne,* also entitled, *An Act to prevent the destroying and murdering of bastard children;* and for making other provisions in lieu thereof. (Passed: 24 June 1803)

This law criminalized for the first time, those who have *'intent'* to procure abortion, and those aiding and abetting that 'intent' before 'quickening'. Previous criminal sanctions had only applied after 'quickening'. A distinction between pre- and post-quickening is maintained in terms of punishment (see p. 171).

TITLE: An act for consolidating and amending the Statutes in *England* relative to Offences against the Person. (Passed: 27 June 1828)

This Act brings abortion under the umbrella of 'Offences against the Person' which are not distinguished from, for example, those against 'property' (such as buildings), in a reorganization of the law.

TITLE: An Act to amend the Laws relating to Offences against the Person. (Passed: 17 July 1837)

In this Act both the distinction between pre- and post-quickening and the term itself are removed from the Statute Book. Any 'intent' to procure 'abortion' or 'procuring of miscarriage' (this distinction is never clearly defined) is made illegal.

TITLE: An Act to consolidate and amend the Statute Law of *England* and *Ireland* relating to Offences Against the Person. (Passed: 6 August 1861)

In this Act women came to be included in the crime of 'intent' to procure their own 'miscarriages', whether they 'be or be not with child'. 'Aiding and abetting' becomes separated from procuring and is reclassified as a lesser crime (a misdemeanour rather than a felony).

TITLE: An Act to amend the law with regard to the destruction of children at or before birth. (Passed: 10 May 1929) (This Act may be cited as the Infant Life (Preservation) Act.)[1]

Here, the 'child' becomes explicitly separated from the woman and is re-categorized in terms of a separate Act for 'it'. The notion of viability of the 'child' is introduced in terms of when it is 'capable of being born alive', in that it could have 'an existence independent of its mother', and a time limit is set at 28 weeks. From this point the crime becomes 'intent . . . by any wilful act' and is renamed 'child destruction'. After 28 weeks the 'intent' of abortion becomes legal only 'for the purpose of preserving the life of the mother'.

TITLE: Abortion Act 1967: An Act to amend and clarify the law relating to termination of pregnancy by registered medical practitioners. (Passed: 27 October 1967)

In this Act all abortions, including those from 'Visiting Forces etc.', become subject to the legal control of the medical profession who are required to regulate them for purposes of collecting information and statistics. The medical profession is given power to decide whether the pregnant woman is eligible for abortion in terms of 'environmental', 'physical' and 'mental' considerations. Viability of the 'fetus' or 'child' is extended to include 'physical' or 'mental' qualities. A conscience clause is introduced for doctors who do not agree with abortion on 'their own' 'moral' grounds. Nothing in this Act affects the provisions of the Infant Life (Preservation) Act 1929, which protects the life of the viable fetus.[2]

First chronology: the shifting power and knowledge of medical men

The early nineteenth century was a critical period in the formation of the medical profession, particularly against competition from 'quackery' which was held in low esteem (McLaren, 1984, p. 129). It was necessary for the medical profession to gain a certain degree of credibility and legitimacy in order for the criminality in relation to abortion to be shifted on to women. Equally, in order for abortion to become legal, the status of the medical profession had to rise. It is against this backdrop, in light of these two overlapping processes, that one begins to make sense of the early Acts. It becomes possible to see them in terms of the increasing ability of the medical profession to determine that their 'expertise' be drawn upon by law-makers. This history is essential to an understanding of the redefinition of abortion in terms of medical knowledge.

The beginning of the nineteenth century was a period that witnessed the increasing emphasis on biological science as a source of 'truth' about sexuality and reproduction. The reproductive process was itself considered a biological mystery which science needed to solve. It was the increasing medical knowledge about the 'biological' process of pregnancy itself that began to lay the grounds for a redefinition of abortion. In turn, this 'factual' account became the basis for the increasing importance of the reproductive sciences in the formation of law and social policy.

An example that demonstrates this increasing power of medical science to define the abortion question, and to influence the terms of the Acts, is the disappearance of the term 'quickening' from the Statute Book. Quickening was a term used by women to denote the feeling of first internal movements. It was also used by the midwives (over whom the medical men were attempting to gain power) and a term the medical profession wanted removed from the law as early as 1803, although this effort failed (McLaren, 1984, p. 129). The disappearance of the term quickening was symbolic of a more general displacement of definitions and meanings used by women. It simultaneously indicated the increase in medical definition and control over reproduction, and the decrease in women's existing control.[3] Both these shifts demonstrate how the process of 'legitimation' is a dual one: women become more *excluded from* by the very act of becoming further *subject to* the law.

These processes of separation were compounded by each successive Act, as women's needs/realities receded and medical knowledge and influence increased. This can be seen most clearly in the shift towards the criminalization of women rather than doctors. It can also be seen in the shift towards protecting the, then unnamed (in law), 'territory' within her, from the now 'criminal' woman herself. The state became the 'guardian' of this newly constituted biological 'territory: 'its' protector from the woman who was increasingly constructed as a 'danger' to it, and as having potentially oppositional interests (see p. 167).

The criminalization of women was also linked to greater medical intervention in reproduction (further exploration into a new mysterious territory which science sought to discover). Criminalization enabled the view that individual women were at the root of the problem rather than, as previously, those who 'enabled' them to have abortions. It was precisely at this point, for example, that those who aided and abetted abortion came to be regarded less seriously, and were explicitly isolated in a separate paragraph of the Act of 1861.

The Infant Life (Preservation) Act of 1929 was a further stage in this process. The 'territory' became a separate issue from other Offences Against the Person within the law, and became explicitly a potential victim in need of state protection. A notion of the 'viability' of the 'child' was introduced on medical grounds. The 'child' was now more 'knowable'. In the law, this status was now determined by the functioning of the heart, regardless of whether the umbilical cord had been 'severed'

(Williams, 1983, pp. 289–291). 'New life' came to be determined by its newly constructed biological capabilities. From this point on, it is changing medical knowledge that defines the abortion debate. Abortion has come to be seen as a medico-biological issue, about which it is possible to be 'factual' and 'objective', and, in this regard, as entirely separate from social relations.

The process of separation effected through medical/legal control (both 'outside' and now 'inside' women's bodies) is also evident in the changing language of the Acts. Whereas women were described as 'being with child' in 1803, by 1929 they were described as 'pregnant *of* a child'. Whereas previously they had been described as 'women', now they were described in terms of their role as 'mothers'. So while, as women, they became separated, as 'mothers'/'hosts' their responsibilities had been extended to include the time from 28 weeks. These linguistic shifts are further evidence of the erosion of women's ability either to define or control their pregnancies in law, and of the duality of women's inclusion and exclusion within it.

The delegation of control to the medical profession was reinforced linguistically in the Acts in terms of personal pronouns. In 1828 there was a specific distinction between female and male procurers in terms of punishment. In 1837 they were referred to as 'his or her'. In 1861 their sex was unspecified, and by 1929 they were referred to as 'he'. There are several possible interpretations of these shifts in the use of pronouns. The earlier use of both pronouns could indicate the inclusion of midwives and other women amongst 'procurers'. The later disappearance of the pronouns altogether, and the reappearance of the term 'he' only, might be read as an indication of increasing male dominance of the profession.

The 1929 Act shows a consolidation of medical 'expertise' in relation to abortion. Although assisting medical practitioners were still deemed criminal, it was they who influenced the terms of the 1929 Act by reinforcing the view that individual women were the problem. Medical practitioners began to be seen as the 'experts' rather than the criminals. Significantly, the British College of Obstetrics and Gynaecology was formed in the same year as this Act, consolidating the organization and promotion of professional medical 'expertise' specifically around this 'territory'.

The emergence of a concept of legal abortion in the Act of 1967 established circumstances (see chart, p. 163) under which medical 'experts' could conduct abortions free of criminal intent. Abortion became legal for women *at the discretion of two registered medical practitioners*. Hence, abortion became 'legalized' in terms of doctors not being criminalized rather than women having legal rights over reproduction. Women had not gained control over their pregnancies, medical practitioners had.

The 1967 Act gave limited recognition to women's needs, in that one of its aims was to stop 'back street' abortions. This at least constituted a recognition of the fact that women need and have abortions. Hence, it could be said that women had been effective in changing the law, despite their position outside it. Organized feminist campaigns did have effects, even though these are not clear-cut or easily quantifiable. But the Abortion Act of 1967 should be seen as part of a more general process by which powerful professional groups sought to redefine the law and to appropriate, or 'contain', women's needs and demands within a move to regain popular consent under a new guise. Crudely, it represents a shift of the patriarchal power relationship between the legal and medical professions; an exchange of women (or control over reproduction) from the former to the latter. Women's inclusion in the law was still premissed on their simultaneous exclusion; it preserved professional control over women's reproductive capacity through limited 'concessions', rather than being women-centred. Women's right to abortion was, and is still, conditional upon the consent of two registered medical practitioners who are licensed by the State. Section 5 of the Abortion Act 1967 stated that this Act was not intended to 'affect the provisions of the Infant Life (Preservation) Act 1929 (protecting the life of the viable foetus)'. It therefore maintained and reinforced the 'separateness' of a woman and a fetus, the fetus being the vehicle for further medical and state intervention.

Both the legal and the medical professions are concerned with their own expertise and power to define and control reproduction, rather than with women, or women's needs or interests. Madeleine Simms makes a number of important points on this issue in regard to the medical profession. For example, she points out the extent to which the concerns of the British College of Obstetricians and Gynaecologists (BCOG) were focused upon restriction of 'the abuse of therapeutic abortion' (Simms, 1974, p. 51) and the ways in which this could be achieved. They made a number of recommendations in an effort to enhance their professional standing in relation to abortion. First, they recommended that doctors 'insist on a second opinion only from a specialist' since 'the family doctor's opinion was suspect . . . likely to be unduly sympathetic to her problem' (Simms, 1984, p. 51). Second, they recommended '[enforced] notification of all legal abortions (i.e. to 'The Home Office') [as a] deterrent to both patients (sic) and doctors' and a means of avoiding any challenge to 'the judgement of the consultants involved' (p. 51). This also reveals divisions within and between the interests of different specializations within the medical profession, and therefore the extent to which it cannot be considered monolithic. Finally,

it was of the opinion that a classified list of conditions justifying abortion was to be avoided. The development of medicine was bound to overtake certain treatments . . 'with such a list, a patient (sic) would consider she had the right to insist upon therapeutic abortion and it would be very dif-ficult for the obstetrician to refuse to perform the operation, even when he disagreed with the indication'. (BCOG quoted in Simms, 1984, p. 51).

These three points are evident in the Abortion Act of 1967, not only showing the power of the medical profession to define the abortion issue, but also to do so unquestioningly as recognized 'experts' in a medically (and legally) defined 'territory' within women's bodies. They also demonstrate the ways in which the Act restricted women's rights in the interests of allowing greater scientific freedom. The Act enabled medical scientists to reproduce their own, now 'legitimated', expertise. Men became further 'legitimated', and included, in an area from which they are 'biologically' excluded – women's pregnancies.

In terms of the 'new territory', the 'separate child', the notion of the viability of the fetus in law became extended to include a construction of 'its health' as 'biological abilities'. This was expressed in terms of the 'child's' capacity to be born alive and well. Not only was the notion of 'viability' explicitly introduced in 1967, but the 'territory' was also named in law for the first time as the 'foetus' (a medical term), in reference to the Act of 1929. The fetus/child 'as separate' became legally defined in eugenic terms. This came about as a result of the ways in which medical knowledge had 'progressed'. The ability of medical and scientific expertise to determine such characteristics was critical to its acquisition of both the power and the legitimacy to redefine women's pregnancies.

Second chronology: shifting cultures

In order to understand how the medical profession gained this power, it is necessary to look beyond the Acts themselves. The nineteenth century has been much documented, and redocumented, by historians in the attempt to account for it as a period of immense socioeconomic change. Factors which have come to be seen as significant during this period include: the emergence of ideologies of the separate spheres and of private/public domains; changing labour patterns and processes associated with industrialization; the formation of the middle and working classes; the development of colonialism; the emergence of the concept of the 'working man'; and the rise of evangelical religion.

The connection to be made between all of these categories, although often complex, is the changing role of women, particularly as mothers and homemakers and (cheap) labourers, throughout this period. By extension/alongside this a new construction of 'childhood' was forming during the Victorian era. Several laws enacted during this period made explicit a number of these changes in women's roles, although it is important to emphasize that women did not necessarily comply with the law or, more often, had little choice.

The laws that will be cited here as an example of these constraints on women are the Poor Laws (1834), the Mines Regulation Act (1842) and the Contagious Diseases Acts (beginning in 1864). The Poor Laws are significant in a number of respects. Previous to this legislation men could be brought before the magistrates and made to take some responsibility for 'bastard' children. From this time onwards it was seen to be the responsibility of the women. On the other hand, married men were to be responsible for 'their wives', 'their children' and, if applicable, all children from their wives' previous marriages who became 'theirs'.

While the Poor Laws involved legal definitions of women as mothers, the Mines Regulation Act concerned women's roles as workers. This Act made it illegal for women to work underground in the mines. It was seen to be work which was 'unfit' for women (dirty, heavy, 'unfeminine'). The moral standing of women mineworkers was seen to be in doubt in that their clothes were often ripped during work and they were 'baring' parts of themselves. They were seen as sexual objects in a manner which threatened their social role of 'good mothers'. Doctors were called upon for evidence in investigations prior to the Act. Cases of stillbirths and miscarriages were also used as reasons why women should not work underground, thereby also giving emphasis to their role as mothers, homemakers and reproducers. The Contagious Diseases Acts, starting in 1864, introduced further redefinitions of women's social roles. Amongst other things, these Acts brought prostitution under the control of the medical profession through the state. The Acts reflected the double standard of female/male sexuality, and the emphasis on women's responsibility for 'moral cleanliness'.[4] In many senses, the abortion debate today is similar to those surrounding the Contagious Diseases Acts, in that both were/are battlegrounds for diverse and competing groups vying with each other and making alliances for power. Just like those around the Contagious Diseases Acts, the abortion debate has become a tool for defending whole world views.

These Acts should also be understood in relation to other debates such as those centring on the 'health (wealth) of the nation', where, again, women were seen as the key agents in terms of 'good mothering'. This was particularly true of white middle-class mothers who were constructed as 'guardians' of the British 'race' in opposition to women from other classes, races and nations. British colonizers/adventurers were part of the construction of empire in the name of progress, civilization and the British nation. These historical processes both enabled and were reinforced by medical intervention. For example, on the one hand, there was a connection made between 'good mothering', health, wealth, cleanliness and nationalism. On the other hand, 'uncontained' sexuality was related to dirt, poverty, sickness and corruption. Both related to the increasing power to define of the medical profession, and the exercise of power over women in the interests of the (white) 'nation'.

This is a rather brief overview of extremely complex historical forces and shifts. However, they are a significant indication of the complex processes through which the medical profession became agents of power, able to define their 'territory' within a wider framework of power relations around sex, race and class. The need to define women in terms of their 'biological', reproductive role and around a particular kind of motherhood took shape in relation to wider cultural shifts through which women's roles were defined. The process of separating women from their ability to define their own pregnancies was a significant component in the redefinition of women's roles.

The effects of such separations continue to be reproduced. For example, as it stands, the abortion debate frames abortion as if it were a separate part of women's lives, as if it were a particular biological moment, measurable in weeks, seconds and heartbeats. From a feminist perspective, the abortion debate could be seen as symptomatic of how women's whole lives and roles are defined and perceived. A woman who never has need for an abortion herself is still affected, is still defined by the issues around it, such as motherhood, sexuality, work, childcare and education. Women are also defined through abortion in terms of the social construction of 'womanly' attributes such as the requirement continually to meet other people's needs and demands; self-denial; sexual availability; and responsibility for childcare and the domestic sphere. In sum, the control of abortion is a central part of patriarchal power, in particular the power to define. The medical profession has played an increasing part in this process, influencing common sense as much as the law. A recent comment made to me by a woman was 'How can you do any research on abortion, you've never studied medicine!' Such a statement could be indicative of the extent to which abortion has become 'medicalized' and separated within women's consciousness.

Third chronology: ambiguities

In addition to examining the power to define which is evident in the history of abortion legislation, it is also important to consider some of the ambiguities within the legal definition of abortion. Three major sources of ambiguities are: to whom the Acts are addressed; how the crime is defined; and how the punishment is structured. Highlighting these ambiguities reveals points of contradiction within the law which are important to those who seek to challenge it. Each of these three sources of ambiguity is addressed below.

Chart 2: who the Acts are addressing

    1803   'All persons'   – Procurers, Aiders & Abetters – as equal
                                    categories

1828   'Any person'   – Procurers, Aiders & Abetters – as equal
                        categories
1837   'Whosoever'   – Procurers
1861   'Every woman'
        'Whosoever' 1   – Procurers
        'Whosoever' 2   – Aiders & Abetters
1929   'Any person'   – Procurers only?
                        – Including women as procurers?
                        – Aiders & Abetters?
1967   'Registered Medical Practitioners'

Throughout the 1929 Act the procurer is referred to as 'he' and therefore it could be said that the procurer does not refer to the pregnant woman – given the preciseness of personal pronouns in previous laws. If this is the case, then, in terms of punishment (see p. 172) for women seeking abortion, the Act of 1861 still stands. The position of women remains as in 1861, and it is the position of the medical profession that shifts. For the medical profession, this means that although they have discovered 'new territory' which has influenced the law, it has become the 'property' of the state, over which the state rather than the medical profession has control.

On the other hand, if the term 'procurer' *does* include women, then it implies that pregnant women and medical practitioners are 'partners in crime' to 'child destruction'. This makes completely invisible the power relations between women and medical practitioners. It appears as if women and medical practitioners have the same interest, whereas women are dependent on doctors to carry out abortions and, later, for these to be legitimated by doctors.

According to *Halisbury's Laws of England*, women were included in the category of those 'aiding and abetting' (in 'administering poison' to themselves). In this interpretation, doctors and 'aiders and abetters' (women seeking abortions) are considered equally culpable. Hence, by the time this interpretation was written, the original (1803) meaning of 'procuring', and 'aiding and abetting' had been completely reversed. Instead of the 'procurers', 'aiders and abetters' 'causing' the miscarriage, the blame is now reversed, thus reinforcing the view that it is women who are culpable and medical practitioners who become allies of the state.

Whichever way one considers whom the Acts are addressing from 1929, women are at the centre of the 'crime', yet ever more marginal to the terms through which it is defined. Increasingly, the terms are defined as who has control of the fetus (as separate from women). This is a continuing battle between the legal profession, the medical profession and the state over expertise and power to define and control reproduction. However, the battle over the fetus, as separate, reflects the battle over control of women.

What is the crime?

The crime of 'intent' to procure abortion has always been regarded as a felony. Yet, it has also meant different things at different times in terms of punishment. The distinction between felonies and misdemeanours was abolished in the Criminal Law Act (1967) whereupon all previous references were to be referred to as misdemeanours or offences (other than treason).

The terms of the felony (now misdemeanour or charges) are both clear and unclear. In 1803, abortion was within an Act encompassing a variety of felonies of which, in title, the destroying of 'bastard children' was explicitly 'murder' yet abortion was not. In 1828, when Offences Against the Person started to be consolidated, abortion was placed in Section 13 after 'Shooting at, or stabbing, cutting, or wounding any Person, with intent to maim', and with murder in the first section. The Act of 1837 confirmed the previous Act, except that the death penalty remained for murder, but not for procuring abortion, implying that they were not regarded as the same. In 1861, in the consolidation of Offences Against the Person, abortion was placed in Sections 58 and 59 after bigamy and, again, with murder in the first sections under homicide. Hence, abortion was not considered as murder but as something different, which was unspecified.

The Act of 1929 introduced the concept of 'child destruction' at the time of 'a child capable of being born alive' (28 weeks). The Act also referred to 'intent' to abort in the 1861 Act in terms of 'murder or manslaughter of any child, or for infanticide', or 'child destruction' at the 'discretion of the court'. This reinforced the importance of the 'child' (as separate from the woman) as it was becoming medically (biologically) 'knowable'. It was as if, in this instance, the medical profession, was influencing the rewriting of previous Acts, as much as the legal profession.

The 1929 Act decriminalized abortion 'for the purpose only of preserving the life of the mother'. This implied both a separation of the fetus from the mother and a potential conflict of interest. However, contrary to the purpose of the Act (to protect the fetus as a separate entity), this clause recognized that the fetus was part of the mother, and that she had greater legal rights. This is only one of many examples of legal confusion over the status of the fetus, or, rather, of how to 'fit' it into the framework of the law (see Williams, 1983). This is again symptomatic of the problem of separating the woman and the fetus.

Chart 3: Punishments

   1803   After quickening – death sentence; before quickening – fines; imprisonment; set in and upon the pillory; publicly or privately whipped; or to suffer one or more of the said punishments; or to be transported beyond the seas for any terms not exceeding fourteen years, at the discretion of the court.

1828   Same – except for before quickening when whipping only applied to men.

1837   At the discretion of the court, to be transported beyond the Seas for the Term of his or her natural Life, or for any term not less than fifteen years, or to be imprisoned for any Term not exceeding Three Years.

1861   Woman and Procurer – at the discretion of the court, to be kept in penal servitude for life or for any term not less than three years, or to be imprisoned for any term not exceeding two years, with or without hard labour, and with or without solitary confinement. Aiders and Abetters – to be kept in penal servitude for the term of three years, or to be imprisoned for any term not exceeding two years, with or without hard labour.

1929   Post 28 weeks – penal servitude for life. Otherwise same as 1861.

1967   Exemptions from the above. Up to £100 fine for registered medical practitioner for not reporting 'termination' to the Chief Medical Officers of the Ministry of Health and the Scottish Home and Health Department respectively.

Some of these changes relate to wider changes in the organization of punishment, such as the abolition of the death sentence, the abolition of transportation beyond the seas, or the abolition of penal servitude which replaced that and which was itself replaced by imprisonment for life or any shorter term in the Criminal Law Act of 1967. However, even considering these factors, it can be seen that there is much ambiguity over punishments. The punishment is presently (under the 1929 Act) 'imprisonment for life or any shorter term', which implies that the crime can be considered very seriously, or not be considered seriously at all. All punishments were and are 'at the discretion of the courts', so severity of punishment is dependent upon who is passing 'judgement'. As stated in the section on crimes, the death penalty for murder was retained in 1837, but not for procuring abortion. This was another point where the growing influence of medical expertise becomes apparent; when the term 'quickening' disappeared, the death sentence disappeared. This exposes a very interesting juxtaposition within legal definitions of fetal life: on the one hand, it was taken more seriously (as potential human life), while on the other less seriously (in terms of retaining the death penalty for murder and abolishing it for abortion).

Another ambiguity is highlighted when examining legal case history and looking at who has actually been prosecuted. In the *Textbook of Criminal Law*, Williams states that

women are not prosecuted for procuring abortion themselves, perhaps because of the difficulty of getting a jury to convict a woman for an act committed in extreme distress, and the unlikelihood that if convicted she will receive anything more than a nominal sentence. A further good reason for not prosecuting (whether or not it weighs with the police) is that a woman who has operated on herself, or taken drugs, will frequently have caused herself such injury as to necessitate medical attention; and it would be most undesirable that she should be deterred from seeking this attention through the threat of punishment. (Williams, 1983, p. 293).

On the other hand, for abortionists (as separate from the pregnant woman):

The maximum sentence is never awarded. In practice, 6 years is the utmost, even for the professional abortionist. Many receive much shorter sentences, and some are merely fined. (Williams, 1983, p. 295).

From this description, it is apparent that the 'wider population', the jury, is reluctant to prosecute a woman who has undergone an abortion. Thus, although women are criminalized, they are not prosecuted. In contrast, if registered medical practitioners do not comply with the Abortion Act of 1967, they are criminalized and have been prosecuted – although not imprisoned for life.

Conclusion

The focus of this analysis has been the duality of women's inclusion and exclusion in the law in the context of abortion legislation. This is seen as a product of the legal construction of pregnancy, as defined by medical experts, which invokes a notion of separation of the woman from the fetus. By these means, women have been excluded from defining their own pregnancies, both in law and through medical expertise. This is related to wider historical, cultural redefinitions of womanhood, in terms of women's roles as mothers, workers and citizens (of the British nation/empire), and in terms of their sexuality. These wider definitions were both reinforced through and informed by medical science within the context of patriarchal social relations. I have shown that rather than having fixed meanings, the Acts are sites of struggle.

I have also recorded the ways in which this representation of women's pregnancies does not 'fit' into the law. Again, this is seen to be indicative of the duality of women's inclusion and exclusion within the law, and symptomatic of the extent to which the issues are defined in non women-centred terms. I have demonstrated how the notion of the fetus as separate is problematic in law, precisely because it is not separate, and how consensus over the meaning of the representation of the fetus as separate is still being fought over by the different interest groups. In addition to this, I have shown how the 'separateness' of the fetus provides justification for 'legitimate' intervention in pregnancy. Similarly, I have addressed the power struggles and shifts between, and within, legal and medical 'expertise', such as the decriminalization of registered medical practitioners.

Finally, by showing the ways in which organized feminist inputs have been effective, I have also illustrated how the power to define is not mono-lithic or complete. It is a process that is continually moving, contested and contradictory. The medical profession did not gain the power to define without many years of struggle. This knowledge is useful and positive in terms of feminist politics and strategies.

Notes

1   This Act does not extend to Scotland and Northern Ireland.
2   This Act does not extend to Northern Ireland.
3   It must also be acknowledged that some women continued to perform abortions (Woodside, 1988) and that there is now a considerable number of women medical practitioners. However, women medical practitioners do not always have a woman-centred perspective, and some male practitioners do. These issues are complex and beyond the scope of this chapter.
4   These Acts are also evidence of alliances which extend beyond the medical and legal professions in defining women as 'the problem'. For example, the Mines Regulation Act was advantageous to working-class men, the Contagious Diseases Acts were advantageous to 'the Forces', etc.

Section 3:

Adversarial politics: the legal construction of abortion

DEBORAH LYNN STEINBERG

Introduction

State regulation and medical management of abortion have been central issues both within women's lives and within the women's liberation movement. The legal status of abortion, as feminists have long pointed out, has a direct impact on women's experience of sexuality, pregnancy and motherhood. The terms of the Alton Bill and parliamentary debate have raised important questions for feminists struggling, particularly within the context of the law, to secure both women's unrestricted access to safe, legal abortion and, more broadly, women's freedom from state and other forms of patriarchal policing and control over sexuality and reproduction.

This section examines one of the most recent constructions of abortion as a legal question through an analysis of the parliamentary debates over the Alton Bill. The parliamentary process reveals both the thinking behind the Bill and how the process of law-making and the framework of law itself shape and constrain the concept of abortion. Thus, this section will examine both the question of how the general framework of law shapes abortion as a legal issue and the specific dimensions of this construction within the context of parliamentary debate. The relevant questions for this section are: (a) how is the act of abortion defined within the law? what is the 'crime'? who are the 'victims'? who are the 'criminals'? and (b) what are the specific implications of this construction of abortion for women?

The terms of the parliamentary debate reflect three fundamental shifts in the broader conceptual construction of abortion. These are: developments since 1967 in prenatal diagnostic capabilities which have given an unprecedented scientific dimension to the construction of fetal personhood and have introduced a modern eugenic[1] dimension to rationales for legal abortion (see also below, Fetal Fascinations); the growth of the currency of the language of rights; and the incorporation and subversion of the language and concepts of the women's liberation movement (including the language of women's 'reproductive rights').

The Alton Bill

The Alton (Abortion [Amendment]) Bill was introduced in Parliament by Private Member, David Alton (Liberal) in October 1987. On 22 January 1988, it was given a second reading in the House of Commons where it passed by a majority of 296 to 251. In March 1988, the Bill went to Committee where 29 amendments were proposed. The Committee was composed of 17 voting members and 2 non-voting members. Nine of the voting Committee members, a majority of one, were Alton supporters, 6 were women, 2 of whom supported Alton, 4 of whom opposed Alton. The pro-Alton bench was dominated by Conservatives, the anti-Alton bench by Labour, and the voting patterns of Committee members consistently reflected the numerical majority of the pro-Alton bench, hence, no amendment proposed by Alton's opponents was passed. The Bill ran out of time at the Report Stage which follows Committee and failed.

The Alton Bill proposed a reduction in the upper time limit for legal abortion from 28 to 18 weeks gestation. The Bill allowed exemptions up to 28 weeks only if: (a) 'the termination is necessary to save the life of the woman', or (b) 'the child is likely to be born dead or with physical abnormalities so serious that its life cannot be independently sustained'. At Committee stage, a further exemption was added for women under 18 years of age who have suffered incest or rape.

The Alton Bill, while anti-abortion in spirit, none the less upheld the legality of abortion under certain conditions. The intent of the Bill was revealed in the following exchange between anti-Alton Committee member, Frank Doran and David Alton:

> Doran: Does the Hon. Gentlemen agree that the Bill, which places a time limit on when an abortion may be carried out, accepts the principle of abortion?
> Alton: If I could legislate for utopia, I certainly would.
> (Doran, Alton in *Parliamentary Debates*, 24 March 1988 (afternoon), col. 83).

Thus, the Bill was deliberately styled to initiate an incremental erosion of legal abortion, beginning with 'late' abortions.

In reducing the time limit for legal abortion, the Bill proposed to extend the definition of infant life provided by the 1929 Act to give 'rights' and 'protection' to fetal life beginning at 18 weeks. This extension of 'fetal rights' rested on the legal principle of the 1929 Act that abortion is 'child destruction'. As we shall see, however, the distinction between 'child destruction' and 'murder' is largely dependent on interpretation. During parliamentary debate, abortion was described (by the pro-Alton bench) as 'murder'. However, like the 1967 Act, which legalized abortion, the fundamental question of the Alton Bill was not *whether* abortion is (effectively) 'murder', but *when* it is so.

'Late' abortion as a crime

What differentiated the Alton Bill from previous legal moves to define the criminality of abortion was the construction of the new criminal category of 'late' abortion. Parliamentary debate on the Alton Bill was dominated by arguments attempting to distinguish 'late' abortion as a new category of abortion crime. What was, perhaps, most significant in the delineation of 'lateness' by the pro-Alton bench was the contradiction between the letter of the Bill and the conceptual shift accomplished by pro-Alton arguments in the broader meaning of abortion. These shifts were manifested in the concept of criminal 'late' abortion; the association of abortion *per se* with murder; and in particular arguments defining the special character of 'late' abortion.

In the wording of the Alton Bill, which proposed that the upper time limit of legal abortion be reduced to 18 weeks, the term 'late' was not used. This concept of 'lateness' emerged directly from the pro-Alton rhetoric of the parliamentary debate, initiated by David Alton himself, who introduced the term in his presentation of the Bill to the House of Commons: 'No upper time limit when abortions may occur is specified in the 1967 Abortion Act. No distinction is made between late and early abortions' (Alton in Hansard, 22 January 1988, col. 1228, p. 631). The Alton category 'late' was notable, furthermore, in terms of its unprecedented association with criminality.

'Late' abortion, according to David Alton, was defined as occurring after the eighteenth week of pregnancy. The 18-week distinction drew some criticism from the anti-Alton bench for being arbitrary, or as one MP put it, 'plucked out of the air' (Mackay in Hansard, 22 January 1988, col. 1236, p. 635). As MP Audrey Wise pointed out, 'There is no legal definition of pregnancy. As a legal matter, the 18th week of gestation does not exist . . . Which day represents the 18th week of gestation? Supporters of the Bill do not know. Doctors do not know. The woman concerned does not really know' (Wise in Hansard, 22 January 1988, col. 1289, p. 662). Anti-Alton MPs also criticized the 18-week cut-off for being too early, arguing instead for a 24-week time limit. A 24-week limit, in their view, could be justified by medical advances in neonatal technology 'during the past 20 years so that today it is perfectly possible for a child [sic] to be born at 24 weeks' (Mackay in Hansard, 22 January 1988, col. 1238, p. 636).

While their criticisms challenged Alton's choice of date, they none the less accepted in principle the category of 'lateness'. Criminal, time-delineated, 'late' abortion now exists, if not (yet) in the letter of the law, in its spirit and in the conceptual framework of law-makers. Moreover, the term 'late' abortion was picked up and proliferated in the mainstream media (see below, The Alton Bill and the media's 'consensual' position) and so effected a significant shift in the broader cultural meaning of abortion.

Abortion as murder

As Wendy Fyfe points out, under existing abortion law (the 1929 Infant Life (Preservation) Act which served as a basis for the Alton Bill), abortion is the crime of 'child destruction' if it is performed 'when the child [sic] is capable of being born alive' (Williams, 1983, p. 291).[2] By law, a 'child' is presumed to be 'capable of being born alive' at 28 weeks. Thus, 'child destruction' is linguistically, and as a matter of legal principle, distinguished from 'homicide' which 'requires the victim to be in *rerum natura* or "in being", which means that he [sic] must be "completely born alive"' (Williams, 1983, p. 292). Homicide, or murder, therefore presupposes the full personhood of the victim. The specific legal precedent in defining a fetus has been that a 'fetus (or unborn child [sic]) is not a legal person, and so cannot (for example) own property, but has its existence recognised by law in some ways. The fetus becomes a legal person when it is born alive' (Williams, 1983, p. 290).

As I have pointed out above, in keeping with legal precedent, the Alton Bill, also defines 'late' abortion as the crime of 'child destruction'. However, throughout the parliamentary debates, the pro-Alton bench discussed abortion in terms of 'killing' and 'murder'. For example, MP Sir Bernard Braine, in a characteristic claim, asserted in Committee that: 'We abhor the legalised killing of helpless infants' (Braine in *Parliamentary Debates*, 24 March 1988 (morning), col. 42). As David Alton implied in his regret that they could not 'legislate for utopia', the philosophical premiss of their desire to legislate against 'late' abortion was that abortion, not only after 18 weeks but at any stage, is 'murder'. Although careful to confine their discussion to 'late' abortion, the pro-Alton bench none the less successfully associated the concept of 'murder' with abortion *per se*. This association, which was in direct contravention of legal precedent, was never adequately or directly challenged, even on this narrow legalistic basis, by anti-Alton parliamentarians.

'Late' abortion: a special case of 'murder'

Sir Bernard Braine situated the 'abortion as murder' premiss specifically within the context of 'late' abortion. He stated before the House that:

The overwhelming proportion of late abortions are performed on babies

1 Leader of the Conservative Party, but also housewife, Margaret Thatcher's use of domestic imagery featured strongly in the early years of her office. In her right hand is a full shopping bag, showing goods bought for one pound in 1974, in her left, a half-filled bag showing goods bought for the same amount under Labour in 1979.   *The Hulton-Deutch Collection*

2 'The Best Man in the Cabinet?' Margaret Thatcher and her Cabinet in 1988.
Press Association Photos

Boats are extremely useful things, let us not forget! For if you set sail without one, you're bound to get terribly wet. Pop stars don't have much luck with boats Simon le 'Bon nearly drowned in his "Drum" And when Bruce "The Boss" Springsteen bought a nice new canoe It broke which was a real bum(mer) ("Pop Stars And Boats: A Study" – D. Rimmer.)

B I T Z

THE RETURN OF THE FRIGHTWIG!!!

Hold onto your hat, viewers – it's disco frenzy time! **Spagna** – she of the most bizarre hair"do" in the history of popular song and of the most mind-numbingly catchy disco tune ever i.e. "Call Me" – is back! Back!! BACK!!! (so to speak). She's got a new tune out called "Every Boy And Girl", which is all about rumpo and is startlingly good and is already number one just about everywhere in the universe (except here, but not for long). And she *hasn't* traded in her frightwig for a new model! Yipppeeee!!(?)

They're "Neat"! They're "Wicked"! They're "Happening"! They're. . . The Royal Family!!!

⭐ And now *Bitz* is overwhelmingly chuffed to un"veil" a brand new portrait of Their Majesties, the Royal Family. Pictured on the lawns of Balmoral they are, from left to right: The Duke Of Edinburgh HRH Prince Phillip, Blushingly Fragrant Princess Diana Of Wales, The Duchess Of York Lady "Fergie" and (centre, seated) HRH The Queen "Mum" (Gawd bless 'er! Roll out the barrel! (*You're fired* – Ed.))
(A corgi writes: "Actually, these fellows are members of popular combo **The Blow Monkeys** who are pictured here to mark the release of their brand new "waxing", "This Is Your Life", in which they'll be hoping to recapture the popular acclaim that followed such much loved hits as "It Doesn't Have To Be That Way" and. . . er. . . the other ones. Thank you and goodnight.")

CRAP JOKE CORNER

Q. Which pop group never washes? A. Grimy Fisher!

Yes, it's more monthly unfamous bit of "humour" that was, eh? It was invented by Janet and Nicola from Glasgow and is genuinely useless. If you can think of something equally feeble send it to **Crap Joke Corner, Smash Hits, 52-55 Carnaby Street, London W1V 1PF.**

Seven Astonishing Facts About Siouxsie (Of "And The Banshees" Fame)

SHE ONCE "FLIPPED" HER WIG!
"I had this idea that I could get into wearing wigs. I thought it would save me a lot of time in the morning, just slipping on a wig like you slip on a hat, instead of an hour or so of crimping and combing my hair. It didn't work. It was too hot, too uncomfortable and I went a bit mad on the dance floor of a nightclub one evening and hauled the wig off. I felt like waving my wig in front of the newspaper photographers, which *wasn't* a very good idea really. I'm not interested in wearing wigs any more."

SHE'S GOT BIGGER MUSCLES THAN ARNOLD SCHWARZEN"EGG"ER (NOT *STRICTLY* TRUE)!
"I've been a regular visitor to a gym for four years now. I always make sure that I go three or four times a week. I do a lot of stretching exercises and work with weights – just toning up generally. It's not a very posh gym. It's a sweaty one. Have I built up muscles now? Look, I've *always* had muscles heh heh . . ."

HER BEST PAL IS A PECCARY CALLED GREGORY (EXCEPT SHE HASN'T SEEN HIM FOR *AGES*)!
"When we adopted him at the zoo he was on the unwanted list. A peccary (*i.e. a small gregarious wild pig*) isn't nearly as lovable as a long-eared rabbit or a panda. I must admit that I haven't been to see Gregory for about 18 months now. He's been moved to Whipsnade Zoo now, but we still pay for his upkeep, his food and things. I do miss him actually, but I've got

a framed photo of him at home. It's a bit sad really because we also adopted an armadillo called Amy, who lives at London Zoo, but she doesn't get as much publicity as Gregory."

SHE'S INTERESTED IN STARING AT HAIRY COATS!
"I'm very interested in solving what seems to be the unsolvable – through science. I really admire the way pathologists can get so much information from a fibre off someone's coat and then match it up to discover where that person bought the coat in the first place. I suppose I've always been very interested in crime, especially when I was very young. Some girls were into dolls, but I was always reading really gruesome murder stories."

SHE'S GOT RATHER A LOT OF TEETH!
"Yes, I suppose you *do* see a lot of my teeth in the video for 'Peek-A-Boo' (Ver *'Shees' new spook-single*), but that's bound to happen if there are lots of close-ups of you singing. Do I always brush my teeth before a video? Oh, of course! But not frantically. As long as you don't eat spinach quiche before you start singing, you're usually OK."

THE GUITARISTS IN HER GROUP KEEP EXPLODING!
"That's because of the fireworks I keep putting down their trousers! Did I start worrying about body odour after our guitarists all started leaving the band? No, I think *they* should have worried about B.O. since they were all asked to leave. . ."

Who The Juggins Are The Funky Worm?!

▲ The Worm (*left to right*): Parrot, Ping Pong and, er, "Julie".

There are some things about The Funky Worm which are *totally* unsecret, like that there are three of them (two blokes and a girlie), that they all live in Sheffield where they are chums with loads of other house music persons like Krush, (who, you may remember, pop fiends, had a hit a while ago with "House Arrest") and that they've got a groovy new single called "Hustle" which is niftily scuttling in the general direction of those charts we call pop. So, in celebration of all of this, *Bitz* is now about to have a jabber with Julie, chief chanteuse with The "Worm", to discover some quite amazing things, like. . .

● **One of them's called Ping Pong!**
"Ping Pong's half Chinese, you see, so it was a nickname given to him when he was at work." (?)

● **One of them's called Parrot!**
"Parrot was called Parrot because his real surname is Barrett and everybody at school rhymed it with Parrot. Barrett, Parrot, Parrot, Barrett. . ." (Bitz *gets the* "*picture*", *thanks*.)

● **They're all turkeys (or something)!**
"We all met at a club in Sheffield called The Jive

Turkey (*i.e. a place where eminent 'house' types 'hang out'*) where Parrot was a DJ. I used to go there every week and dance and we just got talking and became friends. Then Ping Pong came up from London and he became friends with Parrot too. Did I fancy Parrot?! Ahaaaaaaaaa aaaaaaaaaa !!!!!!?! (*At this point Julie goes completely hysterical and is 'rendered' unable to talk to Bitz for at least three weeks.*) No!!! (?) Em. . .I didn't fancy him at all. . . em. . .I don't think I'm allowed to say – he could get done for it! (Bitz *is now completely lost – how about you viewers?*) Oh, well, anyway, no we're just good friends. He fancied Ping Pong anyway!! But they're just good friends too!"

● **Julie is a Yorkshire Pudding Champion!**
"Yes, well I was trained to be a chef, you see. I didn't want to be a pop star, this just happened. Oh dear. . .hahaaaaa!! (*Goes off into another fit of giggling, presumably because Ping 'Pong' and Parrot are doing unspeakable things behind Bitz's back!*) Stop it!! Sorry about that, yes, I'm good at cooking Caribbean food but I'm terrible at cooking the simplest things like beans on toast – I can really muck it up a treat! Have my

soufflés ever flopped? No. My soufflés are always perfect, *actually*. Anyway, once I won this Yorkshire pudding competition and I had to go to France to cook for the French President! Ping Pong and Parrot take the mick out of my old job, though. What did they do before this? Well, Parrot was a gardener and Ping Pong was an audio visual technician in a museum so *that's* not much cop is it?!"

● **She's got a pet goldfish called Beethoven!**
"I live just down the road from Parrot, we all live separately. I live on my own, I haven't got any pets really, except a goldfish called Beethoven. I bought two goldfish but one died as soon as I put it in the tank. I thought I'd put them in contaminated water so I had it tested but it just turned out that it was a dodgy fish in the first place."

● **She invents ancestors!**
"I've got loads of interesting ancestors – they were tribal chiefs from darkest Africa. Am I japing? Er, yes I am actually. I haven't got any famous ancestors at all! Hahaha! Why don't you ask my grandkids if they've got any famous ancestors and then they can say me!!! Heheeeeeeeeeeeeeeeeeeeee-ee!!!!!!"

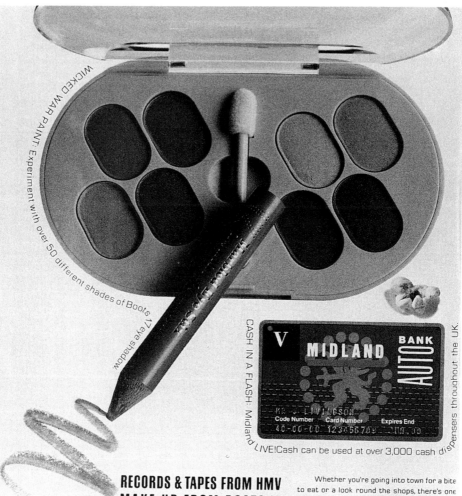

WICKED WAR PAINT: Experiment with over 50 different shades of Boots 17 eye shadow.

CASH IN A FLASH: Midland LIVE!Cash can be used at over 3,000 cash dispensers throughout the UK.

MIDLAND BANK AUTO

MR J LIVINGSON
Code Number   Card Number   Expires End
40-00-00 123456789   JAN 00

RECORDS & TAPES FROM HMV
MAKE-UP FROM BOOTS 17
TICKETS FROM THE BACK ROW
LIVE!CASH FROM MIDLAND

Whether you're going into town for a bite to eat or a look round the shops, there's one thing you can't afford to be without.

A Midland LIVE!Cash Card.

You can use it at any Midland AutoBank to get to your money 24 hours a day. 7 days a week. And as long as there's a minimum

VITAL VINYL: The world's biggest music store, HMV in Oxford Street, sells over

KICKS AT THE FLICKS: Over 200,000 young people visit their local Odeon cinema every week.

To be given up on Admission

ODEON 3759206

PERF. TIME			DATE
			27-2
1	Z	11	
SCREEN	ROW	SEAT	PRICE

THE WORLD'S BEST MUSIC STORES

balance of £20 in your account, you'll earn a good rate of interest.

If you are aged 14-20, you can open a LIVE!Cash account.

Just call in at your nearest Midland Bank and fill in an application form. Or call free on 0800 400 469 for written details.

MIDLAND
The Listening Bank

LIVE! CASH
14
20

4 *Smash Hits*, 10–23 August, 1988, pp. 10–11

Readies when you are.

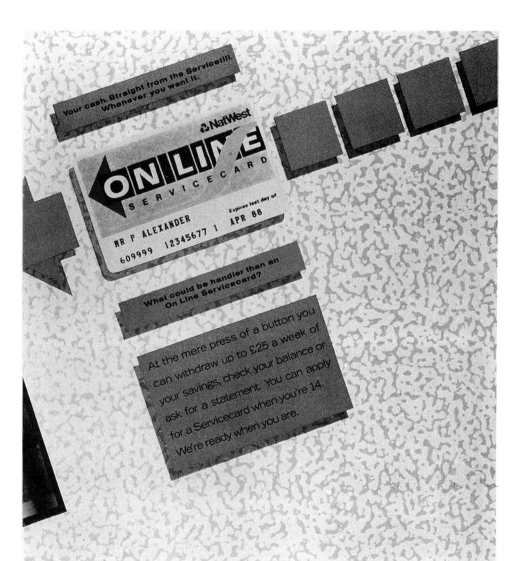

Your cash. Straight from the Servicetill. Whenever you want it.

NatWest

ONLINE

S E R V I C E C A R D

MR P ALEXANDER

Expires last day of APR 88

609999 12345677 1

What could be handier than an On Line Servicecard?

At the mere press of a button you can withdraw up to £25 a week of your savings, check your balance or ask for a statement. You can apply for a Servicecard when you're 14. We're ready when you are.

NatWest The Action Bank

PRESS FOR ACTION

5 *Smash Hits*, 9–22 March, 1988, pp. 8–9.

Just Seventeen girls can think of nothing else.

Just Seventeen girls certainly have an eye for a record.
They buy over 34 million records and cassettes every year
(10 million of which are singles).
One in three teenage girls read Just Seventeen because it's
packed with new bands, artists and records.
In fact, we've just made our own record. An ABC of 285,482'.

Which means Just Seventeen sells more than Melody Maker,
NME and No. 1 put together.
Call Barbara Smith on 01-437 8050. She'll tell you why an ad for a
record in Just Seventeen is one in the eye for other music mags.
Just Seventeen, 52–55 Carnaby
Street, London W1V 1PF

'ABC Jan-June 88

An EMAP-Metro Publication

6 *Music Week*, 10 September, 1988, p. 31.

which if born would have been normal healthy children. There is only one word for that in my book and that is murder . . . Well before 18 weeks, the foetus is recognisably human . . . and it should be basic to our understanding of what the Bill is about. (Braine in Hansard, 22 January 1988, col. 1244, p. 639).

This definition of 'late' abortion as a special case of 'murder' was constructed through arguments elaborating the distinct and special character of 'late' abortions. One such argument rested on the assertion that it is 'late' abortions 'which carry the gravest consequences for the mother, for the child and for the medic alike' (Alton in Hansard, 22 January 1988, col. 1236, p. 635). Hence, 'late' abortions are not only 'murders', but especially gruesome and traumatic 'murders'. In his opening speech in the House, David Alton gave this description of 'late' abortions:

Labour is induced by [prostaglandin] drugs . . . There is a chance that when prostaglandins are used, the child will be born alive. To avoid this, a child is usually poisoned before the abortion . . . With dilation and curetage, the cervix is dilated and the baby's body removed piece by piece. To facilitate its extraction from the womb, the skull is crushed, the spine snapped, and the body removed piece by piece. An attendant nurse then has the job of reassembling the body to ensure that nothing is left behind that might cause infection. Throughout this procedure, no anaesthetic is used on the child. (Alton in Hansard, 22 January 1988, cols. 1232–3, pp. 633–4).

The use of emotive and shocking terms such as 'poisoned' 'removed piece by piece', 'crushed [skull]', 'spine snapped', 'reassembling the body', 'no anaesthetic' imbues the procedure with horror. This characterization lingers on prurient details, evoking a picture of medical torture, inhumanity and moral perversion. Although what was being described here was allegedly the terrible, 'hidden' facts of 'late' abortion, this sort of language has long been used by anti-abortion lobbyists to describe abortion *per se*. Again, underlying the ostensible focus on distinguishing 'late' abortion in order to make a special case for criminalizing it, was the pro-Alton intent to erode the social legitimacy of abortion at any stage.

Another strand of argument positing the special nature of 'late' abortion concerned the fetal-centred construction of abortion victims. Both of the above quotations, for example, focused on the fetus-as-victim. They claimed to represent not only the 'fetal experience' of 'late' abortion, but in so doing, aimed to represent and protect fetal 'interests'. Fetal-centredness in the language and descriptions of abortion ('late' or otherwise) dominated parliamentary debate on both sides. Both pro-Alton and anti-Alton MPs consistently referred to fetuses as 'unborn children' and 'children'. Such language bolstered what became the substantive definition of abortion in the debate: abortion is, in the first order, something done to fetuses/'unborn children', and only secondarily (at most), a procedure women undergo.

Victims of abortion: 'Perfectly normal children', women and medical staff

> The subject of our discussion has been variously called a child, a baby, a foetus, a person and a thing. Perhaps if we settled for a proper name, a proper terminology, that might help many of us to make up our minds. I suggest that we substitute the term human being. (Mallon in Hansard, 22 January 1988, col. 1287, p. 661).

The construction of 'fetal victims' of abortion was constituted by several arguments, again, made specific to the 18-week distinction. One set of such arguments asserted that at 18 weeks the fetus has full legal personhood. As evidence of fetal personhood, MP Cyril Smith asserted, with an illogicality that has come to characterize rhetorical defences of the fetus as a legal person, its supposed anatomical wholeness: '[by] 18 weeks, a foetus is fully formed, with all major organs, *except its lungs*, intact' (Smith in Hansard, 22 January 1988, col. 1257, p. 661; my emphasis). Additionally, Alton supporters asserted fetal size and sentience as evidence of personhood. Sir Bernard Braine, for example, argued that 'the only difference between babies born . . . after 28 weeks and those born at 18 weeks is that the latter are smaller . . . [they] react to outside stimuli and can feel pain' (Braine in Hansard, 22 January 1988, cols. 1244–5, pp. 639–40).

Not only was the primary victim of abortion defined as a 'baby' or a 'child', but frequently as a 'perfectly normal' and 'perfectly healthy' child.

> For over 20 years, I have been concerned at the way in which a civilised country such as ours has permitted, and indeed encouraged, the deliberate destruction every year of 150,000 unborn babies, most of whom, if born, would have been *perfectly normal, healthy children*. (Braine in Hansard, 22 January 1988, col. 1243, p. 639; my emphasis).

> The nurse's observation that aborted babies are perfect is invariably true. Of the 8,276 late abortions undertaken last year, 92 per cent were on *perfectly healthy children*. (Alton in Hansard, 22 January 1988, col. 1234, p. 634; my emphasis).

The categorization of most aborted fetuses as '*perfectly healthy and normal*' explicitly distinguishes these fetuses from those which are presumably 'unhealthy' and 'abnormal'. These qualifiers thus constitute eugenic distinctions. They implicitly assert and reinforce the notion that the 'quality' of 'children' is of central importance in considering both abortion, and by extension, pregnancy and reproduction. They not only reinforce the notions that the fetuses of 'late' abortion are persons and that 'late' abortion is therefore 'murder', but they also imply that it is the 'murder' of 'perfectly normal' children [sic] which is especially repugnant and which is the most pertinent issue.

Alton supporters defined two additional categories of abortion 'victims'; women who undergo 'late' abortions and the medical staff (doctors and nurses) who perform them. These categories of victims are, in several respects, even more contradictory than the construction of the fetus-as-person-as-victim formulation. Pro-Alton MPs made several claims as to how, in their view, women are victims of 'late' abortion. One argument made by David Alton was that men coerce women into having abortions:

> Women are frequently pressurised into abortions by men. Men too often leave a woman in the lurch, having used their sexuality without responsibility. Those who maintain that abortion is purely a woman's issue do women no service; it allows men to evade their responsibilities, and without changes in men's attitudes, *women will not be truly liberated*. (Alton in Hansard, 22 January 1988, col. 1235, p. 635; my emphasis).

What is most significant and disturbing about this argument is the appropriation and recuperation of one of the central concerns within feminism: male sexual exploitation of women. Here David Alton uses the rhetoric of feminist arguments in order to support an anti-abortion initiative under the guise of protecting women's interests. That is, Alton used feminist ideas as a 'pro-woman' veneer obscuring the actual intent of his Bill which is to erode women's access to abortion and to criminalize women who undergo 'late' abortions.

Another 'pro-woman' argument used to justify the criminalization of 'late' abortion was that women inevitably suffer traumatic after-effects of 'late' abortion. David Alton described this condition (given the medicalized title of 'post-abortion trauma') as

> the psychiatric morbidity experienced by women after an abortion . . . That is how people [sic] tic. A late abortion – when a woman has felt her child quicken, when its humanity can be in no doubt – is inevitably the most traumatic abortion of all. (Alton in Hansard, 22 January 1988, col. 1231, p. 633).

The construction of 'post abortion trauma' as a condition that women inevitably suffer as a result of having a 'late' abortion again reinforces the very concept of 'late' abortion. Alton's use of the term 'quickening' is particularly notable, as this woman-oriented term, as Wendy Fyfe has pointed out, is no longer considered legitimate by the medical profession or the law. To use a woman-oriented term, moreover, gives the false impression that both the supposed 'trauma' and the concept 'late' have an essential, empirical, even 'natural' basis in women's lives and consciousness.

David Alton also claimed that women are abused by abortion counsellors and private clinics who coerce them into having abortions for monetary profit:

> Given the psychological and physical consequences to which a woman may be subject, having had an abortion, why do counsellors advise her to have an abortion so late in a pregnancy? . . . About £12 million is estimated to have passed hands in this [private abortion] business last year. (Alton in Hansard, 22 January 1988, cols. 1231–2, p. 633).

Developing this notion that 'late' abortion is a medical racket for profit, Sir Bernard Braine argued that

> With regard to foreign women, can my right Hon. Friend defend a practice whereby we are effectively breaking the law of other countries? Perhaps more importantly, from the point of view of those women, what guarantee is there that a quick abortion at a London clinic will be followed up by the aftercare that is absolutely essential, psychologically and medically, for women who have had an abortion? (Braine in Hansard, 22 January 1988, col. 1267, p. 651).

In portraying women as victims of the medical profession, David Alton again invoked the language of well-established feminist arguments. Again, he constructed an apparent concern for the protection of women which directly contradicted the intent of the Bill to criminalize women and to subordinate them to the so-called 'interests' of the fetus.

This reversal of feminist rhetoric, and reference to feminist political critiques ironically reveals, in one sense, the impact of feminism on the terrain of abortion. However, it also demonstrates the vulnerability of feminism to such anti-feminist reappropriations. There is a profound duplicitousness in the construction of women as victims side-by-side with the construction of the fetus as victim. It is precisely the construction of fetal personhood which threatens women's sovereignty over our own bodies, subordinating us, in the interests of protecting the fetus, to self-appointed (in this case, state) embryo-protectors. Moreover, the construction of women who undergo 'late' abortion as victims of it implies that women who have such abortions would actually want the Bill to pass, would be *advocates* of the Bill and would benefit from the 'protection' it supposedly offered them.

However, statements such as the following by Jill Knight reveal the fallacy of the professed intent of Alton supporters to protect women:

the overwhelming number of babies aborted after 18 weeks, about which we are concerned today, are not handicapped. They are perfectly normal children *whose only crime is that their mothers do not want them* . . . I am worried about the opinion that a handicapped person has a right to live *only as long as its mother wants it.* (Knight in Hansard, 22 January 1988, cols. 1249–50, p. 634; my emphasis).

Here, the interests of pregnant women were explicitly set in opposition to the 'right to life' of their fetuses (whether 'perfectly normal and healthy' or 'handicapped'). The description of the 'crime' of the 'babies' (sic) as being unwanted suggests that not wanting to have a baby is the 'real crime'. Fetal life and fetal 'rights' are construed as dependent upon and endangered by the 'wants' of pregnant women. A woman's desire not to continue pregnancy is constructed as a criminal want.[3] A pregnant woman is implicitly understood as a fetal 'enemy' (an 'enemy without', as it were).

David Alton also argued that the doctors and nurses who perform them are victims of 'late' abortion. As evidence of such victimization, he quoted from a letter which he said he had received from a nurse stating that s/he did not 'know which is worse, those [abortions] done in theatre, where you see the uterine contents being sucked into a bottle or seeing the bruised bodies of these always perfectly formed foetuses . . .' (Alton in Hansard, 22 January 1988, col. 1233, p. 634). Alton further argued that 'late' abortion 'is a corrupting and degrading business for the medical staff who become the destroyer instead of defender of life' (Alton in Hansard, 22 January 1988, col. 1233, p. 634). He also claimed in Committee that obstetricians and gynaecologists are being driven from the profession because of their repugnance for 'late' abortions (Alton in *Parliamentary Debates,* 24 March 1988 (afternoon), col. 5). Given that, by law, doctors may conscientiously object to performing abortions (and in fact, except in emergencies, have the right to refuse to treat any patient as long as they refer her/him to another doctor (British Medical Association, 1988, p. 34)), this latter claim was clearly duplicitous. The implication of all these statements that doctors and nurses are forced to perform abortions, is simply not true, Moreover, this characterization of abortionists as victims contradicts the construction of abortionists as coercing women into having 'late' abortions for their (doctor's) profit. Most importantly, it contradicts the actual intent of the Bill which would have explicitly criminalized medical staff who perform abortions after 18 weeks.

These contradictory definitions of 'criminal' and 'victim' (the adversaries in the abortion context) are underpinned by and reveal the fundamental tension in the definition of ('late') abortion as a criminal act. Abortion is constructed as, in itself, an adversarial act. However, the adversarial definition of abortion in the Alton debate does not simply reflect the idiosyncratic mindsets of particular parliamentarians, but indeed, reflects two, more fundamental, factors. There are, first, the adversarial nature of the legal context wherein the adversarial definition of abortion is elaborated and second, an implicitly adversarial definition of pregnancy.

The adversarial nature of law and pregnancy

The adversarial construction of abortion reflects and derives, in part, from the nature and structure of the legal system itself, which is by nature adversarial. The territory of the law (jurisdiction) is conflict, and the role and process of the law (jurisprudence) is to mediate conflict. In turn, because the law exists to arbitrate, all issues or questions which it addresses are constructed in terms of conflict. Thus, law constructs disputes even as it mediates them. The adversarial character of law is particularly evident in the context of criminal law, where the category 'crime' denotes violation and implies violators (criminals) and violated (victims). Criminal law provides a punitive definition of conflict in terms of offences (against persons, property and the law itself) and provides a framework and sanction for punishment. Thus, criminal law seems implicitly to take a victim-oriented perspective, where the victims of crime are both those entities understood as offended against and the state (which makes laws).[4]

As a legal question, abortion must be framed within the jurisdiction of law and subject to its adversarially oriented jurisprudence. *It must necessarily be defined in terms of conflicts of interest*. However, even within the conflict orientation of the law, it would be possible to imagine illegal abortion being defined as one which involves negligent endangerment by the abortionist of women undergoing the procedure. In this construction of 'criminal abortion', the conflict would be defined in terms of violence against women: the state would be taking the perspective of the woman as victim. Moreover, the conflict in the abortion question could be defined as between the power of the state and the rights of women. Hence, as was the case in Canada (until recently), it could be ruled that state restriction of abortion violates women's rights; thereby effectively removing, by law, its own jurisdiction over abortion.

However, as we have seen, both the existing law on abortion in Britain and the Alton Bill have defined the conflict of abortion as among the alleged interests of women, the fetus and the medical profession. The *site* of conflict is the pregnant woman, that is, between a woman and part of her own pregnant body. Underlying this construction of the abortion crime 'child destruction' are, as I have pointed out, the presumptions that: (a) a pregnant woman is actually two persons; and (b) a woman's fetus is endangered by her (e.g. her potential desire to discontinue her pregnancy is evidence of essentially conflicting interests between mother and fetus). Thus, the definition of abortion as an adversarial act rests on a preconditional construction of pregnancy as a hostile relationship between two entities. As David Alton argued: 'The answer can never be to kill one of the two patients who confronts the doctor' (Alton in Hansard, 22 January, 1988, col. 1235, p. 635). Or, as Sir Bernard Braine reiterated in Committee debates: 'Surely the highest quality of advice and diagnostic experience should be provided when two lives are involved – one of which is to be destroyed' (Braine in *Parliamentary Debates,* 24 March 1988 (morning) col. 49). An understanding of abortion as an adversarial act is predicated on an understanding of pregnancy as an adversarial condition. Without the latter, the former would make no sense.

Abortion as a conflict of 'rights': the question of jurisdiction

The construction of criminal 'late' abortion in the Alton parliamentary debate was expressed in terms of another adversarial legal construct, the language of 'rights'. The legal concept of rights is itself an adversarial territorial concept. Rights are either entitling, that is, claiming territory or liberties (as in property rights or the right to free expression), or protective (as in civil rights, the protection of individuals against violations by the state or by other institutions and individuals). Consistent with the oppositional framework of law, a central focus of the Alton debate was the construction of opposing categories of rights and interests. This construction of conflicts of rights had both a jurisdictional and a eugenic dimension.

The conflict over who has jurisdiction over the question of abortion was articulated through the construction of three categories of rights: the rights of Parliament, the rights of fetuses and the rights of women. It was strongly asserted throughout the Alton debate, mostly by the pro-Alton bench, that the question of abortion belongs under the jurisdiction of Parliament: 'Those who oppose the Bill talk about the right to choose. Parliament has a right to choose too' (Smith in Hansard, 22 January 1988, col. 1256, p. 645). More significantly, the right of Parliament to mediate the question of abortion was seen as expressly derived from the assumption that fetuses have rights, and that it is therefore the role of Parliament to represent those rights:

> On the argument about the right to choose, what about the rights of the unborn child? Since it cannot exercise those rights for itself, is it not the job of the elected Parliament to exercise them on its behalf? It is the job of Parliament to protect the rights of the unborn child and it is the right of Parliament to legislate on the matter. (Smith in Hansard, 22 January 1988, col. 1256, p. 645).

This argument implicitly supported the idea that women's interests are inherently adversarial to fetal 'rights'. It assumed that pregnant women cannot represent the 'interests' of their fetus(es). Only Parliament can speak for the fetus; the right of Parliament is thereby its 'right' to the status of fetus-protector. In this formulation, women's rights are thus subordinated to the 'rights' of fetuses.

> The argument often used against the Bill is that a woman has the right to choose. We have never been so well informed about contraception as we are today, so a woman has the right to choose not to become pregnant. Once she becomes pregnant she does not have an automatic right to destroy the child in her womb, the child has rights too. The child has rights in law. There have been cases in which people have sued on behalf of the unborn child and won. Choice should not be given only to one person. There is no one to speak for the child but us. (Knight in Hansard, 22 January 1988, col. 1251, p. 643).

Because the 'rights' of fetuses were asserted through the 'rights' and voice of Parliament, the fetus-protector, women's rights would actually be subordinated to the will and terms of Parliament. 'Embryo protection' is a construct which locates the agency of the state within a woman's body. It serves as both a justification and a front for state control of women's reproduction. Ironically, parliamentary fetal-centredness was again constructed through subversion of the feminist insistence upon a woman's 'right to choose', which aimed to secure women's access to legal abortion.

The 'right of Parliament' was also a thinly veiled appeal to the right of men to decide about abortion. Replying to Alton opponent Clare Short's criticism of the question of abortion being decided by a male-dominated Parliament, one pro-Alton MP, Elisabeth Peacock, argued that

> The House is now undecided about whether it should be allowed to legislate on issues that affect women, but that has been happening for centuries. There has always been a male-dominated House of Commons legislating for women. Why should that change today? (Peacock in Hansard, 22 January 1988, col. 1292, p. 663).

It is all the more disturbing that this defence of the 'right' of men to decide on questions that only affect women was forwarded by one of the few women in Parliament. However, it is equally true, perhaps owing to the presence of women in Parliament, that even as the legitimacy of men legislating for women was questioned, the state's jurisdictional claim on the issue of abortion also continued to be in question.[5]

Rights and the eugenic opposition

The eugenic dimension of the debate was chiefly introduced by the parliamentary opponents to the Alton Bill. Just as David Alton relied on advances in neonatal technology to justify the restriction of legal abortion, so anti-Alton MPs relied on the limitations in pre-natal diagnostic technology to justify the continuing legality of 'late' abortions. They argued that the limitations of technological capabilities for diagnosing fetal 'disability' (e.g. results of some tests are not available until after 18 weeks) create a moral imperative for women/parents to have the right to terminate pregnancy after 18 weeks. The following extracts represent the anti-Alton eugenics-based argument:

> I do not believe that we should be in the business of bringing more and more unwanted children into our society. I believe that, ultimately, a woman must have the last say on whether she wants to bear a handicapped child. (Moonie in Hansard, 22 January 1988, col. 1248, p. 641).

> It is essential to give a choice to mothers who may be passing on genetic defects. (Wigly in Hansard, 22 January 1988, col. 1270, p. 652).

> It is up to the parents to decide whether they wish to have a grossly disabled child. (Mackay in Hansard, 22 January 1988, col. 1237, p. 636).

These arguments also reconstituted the original feminist meaning of a woman's 'right to choose'. Although, they (arguably) reflected awareness of the fact that women, with no significant social support system, bear the heavy burden of caring for physically 'disabled' children, these arguments none the less constructed the legitimacy of abortion in eugenic, rather than woman-centred terms. Abortion was not considered legitimate because a woman has the 'right' to control her own body (a position which would not dictate the reasons why a woman might want a termination).

The construction of women's 'right' to (late) abortion in relation to eugenic considerations, particularly as an oppositional position to the Alton Bill, has deeply disturbing implications for women. First, it defines women's 'rights' in terms of eugenics; the 'right' to make eugenic decisions. Second, it does not challenge the adversarial construction of abortion, but rather supports this premiss. It is a special-case argument, that women should have access to 'late' abortions on an exemption basis. Like the pro-Alton position, moreover, it is a fetal-centred argument. Thus, the anti-Alton philosophy in the parliamentary debate did not challenge but rather supported the fundamental terms of the pro-Alton philosophy; that abortion is about fetuses. Moreover, as an opposition argument, the eugenic 'rights' position was a weak and contradictory defence for women's access to abortion. Indeed, it established eugenic grounds to justify the extension of state jurisdiction over women's sexuality and reproduction. It also effectively opened the door for David Alton to express repugnance for the idea of selective breeding and to allude to a Nazi-like programme of racial genocide thus articulating an emotively powerful argument against women's access to ('late') abortion.

Conclusion

The parliamentary debate on the Alton Bill, though it did not ultimately pass into law, was successful in several respects in shifting the terrain of the meaning of abortion. These shifts included: the successful introduction of the concept of 'late' abortion at 18 weeks; the increasing degree of reliance on medical/scientific technology (in terms both of its capabilities and limitations) to define the meaning of abortion in both fetalist and eugenic terms; and the expropriation and subversion of feminist rhetoric and political arguments to serve anti-feminist or non woman-centred political agendas (e.g. anti-abortion and eugenic agendas).

These 'successes' of the Alton debate, particularly the latter reconstitution of feminism, raise serious questions for the future of feminist politics in the area of women's 'reproductive rights'. Given the evidence of the Alton debate, I would argue that we must focus our attention at two levels: (a) the question of feminists working within the context of law; and (b) the terms of our arguments.

As I have tried to show in this section, the adversarial construction of abortion is not confined to the specific terms of the Alton debate. Rather, this understanding of abortion reflects the adversarial framework and process of the law itself. Much of the history of feminist politics on the issue of abortion has been within the realm of law-making, including: defensive campaigns against anti-abortion initiatives such as the Alton Bill; strategies for introducing legalized abortion (such as in the US *Roe* v. *Wade* test case); and efforts, such as those in Canada, to decriminalize abortion by removing the question from the scope of the law. The question remains, however, whether it is possible for feminists to operate on feminist terms within the law, and if so, how that might be accomplished. The Alton debate and Bill, at the very least, reflect how uncomfortably the question of abortion fits into the law, but perhaps more significantly, how unable the law, an adversarial model of social relations, is to reflect or serve women's experiences and interests, particularly in the context of reproduction.

The second question facing feminists in Britain in the wake of the Alton Bill and debate is whether we can rely any longer on the terms and slogans of our resistance campaigns for 'reproductive rights' developed over the past two decades. It is clear in the Alton case (and in current cases elsewhere, e.g. the USA, Canada), that attacks on women's 'reproductive rights' are more than simply legislative. They are also rhetorical and ideological. The co-option of feminist language and ideas to attack their spirit and intent is one of the most disturbing and problematic dimensions of current anti-abortion politics. It is clearly necessary for us to re-examine the language, slogans and concepts, such as the adversarial concept of 'rights' and the liberal concept of 'choice', that we have relied upon in our struggles in the past. We must understand the contradictions that inhere in our words because it seems that these contradictions are weak links, points of vulnerability and entry to those who wish to subvert their feminist intent. In particular, we must challenge the construction of pregnant women as two (hostile) persons. Do we accept this strange concept that one is a territorial conflict of two? Is it not also possible to understand a pregnant woman as one person, or as Sarah Franklin has put it, 'one who becomes two', but is still one in that becoming?

It has been, however, equally true in the past that feminist insights have changed the terms of debate in positive ways. We must remember that at the time, the slogans 'woman's reproductive rights', 'women's rights to choose' and the perhaps still viable 'our bodies, ourselves', were conceptual leaps which galvanized the spirit of feminism, not simply in terms of resistance, but also in terms of feminists creating alternatives to improve the quality of life for women. Our task now is one of terrible necessity, but at the same time and in the light of our own history as feminists, part of the continuing project of generating empowering possibilities for women.

Notes

1   Eugenics is the philosophy and science of improvement of the human race by genetic means and the idea of improving physical and mental characteristics by selective parenthood. It was the basis of compulsory sterilization laws passed in many countries in the early twentieth century and the Nazi 'racial hygiene' programme. There are two types of eugenics, 'positive' and 'negative'. 'Positive' eugenics is the idea and practice of increasing the propagation of 'desirable' human types. Pronatalist policies of restricting access to contraception or abortion for women of 'desirable' race, class, etc., for example, can be described as 'positive' eugenics. 'Negative' eugenics is the idea and practice of decreasing the propagation of 'handicapped' or human types otherwise defined as 'undesirable'. The term today is used in particular to describe selective abortion of (for example, 'handicapped') fetuses (also called 'therapeutic abortion'). 'Negative' eugenics are advocated by population control programmes.
2   The Granville Williams text (1983) is a criminal law textbook. As such, it provides an index of current (up to 1983) legal principles, or rules of law.
3   In fact, even within the existing legal precedent, intent is the key concept defining the crime of 'child destruction' as 'limited to *willful* acts' (Williams 1983, p. 289; my emphasis).
4   While on the one hand, the perspective of criminal law can be said to be 'victim oriented', at the same time there are sectors of criminal law, for example rape law, where the opposite appears to be the case.
5   I would like to thank Sarah Franklin for making this observation.

Section 4

Fetal fascinations: new dimensions to the medical-scientific construction of fetal personhood[1]

SARAH FRANKLIN

As is evident from all of the contributions to this chapter, the issue of fetal personhood or fetal rights has become increasingly significant within contemporary public debates over reproduction, and correspondingly within feminist analyses of these. In her introduction contextualizing the Alton Bill, Maureen McNeil has described the fetus as one of the 'new oppressed' under Thatcherism, a development which suggests both a backlash against feminism and a significant shift in the terms of the abortion debate (see further McNeil, Chapter 8). As Wendy Fyfe went on to argue, the emergence of fetal personhood and fetal rights can be seen as a development which is consistent with the increasing medicalization of the abortion debate, and the reliance upon abstract scientific criteria, such as 'viability', to define the abortion question. Deborah Steinberg has further noted the significance of fetal personhood and fetal rights in the context of the legal framing of the abortion question, drawing attention to the implications for women of the construction of a conflict of interest between the fetus and the mother in legal terms. Finally, as Tessa Randles argues in Section 5, fetal personhood and fetal rights figured centrally in the media coverage of the Alton Bill.

What emerges from these investigations is a clear indication of the significance of what has come to be known as 'fetal personhood' in the debate over abortion. Feminists such as Rosalind Petchesky (1984, 1987) and Janet Gallagher (1985) were among the first to note this shift and to develop a feminist critique of its implications for women. Since the early 1980s, it has become an increasingly significant component of feminist analyses of various reproductive issues, from new reproductive technologies, such as prenatal diagnosis and *in vitro* fertilization, to fetal organ transplants, enforced Caesarian sections and, of course, the continuing struggle for abortion rights. The aim of this section is to investigate the concept of fetal personhood more deeply, in an effort to delineate its emerging dimensions as a cultural category. In the analysis offered, the convergence between emerging scientific constructions of fetal personhood and the use of these in arguments against abortion are analyzed from two perspectives: their construction teleologically and ontologically. This is described as the TIME–LIFE construction of the fetus, referring to both its discursive content and the public, high-profile media forms from which it draws its strength.

Fetal ontology: LIFE

The abortion debate is now more than ever an explicit struggle over the definition of a key set of 'natural facts', the so-called 'facts of life'. The staple anti-abortion argument that 'life begins at conception' once referred to the idea that all human life is sacred because it was created by God, and thus for a divine purpose. The Alton campaign was part of a general move away from this argument by anti-abortionists, through which religious definitions of life are replaced by biological ones. As Petchesky has argued,

> Increasingly, in response to accusations of religious bias and violations of church–state separation, the evidence marshaled by the anti-abortionists to affirm the personhood of the fetus is not its alleged possession of a soul, but its possession of a human body and genotype. (Petchesky, 1984, p. 334).

It is now biological life that is referred to in the phrase 'life begins at conception', biological *human* life, which has an inherent *biological* purpose, or teleology. As Petchesky has also noted, the role of medical technologies has been central in bringing about this shift:

> Aware of cultural trends, the current leadership of the anti-abortion movement has made a conscious strategic shift from religious discourses and authorities to medico-technical ones, in its efforts to win over the courts, the legislatures and the popular 'hearts and minds'. (Petchesky, 1987, p. 58).

The construction of the fetus as separate, as an individual in its own right, deserving of state protection and medical attention, has been a central component in the 'biologization' of anti-abortion rhetoric. This construction of fetal separateness can be analyzed from a variety of perspectives, in terms of historical changes, legal discourses, visual representations, or medical expertise. By analyzing the construction of fetal separateness and individuality in terms of *ontology* and *teleology* in this section, I am specifically attempting to investigate its naturalization through *biological* discourses, of which the medico-technical rhetoric described by Petchesky is a primary instance. Hence, in discussing the discursive construction of fetal personhood in terms of ontology and teleology, I will consider the discursive processes which naturalize fetal being (ontology) and fetal development (teleology).

Ontology is the philosophical study of being or existence. It is a necessary concept to describe that aspect of the cultural construction of personhood which concerns the essence and origins of a human being. In Western culture, the origin story of coming into being is a natural one, indeed a biological one, to be precise. Hence, persons 'originate' at conception: it is biological facts that cause them to be, to come into existence, as it were. Biology is also the dominant discourse informing our constructions of ontogeny, the development of the human individual, and phylogeny, the emergence of the human species (through the process of evolution). Consequently, the 'biological facts' of conception, pregnancy and fetal life are not only powerful as authoritative forms of *knowledge*, they are powerful *symbolically*, as key cultural resources in the construction of personhood. It is, therefore, not at all surprising that they should become such powerful sources of meaning in contemporary debates around abortion.

However, it is only since the fetus has emerged as a focus of increasing medical and biological attention that these areas of knowledge and expertise have become so much more valuable to the anti-abortion lobby. A shift away from a primary focus on maternal health within the medical literature was a prerequisite for the anti-abortion lobby to take up this discourse. This shift is explicitly described by the editors of a medical textbook on fetal physiology published in the mid-1970s:

> The practice of perinatal medicine started when obstetricians, *having resolved most of the problems of the mother,* turned their attention to the fetus. Recording of the fetal heart rate has for many years been the only window available to the obstetrician through which to observe the condition of the fetus – a cloudy view on a world full of activity. It was therefore natural that efforts should be made to improve the technology of observation . . . This basic information is vital in the ultimate establishment of successful intra-uterine therapy. (Beard and Nathanielsz, 1976, p. v; emphasis added).

According to this source, these recent developments 'coincided with the growing recognition that the first priority of a mother in particular and of society in general is the delivery of a baby capable of reaching his or her full potential in adult life' (Beard and Nathanielsz, 1976, p. v). Scientists have long found the subject of intra-uterine life and early human development a fascinating puzzle in and of itself, and it is this motive, as much as any altruistic one, which has propelled this area of science forward at such a terrific pace over the last two decades. Just as the anti-abortion lobby, the textbook cited above is dedicated to 'those who have the interests of the fetus at heart' (Beard and Nathanielsz, 1976, p. vi).

The emergence of the fetus in the medical literature is the result of a significant shift away from the perception of it as a passive, semi-parasitic 'passenger' in the womb. As one fetologist describes this shift,

> The fetus is thought of nowadays not as an inert passenger in pregnancy but, rather, as in command of it. The fetus, in collaboration with the placenta, (a) ensures the endocrine success of pregnancy, (b) induces changes in maternal physiology which make her a suitable host, (c) is responsible for solving the immunological problems raised by its intimate contact with its mother, and (d) determines the duration of pregnancy. (Findlay, 1984, p. 96).

Whereas a division of interests between the fetus and the mother had long been seen to exist, even if only as two different biological systems, the fetus was previously regarded as weakly parasitic, but essentially passive – 'an inert passenger'. It is the complete reversal of this previous view which is most strikingly apparent in this passage. Not only is the fetus now the active partner, taking 'command' of pregnancy, but in fact it is the dominant partner, with a determining role in pregnancy. What is also evident in this passage is that the fetus is not only attributed agency, 'induc[ing] changes in maternal physiology', and individuality, but it is attributed a will of its own and even an ability to undertake responsibility for its own interests. In sum, the fetus is here defined as an individual agent, who is separate from the mother and has its own distinct interests of which it is both aware and capable of acting on.

This view of the fetus is now well established. As another fetal expert writes:

> The fetus is far from a quiescent, passively-growing product of conception tucked neatly away in its protected uterine environment. Whilst undoubtedly dependent on the mother's nutrient supplies for its growth and survival, it nonetheless enjoys considerable independence in the regulation of its own development. Indeed, the fetus also exerts effects on *maternal* physiology via hormones secreted by the placenta into the maternal circulation which in part determine the mother's ability to meet the metabolic requirements of pregnancy. (Johnson and Everitt, 1988, p. 265; original emphasis).

Again, the emphasis is not only on fetal separateness and fetal independence, but on its ability to control the mother, rather than being controlled by her. This reversal of agency and attribution to the fetus of a determining role in pregnancy marks a significant departure from previous medical and scientific constructions of fetal life.

The emphasis on fetal separateness is heavily stressed in the pro-Alton campaign literature distributed by LIFE, the anti-abortion lobby that played a major role in the Alton campaign.[2] In a lecture entitled 'The Humanity of the Fetus', which has been reprinted as a LIFE pamphlet, a medical professor claims that

> The genetic pattern of this separate individual is as different to the mother as it is to the father. It can in no way be considered as part of the father, nor can it in any way be considered part of the mother. This new identity is unique. (Zachery, n.d.).

Another LIFE pamphlet, entitled 'Abortion and Human Rights', claims that 'from the beginning the unborn baby is a separate, unique individual. At no stage is he or she "part of" the mother.' Similarly on a wallchart entitled 'How You Grew Before Birth', distributed by Human Life Educational Aids and designed for use in schools, this theme is repeated: '*Your blood system was always quite separate from your mother's, and your blood groups may be different. You are a separate person.* You have your own inherited genes [and] your own unique set of fingerprints' (original emphasis).

The construction of the mother is often ambiguous in these accounts. She is fragmented into being and non-being, at once the mother and the maternal physiology that constitutes the fetal environment. In the passage cited earlier, the mother is not only commanded by the fetus but defined by it. That it is the fetus who makes of her 'a suitable host' defines her role precisely: her existence is defined by the needs of the fetus, the little commander in the womb. Importantly, there is a clear antagonism set up between the fetus and its 'host', thus replicating in scientific discourse the same conflict of interest defined by Steinberg in Section 3 above dealing with the law. The 'problems which are raised' for the fetus 'by its intimate contact with its mother' suggest a threat, as does the suggestion that the mother be made into a 'suitable host'. Finally, the role of the fetus in 'determining the duration of pregnancy' suggests the risk of staying in this hostile environment too long and ensures that the fetus can escape. In sum, as Findlay writes, 'the fetus is an egoist, not merely a helpless dependant. Its purpose is to see that its own needs are served' (Findlay, 1984, p. 83).

Both the description of the mother and the fetus in this new discourse of 'fetology' correspond directly to the rhetoric of the Alton campaign. The emphasis upon the active role of the fetus during pregnancy and the attribution to it of a will that is independent of the mother, of interests that conflict with hers in these scientific accounts give both legitimacy and authority to the argument put forward by the Alton campaign that it is a separate human being, deserving of public protection and sympathy. As a pro-Alton poster claimed:

> He has likes or dislikes for sweet or sour fluids; he is developing tastes for music and may jump up and down to the beat; he is learning to recognise his mother's voice; he can be alarmed by loud bangs, and he is, of course, sensitive to pain.

The emphasis on fetal autonomy evident in the medical scientific texts is visually achieved through the use of scientific photography, such as that of the Swedish photojournalist Lennart Nilsson. Nilsson's close-up colour photography of fetuses, many of which were recovered from late abortions, first became the subject of international acclaim in his photo-essay documenting early human development, published in *LIFE* magazine in 1965.[3] Since then, it has featured centrally in the imagery of anti-abortion campaigns, including Alton's, which drew heavily upon this source of potent photo-realist propaganda. Indeed, the bold, full-colour fetal portraits produced by Nilsson have proved to be an invaluable armature of emotive images, made to order for the anti-abortionists' crusade to make of fetal imagery an iconography of fetal innocence. In the face of these portraits of fetal tranquillity (actually portraits of fetal post-mortems), the spectre of bodily dismemberment strikes an especially powerful chord.

These photographs offer a specific set of points of identification with the fetus which are enhanced by the accompanying texts. The primary emphasis is on the miracle of fetal development and survival through the arduous journey of pregnancy. 'The little fetus that could' might have been the most appropriate subtitle for the article in this respect. The fetus is also presented as *physically very sensitive,* as continually under threat of *something going wrong* with its development, and hence as an agent responsible for the task of its own miraculous transformation from a kidney bean-sized encephaloid into a 'baby' at 28 weeks gestation where the story ends.

LIFE has made extensive use of Nilsson's photography as part of their anti-abortion campaigns. The LIFE poster most commonly seen in support of the Alton Bill was an enlarged section of a Nilsson photograph of a fetus 'sucking its thumb'. Across the top is printed 'Choose Life' in bold letters. LIFE also distributes reprints of Nilsson's 1965 photo-essay from *LIFE* magazine, entitled the 'Drama of Life Before Birth', in which many of the now-famous images of fetal development were originally published (Nilsson, 1965). It was one of Nilsson's photographs that was reproduced as a postcard for the showering of Parliament during the Alton debate, and Nilsson's photographs are also used in LIFE videos which argue for fetal rights.

The position of the spectator constructed by these images is most significantly defined by the structuring absence of the mother, who is replaced by empty space. Equally invisible are the means by which these images were produced, which must have involved highly invasive technological manoeuvres in order to produce 'the first portrait ever made of a living embryo inside its mother's womb', as is claimed in the article where they originally appeared (*TIME* Inc., 1980 [1965], p. 1). Set against a black backdrop, these round fetal orbs resemble nothing more than a sort of organic spacecraft, floating in a void. Through this technique, the conditions for spectator recognition of and identification with the fetus are achieved on the basis of its separation and individuation from the mother. The fetus is here represented as autonomous, intact and at peace, in direct contrast to the Alton portrayal of the fetus in the woman's body as vulnerable to a violent disintegration.

In sum, the convergence between the scientific discourse of 'fetology' and the visual discourse of fetal autonomy produces a specific construction of fetal personhood which has proved highly compatible with the strategy of contemporary anti-abortionists to win state protection for the fetus and thus a ban on all abortions. These discourses have been skilfully popularized and widely disseminated by anti-abortion campaigners both in Britain and in the USA. What is at stake in both the discursive construction of the fetus in scientific accounts and the visual representation of it through scientific photography is the cultural construction of the natural facts of pregnancy. These 'natural facts' have been elaborated in such a manner as to produce a social category of fetal personhood which has an enhanced ontological validity and specificity, which is of particular value to the anti-abortionists because of its authoritative scientific pedigree.

Two components of this ontological construction are of particular importance to the contemporary debate around abortion. One is the extensive reliance upon high technology to construct this definition of fetal being, including both medical scientific and visual technologies. The second is the processes of separation involved in this construction: of the fetus from the mother, and of the social from the biological. The ontology of fetal being is entirely asocial. It is a definition of personhood constructed entirely out of 'natural facts', although these are themselves, of course, socially constructed. In the following subsection, I hope to demonstrate how these processes of separation are enhanced through constructions of fetal teleology. The implications of these constructions for the abortion debate are discussed further in the concluding remarks to this section.

TIME: fetal teleology

In addition to their attentiveness to the details of fetal ontology, medico-scientific constructions of the fetus are particularly notable for their fascination with fetal development. Historically, the science of embryology has held a privileged place in Western definitions of personhood, resulting from the significance attached in all cultures to ideas about conception, or 'coming into being', in the formation of cultural beliefs about kinship, personhood and the body.[4] As has already been noted, biological science provides not only a set of facts about conception, but also a key source of symbolic material through which these various beliefs are given cultural meaning.

A key component of the model of conception ascribed to in Western culture is the idea of the *unique bio-genetic individuality* of each conceptus. Thus, from the moment of fertilization, in every cell that emerges from that first meiotic division, there is the genetic blueprint for a unique individual (except in the case of identical twins). Symbolically, this construction of conception is the basis for the dominant model of bipartisan kinship operative in contemporary society: each parent makes an equal and distinct biogenetic contribution to the formation of a new person who is thus equally a part of both father and mother, a product of their biogenetic union but itself biogenetically unique (see Schneider, 1978).

We are currently living in an era which has seen a significant proliferation of genetic discourses about not only conception but virtually every facet of human existence. Genetic fingerprinting, prenatal diagnosis, genetic counselling, genetic engineering and the project to map the human genome are all evidence of a massive resurgence of genetic determinism which is currently in progress (see Spallone, 1989). The link between the renewed fascination for fetal development and this resurgence of genetic determinism is the embryo, whose processes of development promise to reveal the secrets of genetic determinism, not uncommonly referred to as 'the secrets of life'. The concepts of *development* and *teleology* are thus key loci in the cultural construction of the category of fetal personhood. Consequently, it is not surprising to see their emergence on the abortion front.

Teleology is the study of 'manifestations of design or purpose in natural processes or occurences' *(American Heritage Dictionary, 1969, p. 1323)* and in this context is drawn upon to emphasize the manner in which both the concepts of biological life force and of genetic determinism are used to establish not only fetal personhood and fetal individuality, but fetal potentiality and purpose as well. The 'miracle' of fetal development as a biological process, and the stamp of biogenetic uniqueness which is replicated throughout its development, are drawn upon again and again in the current public debate about abortion. The emphasis upon what the fetus is going to become, upon its genetically determined development, inevitably leads to a focus upon its developmental potential as a person, as an individual human being with an entire life course mapped out for it from the moment of conception. There is thus not only a focus upon the fact that it is constitutionally (ontologically) an individual person, but on the fact that it is developmentally a potential human adult. There is thus a sense in which the conceptus is provided with an entire life cycle through the construction of its developmental potential, which is simultaneously naturalized and authorized through its representation as biological fact.

This teleological construction of the 'natural facts' of pregnancy has become a major component in the anti-abortion argument that 'life begins at conception'. 'Human life begins at conception . . . from the beginning the unborn baby is a separate, unique individual . . . These are scientific facts. Deny them and you fly in the face of modern genetics and embryology', argues a LIFE pamphlet entitled *'Abortion and Human Rights'*. 'At the time fertilisation occurs . . . this new cell has *within itself* all that is necessary to ensure its continuous development into an adult person', argues a medical professor in another LIFE pamphlet (Zachery, n.d., p. 3). Nilsson's photographic series on 'Life Before Birth' also gives priority to the developmental aspect of fetal existence. In the original article in LIFE magazine, each photograph is accompanied by a detailed text explaining the precise stages of physiological development illustrated by the photographs. The fingers and toes, the eyelids and nostrils, the heart and other vital organs are all documented as part of the 'drama' of life's unfolding. Similarly, on the LIFE wallchart entitled 'How You Grew Before Birth' this theme is repeated. The chart claims, 'Bodily and personal characteristics are developing to your own unique pattern laid down at the time of your conception . . . By the end of your first three months of life as an unborn baby everything you will need when born is present in miniature.'

The individuality of the fetus/embryo has also been the basis for the categorization of early human development in terms of stages of growth. This is already evident in the use of the concept of viability to demarcate a critical stage of pregnancy, replacing, as Wendy Fyfe has noted, the previous concept of quickening with a term that specifically refers to the ability of the fetus to survive independently of the mother, in other words, as a separate individual. This use of individuality to demarcate stages of development is also evident in the more recent distinction (established in the wake of the Warnock Report by the Medical Research Council, the Royal College of Obstetricians and Gynaecologists and the Interim Licensing Authority) between an embryo and a 'pre-embryo', which has become the term used to describe the embryo up to 14 days of development. The definitive 'natural fact' used in the establishment of this 'scientific' distinction is the formation of the so-called 'primitive streak', or emergent spinal column. Until this time, it is argued, the cells of the embryo are undifferentiated in terms of which will become the placenta and the embryo proper (see McLaren, 1987). Hence, it is only after the embryo has differentiated itself from the surrounding placental cells and become an individual entity that it is conferred a new status, the status of having potential human life. This 'human potential' is explicitly defined in terms of individuality. It is precisely the emergence of human individuality, out of previously undifferentiated biological life, which is used to demarcate scientifically the emergence of specifically human potential.[5]

Christine Crowe has described the emergence of the term 'pre-embryo' as an instance of 'strategic classification' (Crowe, 1990, p. 52), thus calling attention to the significance of this distinction having been arrived at in the context of competition between powerful interest groups in the struggle for reproductive control. Significantly, the 14-day distinction was proposed as a legal basis for protecting embryos in Britain in the Human Fertilisation and Embryology Bill (1989). Consistent with the longstanding reliance of parliamentarians upon medical expertise in formulating legislation which affects the products and processes of reproduction, the recent medico-scientific decision that human life begins 14 days after conception has been transferred directly into proposed legislation.

The medico-scientific construction of fetal teleology thus not only appeals to a commonsense or popular understanding of fetal personhood, it is also powerful in the context of the legal profession and has sufficient authority to be translated *verbatim* (or *numeratim*) into legislation. It is thus hardly surprising to find fetal teleology arguments used by anti-abortionists, especially as these medico-scientific constructions of embryonic and fetal development precisely recapitulate and thus enhance the features of fetal ontology which are being used by the anti-abortionists: its unique individuality and its human personhood. Given their authority, it is also not surprising to discover arguments based on the medico-scientific construction of fetal teleology among the *pro*-abortion lobbies. While the moral majority uses the Beethoven argument ('every fetus could be a Beethoven'), the pro-abortion lobby uses the Down's syndrome argument ('every fetus could be genetically defective'). In arguments such as '70 per cent of spina bifida babies die within three years', which are being used to support a woman's right to have an abortion, the construction of the fetus is as a potential human person, which is precisely the argument being used by anti-abortionists to protect it.[6]

Notably, therefore, both pro- and anti-abortion campaigners rely on arguments about the individuality of the fetus/embryo, and its developmental potential, in order to make their case. This is evidence of the extent to which particular constructions of fetal personhood have come to determine the parameters of current debate. What is most evident in this disturbing overlap of arguments from both sides is precisely the degree to which the terms of the debate have been shifted in a manner that makes the arguments *in favour* of a woman's right to choose abortion complicit with the arguments of those who *oppose* abortion. Again, this demonstrates the power of medico-scientific discourse in the battle to define the 'natural facts' of pregnancy, which has become the central site of contestation in the contemporary abortion debate. Moreover, it demonstrates what is at stake in terms of the need to account for this shift in order to put forward an effective opposition. The problem of the increasing emphasis on fetal/embryonic individuality for feminist understandings of the abortion question is discussed further in the conclusion to this chapter.

Whereas the construction of fetal ontology in the scientific literature, scientific photography and in the anti-abortion literature invites identification with the fetus on the basis of its morphological individuality and personhood, the teleological construction of the fetus opens up the possibility of identifying with its developmental personhood, its entire imagined life course and its future as a human adult. All of this is achieved by the priority given to certain biological 'facts' in the construction of fetal personhood, most notably its bio-genetic uniqueness and its potential for biological growth. These biological 'facts' are seen as a force unto themselves, entirely independent of social constraints. Thus, not only is the mother made invisible by these constructions of fetal personhood, but so is society and kinship. The potential for biological life completely obscures all other dimensions of human life, and is seen as a justification in itself for the right to exist.

It has been suggested at the outset of this section that the abortion debate has increasingly become a struggle over the cultural definition of a key set of 'natural facts'. The construction of fetal personhood in terms of ontology and teleology is one example of this process. What is occurring here has a two-fold dimension. First, biology as a force, in and of itself, displaces the social, as is evident in the concept of biological viability as a criterion for fetal personhood, independent of any social considerations (such as the significance of social viability (see p. 156)). Second, what is occurring is the replacement of social categories with biological ones, such as biogenetic fetal individuality and personhood. Biology thus not only obscures social categories, but it becomes the basis for their cultural production. It is this double move, of displacing and replacing the social with the biological, that enables a woman's pregnancy, the work of nurturing a child, the meaning of motherhood, the social meaning of personhood (in terms of kinship, identity, naming, reciprocity, interdependence, etc.) all to be reduced to one dimension, which is that of biological life. It is an awesome measure of the power of medico-scientific discourse that it can accomplish this simultaneous erasure and replacement of something so basic to human social life as reproduction through the power of its exclusive claim to represent the truth of 'natural facts'.

Beyond TIME–LIFE: the social construction of biological categories

So far I have looked at two dimensions of the construction of fetal personhood as a cultural category: its construction in terms of biological life, and its construction in terms of biological time. In doing so, I have tried to show both how the meaning of 'natural facts' or 'the facts of life' are socially constructed through the discourses of biology, and also how discourses of biology, such as 'fetology' are socially constructed out of so-called 'natural facts'. In the concluding part of this section, I have attempted to examine an important meta-discourse that runs through this multilayered process, that is, which holds together the social construction of biology and the construction of social/cultural categories through biological science. This theme is *patriarchal individualism,* and it bears particular significance for the domain of reproduction.

Patriarchal individualism holds together the construction of fetal person-hood in a number of respects, including how it is constructed through power/knowledge or discourse, how it is described through language and metaphor, how it is represented visually, how it is narrated and how it is positioned as a masculine subject. Examples of this include: the construction of the fetus as a patriarchal citizen, the construction of the fetus as the object of patriarchal science, the gendered construction of the fetal self as masculine, and the narration of the fetus in terms of masculine heroism and adventure.

The construction of the fetus as patriarchal citizen is clearly evident in the use of the language of rights and entitlements to state protection which have become staple arguments in anti-abortion rhetoric. This rhetoric of human rights, of liberal democratic values, of entitlement to protection by the state, is founded on the values of *liberté, egalité, fraternité* and the patriarchal 'social contract'. It has been argued by feminists that the model of individual citizenship implicit in the social contract is patriarchal to the extent that it excludes women on the basis of both their reproductive capacity (Patemen, 1988) and their sexuality (Wittig, 1988). Nowhere is this more clearly evident than in the assertion of fetal rights. By its very nature, such a concept threatens the bodily integrity, the individual autonomy and the right to bodily sovereignty of women. Fetal citizenship contradicts the citizenship of women; indeed, it contradicts their individuality. Endowing fetuses with full civil rights ironically confers upon them a status in relation to the patriarchal social contract *which women never had to begin with.* It is thus a double blow, extending feminine disenfranchisement from the patriarchal state, and locating within their bodies a citizen with greater rights to bodily integrity than they have.

The construction of fetal personhood also relies on the individualism of the scientific expert, whose independent, detached, objective stance is the basis for authority and claims to truth (see Keller, 1985). This too is a form of patriarchal individualism, rendered explicit in the long history of patriarchal science as a masculinist epistemology, inextricably bound up in the project of 'conquering' nature, and often most extreme at its points of encounter with women's reproductive capacity (Ehrenreich and English, 1979; Martin, 1987; Laqueur, 1986; Oakley, 1984).

The construction of the fetus in terms of patriarchal individualism is well demonstrated in the following surprisingly candid and personal account of work as an embryologist, written by a leading American scientist in the 1940s:

> I hope that the human being whose biography during the first weeks of [intra-uterine] life is being sketched herewith, is already something more to the reader than a diagram in a book . . . I have heard an embryologist who thought himself impersonal and unsentimental talk affectionately of a handsome three-weeks embryo as 'he'; and speaking for myself, I seldom sit at the microscope to study one of these individuals we call 'specimens' without the thought that here is one who but for the turn of circumstance would have taken his place in the army of the living. (Corner, 1945, p. 37).

Here we see not only the degree of identification that is possible between the male scientist and the (assumed to be) male embryo, but also, in precisely this act of merging of identities by both scientists with the embryo, we see the myth of individualism exposed. Clearly, even male scientists who consider themselves 'impersonal and unsentimental' are not incapable of strong sentiments towards 'these individuals we call "specimens"'.

The fetus as bounded object of patriarchal science, through which the body of the woman in whom the fetus exists is rendered invisible, bears a strong, and not unremarked upon (see Keller, 1985), resemblance to the bounded masculine self formed through a similar psychic process of disavowal of maternal dependence (Chodorow, 1978). Hence, the powerful drive to constitute fetal personhood in terms of separateness, independence and individuality must also be located in relation to these characteristic psychic requirements of 'successful' masculine individuation and identity formation.

This is also evident in the forms of masculine identification with the fetus as hero or adventurer. The construction of fetal personhood through descriptions of the arduous developmental journey, the barriers which must be overcome, the threats which must be conquered, the risks which must be faced, and so forth, all invoke a construction of the fetus as a masculine hero, and of the mother as a hostile environment. The metaphor of space travel is a frequent one: 'Just as an astronaut may spend months preparing to live in the weightless environment of space, so we spend nine months before birth preparing to live in the outside world with its environment of air', explains the LIFE wallchart described earlier. The athleticism of the fetus is another example of this. 'Your skin is well protected in its watery environment by an oily cream – like a channel swimmer', explains the wallchart, or 'the 18 week old fetus is very active, and does a lot of muscle flexing' (Rosenfeld, 1980, p. 18 (postscript to Nilsson), 1965). Certainly, the earlier description of the fetus-commander, preparing his defence-mechanisms against the hostile maternal environment speaks of a particularly militaristic genre of the masculine adventure narrative (*Rambo* fetus).

What is significant, therefore, is the extent to which the theme of patriarchal individualism holds together so many different versions of fetal personhood, while at the same time comprising one of the most exclusionary, masculinist perspectives from which to understand the process of reproduction. What is also significant is how deeply patriarchal these forms of individualism are, constituting the powerful mythology of masculine independence at the same time as they maintain the powerful institutions of patriarchal dominance.

The very term 'individual', meaning *one who cannot be divided,* can only represent the male, as it is precisely the process of one individual becoming two which occurs through a woman's pregnancy. Pregnancy is precisely about one body becoming two, two bodies becoming one, the exact antithesis of in-dividuality.[7] This is, claims Donna Haraway,

> why women have had so much trouble counting as individuals in modern western discourses. Their personal, bounded individuality is compromised by their bodies' troubling talent for making other bodies, whose individuality can take precedence over their own. (Haraway, 1988b, p. 39).

The centrality of patriarchal individualism to the construction of fetal personhood – the language of rights, the language of medical science, the language of in-dividuation and the language of masculine adventure– heroism – poses a similar threat to women's reproductive control. The entire basis of this dominant patriarchal construction prohibits the possibility of a woman-centred perspective on pregnancy, in which the term 'individual' has no meaning.

As the abortion debate moves into the 1990s, a new language of reproductive politics must be foregrounded in terms that challenge the process of biologizing the social in the name of natural science and natural fact. In order to develop terms that are woman-centred and responsive to the realities of women's lives as mothers, workers and persons in society, reproduction must be reclaimed as a social process involving social persons, who are interdependent and whose right to exist is not bound up with notions of radical separateness. The construction of the fetus described in this section is one which mythologizes both the social and the biological, constructing of them categories which affirm a deeply patriarchal model of the reproductive process, both before and after birth. Moving beyond these accounts, and challenging the male-defined perspectives they both attempt to create and affirm, will be increasingly difficult as the state, the legal system and the medical profession converge with their versions of the fetal martyr/victim/hero. Shifting the terms of debate, however, is an increasingly significant component in the struggle to establish a woman-centred territory at the heart of reproductive politics.

Notes

1   I would like to acknowledge the contributions of several people to this section. Thanks to both the members of the Science and Technology Subgroup and the Women Thesis Writers' group, Department of Cultural Studies, University of Birmingham. Particular thanks to Celia Lury and Jackie Stacey for their comments and suggestions.
2   LIFE is not the only anti-abortion campaign to rely heavily on fetal personhood arguments and fetal imagery. The Society for the Protection of Unborn Children (SPUC), for example, has made the 'U' in their logo into a fetal form *in utero*, a tidy encapsulation of the increasing centrality of medico-scientific representations of fetal life to the arguments of anti-abortion campaigners.
3   Nilsson's photography has been extensively reprinted and used to illustrate a wide range of conception narratives. A particularly interesting example of the ways in which his photography has been used to illustrate maternal–fetal bonding and maternal–fetal intimacy, rather than fetal separateness, comes from *Being Born* by Sheila Kitzinger. In the preface to this volume, Kitzinger and Nilsson write: 'For a mother and her child, pregnancy is the time when they were in *the closest partnership, intimately joined together* in an experience which is rarely discussed and often forgotten' (Kitzinger and Nilsson, 1986). This pre-Oedipal (and, it is suggested, often repressed) narrative contrasts sharply with the highly individuated fetus of the accounts discussed in this section.
4   Anthropological debates, such as those surrounding the controversy over societies who believed in 'virgin birth', are a significant source of evidence of the importance of accounts of conception to other cultural belief systems. For a recent discussion of these issues see Delaney (1986), Jorgensen (1985) and Weiner (1978, 1979, 1985).
5   The inextricability of notions of individuality from notions of biological development is well demonstrated in William Coleman's study of *Biology in the Nineteenth Century: Problems of Form, Function and Transformation (1977)*. In Chapter 3, 'Form: Individual Development', Coleman traces the move away from 'cell theory' towards the basis for modern genetics, that is, the chromosomal basis of cell differentiation and development. Coleman also notes the inextricability of studies of development from embryology, which, he argues, was the paramount science within nineteenth-century biology: 'The study of the embryo is the study of development *par excellence* . . . and embryology and its students are representative of the broadest interests and activities of nineteenth century biology', he notes (Coleman, 1977, p. 36). He adds,

> One must note that embryology, in addition to its close conceptual bond with the general idea of development, prospered because of the very immediacy of the events it studied. A complete cycle of development was exhibited by the individual embryo. Nothing in the gradual evolution of plant and

animal species corresponded to the beauty and seeming obviousness of the rapid embryonic transformations working themselves out before the observer's eyes. The embryo offered, furthermore, largely virgin terrain for exploration. (Coleman, 1977, p. 37).

In noting the importance of embryological studies not only for the under-standing of individual development, but in terms of classification, through the use of embryonic stages in the formation of distinctions between species, Coleman illustrates convincingly their centrality to the formation of basic concepts in the life sciences.

6 Interestingly, contemporary Christian ethicists, such as Australia's Norman M. Ford, have adopted the primitive streak argument in theological definitions of personhood. This represents further evidence in support of Petchesky's claim that religiously motivated anti-abortionists have increasingly moved over to medico-scientific language in articulating their arguments. Ford writes:

> The appearance of the primitive streak is an important landmark, indi-cating . . . [the formation of] *one whole multicellular individual living being . . . now integrated . . . to form a single heterogeneous organic body that endures with its own ontological as well as biological identity throughout all its subsequent stages of growth and development. A new human individual begins [here], informed or actuated by . . . a life-principle or soul that arises through the power of God. The appearance of [the] primitive streak signals that [the] embryo proper and human individual has been formed and begun to exist.* (Ford 1988, p. 172; original emphasis).

Again, the emphasis on individuality is paramount in this account. It is defini-tive of a distinctive and individual humanity that will inform all subsequent stages of development.

7 A reverse concept, of patriarchal (capitalist) *dividualism,* is suggested by Maria Mies in her challenge to the arguments of Lori Andrews. Andrews advocates a radical free-market approach to reproductive rights (a woman's body is her private property to sell if she so wishes). As Mies points out, the logical conclusion of such an argument is that 'If the *individual* – the undivided person – has been divided up into his/her saleable parts, the individual has disappeared . . . What is left is an assembly of parts. *The bourgeois individual has eliminated itself'* (Mies, 1988, p. 236; original emphasis). Here again, it is the contradiction between the centrality of in-dividuality to the liberal democratic state and the 'dividuality' inherent in women's reproductive potential (or in the commodification of body parts) that is being underscored.

Section 5

The Alton Bill and the media's 'consensual' position

TESS RANDLES

The media's ability to shape public debate, and the position and status it enjoys as 'independent arbiter', are central themes in this section, which is based on a study of some 137 articles covering the Alton Bill debate in the period from October 1987 to May 1988. The reports were obtained from a cross-section of newspapers which included: the *Guardian, The Independent, The Times,* the *Daily Mail,* the *Express,* the *Mirror,* the *Sun* and the *Birmingham Daily News.* By looking at the common themes, assumptions, imagery and language, as well as the suppressions, marginalizations and exclusions of certain issues, a particular picture of the debate as it was portrayed in the press emerged.

One of the aims of this section is to investigate the mechanisms by which a particular agenda of the abortion debate was shaped in the press, and how this became 'the' framework within which 'dominant' meanings were given priority, at the cost of subordinating women's definitions of abortion, as well as women's status as decision-makers. Particular attention will be paid to the ways in which notions of science and objectivity have, in different ways, come to structure the debate. In the following discussion the focus will be first, on how the media are able to secure dominant readings and, second, on their application to the Alton Bill.

The media and the construction of consensus

It has been widely argued (Hall *et al.,* 1978; Hartley, Goulden and O'Sullivan, 1985; Fiske, 1987; Masterman, 1985) that the media are, in general terms, able to promote and give priority to 'preferred' or 'dominant' meanings, the effect of which is to reproduce or maintain rather than challenge the status quo. In part, they are able to do this by drawing on their links with external sources of legitimation, such as, for example, the institutions of the state, religious bodies, Parliament and the legal and medical professions (Althusser, 1969). It is in this context, of 'collaboration' with other 'independent' institutions of power, that the ways in which an interpretive framework was constructed in relation to the abortion debate in the press can be explored. As I shall argue, the timing and nature of the coverage of the Alton Bill clearly illustrate the degree to which the press works intimately with other powerful institutions in its effort to convey what it purports that 'everyone agrees to'.

Adding to the advantages that come with its institutional reputation as impartial arbiter, there are also a number of ways in which the media are able to promote preferred readings through the construction of a 'consensual' stance on a particular subject. The transformation of the random into the familiar, which is part of the process of translating events into representations which both make sense and make news, involves a variety of techniques: the use of rhetorical strategies of 'universalization', 'objectivity' and 'impartiality'; the neutralization and naturalization of antagonisms of class, gender and race (Hartley, Goulden and O'Sullivan, 1985); the use of the language of 'expertise' as a source of accreditation, sometimes juxtaposed with more 'subjective' linguistic forms; and finally, the marginalization or exclusion of 'extra-consensual' ideas.

In addition to its semblance of impartiality and 'freedom', and its ties to other powerful social institutions, the press secures a 'consensus' framework by resorting to the use of a presumed set of shared knowledges and/or familiar languages. In the case of the Alton debate, this took the form of a medico-moral rhetoric which drew upon a fusion of Christian dogma and state-of-the-art medical technological knowledge. The effect of this was to establish an apparently 'consensual' framework for the debate which invited 'objective' decision-making and 'rational' discussion of a very emotive and 'subjective' issue. In turn this facilitated reliance upon established (patriarchal) forms of expertise in the media representation of the arbitration process over what was seen as a public moral concern. The question here is what the formation of a media consensus on this basis represents. Who does or does it not represent, and how does it position women as decision-makers about abortion or contributors to the public debate which informed the law-making process?

The media's presentation of the Alton Bill

Certain distinct processes can be identified through which a consensual position on the issue of abortion was constructed within the press in relation to the revival of public debate provoked by the introduction of the Alton Bill. Although the dynamics at work are more complex, I will concentrate on two key aspects of this process. First, I shall examine how and why the press took up the debate in the language used by Alton, and argue that the contribution of science is central to the construction of an anti-abortion perspective. Second, I shall look in more detail at certain technical aspects of the press coverage, including timing of reports, use of language and the rhetorical strategies of objectivity and impartiality.

The timing of the press coverage of the Alton debate occurred in three major spates, coinciding with the debates in the House of Commons (September–October 1987 and January 1988) and the defeat of the Bill (May 1988). The first reports of the Alton Bill in the quality papers were often placed in the 'home news' sections, and appeared straightforward and factual, as this extract from an early article in the *Guardian* entitled 'Alton faces moral dilemma' shows:

> Mr. Alton, a devout Catholic, believes the Abortion Law Reform Act, introduced by his leader 20 years ago, is outdated by advanced technology and ought to be substantially changed. He is considering proposing that the time limit for legal abortions should be reduced from 28 weeks to 18, and that there should be further restrictions on circumstances when abortions can be allowed. (*Guardian*, 17 September 1987).

In so far as such reports appeared merely to pass on Alton's opinion, without explicit comment, they prepared the ground for the view that the moral and political issue of abortion had been substantially transformed as a result of technological progress. Indeed, the use of the notion of an advancement in technology subsequently became the main focus of further coverage of the Bill in the media, and set the parameters of a consensual framework for understanding abortion as a moral dilemma. This was facilitated by the privileged position given to Alton by the press as the 'primary definer' (Hall *et al.*, 1978) of the issue in question, as evidenced by his being either quoted at length or given the opportunity to present his own view in featured articles or columns.

A perception of the Alton Bill as a contentious issue was also presented at this early stage, but it is clear that even here no substantive challenge was posed to the fundamental assumptions upon which the debate was premised. As this extract from the *Guardian* piece entitled 'Alton Advised to Compromise on Bill' shows, 'opposition' to the Alton Bill very often accepted, rather than questioned, the assumptions upon which the terms of debate were founded: 'the 18 week clause is expected to harden opposition. Mr. Alton had been urged by doctors and fellow MPs to go for a less drastic 24–week limit' (26 September 1988). Instead, the debate was seen as a means of reaching a 'compromise' *within* the terms of a consensual framework, in which medical judgement was used as a basis for establishing the social and political parameters of 'the abortion question'.

Alton's own use of the apparently objective or neutral discourses of sci-ence, and in particular his authoritative use of medical forms of knowledge, rather than those of religion, strengthened his position further, allowing him substantial influence in setting the terms of debate. For example, his attack on 'late' abortion was mediated through a stress on the need for the apparently neutral arbitration of the medical and legal professions:

> The 1929 Life Preservation Act, which sets the 28 week limit, was introduced by the Lord of Appeal to fill the gap between abortion and murder. Its aim was to exclude from murder cases where a foetus was destroyed at a time when it was not capable of being born alive – 28 weeks was then a 'rule of thumb' . . . and, given the gigantic strides in medicine and technology, it is incumbent on any civilised society to do so. (*The Independent*, 23 January 1988).

The use of the language of medical expertise thus helped to lend Alton's anti-abortion argument a veneer of objectivity, making it uncontentious and amenable to a process of 'neutral' presentation by the press.

His arguments also relied heavily on other aspects of medical discourse, especially in the adoption of the notion that the woman is opposed to the fetus. This is evident in a constant press and general media emphasis on the fetus as a separate person with civil rights, the idea of 'fetal viability' and, indirectly, in support for the idea of maternal sacrifice. The elaboration of the conditions of fetal viability, and the associated notion of technological progress, came to represent the key 'common-sense' ingredients of the con-sensual interpretive framework which gradually emerged in the press. The appropriation of medical knowledge thus made possible a new 'fetocentric' element in the abortion debate.

In this way, the use of medical knowledge reinforced the idea of the fetus as a separate entity with full civil rights, contributing to what Petchesky (1984, p. 334) has termed the 'doctrine of fetal personhood'. As noted in the previous section, this process is powerfully illustrated by the widespread presentation, in both visual and linguistic forms, of the fetus as an innocent and sentient child. It is also present in the emphasis on the horror of the bodily destruction of the fetus, critical to Alton's well rehearsed and widely publicized description of abortion:

> The cervix is dilated and the baby's body is removed piece by piece . . . To facilitate its extraction the skull is crushed, the spine is snapped and the body is removed in pieces. An attendant nurse then has the job of reassembling the body to make sure nothing has been left behind that might cause infection. Throughout this procedure no anaesthetic is used on the child. (*The Independent*, 23 January 1988).

The incorporation of medical expertise in support of the anti-abortion arguments had a number of other effects. Most notably, by being brought firmly into the realm of 'medical judgement' through the scientific discussion of time limits and viability, the issue of abortion was 'universalized' (Alton's appeal to 'civilized society') and, in this way, the debate was lifted beyond the (now apparently) 'partial' notion of a woman's right to choose. The prompt uptake and relay of this specific formulation of the terms of the debate by the press is significant for a number of reasons. Most importantly, by accepting Alton's medico-moral terms, the press publicized the anti-abortion position and the set of assumptions about women's status and reproductive control at stake in the Alton debate.

It was not until the Second Reading of the Alton Bill, some three months after the terms of the debate had been set, and in the midst of the abortion furore in Parliament, that the tabloids 'woke up' and began to offer coverage of the Bill. Just as the quality newspapers, their reports tended to concentrate on and to accredit the opinion of the medical bodies involved. However, a number of additional themes were promoted in the popular press, including the dilemma of 'fetal abnormality', and the position taken on the issue by Margaret Thatcher and her Cabinet.

These issues were typically highlighted through the use of 'human interest stories'. So, for example, the dilemma of 'abnormality' was presented through the personal accounts of mothers-to-be who wanted to keep handicapped babies. A front-page headline of a leading tabloid read: 'My Abortion Agony, MP Rosie Reveals Heartache Over her Unborn Babies'. Beneath the headline, the story read:

> She twice agonised over whether to have an abortion . . . She decided to abort two of her unborn children if tests showed they were handicapped . . . But she went ahead with the pregnancies and is now a proud mum. (*Daily Mirror*, 23 January 1988).

What is noticeable here is not only the reference to the fetus as an 'unborn child', but also the construction of abortion as a temptation and a threat to the happy resolution of motherhood. In addition, there were a spate of sensationalized reports of abortion as murder. Under the headline 'Abortion baby took three hours to die', one article read:

> A baby girl of 21 weeks was placed in a metal dish in a back room and left to die after a hospital abortion . . . it was said to have taken three hours. (*Daily Mail*, 8 February 1988).

These extracts are significant not only in terms of their content, but in the modes of address they employ, drawing upon, for example, a popular fascination with gruesome details of death and tragedy which is a staple ingredient of both the tabloid and the quality press.

Noticeably, both the quality and popular press tended (except during the three main stages of parliamentary debate) to place longer feature articles on abortion outside their 'hard news' sections, under such headings as 'Living', or 'Health', or the 'Woman's Page'. Some of these features outlined oppositional views, such as those of the Labour spokeswoman on Women's Affairs, Jo Richardson, who wrote of her fear of a 'partial return to the conditions in which women and doctors were criminalised' (*The Independent*, 23 January 1988), or that of the Labour MP, Clare Short, who asserted that the 'overwhelmingly male dominated Commons should approach the issue with humility . . . every man in this House who has used a woman's body and walked away without knowing the consequence, has no right to vote on this Bill' (*Guardian*, 23 January 1988). However, even some of the anti-Alton views tended to work within the parameters of the debate as it had been constituted, while those that did not were usually isolated, or appeared to be marginal, precisely because they did not appear to address the concerns of the debate.

Nevertheless, there was some representation of feminist attempts to oppose the Alton Bill. However, even the use of the language developed in the context of the struggles to get the 1967 Abortion Act passed had contradictory implications in the very different context of the 1980s. Even the most apparently political of the old feminist terms, such as 'the right to choose', had been appropriated by other groups, including the anti-abortion campaign movement. The idea of 'rights' was extracted from the feminist context of the analysis of sexual inequality and translated into the 'right to fetal life', the effect again being to 'fetalize' the debate. Alternatively, such terms were taken up by the (surprising) body of Conservatives against Alton, in whose rhetoric of 'freedom' the notion of choice had very different implications. For example, the right-wing Conservative MP Teresa Gorman, featured as an anti-Altonite in a *Daily Mail* article, 'Why I believe David Alton should be stopped' (20 January 1988), used the notions of freedom, individual responsibility and the 'right to choose' in a libertarian conservative argument against state intervention in private life:

> I think it is a mercy to a woman and her family to know that the child she is carrying will be born with Spina Bifida, Down's Syndrome or Muscular Dystrophy, so that they can decide whether or not they feel able to cope . . . It is a straightforward case of civil liberty . . . Politicians cherish the absurd illusion that the State should interfere with what common sense dictates. (Gorman, 1988).

The eugenic implications of some anti-Alton views were made explicit in the publicity given to the fears of women of giving birth to 'abnormal' babies, and thus to a specific breed of unwanted offspring. As a report in the *Daily Mirror* put it:

> some experts fear that this will mean more handicapped babies are born. Down's Syndrome is one such handicap. It affects one baby in 600. The risk of having such a child for women under 30 is one in 1,000 but this rises to one in 60 for women over 45. It is caused by a chromosome abnormality – the child has 47 instead of 46 – nobody knows WHY. (*Daily Mail*, 22 January 1988).

Together, both the tabloids and the 'respectable' press managed to unite the many fragmented and often contradictory opinions on the abortion issue into a recognizable framework that established a clear set of parameters and concerns. In so doing, feminist perspectives were largely marginalized from debate and excluded from a consensus framework, which instead gave priority to a narrow set of 'moral' issues. The combination of the purportedly objective status of the 'hard news' papers, and the increasing reliance on medical expertise and new medical technology in the debate over abortion proved too powerful a convergence of authority for feminist arguments to challenge successfully.

Importantly, the establishment of this consensus within the press had significant political consequences. In a style which was characteristic of her government on many previous occasions, it was not until a clear consensus had emerged in the media that Margaret Thatcher made her own position on the Alton Bill clear. On such a contentious issue, it was highly desirable for the government to find a path of least resistance and a rationale for their position which would minimize hostility to their party from the important constituency of morally conservative, New Right and religious anti-abortion voters. In large part, this position was prepared for the Thatcher government by the media, in their reduction of the debate to a narrow range of positions and prioritization of medical and parliamentary technicalities in the later stages of debate. This made it not only possible, but inescapably obvious for the government to be seen to take a 'compromise' position of a reduction to 22 rather than 18 weeks as the upper time-limit for abortion. In turn, this position was put forward as a basis for a vote on abortion in the 1989/90 session of Parliament, in which a virtually identical version of this position provided the basis for a reduction in the upper time limit of abortion to 24 weeks.

The way in which the fight to maintain and widen abortion rights is conducted in the future is a vital question. This analysis has suggested that there are a number of problems in determining what kinds of language feminists can successfully use to convey oppositional meanings within public debate. It has attempted to outline the means by which the media succeeded in winning the consent of diverse groups for their system of signification by accommodating conflicting definitions within an interpretive structure which rested on familiar sources of authority and common sense. The new 'fetocentrism' has not, as yet, been paralleled by an equally radical change in the thinking of those concerned to maintain abortion rights for women. Establishing feminist strategies which can employ a new, popular language of opposition to the anti-abortion movement must thus be seen as a political necessity.

Conclusion

Feminism and abortion: pasts, presents and futures

THE SCIENCE
AND TECHNOLOGY SUBGROUP

In the different areas of our investigations we have shown that those fighting for and against the Alton Bill came to inhabit a similar terrain – associated with a few main themes. The debate focused on fetal viability as the point of arbitration for abortion rights. This focus enhanced the already established role of medical expertise in the adjudications surrounding abortion in Britain. In addition, the enhanced role of medical expertise went hand-in-hand with the harnessing of abortion rights to the technological capacities of modern medicine and an unquestioning faith in scientific progress. Prenatal diagnosis, technological systems for sustaining infants born prematurely and the technology which produces photo-images of fetuses were all invoked frequently during the Alton abortion controversy. In such circumstances, medical judgements and technical possibilities or limitations, not women's needs or lives, set the parameters of debate.

Medical expertise and technological progress were, in turn, key components in the elaboration of notions of a separate (from the mother) fetal personhood. The circulation of visual imagery, the defining of distinct fetal interests, the attribution of separate anatomies and sentient qualities to fetuses and the cultivation of a sense of the potentially adversarial relationship between pregnant women and their fetuses were some of the main strands within this theme. We have shown that the construction of fetal personhood has made it increasingly easy for anti-abortionists to invoke a 'need' for embryo protection laws and for the state to claim 'the right' to act as the 'protector' of fetal 'rights'. Moreover, we have highlighted the fact that fetal personhood has increasingly come to be regarded as an extension of childhood, involving the delineation of an extended ambit of maternal responsibilities.

Our final theme was the growing primacy of the language of rights, particularly as it was used to subvert feminist politics. While feminists reasserted 'a woman's right to choose', Alton supporters were keen to reply with the 'rights of the fetus'. Inevitably adversarial models came easily to mind with such conceptualizations. Many feminists have become increasingly uncomfortable with the dependence on the notion of 'a woman's right to choose' (Himmelweit, 1988; Franklin and McNeil, 1988). In pitting the right to choose against the right to life, feminists run the risk of losing public sympathies, and being constructed as self-indulgent and irresponsible. When two sets of rights are so closely juxtaposed, the developed sense of fetal oppression and the use of fetal imagery referred to above stack the odds against women. Moreover, the justification of 'a woman's right to choose' as a 'right to prevent disability' subverts the original spirit of the slogan, a woman-centred assertion for self-determination and freedom from state control over our reproduction. Finally, the liberal language of rights also encourages individualistic approaches to reproduction which make it difficult to tackle its social dimensions. For example, there was a near total absence of any concrete discussion of childrearing conditions during the debate.

In our assessment, these were the main parameters and legacy of the Alton Bill debate. Feminists were forced to share with Alton supporters this basic terrain: (a) medical expertise as the adjudicator of abortion; (b) technological progress as the factor determining its parameters; (c) a developed public consciousness about 'fetal personhood'; (d) negotiation in the language of rights; and (e) the use (and subversion) of feminist rhetoric in the service of anti-feminist political agendas. Despite the fact that the Bill itself was legislatively unsuccessful, the terms in which abortion was to be considered had been forged in a way which left little opening for women's needs or interests or for exploring reproduction as a social, not just a technological, biological or individual issue.

In the aftermath of Alton, we have witnessed a settlement in which scientific medicine and technology have determined the parameters of abortion possibilities in new and extended ways, as well as familiar ones. One of the distinctive features of the Alton Bill controversy was that it was not a matter of pitting a traditional, religiously based defence of the 'right to life' against a more secular rationalist right to abortion. So, for example, the 'right to life' became linked to estimations of technical and biological viability. Moreover, the defence of (late) abortion was argued in terms of the limitations of prenatal diagnostic technology and the interests of preventing 'disability'. Despite the continuing importance of religious motivations for anti-abortionists, the terrain of science was accepted as the main battle ground for both sides of the debate. It is also significant, we feel, that the scientization of the issue has been realized not through a playoff between rationality and emotionality, nor through the assertion of scientific 'facts' alone. The mobilization of established faith in scientific progress and the public's imaginative engagement through high-technology visual representations of fetuses have been equally significant. In other words, we have seen that science operates not only through authoritative statements and cognitive power, but also through symbolism, imagery and other direct appeals to the popular imagination and common sense.

Abortion politics and feminist resistance

The marginalization of women's voices within the Alton debate should not be taken to mean that feminists have had no input into these developments. One of the most important findings of our investigations was the discovery that anti-abortionists clearly have heard feminists. Indeed, over and over again, we felt we were confronting the impact and legacy of feminism, not just its marginalization or exclusion. From a Foucauldian perspective, what we were seeing was not the repression of feminism, but its proliferation into a myriad divergent, often subverted, forms. Thus, parliamentarians directly addressed arguments about 'a woman's right to choose' and the LIFE campaign presented 'feminists' who supported the Alton Bill in their video. Indeed, Alton frequently presented himself as acting on behalf of women. We became increasingly convinced that feminists perhaps have underestimated the extent to which feminist arguments have been attended to, even if this was in the form of their having been recuperated. We came to see debates about abortion not simply as feminists banging our heads against a brick wall, but rather as a spiral of interactions in which feminism *has* made a difference. In many ways, there was a real attempt to construct the Alton debate as a 'post-feminist' debate: to incorporate a superficial acknowledgement of feminists' concerns and a veneer of acknowledgement of women's interests by those leading the Alton campaign.

Though rarely acknowledged by the visible members of the Alton debate, the anti-feminist construction of 'feminism' and women's interests did not go unchallenged by feminists. There was the FAB (Feminists Against the Alton Bill) campaign itself. The FAB campaign was a 'crisis' campaign of national proportions. Responding to the introduction of the Alton Bill in Parliament, local and regional FAB groups quickly developed all over the country with an infrastructure of communication that facilitated the planning of co-operative lobbying efforts in Parliament and at individual parliamentarian's surgeries and mobilized mass demonstrations, some of which in London attracted unprecedented numbers of 'pro-choice' marchers. FAB groups also published and distributed information and leaflets, organized talks and local actions and made important links with trade unions to gain their support. The FAB campaign was mixed; men were involved both through the trade unions and within many FAB groups. There were also women-only groups, many of which were centrally linked to the National Abortion Campaign (NAC) in London and the Women's Reproductive Rights Campaign (WRRC) in the North.

The central priority of the FAB campaign, as reflected by its name, was the defeat of this one legislative initiative. As such, it lacked a certain continuity with the wider historical struggle by feminists for women's reproductive rights, which have not been limited to the legislative arena. More importantly, perhaps, the FAB campaign suffered from an analysis of the politics of the abortion debate which was, perhaps unavoidably given time and resource constraints, inadequate. For example, one of the main FAB oppositional stances was to protect the deeply problematic existing legislation on abortion. 'Protect the 1967 Abortion Act' was a widely used FAB slogan. Additionally, although the campaign generated large-scale grassroots activism, it also relied rather uncritically on political strategies, e.g. demonstrations, lobbying, etc., which were, in the current climate, disappointingly inadequate and easily ignored and dismissed by both parliamentarians and the mainstream media.

Since in different ways we had all been involved in the FAB campaigns, we have been very much concerned to consider how this project might inform the strategies of feminists around abortion. Clearly, one implication of our analysis is that defensive, one-off campaigns can never be enough when we consider the ways in which the popular consciousness about abortion is shaped on a day-to-day basis. We have suggested some of the elements which have contributed to the current consensus within a framework for debating abortion in Britain today in the hope that they can be given more attention. Feminists can 'win' on the abortion issue not through filibusters or other parliamentary techniques, nor even through the publicity gained by staging a few large demonstrations, but only through changing commonsense presumptions about abortion, medico-scientific intervention in pregnancy and motherhood.

This makes the feminist project on abortion a less defensive, though far more daunting enterprise. But perhaps we could suggest a small beginning. During our research we became disturbed by the manner in which feminist slogans were being 'turned upside-down' by those keen to erode women's access to abortion. 'A woman's right to choose' was constructed as a eugenic right, or a justification for selfishness, or countered with claims to the 'rights' of fetuses (or of Parliament to represent them). We were reminded of how easy and reassuring such slogans had been in FAB demonstrations and lobbying efforts. Our own work makes us now feel that we must be much more aware of the potential recuperation and transformation of feminist meanings in a wider political context. This means being more sensitive to public response and perhaps more innovative in our own imagery and rhetoric. Appeals to 'back-street abortions' may have had resonance for women brought up in 1950s Britain, but they do not mean much to those who see the main issue as the capacity of high-technology medicine to prevent 'disability' or sustain 'life'. In short, we think we have to be more aware of how the debate on abortion has moved on and about how we, as feminists, can orient our strategies around that movement.

The media have, in various ways, been central to the Alton Bill debate and to our analysis. Obviously, we would also hope that there could be more attention given to the media in future feminist campaigns. If transforming popular consciousness is our main goal, we cannot devote all our energies to demonstrations which get little coverage. We have highlighted the fact that the consensual strands which emerged from the coverage were potentially more threatening to feminists than direct 'pro-Alton' rhetoric. Once again, this suggests a need for a rather different feminist orientation towards the media – one which is trying to understand and break with consensus – rather than a need to address our opponents in a confrontational, debating mode. We have also stressed the importance of imagery, symbols, juxtapositions. Overall, we feel a need to depend less on the occasional letters to the quality press or parliamentarians, and instead to build a much more broadly-based, diverse approach to the media around reproductive rights.

Methodological endings and beginnings

Throughout this project, we have been aware of many limitations, from own working process as a group to the broader macro-context in which we were working. Moreover, the Thatcher government proposed a parliamentary amendment to lower the upper time limit of abortion to 24 weeks shortly after we completed this project, which was passed in April of 1990 by a considerable majority. While, on the one hand, this led us to feel pessimistic about the potential for feminist efforts to protect abortion rights, it also confirmed some of our own assessments of the extent to which the Alton Bill had marked a significant turning point in the redefinition of the abortion debate. In addition, the importance placed on the various scientific, medical and technological criteria outlined in this chapter, as well as the role of the media, the law and the medical profession outlined in our analysis of the Alton Bill, were very much in evidence in the arguments surrounding the recent reduction in access to abortion. Meeting this challenge, by continuing to protect women's access to abortion and by resisting the narrow parameters of the abortion debate, will continue to be a priority. In particular, addressing the power of science, medicine and technology to determine commonsense assumptions concerning reproductive issues will be an increasingly important focus for feminists struggling within the contested territory of reproductive politics.

Part Four:
Thatcherism and the enterprise culture

8

Making and not making the difference: the gender politics of Thatcherism

MAUREEN McNEIL

> It is this gendering of the mainstream political agenda that has created such trials and difficulties for feminists. (Loach, 1987, p. 28)

Introduction

This chapter is the product of my unease. In the first instance, it is about nothing less than the state of the nation as it was under the first British woman Prime Minister. After just over a decade of feminist struggles, Britain elected Margaret Thatcher in 1979. These two political facts constitute stark dichotomies. The first two sections of this chapter attempt to comprehend how this dichotomy has worked. My analysis of Thatcher's image and rhetoric explores the ways in which Thatcher has inhabited and related to femininity in her culture. The specific forms of these 'takes' on femininity have diffused any possible feminist connotations or reappropriations of her period in office, building a wall, as it were, between the decade of feminism and the decade of the first woman Prime Minister.

However, my discomfort about the state of the nation revolves more around the lives of other women than it does around the life of this particular woman. It is my firm belief that there has been a strong gender politics within the policies and interests of the Conservative governments of the last decade. And yet, this has been very elusive. The first systematic studies of Thatcherism marginalized this dimension of it (for a discussion of this absence, see ten Tusscher (1986, esp. pp. 67–72)).[1] In recent years, several critics of Thatcherism have allowed some of the language and conceptual frameworks of feminism to shape their picture. Hence, Stuart Hall now speaks of Thatcherism constructing a 'patriarchal, entrepreneurial subject' (Hall, 1988a, p. 8) and of it addressing, at some moments, 'Thatcherite men (or the Thatcherite man in all of us)' and at others, 'the little Thatcherite "woman" in us all' (Hall, 1988a, pp. 85–6).[2] Likewise, Andrew Gamble briefly alludes to the 'feminist perspective' on Thatcherism (1988, pp. 175, 197–201). But these forays do not even begin to assess adequately the gender politics of this period. In taking issue with many of the tenets of those who have proffered analyses of Thatcherism, Elizabeth Wilson offers a much broader profile of gender relations in Thatcher's Britain (Wilson, 1987). Unfortunately, however, she tends to restrict her focus to the question of whether or not this has involved a push to return women to the home. Moreover, much of her exposition is channelled into the insidious and misleading choice between Thatcherism as a politics of either class or gender oppression.[3]

My own unease about the gender relations I have witnessed developing during the past decade made me suspicious about left marginalizations or denials of gender politics. Increasingly, I came to see these readings of the Thatcher era as indicative rather than definitive, indicative of the complexity rather than the absence of gender politics. So, when I move away from Thatcher herself to deal with concrete aspects of gender relations during the past decade in Britain, I am teasing out a gender politics which is not on the surface. In a sense I am suggesting that, despite the sophistication of recent work on sexuality, sexual politics and gender issues, the left has been rather flat-footed in its approach to recent government policy and practices. It is as if we have been looking for the manifesto and it has not appeared![4] As I will suggest below, the reification of Thatcherism in some political analyses has been part of the problem here as well.

The four subsequent sections of this chapter attempt to draw out some of the more salient features of the gender politics of recent years. I begin with reinvigorated modes of consumption in the section on 'consuming families' and then move on to the cultivation of concern for what I label 'the new oppressed'. In both these instances I suggest that, without announcing it, the Conservatives have launched initiatives which have had profound implications for gender relations. In the subsequent considerations of the public–private divide in work and of sexual mores, the indirect, yet forceful nature of recent Conservative initiatives around gender and sexual politics are brought to the fore.

Thus far I have chosen to avoid the term 'Thatcherism' in my own references to the politics of Britain in the 1980s. This brings me to the final facet of my unease. Although I myself have used this term, and shall continue to do so as a shorthand in this chapter, I have definite reservations about it.[5] The packaging of politics into the bundle 'Thatcherism' can contribute to a certain reification of culture and politics. Complex patterns of opposition, government policies and popular culture emerge in each of my case studies, rather than boiled down 'effects of Thatcherism'. Furthermore, I am worried about the pull of, what might be labelled rather facetiously, *Spitting Image* politics.[6] Here I am hinting not so much at a critique of one of the most popular public critical portrayals of the Thatcher government but at the significance of its appeal. Is there not something rather limiting about its personalizations? Is it not reassuring to have politics cut down to personal caricatures – to puppet size – to have something or someone to spit at?

In all of this I detect a rather disturbing pattern of personalization in the forms of opposition to the politics and practices of the Thatcher government. My own reading of Thatcher's image and rhetoric, as I shall indicate below, leads me to believe that at best this could be a stubborn insistence on her absent presence – a reading against the grain of the cultivated political texture. But it is fraught with dangers: false expectations that the end of Thatcher was the end of the political problems which have emerged in this period; oppositional tactics and forms which are rather misogynistic; and real confusions about the sexual and gender politics of the period. These are issues I will return to in my conclusion.

The image of Thatcher: making it like a man?

A woman in power has to put away feminine things, has to prove that she doesn't quail before the sword, that she too can 'be man enough to press the button'. (Warner, 1988, p. 43).

The Eighties have given us many female icons . . . But the greatest of these is Margaret Thatcher.

(Polan, 1988)

The significance of having had a woman as Prime Minister should not be denied. Across the political spectrum, the tenth anniversary of Thatcher's leadership confirmed that a woman *can* manage the job (see Brunt, 1987). Yet, this has been no victory for women, and there has not been much optimism about 'jobs for the girls' as a result of Thatcher's establishment. Her attachment to an almost exclusively male Cabinet exemplifies this. Thatcher continually presented herself as unique, as a loner, as 'the "exceptional woman"' (Wilson, 1987, p. 199), a woman who had succeeded without challenging the fundamental rules of the boys' game of mainstream politics. Hence, perhaps the most fundamental comment that can be made about Thatcher's image is that it was thoroughly conservative: she was a woman who succeeded by not challenging the status quo, by not changing precedents or improving the opportunities for other women in politics.

Nevertheless, Thatcher *is* a woman: she dresses like a woman, carries a

handbag, has a feminine speaking voice, and so on.[7] Robert Harris, writing
in the *Observer*, even reported that she indulged in such feminine activities as
making bacon and eggs for Cabinet ministers during late-night meetings at
Downing Street, and that she was susceptible to masculine charms and good
looks (Harris, 1989). Thus, in many ways, Margaret Thatcher declared that
she was feminine. Yet, as Ros Brunt claims, Thatcher also appeared to
'disavow femininity'. For example, she did not appear as a highly sexualized
figure. It could be argued that this relates to her age. But as Joan Collins and
others have demonstrated, there are no essential prohibitions against the
sexualization of older women. Moreover, Thatcher made little use of more
specific female role playing – for example, as mother or even grandmother
– in her daily demeanour. It was as if she wanted to be seen as a woman
but she did not want to offer much specific content. To be feminine, in our
society, is to be vulnerable, and it would appear that Thatcher wanted to
maintain established gender codes without a big investment in femininity,
with its concomitant vulnerabilities. In contrast she has been associated with
a tradition of female imagery identified with Boadicea – the invulnerable
female warrior (see Fraser, 1988; Warner, 1988).[8]

Indeed, this mode of inhabiting femininity fits easily with a rather depersonalized political image. It is striking that, despite the tenth anniversary
focus on Thatcher in the spring of 1989, there has been little public sense of
her personality. While the press and public mutually cultivated fascination
with the details of the royal family's life, relationships and emotions,
there was little concern for the personal life of the Prime Minister.
Even the antics of her erstwhile spendthrift son, Mark, did not hold
public interest for long. Neither is her husband Dennis an explanation
for this, since, as the royal family aptly illustrates, dull husbands do not
necessarily inhibit popular curiosity. Indeed, it may be one of the ironies
of Thatcher's term in office that, despite the identification of the period
with her, the content of Thatcher's personality seldom entered into the
political arena. The very notion of an 'Iron Lady' seemed to denote not
only a woman without weakness, but a woman with little distinctive
character.

In these various ways, Thatcher's image did not expose the contradictions
or tensions inherent in being a woman Prime Minister. Rather, this image
bolstered the male-dominant nature of mainstream political institutions and
conventional notions of femininity. The world of public politics was at
once declared to be a realm that is open to women and yet not; it was
so in form, but not in content. There was no need for change. Indeed,
it was this distancing from the vulnerability of femininity which denied
the specificity of women's problems in contemporary Britain. Moreover,
it was ironic that the first woman Prime Minister should so rigidly reinforce
the boundary between the public and the private – the boundary which the
recent phase of feminism sought to break down.

The rhetoric of Thatcherism: ladies, housewives and nannies

Standing back from Thatcher's personal image, the gendered dimensions of the rhetoric of Thatcherism are apparent. There are three invocations which were familiar parts of her rhetoric: 'the lady's not for turning'; 'as every housewife knows'; and 'fighting against the nanny state'. By considering each of these key phrases we get a clearer sense of the gender politics of Thatcherism.

Perhaps the most memorable phrase from Thatcher's rhetoric was first uttered at the Conservative Party Conference in October 1980 and written for her by the playwright Ronald Millar. Associated with her distancing from Tory 'wets', it constituted her most direct public self-reference. In her pronouncements that 'the lady's not for turning', Thatcher was emphasizing her power and control, expressed in a rather depersonalized manner. Used to insist upon her strength and determination, this is a declaration that she was neither vulnerable nor subject to persuasion. Unlike the stereotypical female, she could not be wooed; her head could not be turned. She displayed, instead, what Loretta Loach describes as a 'female triumphalism': 'She is a woman who can sustain the conflicting qualities of drive and femininity and still be part of the world – not loved or liked as women feel they need to be, but successful, assured and admired' (Loach, 1987, p. 26). It is not insignificant that this image of feminine strength was not collective, but rather exclusive and individual. It is not the power of women, or even of ladies, but of THE Lady which Thatcher insisted upon.[9]

The second key gendered phrase in the rhetoric of Thatcherism relates to the domestic budget. 'As every housewife knows', the Thatcherite phrase labelled as immortal by Bea Campbell (Campbell, 1987, p. 234), was repeatedly drawn upon by Thatcher in her attempt to establish parallels between the domestic and the national economies (see Hall, 1988a, pp. 47, 206). This was part of a more general appeal to common sense which has characterized recent British conservatism. Just as other such invocations, it appeared to be crediting 'ordinary people' (in this case housewives) with knowing what the nation needed.

However, when Thatcher refered to what 'every housewife knows' she was invoking rhetoric about, not the experience of, housewives in contemporary Britain. There is a certain irony in Thatcher's choice of this phrase during a period in which, as Lynne Segal points out, 'most women [in Britain] for most of their lives are no longer full-time housewives' (Segal, 1983, p. 206). Nevertheless, this indirect address to housewives had crucial implications for women. It had a double significance. On the one hand, it was a message about how housewives should be managing their domestic economies. For those with little financial leeway, this was no easy task. As I shall suggest below, many of the policies of Thatcher's government made this more difficult. So, in effect, she was asking them to make a virtue of necessity in coping with new hardships experienced under her regime (see Gardiner, 1983; Segal, 1983; Brunt, 1987; Loach, 1987, p. 26). On the other hand, this invocation proposed that housewives were responsible not only for their own domestic units, but for the state of the nation. Hence, while appearing to include housewives and their daily reality in the public negotiation of state management, Thatcher denied the concrete features of their actual experience in contemporary Britain and thus increased the pressures upon them.

The form and language of this invocation is itself noteworthy. Thatcher did not address herself directly to housewives. They were referred to as she spoke to the rest of her political constituency – by implication a mainly male audience, unfamiliar with the ways of domestic budgets. Moreover, this invocation of housewives' common sense endorsed a language of individualism and privatization since, as Brunt argues, it is 'pre-eminently . . . the language of "making the best of yourself" and "making do"' (Brunt, 1987, p. 24). Thus, harking back to the wartime conventions strongly associated with British nationalism and nostalgia, women were encouraged to carry heavy domestic burdens and to make great self-sacrifices in the 'national interest'.

A further example of gendered rhetoric associated with Thatcher's campaign against the welfare state was its depiction as the 'nanny' state (Hall, 1988a, p. 227). The discrediting and dismantling of the latter was one of the main aims of the Thatcherite programme. It is revealing that this was so often conceptualized in explicitly gendered terms. The disdain for the 'nanny state' conveyed the view that people should be 'real men' (sic) and take care of themselves. It constructed a set of dichotomies: welfare state, socialism, femininity, dependence and indulgence versus the market, *laissez-faire* values, masculinity, independence and austerity.

The negative associations implicit in this phrase attach not only to the state, but to a distinctive kind of feminine labour. The work of nannies (mainly working-class women) is associated with weakness and decadence. Indeed, the caring labour which has been the traditional domain of women is thereby rendered despicable (see Finch and Groves, 1983). There is an irony about the use of this particular piece of Thatcherite rhetoric, because (as I shall show below) nannies became more essential to middle-class women in paid employment during her years in office.[10] As noted in the editors' second introduction to this volume, a 'first rate nanny' was indeed an essential component in Thatcher's own recipe for successful career women such as herself. A particularly ironic twist occurred when some members of Thatcher's government actually invoked fears of the 'nanny state' to justify the current government's refusal to provide state support for childcare.

The personal image of Thatcher and the gendered dimensions of Thatcherite rhetoric were complementary. They shared a common emphasis on the uniqueness of Thatcher's feminine strength, a disdain for many aspects of women's experience and a distaste for some features of 'the feminine' in our culture. Significantly, femininity was also used to distance Thatcher from her male colleagues and to address them in an idiom from which they were excluded – 'as every housewife knows'. Throughout, the message is clearly conveyed that this woman Prime Minister was not going to challenge established modes of gender politics; the wall between feminism and Thatcher's power had been constructed and was continually reinforced.

Consuming families

> What I am desperately trying to do . . . is to create one nation with everyone being a man of property. (Thatcher (1983) quoted in Wilson (1987, p. 221)).

Moving from gendered imagery and rhetoric to policy, it would seem that the family was one of the centres of tension between the conservative social and liberal economic policies which characterized Thatcherism. At some points, as in the flurry of attention given to the Family Policy Unit in 1982–3, conservative social priorities seemed to be in the ascendancy. Moreover, amongst her strongest supporters, Thatcher undoubtedly found some lieutenants – most notably including Ferdinand Mount – who would have her give the family a much higher profile within her political programme (see Mount, 1982). However, except for these occasional flurries of attention, explicit social politics on the family remained on the backburner.[11] The family appeared in Thatcher's speeches mainly as the background to her political projects. Other policies were endorsed and pushed forward on behalf of 'individuals and their families' – the latter being the main, indeed the *only*, social unit which Thatcher countenanced (see Hall, 1988a, p. 12).

Indeed, the traditional values of the nuclear family have been far more effectively promulgated as an offshoot of the cultivation of the liberal economic framework than through explicit social policy. It was the implicit gender politics embodied in the 'free' market consumerism of Thatcherism which was its most powerful dimension. 'Popular capitalism' was cultivated, in part, through the encouragement of purchases of homes, private education and healthcare. Domestic products and family-oriented services were primary areas of privatization and market proliferation. This was evident in the importance of conventional notions of masculinity in the articulation of the Thatcherite enterprise–consumer discourse. As Andrew

Tolson has argued in *The Limits of Masculinity* (1977), such purchases are important vehicles for the construction of middle-class masculinity. In the contemporary West, the identities and powers of middle-class men have become closely linked to their ability to provide precisely these goods and services for their families. From this perspective, Thatcherism can be seen to have promoted a politics which intensified and reinforced these dominant modes of masculinity.

But this reinforcement of dominant gender roles is not merely a matter of degree. The enticement of the aspiring working class into this form of consumerism may also involve changes in the modes of working-class masculinity.[12] When buying one's own council house or purchasing education or healthcare are presented as essentials for working-class families, there can be profound implications for gender relations. Through investing, emotionally and financially, in a new range of consumer goods and services, working-class men are adapting to more middle-class modes of masculinity. Of course, in the case of men of both classes, the concern for the heroic burden of the male breadwinner obscures the increasing participation of women in paid employment and the domestic labour through which women also contribute to these new consumer patterns. Although new forms of consumption assume models of male independence, there is much hidden dependence in these developments.

The intensification of the significance of the family as a consuming unit has thus worked both to tighten the hold of capitalism and to reinforce conservative gender roles. As other freedoms (including, for example, freedom of speech, freedom of political organization and freedom of movement) were diminished during Thatcher's period in office, the realm of domestic consumption was designated as the pre-eminent sphere of independence, freedom and self-expression.[13] Meanwhile, the largely unsuccessful campaign against relatively high rates of inflation, together with high interest rates and the Thatcherite dictum that families must 'make ends meet', made for potentially explosive domestic situations.[14] Enticing more family spending, while cutting key domestic resources[15] in these economic circumstances made low-income families into domestic pressure-cookers.[16] Moreover, all of this occurred at a time when the range of domestic technologies for both work and leisure expanded. These provided yet another set of consumer options (or traps), and another set of enticements for investments in the family unit.

The 'new' oppressed

One of the characteristics of Thatcher's term in office was the attention given to a range of social groups who can be brought together under the label 'the new oppressed'. The construction of an agenda of social oppressions which countervails the struggles against class, racial, sexual and gender oppressions of the 1960s and 1970s permitted the cultivation of 'the caring face of Conservatism'. Simultaneously, it proclaimed that class, race, sexual and gender oppressions were largely irrelevant. The list of those on whose behalf the Thatcher government acted in some way includes: parents, fathers, burdened taxpayers and fetuses. Thatcher and her ministers were not necessarily involved in specific campaigns to defend the rights of these groups, but campaigns on their behalf flourished during her period as Prime Minister.

In considering each of the groups mentioned above we see that frequently the rights of these so-called oppressed groups were defined and defended through the cultivation of female or feminist bogeys. For example, parental rights were defended and ostensibly extended under the Thatcher governments. The Educational Reform Bill of 1987, for example, was celebrated by its supporters as the guarantor of new parental powers. The social relations derived from this and other parts of the Conservative education reform programme have been played out, through which established patterns of racism and class privilege were likely to be reinforced. Hence, it would seem that middle-class white parents were those with the best chance of benefiting from these changes. Moreover, it was not altogether clear whether this would involve more scope for mothers or simply more invisible labour for them – fund-raising, filling in as support staff, etc. The championing of parents' rights was directed against the supposed encroachments of professions in which women predominate – teaching and social work, in particular.

The second group for whom popular conservative support has been garnered is fathers. Their legal rights in custody cases, divorce settlements and in claims to rights in the abortion decisions of women with whom they have been sexually involved have all been given considerable attention during the past few years. Here the consistent bogey has been the threatening, but increasingly prevalent, single mother. The immediate context is the increase in the number of single mothers, the indications that some women are deliberately opting to bring up children without men and the publicity given to sperm banks and the technique of artificial insemination. In these circumstances, the single mother was easily regarded as threatening the traditional role of the father and the coherence of society in general. These anxieties were reinforced when single mothers were portrayed, as they have increasingly been in the British media, as an economic threat through their claims on the welfare state.

This brings us to the 'decent, hardworking, over-burdened' taxpayer typified by the male breadwinner of the working- and lower middle-class family, who is 'unfairly' burdened by those making 'excessive' claims on the state. This 'oppressed' taxpayer was most directly threatened by the 'scrounger'. The latter was a generic term (see Hall, 1988a, pp. 47, 145), but one specific variety has been the single mother on welfare. Stories of irresponsible young women who have babies as a way of getting council flats and state support have become the stock and trade of recent popular mythology. In *Wigan Pier Revisited* (1984) Bea Campbell presents single mothers as typifying the plight of the contemporary working class in Britain.[17] In her sketch of contemporary Britain, they occupy the position formerly accorded to miners in Orwell's earlier profile of the English working class (see Orwell, 1937). What Campbell does not draw out is that, in her new role, the single mother has been viewed as the 'enemy within' both her nation and her class, soaking up resources more justly 'earned' by the hard-working father cum breadwinner – the respectable male taxpayer.[18]

A similar form of reversal has occurred in relation to women who are pregnant. During recent years in Britain, as in the USA,

> the pregnant woman is increasingly put in the position of adversary to her own pregnancy/fetus, either by having presented a 'hostile environment' to its development or by actively refusing some medically proposed intervention. (Petchesky, 1987, pp. 64–5; see also Stanworth, 1987).

The recurring attempts to tighten the restrictions on abortion in Britain have both fed off and contributed to this trend. Although Thatcher's governments allowed other political forces to take the lead in the campaigns to tighten abortion legislation, it was quite clear about the need to regulate women through control over their reproduction in this and other spheres.[19] Thatcher's belated but strategic support for 'the consensual' position that there should be a reduction in the upper time limit on abortion in the wake of the Alton debate indicated this (see Chapter 7 on the Alton Bill).

The Thatcher government more or less directly identified itself with support for the various groups mentioned above. The degree and form of support varied but, in each of these cases, groups were constructed as oppressed and their rights were seen as undermined by the independence of women. Particularly significant was the reversal of agency such constructions invoked, whereby those, less powerful, groups who have demanded greater social justice, came to be seen therefore as agents in the oppression of other, more powerful groups. This championing of the rights of parents, fathers, burdened taxpayers and fetuses in turn threatened some of the hard-won gains of British feminism in the spheres of the professions, education, welfare and reproductive rights. The cultivation of sympathies for the 'new oppressed' was a crucial but neglected aspect of the ideological face of Thatcherism and a key component of its gendered dimensions.

Work: negotiating the public-private divide

It would be impossible to provide a full profile of how women's work changed during the Thatcherite regime. Moreover, simultaneous with the impact of these policies were major global alterations (including new technological developments) in the divisions of labour and the broader 'feminisation of poverty' (Scott, 1984; Wilson, 1987, p. 207) which were significant in the changing international profile of women's employment. Nevertheless, there was at least one general trend that characterized the policies of Thatcher's governments which merits comment. This can be described as a three-fold push towards privatization of aspects of work.

To begin with, work formerly undertaken in the public sphere has been increasingly pushed into the private realm, thereby increasing women's domestic labour. In the name of community care, the Thatcher governments withdrew many state services for the sick, the mentally ill and the elderly (see Finch and Groves, 1983). In addition, cuts in home-helps and school meals were amongst the measures that increased the domestic labour which has been mainly done by women in Britain (Wilson, 1987, p. 219). Likewise, women's educational responsibilities have been extended as they have been asked to make a greater contribution to the teaching of children, in running and helping to finance schools and in disciplining their children.[20] In general, women have been called upon to make up the difference which has resulted from the cuts in public services: unpaid domestic labour (mainly that of women) in the private sphere has been used as a substitute for previously paid labour in the public sphere.

The second strand of this privatization process relates to the Thatcherite advocacy of the free-rein of the market. Both Angela Coyle and Elizabeth Wilson have highlighted 'deregulation' as a key aspect of the Thatcher governments' employment policies (Coyle, 1983, 1985; Wilson, 1987, pp. 207–8).[21] Although the origins and role of so-called 'protective legislation' were dubious and double-edged, this legislation did highlight the fact that women were differently positioned in the labour market in comparison with men. The Thatcher government abolished some of this legislation, indicating its refusal to acknowledge the gender divisions within the labour market of the 1990s.[22] Women are differently positioned to deal with these pressures (see Wilson, 1987), but in all instances they have been expected to manage privately the problems associated with participation in paid employment.

The final dimension of privatization is its most obvious and literal form. One of the clearest and most distinctive policies of the Thatcher government(s) was the impetus to privatize many public services. School kitchen staff were among the first and most publicized targets of this policy. Much of the Tory offensive was focused on the most highly unionized parts of the public sector – where there is a predominantly female labour force (see Coyle, 1985).

This three-fold process of privatization of public domestic labour, deregulation and literal privatization of public services was not a policy specifically addressed to (or against) women. Nevertheless, these processes become issues of gender politics because they resulted in the intensification of women's domestic labour, the individualization of women in dealing with their particular problems as paid workers and the changes experienced by women workers in parts of the public sector which have been privatized. In these various ways, women's work has been increased, while the gendered dimensions of these transformations and their implications for women have been hidden.

The undermining of women's position in paid employment is not the only disturbing feature of this dimension of Thatcher's decade. If we turn to the public profile of women workers we see an equally disturbing pattern. It has been well established that the recent Conservative government has directed considerable attack against the liberal professions associated with the welfare state (Gamble, 1989, pp. 58–9). However, it is much less commonly noted that the two professions which have been most consistently cited as responsible for national problems are female-dominated: teaching and social work. Moreover, there has been little comment about the fact that the professions which suffered the most serious erosion of conditions, pay and status in recent years were also those in which women predominate: nursing, social work and teaching. It was not coincidental that the professional conduct of two women doctors – Wendy Savage and Marietta Higgs – became the subject of major public debate.[23] These public cases were not the direct result of government policy. Nevertheless, Thatcherism arguably promoted a climate in which the scapegoating of women professionals was a predictable outcome.

Thus, overall, Thatcher's term was associated with a number of public challenges to and attacks on women professionals. The gender politics of work in Thatcher's Britain affected not only the renegotiation of the public–private division but a range of labour issues. While there was no frontal attack on women workers by the Thatcher governments, public expenditure cuts, off-loading of state responsibilities, deregulation, privatization and demoralization hit women workers as hard as any explicit attack might have done.

Sexual mores: see no evil, speak no evil

It is clear that for Thatcher and many of her supporters the 1960s were associated with sexual permissiveness but, perhaps more importantly, that decade was linked to the proliferation of discourses about sexuality. The

Thatcherite era disassociated itself from this 'permissive society'.[24] In a Foucauldian sense, this rejection of the ethos of the 1960s was sought not through an explicit stand, but by refusing to articulate the discourse of sexuality.[25] (Although there were some forces pushing in this direction.) The Thatcherite regime seemed for the most part to have been hesitant to enter the discourse of the sexual since, despite its strong moralistic image, such engagement might have proliferated, rather than eliminated, that which it wished to destroy.[26] In this sense, Thatcherism distanced itself much more systematically than Reaganism from undiluted new right morality and sexual puritanism.[27] This is best illustrated by observing that Thatcherism did not link up with Mary Whitehouse and other would-be puritan reformers of sexual morality in 1980s Britain.

The most systematic instance of this feature of Thatcherite strategy can be discerned in the efforts to prise the family as the quintessential unit of social stability and economic transactions from the unsettling realm of sexuality. This was apparent in the dictates of some of the leading philosophers of the new right in Britain. Roger Scruton, for example, advocated that women should tame the unruly force of male sexuality (1983) and that marriage and the family accordingly were units which socialize men and guarantee social stability. In contrast, Ferdinand Mount (1982) constructed a full-blown historical and theoretical account of the family as the institution of radical autonomy – as the primary social unit fighting the forces of church and state. In both instances, the sexual dimensions of family life were contained or denied. As I have indicated above, the heavy investment in the economic dimensions of family life and in domestic consumption as the quintessential realm of freedom underscored the containment of the family. As the only social unit acknowledged by Thatcherism, the family had to carry the whole weight of responsibility for socialization – for conservative adaptation to the status quo. Given this expectation, sexuality could only be seen as a potentially disruptive force.

Issues of sexuality none the less entered the Thatcherite agenda. In what might be labelled the 'return of the repressed', sexuality raised its ugly head and more or less forced Thatcher and her ministers to enter the discourse they sought to avoid. To illustrate how this occurred, I shall consider three key moments when Thatcher and her supporters could be seen as being pulled into the discourse of sexuality.

It would be a mistake to portray the Thatcherite position on sexuality as totally monolithic and unified. There were more moralistic elements within her camp who were troubled by the avoidance of explicit policies on sexuality and sought more active measures against sexual permissiveness. Hence, occasions such as Victoria Gillick's campaign to assert parents' rights to control their daughters' access to contraceptives exposed divisions within Conservative ranks on these issues.[28]

However, in the eyes of many Thatcherites, if there was any form of sexuality which must be spoken against, it was homosexuality; if there was any consensus, it was around heterosexuality. The introduction of Section 28, a government-sponsored amendment to a Bill concerning local government, which banned 'the promotion of homosexuality' by local councils, represented a key policy initiative by the Thatcher government concerning sexuality. (A full account of the public debate concerning Section 28 is provided in Chapter 12.) Assessing this from the vantage point of what it demonstrates regarding Thatcherite strategy, I would argue it can be seen as a response both to the image of the 1960s and the threat of oppositional local governments. Seen in this light, Section 28 was first and foremost (and rather contradictorily) about interdicting discourses on sexuality within local government.[29] Of course, for those more moralistic and determinedly homophobic supporters of Thatcher, this legislation was embraced for other reasons, and seen as a sign that the government was finally taking on its moral mission regarding sexuality. In my interpretation, Section 28, despite ostensible contradictions, was not inconsistent with the Thatcherite course of abstention from the discourse of sexuality.

The emergence of AIDS as a full-blown international health problem was another situation in which the government was unable to avoid engaging, publicly and explicitly, with the issue of sexuality. Unlike Section 28, however, it could not be so easily accommodated. The Health Department's pamphlets and the advertisements relating to AIDS were the most widely circulated indications that the government had been pulled into the discourse of sexuality. The government was literally cajoled into taking the issue on and assuming the mantle it had refused in relation to sex education within schools – that of public educator. Once into this discourse the conventions of more traditional conservative attitudes towards sexuality again came to the fore: homophobia and moralism. None the less, the point remains that it took the international mobilization of fears about AIDS, nothing short of a major international health crisis, before the Thatcher government would intervene.

Within their own ranks, the repressed also came back to haunt them. The most publicized occasion of this was the case of Cecil Parkinson and Sara Keays.[30] Here was an example of the serenity of the stable nuclear family being blown open by *hetero*sexuality. In this case, the government distanced itself by temporarily suspending Parkinson from service and effectively waiting for it all to 'blow over'.[31] The public response to the clear misdemeanours of Cecil Parkinson and the behaviour of Jeffrey Archer[32] suggested that men could stray from the straight and narrow, but that women must 'stand by their men'. The examples of Mrs Parkinson and Mrs Archer celebrated the virtues of quiet, long-suffering and loyal wives. These were models of femininity – of very different sorts of 'Iron Ladies'.

In each of the instances I have cited there was some tension about the Conservative governments' abstention from the discourse of sexuality. In the case of Section 28, with mixed motivations, their main avoidance strategy was bolstered. AIDS and the naughty behaviour of some of Thatcher's boys blew this framework open. The responses were containment operations. This was facilitated through models of female loyalty and martyrdom in the latter case. However, AIDS continues to give impetus to the moralistic and homophobic tendencies within the Conservative alliance and to beckon them into the dangerous discourse of sexuality.

Conclusion: Thatcherism, feminism and the difference(s) they make

Finally, let me return to the term Thatcherism. This chapter has been written in and against this category. I have already outlined some of my reservations about the term. I want to add to this two further points. First, as my specific analyses suggest, there are disparate forces at play in the contemporary Conservative alliance: ideologists of the traditional family, puritan secular 'reformers', free-market prophets, etc. This is a precarious and ever-shifting alliance as certain moments I have highlighted (the Gillick campaign, the dilemmas about dealing with AIDS, etc.) illustrate (and the dismissals in Thatcher's Cabinet continually reminded us).

The missing ingredient in this picture is feminism. Let me return to where I began: Thatcher's decade followed immediately on the heels of a decade of feminism. Feminism did make a difference; perhaps more of a difference than we have realized. At the core of virtually every aspect of the Thatcherite programme I have examined there was some contestation with feminism: the reinforcement of the public–private divide; profound individualism and devaluing of women's experience within Thatcher's image and rhetoric; the entrenchment of middle-class models of the masculine breadwinner through the reinvigoration of domestic consumption; the attacks on women's autonomy through the championing of the rights of fathers, burdened male taxpayers and fetuses; the undermining of concrete gains made in struggles over women's welfare, employment and professional possibilities; the closing down of the discourse of sexuality. Indeed, the very indirectness of the sexual and gender politics of the past decade is testimony to the achievements of feminist struggles – in its implicit acknowledgement that, in the wake of the latest phase of the movement, a direct assault on feminism and women was no longer possible.[33]

An historical perspective is important because it places some of the central dilemmas of contemporary feminism in context (for Britain, at least). One of the most pressing issues on feminist agendas in the West in recent years has been the problem of difference or, more accurately, the problems of differences. There is some confusion about these problems. At theoretical levels, there are at least three issues: dealing with differences amongst women as a political and analytical group (Barrett, 1987); claiming that women are or are not clearly distinguishable from men as a social and analytical group (Epstein, 1988); and questioning whether there is a unified self (essence) which can be identified as 'woman' or 'man'.[34] In terms of practice, there have been pessimistic readings which speak of the fragmentation or dispersal of the women's movement and more optimistic interpretations of the desirable emergence of pluralism within the movement.

These theoretical debates about difference take on a strange, distorted and sometimes even perverse dimension in light of recent politics in Thatcher's Britain. For what we encountered was the construction of identities in and around their differences. I have shown that the encounter with the gender politics of Thatcherism took a wide variety of forms: middle-class women running up against the barriers of mythical fears of the female professional: black, single mothers dealing with cuts in welfare, racist constructions of their domestic lives and of welfare scroungers. In these and countless other instances women were constructed as a political category which they experienced as gender difference. In short, the differences amongst women were constructed in such moments. The result was not only different experiences of Thatcherism, but a similar encounter with the persistence of gender difference as a mode of political categorization and oppression.

The differences amongst women are important (and they must be addressed), but they by no means necessarily undermine feminist struggles. Moreover, whatever the dangers of overemphasizing gender difference, we cannot afford to ignore the fact that many women experienced and lived the politics of difference in Thatcher's Britain. While not advocating a reductionist version of the category 'woman', there clearly are occasions when battles must be fought in the name of 'women' and through bringing attention to gender differences.

As this chapter has suggested, mounting an oppositional sexual politics in contemporary Britain is a complex matter. We were waiting for the manifesto to appear and meanwhile the Thatcherite revolution was being waged in disparate and, sometimes, unexpected quarters. We were dealing with a sexual politics which did not generally declare itself. As some of my examples illustrate, this required quick-footed manoeuvres: sometimes fighting against 'over-' and sometimes against 'under-feminization' (Riley, 1988, p. 4), campaigning with and against the category 'women' (Riley, 1988).[35]

My interpretation of the past decade in Britain should untap some cautious optimism. For not only does it provide a more positive reading of feminism's impact in Britain, it enables us to view what many have seen as the dispersal or 'fragmentation of contemporary feminism' (Delmar, 1986, p. 9) as, in part, a sign of our times, rather than an inauspicious condition. In this respect, there are certain similarities between the recent period and the immediate aftermath of the first wave of the women's movement associated with the struggles for female suffrage in Britain.[36] Both that episode and the recent decade of Thatcherism, follow periods of strong identity politics and have been times of the unravelling of that unity.[37] The point about my historical comparison, following Riley, is that it makes it less surprising that this should be a time of confusion about priorities and goals. These are periods when the ever-present difficulties in and around the category 'women' are most acute. Riley suggests that this produces the need for contemporary feminists to 'insist on attention to "women", and yet challenge what it takes to be inappropriate insistences on "women" which spring from sexual conservatism' (Riley, 1988, p. 68). Taking this together with the other facets of this chapter I would suggest that feminism has both made more and less of a difference to the gender politics of the period of Thatcher than is generally believed.

Notes

1 Hall and Jacques (1983) contained only two articles which dealt with gender politics (see Gardiner (1983) and Segal (1983)). Gardiner observed: 'The Tory government is neither explicit about its attacks on women nor even probably aware that its policies have this effect' (1983, p. 13) and Segal argued that Thatcherism has been ambivalent in its attitude towards women's rights. Thus, as noted in Introduction Two, neither author took a perspective on Thatcherism as itself a gendered phenomenon.

2 I confess that I find it bewildering that Hall should use the diminutive 'little' for the female designation. I trust that this is a straight quotation from the Thatcherite repertoire, but I think he should have made this clear!

3 Despite her own framing of these issues, Wilson's analysis seems clearly to demonstrate the class, race and gender oppressions resulting from the policies of Thatcher's government(s). These are just some of her concerns since, amongst other arguments, she is also objecting to the positing of too sharp a break between the policies of the Thatcher governments and certain Labour Party policies during the period of social democratic consensus.

4 There is a sense of the elusiveness of the gender politics of Thatcherism within Gardiner's article (1983) – at some points almost implying either that the only thing which would count as a gender politics would be that which proclaims itself as such, or that the Conservatives did not mean to introduce policies which would have an adverse effect on women (see n. 1 above).

5 In using the term Thatcherism as a shorthand, my working definition is that offered by Andrew Gamble: 'Thatcherism has come to stand for the distinctive ideology, political style and programme of policies with which the British Conservative party has been identified since Margaret Thatcher became their leader' (Gamble, 1988, p. 20). I also acknowledge the ways in

which this has come to be 'an hegemonic project' (Gamble, 1988, p. 24; see also Hall, 1988, p. 7).

6   *Spitting Image* is a popular British television programme in which puppet caricatures of leading public figures are used for the purpose of political satire.

7   For an examination of the significance of the handbag as a 'female symbol', see Polan (1988). In fact, it was a male actor whose voice was used for Thatcher in *Spitting Image*.

8   As Jean Bethke Elshtain points out, Thatcher is one of the few women in history to have started a war (Elshtain, 1987, p. 166).

9   My reading of this piece of Thatcher's rhetoric draws out a somewhat different interpretation than that offered by Loach (1987, p. 26). However, we agree that the crucial problem is that Thatcher did not address issues of power within gender relations.

10   Indeed, Thatcher herself advocated the use of nannies well before she assumed her position as Prime Minister:

> It is possible, in my view, for a woman to run a home and continue with her career provided two conditions are fulfilled. First, her husband must be in sympathy with her wish to do another job. Secondly, where there is a young family, the joint incomes of husband and wife must be sufficient to employ a first class nanny–housekeeper to look after things in the wife's absence. The second is the key to the whole plan. (Thatcher (1960), quoted in ten Tusscher (1986, p. 79)).

See also the statement by Geoffrey Finsberg (Undersecretary of State for Health and Social Security, 1981–3), when justifying cuts in nursery provision:

> I do not see it as the state's job to say that the parents of young children should or should not work. This is the parents' decision. But they should recognize their responsibility for their children's welfare when making that decision. (Finsberg, quoted in David (1983, p. 41)).

11   This is not to say these policies do not have effects on families – different effects relating to class and race. Here I view the significance of the family within the Thatcherite era rather differently from some preceding feminist assessors (e.g. David, 1983). To some extent, this reflects my assessment of changes since these analyses.

12   This class specificity is neglected in Stuart Hall's reference to Thatcherism's appeal to 'the Thatcherite man in all of us' and 'the little Thatcherite "woman" in all of us' (Hall, 1988a, pp. 85–6). I also think that much of Jeremy Seabrook's political critique takes the form of a rather conservative retreat to traditional gender divisions partly because he does not recognize this dimension of recent developments.

13   On the notion of 'freedom and equality being achieved through the daily plebiscite of the market', rather than through other forms of political enfranchisement, see Gamble (1988, p. 50).

14   On women's assumption of responsibility for making ends meet see Wilson (1987, pp. 216–17).

15   Significant cuts were made in welfare benefits, council housing provision, school meal services and child allowances, to mention but a few key areas. As

Elizabeth Wilson emphasizes, these have meant very significant changes for different families (Wilson, 1987, p. 219).

16 The problems of mortgage defaults and arrears, lack of repairs and bad housing are amongst those delineated by Wilson (1987, p. 221).

17 While disagreeing with elements of Campbell's picture, Elizabeth Wilson also attaches importance to the growing numbers of single mothers and of female breadwinners (Wilson, 1987, p. 216).

18 Of course, the reality is that there was a considerable reduction in welfare provisions during Thatcher's period as Prime Minister (Wilson, 1987, p. 219). It is undoubtedly true that black single mothers are further stigmatized through the racist pathologizing of the black family and of blacks as burdens on the welfare system.

19 In March 1990, the Thatcher government sponsored an amendment to the Human Fertilization and Embryology Bill to lower the upper time limit on abortion by four weeks (from 28 to 24). Although this was a departure from the more characteristic non-interventionist stance of the Thatcher government(s) on this issue, their intervention in this instance was considerably less controversial, due to the degree of 'consensus' formation, particularly through parliamentary debate and the media, which preceded their amendment (see above, Chap. 7).

20 In the aftermath of the urban uprisings of 1981 and later there were calls – particularly addressed to the black community – for parents to 'police' their children more adequately. More generally, mothers' responsibilities for youth misbehaviour in riots, muggings, or on the football pitch have come under scrutiny (see David, 1983, p. 40).

21 Notably, such deregulation particularly affects part-time workers, who, in Britain, as in most other places, are mostly women (see Wilson, 1987, pp. 208–9).

22 For example, the 1980 Employment Act withdrew the rights to maternity leave and job retention in firms with fewer than ten workers.

23 Wendy Savage, an obstetrician, and Marrietta Higgs, a paediatrician, were both at the centre of widely publicized controversies in which their professional expertise was severely challenged and their competence subjected to often hostile public interrogation. The Savage case revolved around her use of 'unprofessional' childbirth techniques. In the case of Higgs, her professionalism was questioned on the basis of the criteria she had used to diagnose child sexual abuse.

24 There has been no moral backlash in Britain comparable to that experienced in the USA (see Wilson, 1987, p. 201).

25 One of Michel Foucault's most original and challenging theses was that the repression model of sexuality is misconceived. Hence, the Victorian era must be understood, he argued, not as a period in which there were social prohibitions on the expression of sexuality, but rather as a period in which these discourses proliferated (Foucault, 1978). One lesson which could be drawn from this interpretation is that prohibitions fuel the flames of the discourses of sexuality.

26 I am not claiming that this is an explicit philosophy, and whether it has been a more or less conscious orientation is not my concern here.

27 In this sense, I agree with Lynne Segal's argument that Thatcherism was quite different from the American Moral Majority. The Foucauldian framework, however, seems a more adequate one for conceptualizing the Thatcherite approach to sexuality. Moreover, it makes it possible to move away from

more monolithic views of Thatcherism and to see the divisions within the recent Conservative alliance.

28 Victoria Gillick won an Appeal Court decision to prevent the prescription of contraceptives for women under the age of 16 without parental consent. The decision was overthrown by the Law Lords in 1985.

29 My argument here is similar to that made by Andrew Gamble (1988) about the contradictions within the Thatcherite strategy towards the state, i.e. that a strong state is required to deconstruct some of the functions of the welfare state. Similarly, a strong intervention within the discourse of sexuality was required to deconstruct the proliferation of this discourse within local government.

30 Cecil Parkinson, a senior government minister discovered to have fathered his secretary's (Sara Keays') child, was the subject of a major scandal.

31 I cannot help but observe that this seems to have been played out as the Conservatives' own version of the narrative of *Fatal Attraction*.

32 Jeffrey Archer, an ex-Conservative MP and best-selling novelist, was the subject of considerable media attention concerning allegations about an extra-marital affair with a prostitute. He eventually won a major libel case against these allegations.

33 This is not a claim that 'patriarchy was perceived to be in crisis and the material base of men's control of women's power was under threat', such as that put forward previously by Tessa ten Tusscher (1986, p. 150). The latter evaluation seems too sweeping and male power too entrenched for it to be accurate.

34 Riley (1988) is concerned with the first and third of these aspects of the 'difference' question. She is most concerned with the ways in which the category of 'woman' and the attention to gender differences can be mobilized against women. This is a concern I share, but there are also dangers in failing to address the political constructions of difference. I share her emphasis on the need to be 'pragmatic' or, I would say, strategic about these issues.

35 This point is similar to that made by Loach in relation to feminist strategies under Thatcher:

> An alliance politics which attaches too much significance to sex is especially problematic under Thatcher, where gender is not only part of her project and behaviour but it is also the basis of conflicting definitions about women's politics.

As this chapter suggests, I have more difficulty with her observation that 'Margaret Thatcher, women and feminism all look alike', but I would agree that Thatcher and feminism, but not necessarily women 'differ completely, yet still flourish in the same garden' (Loach, 1987, p. 23).

36 Riley's reading of this is the most helpful one I have encountered, illustrating as it does the symptomatic confusions amongst feminists in Britain during the interwar period (Riley, 1988).

37 Also, they are periods of facing up to the spurious universality of the concept of 'women' which dominated earlier struggles, as Riley points out. As many black feminists have claimed, this has been required in the recent period. Although I disagree with much of her analysis, Juliet Mitchell raises related issues about the class-specific orientation of the recent phase of the women's movement in Britain (see Mitchell, 1986).

9
Enterprising women: images of success
JANET NEWMAN

A central strand of the political terrain of the 1980s has been the rise of enterprise culture. This well-worn term masks a complex set of meanings. At one level it signifies a nexus of political and commercial strategies which have unleashed market forces in both the public and private sectors, with the aim either of sharpening the competitive capability of business, or of restructuring state organizations through privatization and the introduction of internal markets. But the term has also been part of the ideological onslaught of Thatcherism, invoking the qualities of individual enterprise in the free market ethos of Thatcher's Britain. The term suggests a mobile, open society offering new opportunities for individual success – for women as well as men. It suggests that you do not have to follow the traditional routes, struggling up long organizational ladders or resigning yourself to the traditional limits placed on part-time or temporary work for women, but can find your own niche in the marketplace of the world of work – that is, if you have enough self reliance, financial nous, competitive spirit and the determination to overcome the barriers you might find on the way.

This is an attractive message for many women, for whom traditional occupational routes and ladders have offered limited opportunities. The attraction also lies in the way in which notions of agency and self-determination seem to echo earlier feminist messages. This chapter explores the way in which such ideas of enterprise are being packaged for women in texts which invite them to join the culture of success, by starting their own business or by grooming themselves for managerial roles.

The 'enterprising woman' has become the subject of an extraordinary explosion in the publication of books of advice for women, including *The Competitive Woman: A Survival Guide for the Woman who Aims to be Boss* (Cameron, 1989); *When a Woman Means Business* (Moore, 1989); *Working the System: 12 Ways for Women to Achieve Career Breakthroughs* (Ward, 1989); *The Influential Woman: How to Achieve Success without Losing your Femininity* (Bryce, 1989); and the US title, *Trading Up: One Woman's Story of Survival in the Wall Street Jungle* (Goldstone, 1988). The messages of these texts are echoed elsewhere in contemporary images of women and work. Features in women's magazines offer advice to women who want to make it in the world of work alongside advertising which presents images of the smoothly sophisticated successful woman as the consumer of products. Mike Nicholl's film *Working Girl* tells the story of a woman who steps into the shoes of her female executive boss, learns to play the system and gets her man: a modern Cinderella story of competition between women for success in business as well as romance.

It is notable that these enterprise promotions are all addressed to white women, and ignore the way in which black women's labour is being exploited in particular ways in the new economic patterns of the enterprise culture (see Westwood and Bhachu, 1988). However, the books with which I am dealing are interesting for two reasons. First, they address a missing dimension in most feminist analyses of work – women's experience of the structures and cultures of the workplace and business world. The feminist analysis of women and work has focused on the analysis of the sexual division of labour, pay and conditions, the relationship between work and the family, between waged and unwaged work, and so on. Women's experience of work organizations has not been central to this analysis. As Angela Coyle notes,

> Even studies of women's employment have tended to focus on women's experience of work in relation to their childcare and family responsibil-ities, and thus ignored the very concrete structures and very real social relations which keep women 'in place' in the employment structure. (Coyle, 1988, p. 12).

Second, they provide an insight into the way in which the ideological themes of mobility, opportunity and self-help are being presented to women in a manner which makes light of the structural inequalities which they face at work. They address women as individuals aspiring to develop their careers, and present them with a series of 'true life' success stories, linked to practical advice on how to 'work the system' to get ahead. Many of the stories are based on women responding to the increased demand for services through the small business sector; others on women struggling for success in the corporate organization. All combine elements of a 'rags to riches' narrative with advice for the reader. The stories hold out fantasy images of dramatic success to women; they offer a Thatcherite version of the Cinderella fable, in which *any* woman can find her life transformed and the problems of existence on the lower rungs of the labour market (or in the kitchen) miraculously solved.

The class-based nature of the images of femininity offered, and of the advice women are given through the texts, is striking. The women in

Moore's *When a Woman Means Business* and the heroine in Goldstone's *Trading Up* are shown using their class advantage, together with energy and risk-taking to break into the business world, while the aspiring office workers in Ward's *Working the System* are advised that success is to be gained only through hard work and conformity. Ward repeatedly links personal advancement to increased effectiveness to an employer: 'Jenna decided she wanted to change jobs within two years . . . First, she tried to make herself a model employee in her current job' (Ward, 1989, p. 24). Personal and company goals are seen to be in harmony; different interests, and any conflicts between them, are magically dissolved in the ethos of hard work and conformity. The injunction to women is to conform to the organizational culture, to the norms and values of the workplace, and especially to the traditional expectations of appropriate feminine behaviour. Conformity and deportment are rewarded, and women are advised that they must not challenge the culture they meet, however anti-woman it may be in its informal values and practices. This approach denies the reality of women's experiences of the blocks and barriers they will meet in attempting to develop their work prospects. Conforming means conforming to the norms of organizations which have been built around the interests and experiences of men, and which systematically block advancement for women. Career routes out of what has become known as the 'secretarial trap', for example, are virtually non-existent in most organizations, and conformity is certainly unlikely to help women break through this barrier. Only in Bryce's *The Influential Woman*, which is directed towards women in, or aspiring to, managerial jobs, is there any recognition of possible tension between the culture of organizations and the development of opportunities for women; but even here the author offers the prospect of individual advancement through women learning to negotiate their way to success and to present themselves in a manner which the organizational culture will accept.

However, all these books offer the fantasy of barriers melting away if women act and perform appropriately, a fantasy which appeals to women precisely because it invokes notions of agency and power:

> Women absolutely need to develop their careers if they aspire to enjoy real security and fulfillment. Now that we have faced the economic reality of having to work, we must go to the next step of advancing as far as we can. Smart women are accepting the challenge. They are finding creative ways of going beyond phase one. They are taking the responsibility of helping themselves and are no longer waiting for husbands, employers or the women's movement to save them. (Ward, 1989, p. 81).

In this fantasy the systematic discrimination in work organizations – against many groups, particularly black employees, as well as against women –

is denied. Whatever the nuances of the advice, the model on which it is based is of self-help and responsibility. This notion of self-reliance is a central strand of Thatcherite ideology and links the moral theme of independence (from the 'nanny state') and the economic theme of personal success. Success itself is depicted as the product of individual energy and risk-taking. Moore comments:

> I honestly believe that anyone who has a depth of commonsense, a lot of courage and capacity for very hard work can be successful in business. I am constantly being told how lucky I am, and, as Prime Minister Margaret Thatcher is fond of quoting, 'Luck is only opportunity meeting readiness', and I must admit the harder I work the luckier I become. (Moore, 1989, p. 10).

This reference to Thatcher suggests the possible significance of Britain's first woman Prime Minister as a symbol of success for women. Her own success has perhaps allowed the emergence of the assertively female model of the successful businesswoman or manager which is found in some of these texts. As in these texts, her success and power in the male world of government has been presented as an essentially individual achievement, not an achievement linked to the advancement of women as a group. While Thatcher articulates images which link her experience to that of other women (housewife, home budgetter, mother and, more recently, grandmother), she does not identify herself with women's interests. Ros Brunt comments:

> She [Thatcher] set out to make it in a man's world and was never interested in even negotiating the terms of patriarchy. Thatcher's success in the realms of patriarchal politics is precisely to do with her effectiveness as a woman and the way she inhabits particular feminine roles while appearing to disavow femininity. (Brunt, 1987, p. 23).

The self-help ethos, so dominant in the texts, largely excludes any notion of the specificity of women's collective interests, denying gender as a social division through the discourses of individualism and enterprise. The texts offer an image of woman as a successful individual in the competitive world of business and work, as entering the enterprise culture on equal terms with men, and able to succeed on equal terms, provided she follows certain rules. Opportunities are portrayed as open to all, whether male or female, if they are enterprising; and class differences are magically dissolved in the images of women with affluent and well-ordered life styles. These images portray women who know how to 'properly package' themselves in terms of personality as well as dress (Ward, 1989); who can afford to use consultants to help in this process, and to buy domestic help to resolve the dilemmas of the working woman (Bryce, 1989); and whose domestic struggles concern who should load the dishwasher (Moore, 1989). The road to success is essentially white and middle-class, and is one which opens up for women who began from advantageous positions in the organizational hierarchy, or from positions where they could impress bank managers with their (or their husbands') economic collateral.

However, the texts contain contradictory messages. In some cases, women are addressed as new entrants to the traditionally masculine cultures of work, having to adopt masculine values to succeed. The imagery in Cameron is highly competitive; it is subtitled *A Survival Guide for the Woman who Aims to be Boss*, and has a cover picture depicting two men and one woman poised on starting blocks for the beginning of a race. Its message is expressed in terms such as 'progress', 'win', 'battle' and 'war'. Her advice is concerned with selling the self in a competitive market (for example, how to 'dress to succeed'). This kind of language is also much used in Goldstone, who is urged by her husband to 'go out there and win, win, win!' (Cameron, 1989, p. 160).

At the same time, the texts recognize that women are positioned in this race in particular ways, and are preoccupied with advising women on how to manage their femininity and to balance work with the traditionally feminine domains of family, domesticity and romance. In short, the theme of the dissolution of gender as a social division is in tension with the theme of advising women on the importance of 'managing' their femininity. However, the overarching discourse of individualism, which dissolves difference by positing equivalence and invoking ideologies of equality, conceals the contradictory ways in which women are addressed. The following sections explore how these contradictions underpin the messages of these texts about balancing femininity and success, and work with family, domesticity and romance.

Having it all? Femininity and success

The gendered nature of the discourse of success is suggested by the difference between the female success stories of these texts and the cultural images of the male entrepreneur. The latter is often portrayed in popular cultural forms through the conventions of the masculine adventure narrative[1] – he is tough, ruthless, has to fight to overcome obstacles, and has to struggle to win the race (supported at every step by women, managing and servicing both home and office). In contrast, while the image of the successful woman is of one who no longer has to wait for her Prince Charming but can take responsibility for her own success, her task is still the feminine one of learning to manage herself and her image. In all the texts under discussion, image is depicted as the vital ingredient of success for women: typical chapter headings include 'Your image – don't underrate yourself' (Cameron, 1989), 'Managing your image' (Bryce, 1989), and 'Assess your image' (Moore, 1989). But what kind of image should women present? How can we be both powerful and feminine, both competitive and caring?

In the texts for those low on the rungs of the organizational ladder, stereotypical female qualities of passivity, modesty and even stupidity are invoked in the construction of what Ward terms the 'properly packaged' woman (p. 114). This is a woman who is 'so smart that you know when to be ignorant' (p. 58); and who knows how to present herself modestly in speech as well as appearance: 'don't try to steal the show or keep the floor. Do exercise good judgement in timing, phrasing and articulating thoughtful questions so you come off looking helpful and interested instead of egotistical or adversative (sic)' (p. 113). Appearance is a major preoccupation: 'You must be immaculate at all times, polished nails, perfect make-up and hair . . . It is more expected of a woman than it is of a man' (Cameron, 1989, p. 37).

Each text talks about the need to conform to the business environment in style and image. However, Bryce, Cameron and Moore all emphasize that this does not mean denying one's femininity; indeed, they link an assertive femininity to the projection of power: 'The theme of this chapter is how we signal to the outside world through the way we stand, sit, move and dress that we are powerful, influential, assertive – and feminine' (Bryce, 1989, p. 73). Femininity itself is inflected by the Thatcherite discourse of choice: here as elsewhere the individualism of the enterprise culture is linked to power through consumer choice in the marketplace. Feminine style can now be selected along with a choice of lifestyle (that telling concept of the marketing world), choice at work, choice as consumers. In Bryce, for example, women speak about how they developed their own style – one always wears high heels and make-up, one wears low heels and switches between jeans and designer clothes, with lots of big jackets to make her feel powerful, and one gives an account of how she changed styles: '"I still wear a suit when I want to be one of the men, as it carries an air of authority. But I have moved away from the slightly male picture I used to present. I prefer to wear more feminine suits now"' (Bryce, 1989, p. 77). Any problems in selecting the right style can be resolved through the market itself by using a range of wardrobe consultants, colour analysts and other services which are recommended in Cameron and Bryce.

These ideas of choice for women at the level of style can perhaps be read as a kind of co-option of the earlier feminist rhetoric of 'women's right to choose' in the spheres of work, sexuality and reproduction. Perhaps as these demands have become less publicly credible in the 1980s, they have been supplanted by notions of choice of style and choice in the marketplace, and by notions that it is valid to choose to do what feminists had identified as activities linked to female subjugation. Cameron encourages the reader to 'accept your femininity, it is not something to be ashamed of or suppressed. If it pleases you, read Catherine Cookson or *Woman*. Paint your toenails. Three hours spent piping a gateau for your man is not subjugation *if that is what you choose to do*' (Cameron, 1989, p. 15; my emphasis).

Traditionally, public power has been the preserve of men and with notable exceptions women have only been permitted power through their association with powerful men, or through the exercise of indirect strategies compatible with femininity (such as manipulation and deviousness). Such indirect strategies are recommended by the texts. Power is to be gained through the deployment of stereotypically feminine skills: 'there are sometimes positive advantages in being a woman, if only one is aware of them and willing to apply them' (Cameron, 1989, p. 15). Key advantages are visibility, winning confidences from men and women's 'natural' cunning:

> Owing to our sex's long history of subjugation, cunning is inborn. It was one of the few weapons our female ancestors possessed and is part of our evolution . . . Why should all these years of oppression have been in vain? . . . Your natural cunning is your best defense while preparing to progress and win. (Cameron, 1989, p. 16).

The experience of women's subjugation is transformed within the discourse of success into a positive asset for women. Indeed, these texts tend to see difference rather than equality as the route to power – in short, difference can be used as an asset.

At the same time, however, difference is never allowed to become division, through the denial of the specificity of women's positions in the labour market, and placings within organizational cultures and hierarchies. The message is that opportunities are there for the taking, that gender is no longer a barrier. Women are, then, addressed as gendered and as ungendered subjects at the same moment; and consequently the notion of power for women remains beset by tensions and contradictions which these texts do not even attempt to resolve.

Women who become powerful are warned to be careful to retain elements of traditional femininity; and different elements of female identity are articulated so that passivity or subordination in one area is set against power in another. In the competitive world of high finance, Goldstone's success on Wall Street is portrayed as compatible with her femininity because it is based on the use of intuition, not knowledge. She is described as hugely successful, but her success comes from trusting her 'gut' reactions, and from playing hunches. This approach is contrasted with those of male financiers who continually exhibit knowledge which she does not understand; and with that of her husband who patiently explains things to her when she gets home at night, and who gives her advice, which later turns out to have been right all along as she reels from the heavy losses or bureaucratic disasters incurred after not following his advice (Goldstone, 1988, pp. 112, 208). Goldstone also finds ways of relating to the men in the financial 'jungle' which are non-competitive and non-threatening, becoming 'surrogate girlfriend, cheerleader, and den mother' (p. 102).

It does not matter which attributes of femininity remain to offset the images of success and power. What is significant is that in each text at least one such attribute is deployed to ground women in traditional feminine domains, and thus guarantee their femininity. It is striking that all the texts emphasize how success at work is compatible with home and family life, and with successful relationships with male partners. In this respect, heterosexuality plays an unchallenged role as a crucial means of confirming femininity, and women's power in the workplace is offset against the reproduction of femininity within domestic heterosexual relationships.

However, these happy assumptions about domestic heterosexuality take a different form when transferred to the workplace. At the core of the dilemmas and difficulties dealt with by the texts is that of how women are to manage sexuality at work. The resolution, we read, is for women, at least those in corporate organizations, to learn how to present a feminine but not a sexualized image: 'We also have to face up to the dilemma that if we are very sexually attractive to men, then we may not seem very powerful and influential to them' (Bryce, 1989, p. 77). This comment highlights the contradictions between the patriarchal relations which pervade the organizational worlds of work and women's attempts to gain equality. Male power in the sexual domain crosscuts and subverts the power based on formal roles and hierarchies; for example, the pervasiveness of male sexual stereotyping of women undermines their attempts to gain recognition through skills and abilities. The texts might advise women to downplay their sexuality, but this hardly provides us with any help in dealing with either the problem of the constant sexualizing of women in the workplace, or its consequences (whether by the erosion of women's confidence and competence, or explicit sexual harassment).

Cameron is the only author to deal with sexual harassment, and here women are advised to develop avoidance techniques, and not to take up harassment as a formal issue. In a personal anecdote, she recalls one experience of repeated harassment, and her own decision: 'It seemed somehow unprofessional to report him to his MD. If I had taken this course, I am sure I would have been the one to drown in the waves that I was making' (Cameron, 1989, p. 76). Implicit here is the view that sexual harassment is a woman's problem, not that of men, or of the organization. Indeed, the problem is seen to lie in the use of faulty interpersonal strategies by women themselves, and the suggestion is that solutions are to be found in women changing their behaviour towards men.

In contrast to the texts dealing with women in corporate organizations, in which women are advised to downplay their sexuality, those depicting women in the entrepreneurial world of consumer capitalism convey a different message about sexuality and power. Moore, for example, presents an explicitly sexualized image of success; the women she describes have beautiful, well exercised, well groomed and expensively dressed bodies, and they also wield considerable financial power. The contradictions between work and sexuality, resolved in other texts by advice on 'managing' sexuality to gain success, are masked through notions of success in both. Sexuality is no longer to be used to manipulate the men who wield power, but is linked to a very specifically female version of success through both the image of the product itself (such as the body transformed by dancing, or by natural beauty products) and through the images of the women who head the companies that produce it. In the late 1980s enterprise culture it is clearly 'sexy' to be successful, and sexual power and financial power are entwined in the images of women who provide products for the 'new woman' of the entrepreneurial culture with money to spend on enhancing her body and life style.

Beyond superwoman? Managing paid work and the family

Paid work and the family are sites of competing pressures for women, pressures which are experienced in different ways by working-class and middle-class women, by black and white women. For the middle-class women whom these texts address the sexual division of labour has traditionally been individualized into a matter of personal choice between work and the family. In the 1970s, Shirley Conran's *Superwoman* (1975) suggested to middle-class women that this choice was resolvable through individual effort in both home and work – women could have it all, albeit at great cost to themselves. Not surprisingly, the 'superwoman' syndrome was heavily criticized by feminists, since it left unchallenged the sexual division of labour within the home.

The 'superwoman' resolution of the 1970s is also addressed explicitly in the success stories of the 1980s, and the texts contrast their own message, which claims to take the interests of women themselves into account, with the 1970s message of piling work at home on top of work in the labour market and trying to be perfect in each sphere. Yet, in the 1980s life for women became more than balancing work and home lives – time for the self became a third element in the equation. Cameron talks of the need for leisure and exercise, and for taking time out to enjoy life; Moore stresses that women should take time for themselves, by using the new support services, visiting health farms and taking leisure seriously, as well as juggling work and the family.

Leisure and home become constituted as things which are to be *managed* in the same way that work is to be managed; the same skills are to be deployed, the same tactics used:

> I've always worked, I've always played tennis, I've always enjoyed my husband and children. Sure, different things take precedence at different times, but everyone has to do a certain amount of juggling whether she works or not. My secret to handling everything is *setting priorities* and *planning my time*. (Quote from a woman manager in Ward (1989, p. 31); emphasis in original).

Bryce uses managerial language to discuss non-work issues. Chapter 10 is entitled '*Managing* your domestic life', and includes sections on 'Trying to be superwoman', '*Negotiating* help', '*Priorities* at work and at home', '*Crisis management*'. Even relationships are to be seen as a form of work: Goldstone realizes that 'romance and passion' have to be *worked* at 'just like everything else' (Bryce, 1989, p. 194; my emphases). Husbands and children are to be '*negotiated*' with and '*influenced*'; housework is to be '*delegated*' and '*organised*'; leisure is to be '*planned*', and time for different activities is to be '*managed*'. In this way it is suggested that the problems women experience in coping can be attributed to a lack of management skills, rather than to the pressures of women's multiple roles.

The whole of life is thus constructed within the discursive practices of managerialism; and the potential contradictions between different elements of women's lives and identities can be resolved – if only women work hard enough and manage well enough they can have it all (or nearly). However, unlike the 'superwoman' of the 1970s, middle-class women now do not have to strive to do all the domestic labour themselves. The ethos of many of these texts is that services – nannies, cleaners, laundry services, shopping delivery services, outside catering services, and so on – should be purchased to resolve some of the problems of domestic labour, and that women must learn not to feel guilty about it.

The tensions between the familial ideology of Thatcherism and the need for women to play an increasing economic role are thus seen to be lessened by the expansion of a substratum of other women workers – some in highly traditional roles (cleaners, childminders), and some in the mushrooming sector of small businesses providing domestic services. As a result, the contradictions between paid work and domestic labour are resolved through the market in a way which presents little challenge to the traditional social relations of housework. Personal solutions to how domestic labour and childcare are to be organized may be negotiated either within the family (as in Bryce, when women have to take the lead in organizing and motivating others) or through the marketplace (as in Moore), but the new choices which these texts seem to offer mask the fact that in every case the responsibility for this work remains with women.

The message of all but one of these texts is that women can have it all – family life, and success and power at work – and more: time to nourish and take care of themselves, and for rewarding relationships with their husbands and children. Heterosexuality is a key dimension of the 'femininity' which women must retain if they are to achieve all this. The successful marriage is part of the overall image of success – behind each of the women in business lies a man successful in his own right, unthreatened by his wife, supportive both personally and financially. Marital partnerships are often combined with business partnerships, though usually in a clearly role-segregated way: in Moore, husbands accompany wives at interviews with bank managers to lend financial credibility, look after the business, property and financial side, while women concentrate on the 'creative' aspects of design and development.

However, these relationships are to be nourished and worked for. Every text discusses the problems for women of carrying over power at work into power in the home. Moore advises,

> If the man in your life does have a chip about your success, then you must be prepared to massage his ego. Don't hog the conversation when you're with friends or colleagues. Of course you're excited about what you're doing and want to tell everyone who's willing to listen, but make sure you balance that by asking his advice on subjects he is experienced in or where you value his opinion. Just because you become used to making unilateral decisions at work, don't start doing the same thing at home, even if it is your money you're spending. (Moore, 1989, p. 79).

Women's power must not challenge that of men, and must not be fought for at work at the expense of building family life and marital relationships. Above all, it must not challenge the dominance of heterosexuality as the institution within which women's identities are constructed.

Indeed, one text presents a cautionary tale to warn women against getting too absorbed in work at the expense of marriage. Nancy Goldstone's power on Wall Street may be portrayed as perfectly compatible with her femininity in the workplace, but at home things are different: 'On the trading desk, my word was law. No-one questioned my decisions, or my right to throw ever increasing sums of money at the market. If I told Peter or Phillip to do something, they did it. Fast. This approach, however, did not seem to work as well at home' (Goldstone, 1988, p. 111).

Goldstone's story is at heart a romance – the chapters on her experience at work are interposed with those showing the development of her relationship with Larry, a paragon of knowledge, good advice, understanding and support. Her success leads to a key point of tension in her relationship, not because Larry is insecure in his masculinity, but because of Nancy's own insecurity and need to prove herself. The tension in the relationship builds up, and eventually she realizes that she is faced with a choice when she is offered an even more prestigious position: 'something inside me said no. It was a purely instinctive reaction. I guess I was beginning to understand at just what price such power is bought. It would be bought at the price of my marriage' (Goldstone, 1988, p. 228). She decides not to go for the position, and leaves work altogether. This moral tale illustrates how the conflicts for women endemic in the sexual division of labour can be resolved through the ethos of choice; a choice in which the family must always in the end come first, and in which women's power must be curtailed when it comes to threaten that of men.

The notion of 'having it all' in the other texts can be understood as a different form of resolution, and one perhaps more in keeping with the entrepreneurial spirit of Thatcherism. Wilson (1987) notes that Thatcherism has not meant 'back to the home' for women (though this is not a view which would be accepted throughout government circles[2]). Women's paid labour is an essential factor in economic expansion and the development of the flexible labour force, but at the same time women's work in the home has increased as a result of the cut-backs in social welfare provision. In other words, women's labour is needed in both spheres. But what is hidden in the ethos of 'having it all' is the way in which the tension between work and family for middle-class women is increasingly being resolved through the market; a market in which middle-class women buy the labour of working-class women; in which white women buy the labour of black women; and in which enterprise for women means the creation of businesses which essentially service other women in a way which offers no challenge to the sexual division of labour. The race and class blindness of entrepreneurial ideology masks the way in which different women experience the enterprise culture. While for some it may mean (limited) new opportunities, for many black and working-class women it means an expansion of low-paid and low status work in traditionally female areas of the economy.

These differences are, however, dissolved in the overarching individualist ethos of entrepreneurialism. This individualism underpins the advice on managing work and domesticity. We may no longer have to strive to be superwomen, but the family and domesticity are added to the list of things we have to 'manage' to be a successful *woman* manager. Sexual exploitation and harassment are, too, aspects of the workplace which the sensible and successful woman must manage. It is as individuals that women now have to hold together their domestic and economic lives; and in the texts the personal nature of the offered solutions reinforces this model of the family as an individual, not political, domain. The problems women face in finding a foothold in the enterprise culture are personal problems, not political issues; and solutions are to be found through individual, not collective strategies.

Women in the post-feminist world

> Have you ever criticized men as a group for the way they treat women at work? If so, have you stopped to think about your grievance in an historical context or from the male point of view? Do you really, honestly believe that men are the enemy? (Ward, 1989, p. 50).

In the texts of Ward, Moore, Cameron and Bryce discussed above, an image of a truly post-feminist world is constructed, in which the last bastions of discrimination against women are fast disappearing. Ward identifies the view that women encounter too many blocks and problems at work to get ahead as one of the 'myths' about women and work, and argues that by accepting these myths women block their own development. Moore focuses on the advances which women have made in business over the last ten years, and relates these to the wider acceptance of women in many spheres of activity. She notes, 'We still have a long way to go, but I have no doubt we will get there in the end. Many of the young women I meet are so full of confidence and energy, not even recognising the existence of the obstacles that we have had to overcome' (Moore, 1989, p. 9).

Any lingering barriers – unfriendly bank managers, business partners who exploit your success, unsupportive families, discriminating interviewers, or sexual harassment – can be overcome by women getting their attitudes right, developing personal and professional skills and negotiating with those who hold power. Cameron advises women how to manage different kinds of men in the business world, but part of her advice – to look interested but to 'Think of England' – is essentially concerned with containing the problem, not meeting it (and resonates with connotations of sexual oppression).

Any residual problems are constructed as personal, not related to systematic discrimination. Where discrimination is acknowledged, it is trivialized:

> As a woman making out in business, therefore, you may be susceptible to prejudice. To a greater or lesser extent, so are cockneys, coloured people, ginger haired people, lapsed freemasons, very short people, atheists and many, many more. It isn't fair, but that's how it is. Occasionally you may even benefit as some people tend to overcompensate to assuage their guilt. (Cameron, 1989, p. 53).

Sexism is a matter of personal prejudice, removed from the social relations of the business world. And this prejudice is trivialized and normalized, alongside racism, in Cameron's flip dismissal. The message of the texts is that with the end of serious discrimination we have moved beyond the need for feminism. Successful women are portrayed as those who do not engage with women's issues or struggle against male power strategies – this is counterproductive to your own advancement. To reinforce the message, feminism itself is often explicitly attacked by being opposed to femininity, professionalism and co-operation:

> I am not suggesting that a woman should deny her femininity and operate like a hard line feminist; indeed such a 'bulldozing' approach would be incompatible with the technique of a commercially minded businesswoman. (Cameron, 1989, p. 13).

> Some women have used a shrill tone in documenting the 'rights and claims' of women. Basically, they've issued two lists: Things we should not tolerate; and Things we should demand. It is time to compile a third list labelled, Things we should learn about are professionalism, cooperation, getting along and contribution. (Ward, 1989, p. 67).

It is further argued that the feminist agenda can be abandoned since the very presence of successful women as role models will be of benefit to other women:

> Concentrate on your individual effort toward getting ahead rather than depending on women as a group to help you. If you make breakthroughs for yourself, you'll pave the way for other women to do the same. Remember, any successful group is made up of individuals who realise they must help themselves before they can help others. Approach your advancement as an individual, not as a crusader for a cause. Women who excel individually lend a degree of credibility to all women. (Ward, 1989, p. 49).

This is a highly depoliticized view of the world, and a strongly argued rejection of feminist struggles. Power is offered to women as individuals on condition that they reject the notion of the need for women to articulate demands at a collective level.[3]

The costs for women of drawing attention to inequalities are constantly stressed. Moving away from the shrill demands of feminism is represented as a move towards 'realism' for women:

> Think broadly about work . . . Men and women as groups are at different levels developmentally in the world of work. Don't think of this in terms of bad or good; think of it in terms of what is real. You

will make better decisions if you make them based on reality. (Ward, 1989, p. 48).

Women are enjoined to stop complaining and conform to this 'new realism'. Over and over again we find the formulation 'this may be unfair, but it's how it is so get on with it rather than complaining' – whether this is the treatment of women in the business world as a whole, in organizational life, or within the family. But this representation of what is real denies that other reality of structural inequalities.

The framework of these texts can be linked to the notion of a post-feminist ethos, a term from the US which Rosenfelt and Stacey (1987) describe as demarcating 'an emerging culture and ideology that simulta-neously incorporates, revises and depoliticises many of the fundamental issues advanced by second-wave feminism' (Rosenfelt and Stacey, 1987, p. 77). In the texts, liberal feminist views are echoed in the emphasis on notions of individual advancement and the legitimacy of women gaining entry to male preserves. These liberal notions are incorporated and revised in the individualist ethos of entrepreneurial ideology, in a way which strips them of their earlier feminist context. Success is conditional on abandoning feminist rhetoric and collective action. To confront issues means not only potentially being stigmatized at work, but falling into the category of Thatcher's 'moaning Minnies'. Success for individual women, we learn, can only be won by abandoning feminism; but this would represent a victory which leaves the basic structures of patriarchy unchallenged.[4]

These texts are depoliticizing because they construct an image of a world in which opportunities appear to be open, in which gender seems no longer to be a problem to be addressed except at the level of which image of fem-ininity to choose. They neutralize the issues of work, family and sexuality which feminism struggled to put on the political agenda. All reject the possibility of confronting and challenging male values and behaviour; all accept the legitimacy of the structures and cultures of organizational life and merely debate how women can best gain entry.

However, organizations have remained profoundly gendered, and women experience them in specific ways depending on class, gender and whether or not they confront the culture of the office, shopfloor or boardroom. These texts do acknowledge the particular ways in which women experience the world of business and management – the conditions of entry, and the rules of engagement – and attempt to guide other women through this unfamiliar terrain. The guidance concerns how women must act to please men: how we should look, how we should soften our strident feminist tones in order to reap the rewards of admission to the male preserves of power. The texts offer a framework through which women address other women and seemingly help them on their way; however, they do so within an overarching framework of patriarchal assumptions. The structures that create the 'special' problems women face, and which elicit the need for advice for women, are never addressed. Any extension of opportunities for women, any acceptance of the idea of women's success at work, is limited by the insistence that this should not disturb or challenge the sexual division of labour.

Women, enterprise and change

In spite of the rhetoric of Thatcherite ideology, refashioned in these texts to highlight new opportunities, the rise of the enterprise culture has had high costs for women. The gains linked to the equal opportunities and equal pay legislation of earlier decades, limited as they were,[5] have been eroded with the decline of trade union power, the attacks on equal opportunity policies and the dismantling of the regulation and control of employment. The exploitation of women in the labour force has increased with the growth of part-time and contract labour (including new categories of homeworker) to meet the needs of the 'flexible firm' (and increasingly the flexible public sector employer). At the same time the redrawing of the public–private divide, with the demise of the welfare state, has added to the burden of women's work in the household, community and voluntary sector, while reducing opportunities for women in public sector employment (Phillips, 1987).

However, while the changes are damaging to women's employment in traditional areas of female work, they have also opened up some new spaces for women – more women are starting their own business, and more are entering managerial posts. These changes should not be overestimated; women in business are more likely than men to be sole trader enterprises rather than heading new companies employing others. The numbers of women in management have increased as management has become a label attached to lower status jobs; and male managers and finance directors have displaced many women from top management jobs in the professions. Nevertheless, these texts do relate to greater mobility in some limited areas of the female labour market. And they address questions which feminism has largely ignored: of how women actually experience the workplace. How should women who have gained some power at work proceed? Where should they direct their energy – towards change or accommodation? What kinds of personal solutions can be crafted in response to the problems women face when entering the male dominated organizations of work? What kinds of personal and career choices might they face, and how should they respond? These are important questions and deserve a different framework of analysis from that offered by the texts, a framework which acknowledges and politicizes women's collective interests. This is, however, difficult for a number of reasons.

Most significant is the dominance of the discourse of choice and individualism. The willingness to perceive problems and blocks as individual dilemmas, and the lack of political vocabulary for taking on collective issues, are both derived directly from this discourse. It has the consequences of depoliticizing experience and of obscuring the material powerlessness of workers faced with such 'choices'. Within this discourse the ethos of post-feminism interacts with that of equal opportunities legislation and practices in complex and contradictory ways. First, both individualize problems and solutions; and both suggest that the barriers facing women in paid work have been removed, except for residual pockets of discrimination which can be overcome (through women's own efforts, or through the law). Indeed, it is possible to go further and suggest that perhaps one of the main impacts of equal opportunities has been to establish and reinforce the discourse of gender neutrality in the workplace. Organizations now pretend to be 'gender blind' in a spurious attempt to be seen to be treating men and women equally.

Second, the articulation of women's collective interests has become more problematic with the co-option of a progressive vocabulary and feminist demands. For example, job sharing is now a tool used by management to facilitate the employment of women in the short-term, part-time flexible workforce; training opportunities for women are now linked to the needs of employers in the light of future skill shortages; even crèches may be provided, but to meet the needs of hard pressed employers rather than the needs of women themselves. It has yet to be revealed how severely limited the opportunities for women promised by the new era of skill shortages will be.

Third, this has happened at a time when the 1970s feminist version of women's collective interests has been challenged as black women have revealed the racist assumptions of the white women's movement, and research has pointed to the failures of equal opportunity policies to address the structural racism of the workplace (Bruegel, 1989; Phizacklea, 1988). Notions of collective interests have masked the divisions between women positioned differently in the enterprise culture: between black and white women; between those in managerial positions and those working within trade unions; between those in the core labour market and those struggling for survival on the contractual and part-time fringes.

Despite these problems, oppositional frameworks are urgently needed in order to reject or transcend notions of individual success, and to include the possibility of bringing about change in the patterns of power and dominance within work organizations. To do this feminism must move beyond the framework of equal opportunities, not only because this has worked against the recognition of the different interests of different women, but because it has given priority to the goal of achieving equal representation with men in the context of a competition in which it is clear that only some can win. It leaves the basic structures of patriarchal organizations unchallenged. Attention needs to be focused not only on women's access to employment opportunities, but on the internal gender dynamics of work organizations: what Coyle terms the 'very concrete structures and very real social relations which keep women "in place" in the employment structure' (Coyle, 1988, p. 12).

These structures and relationships, the culture which ascribes different kinds of value to women's and men's work, and the everyday routines and practices of the workplace which embody a multiplicity of coded messages and signs, all work to inform women of their marginality to the cultures of power, whether on the assembly line or in an office, in a trade union or in management. Women struggling for change within organizations face hard decisions about how far to challenge the cultures and social relations which confront them. Developments such as the Women and Work Programme[6] and other initiatives have exposed the marginality of most of us to dominant cultural practices and our exclusion from informal power networks. They have revealed that the dominant organizational practices through which value is ascribed to different kinds of work and groups of workers obscures our contribution to the workplace, and marginalizes the concerns about values, quality and equity to which women give priority. It has revealed the stress which women in the public sector experience under the double burden of striving for organizational change at the same time that they are working to defend services – struggles which are at many points contradictory. Above all, this work has shown how powerful gender divisions are in structuring women's experience of work organizations, despite the gender-neutral discourse of post-feminism.

What the notion of enterprise and the other discourses of Thatcherism offer women is a route through these problems and contradictions based on success for women as individuals:

> Thatcher has welcomed the spirit of the modern go-getting woman who has been made to feel guilty about her desire for success. The Prime Minister is their model . . . In opposition to feminism, Thatcher represents a female triumphalism which speaks to collective identity but then disregards it at the point where it is marginal to power. (Loach, 1987, p. 24).

Women are permitted access to the goods of the enterprise culture, are permitted to succeed, but only so long as they do this in a way which does not challenge the basic structures of power. The texts discussed in this chapter set out the 'rules' which women must follow in order to succeed while leaving these structures intact. The rules concern how femininity is to be balanced against power; how work is to be balanced against women's traditional responsibilities for the family (supported for some through the market); and how any tensions which arise when women's pursuit of work opportunities confronts structural sources of power (in the home or at work) are to be 'managed' at a personal level, thus magically dissolving their potential political content. The first and most important rule which these texts enforce is that women who want to get on must abandon any identification with the needs and interests of other women. The individualist ethos of success can, however, be challenged by enabling groups of women to address their collective experiences in a way which acknowledges difference, and to develop collaborative strategies for change.

Notes

1   These comments are based on the work of Richard Johnson at the Department of Cultural Studies, University of Birmingham (unpublished).
2   Despite this claim, it must be recognized that many exponents of Tory family policy have not accepted the validity of women with children entering the labour market. The benefit structure and other aspects of social welfare policy, especially on childcare provision, severely limit women's opportunities in the labour market.
3   Notions of collective interests are included as a marginal theme in Cameron (1989) and Bryce (1989), with women being encouraged to join women's business and professional organizations and women's support networks, but this is subordinate to the individualist ethos of the texts as a whole.
4   Others, outside the framework of these texts, offer a different 'post-feminist' view based on economic change as 'solving' the problems which feminism addressed. A Women's Education Conference, 'Harnessing the Female Resource' at Croydon in July 1989 drew together a number of notable speakers who argued that the battle for women's progress must be through harnessing women's contribution to the economy to improve Britain's competitive edge, especially in the light of skill shortages and the development of the single European market, rather than by reiterating the dated messages of feminism. However, arguments which deny the specificities of gender and foreground those of economic necessity will not, as history has shown, be of any lasting benefit to women.
5   See Snell *et al.*, 1981; Atkins, 1986; Beechey, 1987; Coyle, 1989.
6   The Women and Work Programme, based at Coventry Polytechnic, is a national centre for positive action in women's employment. We work with women in organizations, through training, research and consultancy, to develop strategies for intervention and change; run programmes for women seeking to enter or re-enter the labour market; and research into women's experience of work and access to work opportunities. We also provide a forum for debate through seminar programmes and publications.

10

Enterprise fictions: women of substance

ESTELLA TINCKNELL

The bookshops of Britain are full of enterprising women these days. Women who have built up multi-million pound businesses from nothing, using only their own gritty determination and a unique flair for entrepreneurial activity to help them. Women who take and discard lovers at will in the search for the one man who will cherish them. Women who know both grinding poverty and delicious luxury, birth and death, joy and grief. In sum, women who have taken all that life has to offer and have survived – magnificently.

These splendid women do not actually work in the bookshops, of course; instead, they stalk the pages of popular fiction, satisfying an ever growing demand for fat paperbacks crammed with female triumphs. Such books are primarily bought and read by women, and that is how they are marketed. Some may be familiar through their translation to the television screen as highly polished mini-series: *Scruples, Princess Daisy, Hold the Dream*. All are salty with a transatlantic tang.

One thing is certain: all these 'wannabe' fictions – as they have been jocularly tagged – are immensely popular; they speak to women in a very particular way, articulating perspectives on issues of consumption, power and femininity which are profoundly important but which remain marginalized by a discursive agenda that continues to identify women's concerns as trivial. Such stories seem to be offering new sorts of heroines: women who know what they want and how to go about getting it, and who are prepared to earn their wealth in the public arena of business, apparently unconfined by the traditional restrictions of femininity. These women, with their ambitions and their lovers, their material wealth are, of course, fictional – figures of fantasy. But their success as models of promise, of what women might be, represents, too, a very real shift in attitudes and assumptions that is wholly political and is part of a much broader social response to the feminist critique of patriarchy. For they are, in effect, women who are 'having it all'.

Reading is very much a private pleasure and that is why it is so important both to women, who make up the bulk of fiction readers in this country, and to feminist critics who have focused on the discourses of popular romance as a means of understanding the ways in which notions of masculinity and femininity are imaginatively deployed and reproduced. For in so far as fictional narratives offer a way to explore and negotiate questions of who and what we are within an imaginative framework, these 'wannabe' narratives of glamorous, active women confronting and challenging the public, masculine domain of work clearly offer their readers – on one level at least – some sort of solution to the 'problem of femininity': for their heroines effectively resolve the conditions of their gender not by denying femininity or even transcending it, but by celebrating it.

In this chapter I want to concentrate on one particular example of 'wannabe' fiction. I have chosen it because I believe it has special significance both in what it contains and offers the reader and in what it seeks to leave out or deny. The book in question is *A Woman of Substance* by Barbara Taylor Bradford. The book was first published – interestingly! – in 1979 and proved a steady bestseller throughout the 1980s. It has been reprinted in paperback alone a total of seventeen times and is still, ten years after its initial appearance, in great demand. It can be found at almost every available paperback outlet, from bookshops to newsagents and supermarkets, and for that reason alone must by now be amongst the all-time bestsellers.

A Woman of Substance was one of the first of the 'wannabe' (or what I would prefer to term the 'enterprise') fictions to reach the bookstalls, and for that reason helped to shape the format of what remains a highly nebulous, ill-defined genre. For, despite the blurb of its covers which seeks to place it as a 'dynastic saga', the book defies formulaic definition in many respects. It is a saga in the sense that it spans over sixty years of this century, yet its primary preoccupation is with the career of its heroine, Emma Harte, and in that sense it is not at all a 'family romance' in the way, for example, of Susan Howatch's *Cashelmara*.[1] Indeed, the character of Emma Harte thoroughly dominates the book in a way which leaves little space for others, as I shall discuss below.

Before examining some aspects of the book in detail I will give a brief outline of the plot, which is fairly simple. *A Woman of Substance* is the story of Emma Harte, a Yorkshire lass born into a poor but honest working-class family at the turn of the century. Her mother is dying of tuberculosis as the story opens, her father and brothers are employed by the local mill which is owned by the Fairley family who occupy Fairley Hall, the local 'big house' where Emma works as a maid. Emma is seduced by Edwin Fairley, the younger son of the house, and finds herself pregnant and abandoned by him. She runs away to Leeds where she finds work in a clothing factory and eventually opens a small general store in the suburb of Armley. Through hard work and extraordinary business skill she is able to expand her shop and to open the first of a chain of department stores which, with her unique skills and talent, she later develops into a multinational empire. In the process Emma works her way through several proposals of marriage, a rape attempt, two unsatisfactory husbands (Joe Lowther and Arthur Ainsley) and one great love (Paul McGill), a number of loyal friends and five children. By the end of the novel Emma is firmly established as the undisputed matriarch of her domain.

One immediate issue linked to this text's status as a key example of enterprise fiction needs to be noted at the outset and that is the historical moment of its appearance. The publication date of 1979 is, as I observed above, interesting. For more than one 'woman of substance' made her debut on the public stage in that year and there is no doubt that both Emma Harte and Margaret Thatcher share certain characteristics. Both are gutsy, determined women, contemptuous of perceived weaknesses in the men and women around them, and it is hardly coincidental that two such models of femininity have emerged in the same decade. For both represent, in their own ways, a response to contemporary feminist critiques of an overwhelmingly patriarchal society; Margaret Thatcher as a 'real' woman within a 'real' public world of political debate, Emma Harte as a fictional symbol of achieving, anti-feminist womanhood. And the simultaneous emergence of both Margaret Thatcher and Emma Harte indicates separate yet linked attempts to demonstrate that traditional notions of femininity can be reworked to accommodate the new demands awakened by feminism without either disturbing existing social structures or questioning their validity. Indeed, both figures are part of a project to make space for women within capitalism through the mythology of the unique individual with its promise of self-fulfilment.

Indeed, although *A Woman of Substance* is marketed (as I have noted above) as a saga – and therefore, implicitly, as a *family* saga – the narrative constitutes, in many respects, a clear flight from maternity. There is barely space to accommodate Emma's children within the structure of the text and the plot tends to render them invisible or superfluous, while key moments in the story focus upon Emma's personal desires rather than the needs of her children. For example, when she gives birth to her illegitimate daughter by Edwin Fairley, Edwina, the event tends to be presented as a potential obstacle to Emma's success rather than as an opportunity for domestic intimacy. Edwina is conveniently removed from the plot by being farmed out to an obliging relative, and the later children barely function at all within the narrative. Indeed, Emma's five offspring only become fully visible at the end of the story when, in an extraordinary twist, four of them are found to have conspired together to deprive their mother of some of her business assets! Fortunately, this plot is foiled by Emma herself.

So maternity is clearly problematic to *A Woman of Substance* and the text's discomfort with Emma's children makes this difficulty visible and potentially puzzling to the reader. For the planned betrayal of their mother by the children at the end of the story is never satisfactorily explained. Instead, their apparent alienation is ascribed to the genetic deficiencies of their disappointing fathers and it is only Daisy, the daughter of Emma's real love, Paul McGill, who has nothing to do with the plot. Indeed, the text repeatedly seeks to deny any responsibility on the part of Emma herself for the faults of her children, emphasizing a care and concern which is never given space in the narrative. For example, at the beginning of the book, in a framing section set in 1968 when Emma is an old and successful woman and has just discovered the plot against her, she is shown pondering on her children's duplicity:

> Years ago, when Emma had been a young woman and had seen traits developing in her children which alarmed her, she had thought: It's my fault. I have made them what they are . . . But as she had grown older and wiser, her guilt was diluted as she came to believe that each man [sic] was responsible for his own destiny . . . She had refrained from agonizing over them and she had stopped blaming herself for their weaknesses and their faults . . .
>
> All this came back to her now as she remembered Paul's words and she thought: *No, I'm not guilty. They are motivated by their own greed, their own vaunting and misplaced ambitions.* (Bradford, 1980, p. 45; italics in original).

Yet this explicit assertion of Emma's concern is never convincingly demonstrated within the main body of the text where her years as a young mother are dealt with sparingly, and there is a sense that what is being concealed is the impossibility of reconciling a narrative of domesticity with one of enterprise. Emma cannot be both selfish in her desire for success and selfless in satisfying the needs of her children, even though the text demands that both these conditions be fulfilled, and this is where the incoherence over her position as an enterprising matriarch is most evident.

The conspiracy is intended to deprive Emma of some of her business interests, thus neatly locating a battle over the control of capital into the heart of the family. Yet while Emma is shown defeating the plotters and reasserting herself as the absolute controller of her empire, the turn from maternity which this episode encapsulates remains evident. So while familialism is part of the *rhetoric* of the book – both as a text and as a commodity (that is, the way in which it is marketed) – the narrative actually reveals the difficulty of reconciling the nurturing demands of motherhood with the ruthlessness of the entrepreneur.

Emma Harte begins her successful career as a businesswoman with a small shop, as I outlined above, going on to open first one and then a chain of department stores. The Harte empire expands beyond the retail trade but the text makes it clear that Emma herself regards the store chain as the jewel of her trading interests, the epicentre of all her activities. Indeed, at the beginning of the book, in the framing section set in 1968, Emma is shown going into her flagship store in Knightsbridge (obviously based on Harrods) to wander through one night, gloating on her success:

> To Emma the food halls would always be the nucleus of the store, for in essence they had been the beginning of it all, the tiny seed from which the Harte chain had grown and flowered to become the mighty business empire it was today . . . Emma knew there were no other food halls, in any store anywhere in the world, which could challenge these, and she smiled to herself with a profound and complete satisfaction. Each one was an extension of her instinctive good taste, her inspired planning and diligent purchasing; in the whole hierarchy of Harte Enterprises no one could lay claim to their creation but she herself. (Bradford, 1980, p. 62).

As this passage makes clear, Emma regards her department stores as the linchpin of her material success and this is of particular significance. Retailing has long been seen as a legitimate sphere for female business interests, perhaps primarily because of women's traditional role as shoppers and consumers on behalf of families – symbolic intermediaries between the external machinations of capital and the internal mechanisms of the family. But shopping has also acquired the status of a hobby, a pleasurable and particularly feminine pursuit which is offered to women both as an indulgence and as part of the work of femininity.[2]

Indeed, the department store in its heyday in the early years of this century constituted both a monument to the miracle of retail capitalism and a special site of safety for women in the dangerous public world; for it offered quantities of commodities in a seductive display of abundance – capitalism's utopia – together with facilities such as coffee shops, powder rooms and hairdressers for the comfort and pleasure of the female shopper.[3] So Emma's identification of her department store chain as the special centre of her enterprise represents a link with a much broader discourse, one which identifies shopping – and therefore the whole paraphernalia of retailing – as 'women's business' in a way which is vital to the contemporary notion of consumer culture.

Moreover, Emma's opening of that first small shop in Armley is articu-lated in the text as the result of her 'innate' energy and entrepreneurial spirit, the physical manifestation of what has been characterized as her natural good taste and judgement. This effectively leaves no space for any debate over the nature of her project or of the terms of capitalism itself, which is consistently presented throughout the text as wholly natural and given; as a matter of the individual's desire to do the best for him or herself through talent, ingenuity and enterprising zeal coupled, significantly, with sheer hard work. Indeed, Emma's success is repeatedly presented as the direct consequence of her own tireless graft plus her extraordinary capacity for sacrifice, as this passage illustrates: 'She had given up her youth, her family, her family life, much of her personal happiness, all of her free time, and countless other, small, frivolous, yet necessary pleasures enjoyed by most women' (Bradford, 1980, p. 63).

The text never elaborates on those 'necessary pleasures' which Emma has nobly denied herself, which is probably just as well since there is no evidence of her going without sex, food, beautiful clothes, or, indeed, a thoroughly luxurious life style as soon as she can afford it. Indeed, this lack of fit between the ideology of puritan denial which the book seems to be offering as the route to success and its simultaneous enjoyment of consumption and commodities leads to a certain amount of incoherence. Emma begins her climb, we are told, with 'the most grinding and merciless work schedule ever conceived and willingly undertaken by a seventeen year old girl' (Bradford, 1980, p. 512), applying business ingenuity to what are essentially, and significantly, domestic skills, and building up trade for her shop through word of mouth. But this deeply puritanical emphasis on hard work and sacrifice, together with its amply fulfilled promise of deferred gratification, leaves a massive absence with which the narrative cannot deal: the possibility – indeed, probability – that a life spent in hard work will not offer these rewards which Emma Harte enjoys.

Furthermore, while much is made of the hard toil of the early days, the actual work involved in building up the business and Emma's technique as a businesswoman – negotiating deals, building alliances, and so on – remains an absent presence, endlessly ruminated on by friends and colleagues but rarely displayed. Indeed, it is naturalized back into definitions of 'innate' ability, so that what emerges finally is a testament to individual achievement and a very special sort of female magic. As Emma's brother, Winston, and her great friend, Blackie O'Neill, agree, her success is the outcome of exceptional qualities:

> Winston eyed Blackie thoughtfully . . . 'Do you know the secret of my sister's great success?'
> 'Sure and I do. I attribute it to a number of qualities. Shrewdness, courage, ambition, and drive, to name only a few.'
> '*Abnormal* ambition. *Abnormal* drive, Blackie. That's the difference between Emma and most people.' (Bradford, 1980, p. 701; italics in original).

Moreover, Emma's femininity is repeatedly presented as a positive advantage in her enterprises and at no point is it shown to be a handicap to her activities in the world of business. Male rivals are surprised yet charmed, disarmed by the combined effects of her tenacity and her beauty.

This identification of Emma's success as a matter of individual genius, plus a magical and essential femininity which defies male comprehension or control, profoundly depoliticizes both Emma's own actions and the social context in which they are supposedly conducted. It is salutary to compare such representations with Margaret Thatcher's personal mythology of womanly know-how and self-defined route to power paved with individual will-power rather than feminist struggle,[4] for both Emma Harte's story and that of Margaret Thatcher in the 'authorized version' omit as much as they tell. In the case of *A Woman of Substance* although historical authenticity is made much of by the book as a commodity (with a page of acknowledgements for help from museums and individuals at the beginning), any sense of specificity is largely absent. Emma is removed from her historical context by her identification in the text as 'naturally' superior, and her struggles are defined as those of an individual, not of a class or gender. In this way, potential problems or moments of conflict, which might seem more than probable for a woman establishing a business empire in the troubled world of Britain in the 1920s, are completely absent. Indeed, there is little sense of any sort of historical time-scale throughout the narrative, for the external world is consistently marginalized and the passage of time is not consistently marked by any sort of authenticating device. The only major political events to be incorporated into the text are the two world wars -- which it would clearly be difficult to ignore. Yet the changing economic conditions of nearly half a century, which it would be reasonable to assume might have some effect on Emma's business enterprises, are barely registered unless they impinge directly on to the separate sphere of Emma's personal desires.

This is not entirely surprising. *A Woman of Substance*, although grounded in the tradition of realist fiction, is essentially a fantasy of desire, revenge and female triumph and in that sense occupies the romantic space of timelessness. Emma Harte's ambitions are important only in so far as they place her in a position of power from which she can satisfactorily direct her emotional life. Time and again, Emma's business interests are dealt with in a matter of paragraphs, while whole chapters are devoted to her personal relationships in which the external world falls away, leaving the lovers in a void. In this way, any sort of political consciousness becomes not only irrelevant, it is actually absent from the narrative, rendered irreconcilable with the timelessness of romance by its historical and social specificity. Emma Harte's story is a narrative not of political change but of feminine survival.

Indeed, what becomes clear in the text is that Emma operates by using her femininity productively, as a way of getting what she wants, either through its ultra-natural powers – 'intuition', 'feminine wiles' – or by exploiting her sexual desirability and the rarity of her status. The identification of Emma's abilities as natural and innate effectively separates her from the 'masculine' structures of political and legal decision-making, rendering her dependent on powers which are deemed peculiarly feminine and therefore outside the social, and wholly unconnected with any sort of political intervention.

This means that although *A Woman of Substance* is a tale of triumph it is very far from being a feminist fable. Emma Harte succeeds not by working with other women but by ignoring them. Her business partners are men – Blackie, David Kallinski – her secretaries are women. For this text is not about confronting or changing social relations, and part of its project is the demonstration that what is reluctantly admitted to be a system can be made to work for those who abide by its rules. What it is about is the potential of exceptional women – women like Margaret Thatcher and Emma Harte – to achieve success within existing structures, and on condition that they remain the exception. For Emma Harte's power, just as that of Margaret Thatcher, depends on the continued oppression of other women. Ideals of sisterhood are nowhere in a text like this, especially since any idea of collective struggle is irreconcilable with a story of individual triumph. For Emma Harte's success is clearly delineated as the product of her exceptional qualities – the endlessly debated issue of her 'difference'. '"Emma's hardly like most women,"' (Bradford, 1980, p. 757) observes her lover, Paul McGill, at one point, and that is one of the keys to her status.

For Emma has been identified as different from the very beginning of the story: she is extra beautiful, extra clever, extra ambitious, extra-ordinary, and that is what sets her apart from other women. Yet there is a dual implication in this definition of Emma's difference. First, it is that she chooses not to accept the limitations by which other women abide, as though it were simply a matter of individual determination. Second, Emma is 'different' only in her dealings with the outside world of business. When it comes to the foregrounded emotional tangles she is very clearly positioned as identifiably 'the same' as other women. There is space in such a representation for the reader to insert herself through a close identification with Emma's personal desires.

Indeed, the difficulties which Emma confronts as a businesswoman are explicitly linked to her own emotional history, primarily through her desire for revenge on the Fairley family, but also via the small circle of characters who prosper with her. In this way, capitalism itself is personalized, transformed into a matter of specifically individualized power, and at the very end of the book we are presented with a picture of capital and the family explicitly linked together by generational decree and the motor of inheritance when Emma routs her children's plot and hands over her business to her trustworthy grandchildren. Emma is thus located in a matriarchal role which tends to reinforce both the capital–family axis and her own position as a woman.

What I am trying to consider here is the specific way in which the reader identifies with Emma Harte and how that identification might locate her – the reader – into the ideological discourses of which the novel itself is only a fragment. In this instance, the relationship of the reader to the achieving heroine is both *in*clusive and *ex*clusive, for it depends on the reader's recognition of individuality with regard to herself, and a belief that she too is potentially 'different' and, by implication, better than other women. This difference is defined in many ways, of course, but it is especially characterized through a textual concentration on Emma Harte's appearance and sexual desirability. Emma is thus repeatedly presented to the reader through the eyes of a defining male observer, so that her actions, responses and emotions are the subject of an almost continuous masculine commentary. The relationship of this observer to the heroine is often quite unimportant: it is not unusual for an enemy such as Gerald Fairley, the elder son of the Fairley household who at one point tries to rape Emma, to comment on her appearance or behaviour, or for authorial commentary to be conducted via a male character. This masculine voyeur effectively validates Emma's actions and is present at moments of pathos or drama in the text. Indeed, the reader is rarely directly privy to Emma's emotions at such times without the interpretive intervention occasioned by the 'male gaze' of an observer.[5]

For example, when Emma first breaks the news of her pregnancy to her seducer, Edwin Fairley (a development of which the reader, too, has been ignorant until that point), the text concentrates not on Emma's fears and hopes as she tells her news but on Edwin's observations of her appearance and behaviour:

> His eyes roved over her. She *was* a beautiful girl. This morning her russet-brown hair was swept up and away from her face, plaits forming a circle on top of her shapely head like a crown. The oval face paler than usual, was like gleaming porcelain, exquisite and refined. The widows peak, protruding onto her wide brow, and those large emerald eyes lifted her beauty out of the ordinary. She was startling, there was no question about that. (Bradford, 1980, p. 377; italics in original).

This textual emphasis on Emma's appearance at a moment of supposed drama is quite unintentionally comic, but it also clearly illustrates the overwhelming importance of her beauty as an element in her success. For it is her sexual desirability that defuses her potential as a threat to men and also serves to reassure the reader of her femininity. Emma is 'made safe' because she is desirable.

For Emma Harte is, above all, a romantic heroine and if she is to succeed in that role she must be both the *subject* of the reader's identification and the *object* of male desire. So Emma becomes the persistent object of a male gaze, but never her own. Her interest in beautiful clothes is characterized as the consequence, not of vanity, but of her innate good taste, and unknowing innocence differentiates her from those guilty women who set out to entrap men with their beauty and are therefore wholly responsible for the desire they 'provoke'.

But Emma's lack of guilt is not confined to her sexuality. It extends to all aspects of her life, so that actions or decisions which might otherwise be interpreted as selfish or manipulative are represented through the prism of authorial intervention as unavoidable or reasonable. In this way Emma's actions are 'explained' to the reader and consistently justified in an attempt to reconcile the problems posed by Emma's role as a self-determining woman within the conventions and demands of romance.

Emma is often presented as both a 'natural' entrepreneur and a 'natural' aristocrat throughout the text – with all that the latter description might imply in terms of integrity and rectitude. When Blackie O'Neill first meets her, for example, he immediately recognizes her outstanding qualities and is able, through his own superior judgement, to identify her difference from the lesser creatures around her:

> He knew she was a poor girl from the working class, yet her face was that of an aristocrat, for it contained breeding and refinement. It was these aspects that combined to create that indefinable quality he had detected earlier. She was patrician and she had an inbred dignity that was unique. (Bradford, 1980, p. 153).

Setting aside some of the absurdities of snobbery that this passage reveals, it remains clear that the text's attempt to incorporate feudal concepts of aristocracy and gentility into its handling of the entrepreneurial project tends to produce moments of great incoherence and confusion when Emma is required to behave in ways that are appropriate to her ambition – but not to the codes of gentility already valorized. Emma becomes at such moments a figure of barely sustainable contradictions as the 'naturalness' of her many qualities seem to be cancelling each other out.

Such contradictions are at least partly the result of the text's insistent denial of oppression or struggle. For *A Woman of Substance* is a tale of bourgeois triumph and Emma's success is repeatedly characterized as positive and progressive. Issues of class and gender are presented yet obscured, so that Emma's story remains a matter of individual achievement heightened by femininity. Indeed, Emma's eventual return to her native village as the new owner of the mill in the 1930s is greeted with a response of cringing gratitude from the male workforce:

> They cheered her rousingly; and one by one, clutching their cloth caps, the men came to shake her hand, to thank her, and to welcome her

back to Fairley. 'I knew yer dad, love,' one man told her, and another added, 'By gum, Big Jack'd be right proud of yer, lass.' (Bradford, 1980, p. 737).

Textual tensions over class become especially clear in the handling of the Fairley family, who are required to perform a dual function in the narrative: that of the tyrannical and semi-feudal masters of the village and the pattern of gentility which Emma seeks to emulate. They are both the manorial lords of Fairley with an ancestral claim to power (or at least we must assume that they are since they share the village's name) and local capitalists, owning and controlling the mill and brickworks where Emma's father and brothers work. But while the Fairleys begin the novel as leading players they are gradually reduced to bit-parts as the story progresses and as their symbolic power is defused by the text's need to obscure the problems posed by the issue of class. For the Fairleys are called upon to impersonate as individuals the tyrannies of class oppression while simultaneously sustaining some semblance of realism. This is clearly impossible and produces a situation whereby all the evils of a class system are loaded on to one character – Gerald Fairley – who becomes an absurd stooge figure, a 'Sir Jasper' straight out of Victorian melodrama, and both morally and physically repulsive.

Yet Emma's ambitions are explicitly characterized as having been fuelled by a dream of vengeance on the Fairleys for their presumed cruelty; and her dislike of the family, and particularly Adam Fairley, the squire, is partially acknowledged in the text as an issue of class: 'Emma thought: he's a mean and wicked man, living off the toil of others, and her young and trembling heart hardened against him more resolutely' (Bradford, 1980, p. 173). But this element in the story is difficult to sustain and barely plausible, for Emma's triumph is hardly a matter of class war and Adam Fairley is clearly represented as a kind-hearted man and a 'good' employer. Indeed, Emma succeeds by transforming herself into a woman every bit as powerful as the Fairleys, and by the end of the story has acquired a large country house in Yorkshire, Pennistone Royal, and a devoted housekeeper not unlike the Fairley's Mrs Turner. So Emma ultimately appropriates both the actual power and the symbols of power which the Fairley family bear, not by changing or breaking the structures of class, but by assuming a new class position herself – and one that she is, very importantly, presented as having earned.

A Woman of Substance thus recognizes class conflict but not class struggle. The hardship and poverty experienced by Emma in her early years, and on which the text dwells in great detail, are characterized not as the result of oppression but as the natural and inevitable consequence of progress, deplorable but necessary. Furthermore, Emma's eventual assumption of the Fairley's position is justified by the deployment of other discourses which obscure the issue of class relations.

For class in *A Woman of Substance* is effectively displaced by the rubric of good taste which is presented as the natural property of Emma and her successful friends, but not of the Fairleys in their hideous gothic horror of a house nor of the forelock-tugging workers. Emma uses her 'natural good taste and judgment' in establishing her chain of shops and it is this talent which, allied with her skills as a businesswoman, makes her so successful. And this device of her 'innate' good taste tends to be linked in the text with issues of national identity, so that Englishness becomes a metaphor for, or symbol of, value. It is Emma's 'good taste' which sets her apart from her family and others of her class, and 'taste' which is deployed as the measure of the social and moral worth of other characters.

Indeed, throughout the text significant chunks of the narrative are devoted to detailed descriptions of Emma's houses and apartments. At the beginning of the book, for example, we are treated to a virtual inventory of the drawing room at Pennistone Royal. Here are some examples of the lavish prose, heavily edited by necessity:

> [The room was] distinguished by a gentle beauty, refinement and good taste. It was understated and unpretentious . . . exquisite Savonnerie carpet . . . everywhere sparkling silver and crystal gleamed richly against the mellow patina of the handsome Georgian tables, consoles and cabinets . . . a Chippendale cabinet, of great elegance and beauty, was filled with matchless Rose Medallion china . . . the Turner landscape dominated the wall. (Bradford, 1980, pp. 75–6).

This passage continues in much the same vein for a page and a half and ends with this assertion: 'Emma's unerring eye for colour and form and her skill at placing and arranging furniture were in evidence everywhere' (Bradford, 1980, p. 76). Yet this particular extract and other passages like it seem only to demonstrate that the 'good taste' so determinedly trumpeted within the text is hardly exceptional; indeed, it is clearly dependent for its exercise on ample financial resources and a very conventional appreciation of antique furniture. Emma's judgements, in fact, constitute nothing more than an expression of bourgeois values: rather than having 'good taste' she simply has the 'right' taste in so far as she is able to recognize what had already been sanctioned as valuable and can afford to buy it.

Yet such detailed descriptions also function as a direct address to the pleasure the reader herself experiences, as each item is lovingly catalogued as precisely as the products on offer in a glossy magazine. And there is a direct appeal to what the reader will also understand as 'good taste' as bourgeois value judgements are here paraded as moral absolutes with an apparent basis in unchanging nature. Moreover, the chintz covers and the Chippendale cabinets represent a very particular version of English taste, one that is, in fact, wholly class-bound but which has been frequently mobilized – as it is here – as a symbol of classless nationhood, in which England features as a timeless Arcadia untouched by the grime of industrial history, and any sort of struggle is denied by the assertion of an organic unity.

And the final episode of the story, wherein Emma successfully prevents the plot against her, effectively reinserts Emma into a family location after her adventures in the public world, and also places her at the crucial centre of that family; controlling its members with the assertion of her will and demonstrating her clear authority as the 'woman of substance'.

Conclusion

In this chapter, then, I have sought to demonstrate the way in which one text, *A Woman of Substance*, engages with the themes of femininity, consumption and power, reworking certain elements of a discourse in its attempt to prove the possibility of capital's promise for women. I do not want to argue that such discourses have been produced as a phenomenon of the narrative's production, but rather that they are already current and identifiable and that popular fiction merely represents those currents as self-evident truth, as a natural reality. None the less, what I hope has become clear in this chapter is the convergence in a single text of certain themes and issues which have been a feature of cultural change in the 1980s. This has taken the form of the public emergence of the individual bourgeois woman who has made a space for herself within capitalism, and of aspirational fantasies, which have effectively laid some of the ideological groundwork for that project, by offering models to women of the possibilities open to them. Yet narratives such as *A Woman of Substance* hardly offer a blueprint for success in the world of business, especially since they clearly evade any sort of discussion of the obstacles in the way of aspiring female entrepreneurs. What they offer instead is the assurance that magical femininity will be the key to individual success in a world which demands that only one woman at a time can sit at the boardroom table.

A Woman of Substance has been a key text for the 1980s, but its promise of individual bourgeois pleasures for the achieving woman within the structures of patriarchy is hardly a reassuring prospect for feminism.

Notes

1 For an interesting analysis of the family saga, see Bridgewood in Radford (1986).
2 For an interesting discussion of issues of femininity and consumer culture, see Bowlby (1985).

3 See Chaney, 1983.
4 Note also the absence of Dennis Thatcher, millionaire, from this personal narrative!
5 All references to the idea of the male gaze in this section are used in the psychoanalytic sense first outlined by Mulvey (1989) and elaborated on by Modleski (1982).

11

Redefining cultural identities

EVELYN REID

Over the past two decades, national identity has become a central and contested issue within right-wing discourses with protagonists asserting who can and who cannot belong to the British nation. Cultural differences have been used as a defining category, a categorization which is constructed to exclude certain groups, who have in turn challenged that construction by arguing for a legitimate right to be part of the nation. The contestation has included a struggle to shift the boundaries of that definition.

The first part of this chapter will analyze the new definition of Britishness and the prerequisites for belonging to that nation, and the second part will outline the critique of that definition put forward by black practitioners involved in cultural production, particularly those involved in the audio-visual field. The third part addresses the shifts in black cultural politics which itself has been rearticulated in the name of a politics of diversity. The difficulty of such a position, however, is the maintenance of alliances and solidarity; this dilemma has many similarities with the debates about the category 'woman' within feminist theory and practice (see Introduction 1).

The resurgence in right-wing nationalist discourse can be identified with the rise of a new form of racism from groups on the far right. However, analysis will reveal that the new racism is not so new, but merely a revival of old ideas presented in a new populist form, and falling on fertile ground during the last decade as Thatcherism has provided a context within which these groups have been able to flourish. The new right is drawn from two distinct, and in some ways competing, traditions. One tradition is based on the free market philosophy of nineteenth-century liberalism, updated and expanded by neo-liberals; the other can be described as social authoritarianism. Their basic concern is to uphold traditional definitions of authority and morality and to preserve the British nation from what they regard as cultural decline, namely, black immigration and a breakdown of law and order.

The origins of the new right can be traced back to the struggle of right-wing groups to reclaim the centre ground from the cultural dissidents of the

1960s. Those dissidents threatened traditional beliefs and values such as the integrity of the nuclear family, the work ethic, discipline and law and order which the authoritarian right claim had previously underpinned the British way of life. During and following this moment of crisis the authoritarian right sought to attribute the discontent of that period to the influx of black people to Britain, whom they claimed also threatened the British way of life. On television and in the press the black community was presented as a threatening ghetto existing on the fringes of civil society.

Both Labour and Conservative governments responded to the crisis with stricter immigration controls on the one hand and compensatory social policies on the other. For example, the Race Relations Acts of 1965, 1968 and 1976, and particularly the Section 11 funding, introduced in 1967 and made available to local authorities 'burdened' with the presence of large numbers of immigrants, formed part of the compensatory social policies (see Layton-Henry and Rich, 1986). The intention behind these policies was to foster the assimilation of black people into white society and at the same time to restrict those wishing to enter Britain. This can be described as the era of British paternalism which gave way, from the mid-1970s, to multiculturalism.

The period also saw the formation of ultra-right groups such as the National Front, but while the policies of the left held the centre ground in the form of liberal paternalism, the ideologies of the right were discredited. However, as the economic recession worsened, hastened by the floating of the dollar in 1971, the oil price rise of 1973 and the rapid downturn in advanced industrial economies, capital could no longer fulfil its promise of affluence – higher wages, better housing. Its failure to deliver these intensified ideological conflicts and resulted in the emergence of the right and the revival of free-market capitalism.

With the election of Margaret Thatcher in 1979 there was a departure from consensus politics and many of the sentiments of multiculturalism. It was argued that the interventionist policies of postwar governments had produced a 'collectivist nightmare of bureaucratic regimentation and unwholesome paternalism' (Eccleshall, 1984, p. 17). Members of the Thatcher government pledged themselves to rid the nation of the constraints which had produced this nightmare, such as subsidies for unprofitable industries and the burden of greater taxation for those producing the wealth of the nation. Legislation to weaken trade union powers, restore law and order and to reinstate personal responsibilities was promised. As Eccleshall states:

> The modern Conservative ideal of minimal government is not a licence to social indiscipline . . . Conservatives blend their laissez-faire economic policies with a firm programme of 'law and order'. They have assembled the traditional values of self-restraint, family life, social deference and

patriotism, into an image of a nation threatened by internal laxity and external aggression. (Eccleshall, 1984, p. 18).

This agenda provided the climate within which the authoritarian strand within right-wing politics sought to win back the souls of the nation. To do this they appealed to a broad public audience using the language and imagery of patriotism and nationalism, redefining who belonged within the nation and who did not. In redefining the nation a distinction was made between those who were of the nation and those who were merely citizens within it. Protagonists claimed that the nation could be identified by a national consciousness based on a shared language, religion, beliefs and social homogeneity, in other words a shared national culture. Black people, it was argued, fell outside this definition, because of their alien cultures of origin. But few societies correspond to the prerequisites of this nationalist demand, which requires the welding together of popular alliances that cut across existing political and social divisions to attract an emotional identification based on a presumed national cultural homogeneity (see Jay, 1984).

The new right drew in particular on arguments put forward by Enoch Powell, which had stirred emotional responses as far back as 1968. At a speech in Eastbourne, he claimed that by virtue of their alienness black people could not be part of the nation, and that although a West Indian or Asian was born in England, he did not become an 'Englishman'. Although in law he became a United Kingdom citizen, 'in fact he is a West Indian or an Asian still. Unless he be one of a small minority . . . he will by the very nature of things have lost one country without gaining another, lost one nationality without acquiring a new one' (Gordon, 1988, p. 17). Alfred Sherman, a former director of the Centre for Policy Studies (a Conservative think-tank) argued that citizenship could be conferred by law and could be taken away, it reflected membership of a nation but did not confer it.

In an attempt to legitimate their definition of the nation the new right based their categorization on cultural differences rather than on biological differences, which had been publicly discredited since the atrocities committed by Hitler in the name of a biologically superior Aryan race. Nationalism was now articulated in the name of 'natural' 'instinctual' differences, as a result of which people desire the company of their own ethnic stock because of a shared culture, and an innate inclination to stick together. As Gordon argues:

By resorting to theories of human nature and human instinct the new racism can avoid arguments about prejudice and racism on rational, moral or political grounds, for it does not matter what people ought to think or feel, since their nature has determined their reaction. (Gordon, 1988, p. 15).

However, nationalism is a medium through which conflict is waged among different cultural groups striving for control, as Jay notes:

> For them, the battle is not over economic and political goals, but over the 'soul' of the nation – its moral life, potential for creative thought and art, its capacity to provide mankind with an instrument for fulfilling the 'higher' things of life. (Jay, 1984, p. 192).

In the struggle for social control the new right has engaged the powers of the press to mobilize the imagery of the nation-state. Graphic headlines in the popular press attest to this. In its articulation, the press has revitalized the image of the black community as a threat to the stability of white British society through the popularization of stereotypes of black people as rioters, muggers and rapists. But the black community mounted a counter-attack. Challenges have come from all quarters and significantly from black practitioners concerned with cultural production – theatre, print, film and video production, photography, literature. Black artists entered the contestation over the definition of Britishness and the rights of black people to be included in that definition. They counterposed the simplistic definition of a fixed national identity and so demonstrated that a national culture is continually redeveloped and the contours of national identity continually redrawn.

In *Signs of Empire* (1983), for example, Black Audio Film Collective combined images and sounds from articles, books and speeches of British history, including those of eighteenth-century administrators in India, Africa and various parts of the colonies in order to expose the relationship between race and power, and between British cultural identity and colonialism. The film exposes the discourse around empire by interrogating the iconography of key moments, such as the Indian Mutiny of 1857–8, images of missionaries at work, the serving of tea in the colonies. It also reworks the politics of signification by asking how the black subject was placed within this discourse, and asking what constituted English social life, how people are enfranchised and disenfranchised.

The articulation of black creativity problematizes the popular concept of the national culture, interrogates the strategies and mechanisms whereby it is maintained and challenges its role in securing the dominance of given groups in a society. It demonstrates that subjects are socially constituted within a system of social relations, rather than being defined by essential cultural or national traits.

Challenging cultural domination is not a new scenario for the black community. Since their arrival in postwar Britain they have been engaged in this struggle as they have been marginalized, misrepresented and underrepresented primarily because they have been positioned as the unspoken and invisible 'other' of white cultural discourse: the object but rarely the subject of the practices of representation. In the field of audio-visual image-making, black practitioners have challenged this portrayal which has entailed deconstructing existing dominant discourses and rearticulating new ones. However, redefining the meaning of cultural construction necessitates access to the means of production and representation in the political process. The struggle to ensure this has come from black educationalists, social workers, community leaders, media workers and black youths.

In the mid 1970s many of their protests were taken up by the left and resulted in a number of multicultural policies which gave rise to a politics of positive representation to counteract notions of negative self-conception which they claimed were at the heart of black discontent, due in part, to the failure of society to recognize their unique cultural identities.

Multicultural pluralism represented a departure from the assimilationist and essentially paternalistic policies of the 1960s. Under multiculturalism cultural differences were recognized as legitimate, albeit within the framework of the dominant culture. However, differences within minority communities were not recognized. Moreover, the black community was still an undifferentiated whole and the specificities of the class or gendered black ethnic subjects were not recognized. In fact, the term 'black community' was a definition attributed by the dominant culture which merely replaced earlier labels such as 'immigrants' and 'coloured people', and did not change the negative imagery in the minds of the general public. None the less, Asians and Afro-Caribbeans united under black community politics to fight racism.

Multiculturalism gave rise to a number of programmes on radio and television designed to cater for the needs of the black community: *Black Londoners* (Radio London), *Skin* (London Weekend Television), *Rice An' Peas* (London Broadcasting Company) and other ethnic music programmes on local radio stations. At the same time magazines such as *Dragons Teeth* challenged negative and racist representations in children's books. The discourses of pluralism also facilitated the introduction of steel bands and 'sari and samosa' evenings in schools, as a positive representation of black cultures. The negative/positive image lobby united a number of groups who claimed that they were opposed to racism.

Many black film practitioners, however, felt that the representation of the black experience should present the dilemma of the crisis of living in Britain – alienation and conflict with white society – and thus sought to challenge the cosy scenario of multi-culturalism.

Pressure (1975), the first black feature film made in Britain, is typical of this genre. The film deals with the alienation of a young British-born black male from both the dominant society through his growing awareness of racism, and from his immediate family, who either do not understand what he is experiencing (his parents), or refuse to accept him on his own terms as black British (his Caribbean-born brother). Running parallel to this domestic conflict is his growing interest in black politics through his relationship with his militant brother and a female activist. Through involvement in the black movement and an encounter with the police, he becomes 'enlightened' as to the 'true' political nature of his alienation and recognizes the contradictions inherent in a black British identity in a society which regards the two terms as mutually exclusive.

Similarly, *Burning An Illusion* (1981) represents a mixture of class, political and sexual conflicts which the female protagonist has to confront in order to rediscover her roots and a politicized self-image. Set in London in the 1980s, the film tells the story of the transformation of Pat, a young black woman, from a state of 'ignorance' to one of 'knowledge'. Pat is an office worker who lives alone in a council flat, reads Barbara Cartland novels and dreams of meeting somebody with whom to 'settle down'. She meets Del, a young toolmaker. But when Del loses his job the conflict in their desires becomes acute as he idles away the day with his friends while Pat goes out to work. Thus the lines of gender conflict are drawn. A fight over a woman at a night club leads to scuffles with the police, Del is victimized and is eventually sentenced to four years for assaulting a policeman. The imprisonment leads to the politicization of both Del and Pat.

Films of this era sought to make the crisis speak. However, they were couched within the dominant realist discourse which attempted to reflect authentic experience. Yet since that experience is contradictory, as is inevitable in the case of black British identities, the language of realism, with its narrative closure of cause and effect, came to be seen as increasingly inadequate and problematic. The conflict-oriented discourse also burdened the black artist with the role of race relations officer.

In sum, the problem that black film-makers encountered was that they entered into an operation where the parameters had already been established. The dilemma they faced was thus that of how to express and articulate what they felt to be an alternative version of reality within the codes and framework which they were actually counterposing.

It could be argued that the political urgency of the period in which the black presence had become problematized necessitated that content took priority over form. The message, the description of the dilemma was more important than stylistic or formal elements. Similarly, films such as *Blood Ah Go Run* (1982), *Riots and Rumours of Riots* (1981) (see Givanni (1988) for a comprehensive list of black and Asian films) voiced the frustrations and uncertainties of young black people. Clearly, these films were important in that they attempted to define black political consciousness and extended the content of black imagery from a black perspective, aims which were beyond the reach of the mainstream media. They also provided the base from which the new generations of black film practitioners could start.

The shift in political policies from assimilationism to multiculturalism was an attempt to contain black discontent. However, the uprisings of 1981 demonstrated that the aspirations of the black community were not being met. As Owusu points out:

> There is a particular sense in which the inner city uprisings of 1981, involving black people and some white youths, spurred changes in places they never intended to . . . The new mood called for action. Almost every institution tapped its feet with anxiety, poised to respond. (Owusu, 1986, p. 84).

The events of 1981 hastened a departure from multiculturalism to anti-racism and consequently a radical shift in cultural policies from funding bodies such as the late Greater London Council, the British Film Institute, Channel 4, various regional arts associations, local governments and the union of the television and film industry. This enabled a broadening of the black independent film and video sector bringing with it an increase in the diversity of groups and individuals involved in production. New groups such as Black Audio Film Collective, Sankofa, Retake and Ceddo were formed within the grant-aided workshop sector and independent companies in the commercial sector experienced renewed interest in their work. The advent of Channel 4 in 1982, although lodged within the multicultural framework, was also a particularly important outlet for black arts. As Pines states:

> For the first time in British race media history, the media had become a primary site of race relations struggle of various kinds: here was an opportunity for us to occupy a new 'space' created by some notion of multiculturalism, which was to be fought over by a range of social and political persuasions, including those positions which formerly had rejected mainstream television's intentions to incorporate black people. (Pines, 1983, p. 1).

Diaspora cinema: a politics of diversity

With the advent of the workshops a new language to represent the black experience began to emerge. Writers and artists were challenging monoculturalism in the name of cultural difference and unity in that difference.

Territories (1984) was the first film to address the questions of race, class, gender and sexuality as a range of identities denied and excluded from mainstream discourses. On another level the film problematizes the representation of black people and offers a critique on the one-dimensional discourse that has fixed and objectified the representation of the black subject. It presented an image of plural identities within the black community and the range of plural ethnicities that make up British post-imperial national identity. As Mercer states: 'the image of the two youths embracing while the Union Jack burns in the background replays the antimonies of black Britishness as merely one ambivalent identity amongst others.' (Mercer, 1988, p. 11).

Using a collage of sound and image, the film selects moments of black culture to explore the black identity, such as the Notting Hill Carnival. The film moves towards a semiological reading of the Carnival considering its meaning in a new landscape, just as the black identity was being considered in a new terrain. Similarly, *Passion of Remembrance* (1986) takes as its main theme the redefinition of what it means to be black and British in the 1980s, using the family to explore not only the public political history but the private spaces which have been ignored or denied in past articulation of the diasporic experience in Britain. The exploration entails travelling back in time and reconstructing histories/herstories, and providing critiques of moments in that struggle. In one of its dialogic moments of reconstruction, the film flashes back to the Black Power Movement to explore black sexual politics, uncovering the fact that within a movement against oppression black women were oppressed. It reveals the invisibility of other minorities such as black lesbians and gays, who were also denied a space. *Passion* thus represents the tension of the black experience.

Two landscapes are used in the film: an urban landscape and an open landscape. The urban landscape represents the histories of the past and the latter the possibility of a new identity, constructed out of the old but informed by the present.

In *Handsworth Songs* (1986) Black Audio explores the contours of race and civil disorder using a mixture of poetry and politics to highlight the histories and politics that hover behind the process of media mythology. Images of urban decay are juxtaposed with images of the black experience in Britain to indicate that between the abyss of the images are untold stories.

In the process of addressing the multifaceted nature of cultural-historical formation, and specifically the diaspora experience of colonization, imperialism, migration, displacement, domination, marginalization, exclusion and personal fragmentation, black artists have searched for a form and a structure to articulate their experience. As Parmar argues:

Of necessity we have had to move between cultures and languages of domination, and in doing so have developed unique responses to questions of identity. In becoming distant from our pasts and struggling against the insecurity of our present, we have searched for a vocabulary to intervene into certain spaces. (Parmar, 1988, p. 47).

In every era each generation rewrites its own history which sometimes necessitates rupture and new beginnings which may involve a struggle for radical forms, new reference points and narrative styles. The new generation of black practitioners in the 1980s has done this in the struggle to tell their story. They have jettisoned the discursive narrative of multiculturalism and the positive/negative image of that period in an attempt to develop a cinema of relevance. This has entailed the interrogation and deconstruction of the rhetoric of racial imagery. As Hebdige suggests:

> Deconstruction here takes a different turn as it moves outside the gallery, the academy, the library to mobilise the crucial forms of lived experience and resistance embedded in the streets, the shops and clubs of modern life. Deconstruction here is used publicly to cut across the categories of 'body' and 'critique', the 'intellectual' and 'the masses', 'Them' and 'Us' to bring into being a new eroticised body of critique, a sensuous and pointed logic – and to make it bear on the situation, to make the crisis speak. (Hebdige, 1987b).

This new language has been informed by the cultures of Europe, Afro-America, Africa and the aesthetics of postmodernism.

Productions such as *Handsworth Songs* and *Passion of Remembrance* use a dialogic, fragmentary discourse which disrupts the linear logic of the narrative to convey a plural reading. They suggest that the black community is a community with similarities and differences, and suggest that with the acceptance of diversities comes a wealth of images and themes derived from within the various communities, and thus attempt to formulate different ways of seeing, and conversely different types of audiences. They challenge the idea of an authentic black experience posited within the realist tradition. They also call into question the limits of the category 'black', a move which, as Hall (1988b) argues, marks the end of innocence, or the end of an essential black subject:

> What is at issue here is the recognition of the extraordinary diversity of subjective positions, social experiences and cultural identities which compose the category 'black'; that is, the recognition that 'black' is essentially a politically and culturally constructed category, which cannot be grounded in a set of fixed trans-cultural or transcendental racial categories and which therefore has no guarantees in Nature. (Hall, 1988b, p. 28).

In short, as the politics of representation around the black subject and the black experience shifted, so the definition concerning the term 'black' has become problematic. Throughout the 1970s and 1980s people of African-Caribbean and Asian descent formed alliances under a black politics which obscured specificities within the community. However, with the shift in black cultural politics there is now a realization that blackness is a multiaccentual category. The end of innocence means that various groups can explore the specificities of their black identities. There is no essential black subject, nor has any one group a monopoly on the black experience.

The shift to a politics of diversity presents a dilemma: the dilemma is how to maintain solidarity around a politics that is endlessly defining and redefining its position. As Hall states:

> This does not make it any easier to conceive of how a politics can be constructed which works with and through difference, which is able to build those forms of solidarity and identification which make common struggle and resistance possible but without suppressing the real hetero- geneity of interests and identities, and which can effectively draw the political boundary lines without which political contestation is impos- sible, without fixing those boundaries for eternity. (Hall, 1988b, p. 28).

Those subscribing to such a politics must recognize their specific subjec- tivities and form alliances to counterpose the divide and rule tactic of the dominant ideology to which such a politics is susceptible.

The task of those engaged in the politics of diversity is to retheorize and reinscribe difference so that it is not synonymous with exclusion as the far right would have us believe; to inscribe in the social body a multiplicity of differences so as to destabilize the dominant political and cultural discourses which, themselves, are ethnic discourses but which are presented as universal.

The politics of diversity which is itself ethnically located must rescue ethnicity from its negative equivalences of inclusion and exclusion, repres- sion, dispossession and displacement, uncouple it from its connection with nation and race and move to an ethnicity which enables syncretism.

12

Promoting normality: Section 28 and the regulation of sexuality

JACKIE STACEY

In the introduction to this collection a number of issues are raised about the relationship between feminist theory and cultural studies. Within this context, the introduction of Section 28 of the Local Government Act, and the public debate about legitimate and illegitimate forms of sexuality which took place during its passage on to the statute book, raise very particular questions. On the one hand, drawing upon feminist perspectives on sexuality, Section 28 might be seen as yet another example of patriarchal control of sexuality, the reinforcement of compulsory heterosexuality and the protection of the patriarchal nuclear family. On the other hand, within cultural studies, Section 28 might be seen in the context of Thatcherism as a moral panic through which sexual identities have been regulated and defined. In both contexts, Section 28 demonstrates the importance of the power to define the terms of sexuality for the successful reproduction of dominant culture. In this chapter the controversy over Section 28 is explored using approaches from both feminist and cultural studies in order to analyze the relationship between sexuality, power and the reproduction of dominant culture.

In particular this chapter looks at the discursive construction of sexuality in the debate about homosexuality and lesbianism which surrounded Section 28. Specifically, it will look at these debates in terms of which definitions of sexuality were included and excluded from the public debate. In this analysis the processes through which particular discourses of sexuality were legitimated and others marginalized will be highlighted. Of particular concern in the final section of this chapter is the reworking of certain feminist discourses of sexuality which had gained some degree of public currency and legitimacy in the 1970s and early 1980s.

The context and background of Section 28

The introduction of Section 28 needs to be considered in relation to several other issues informing the political context at the time. First, the AIDS crisis had been used as an opportunity for renewed homophobic attacks on gay men. Underlying this increased hostility was an increased pathologization of homosexuality, associating it with promiscuity, disease and a risk to both public health and morality.[1] The 'dangers' of homosexuality had thus been firmly implanted in the popular imagination, and the prevention of the spread of AIDS was easily associated with the prevention of the spreading of homosexuality itself.

A second important feature of the context of Section 28 was the association of lesbian and gay issues with Labour Party politics in attempts to discredit them by the Conservatives. Many Labour councils were continuing to have substantial effects on the political and social life of people in Britain, particularly in major cities such as London, Manchester and Sheffield, despite the tightening grip of Thatcher's regime. Gender, sexual and anti-racist politics were a central part of the activities of the Greater London Council and other local councils, before the central government stepped up their attacks on these bodies. The appearance of Section 28 in the Local Government Act, then, is no coincidence, since the attacks on the 'loony lefties' in local government were fuelled by their association with lesbian and gay rights and used to discredit their position. Hence, Section 28 was introduced in the context of a particular series of political conjunctures which shaped the debates surrounding its passage through Parliament.

Third, Section 28 was one of many legislative initiatives which have intervened in the areas of sexuality and reproduction. Other initiatives such as the Alton Bill, the Warnock Report and later the Children's Bill have together, though in different ways, contributed to the increased regulation of sexuality and reproduction.[2]

'Clause 28'[3] was conceived as a legislative initiative by MPs Dame Jill Knight and David Wiltshire in December 1987. Originally introduced in 1986, the amendment fell in the Commons when the government did not support it, arguing 'that the distinction between abuses of . . . and the proper teaching of homosexuality cannot be drawn sufficiently clearly in legislation to avoid harmful misinterpretation . . . In these circumstances, in the Government's view the Bill is unnecessary' (quoted in Roelofs (1988, p. 38)). Following Thatcher's third re-election, this legislation was reintroduced on 9 December 1987 by Tory back-benchers as an amendment to the Local Government Bill. With the full support of the government, this Bill was passed into law on 24 May 1988. It laid down that

(1)   a local authority shall not:
    (a)   promote homosexuality or publish material for the promotion of homosexuality;
    (b)   promote the teaching in any maintained school of the acceptability of homosexuality as a pretended family relationship by the publication of such material or otherwise;

(c)   give financial or other assistance to any person for either of the
purposes referred to in paragraphs (a) and (b) above.
(2)   Nothing in subsection (1) above shall be taken to prohibit the doing
of anything for the purpose of treating or preventing the spread of disease.
(Section 28, Local Government Act, 1988).

Once passed, it was revealed that one of the chief targets of the section,
education, was covered by the Education Bill, rather than the Local
Government Bill, thus rendering the section legally redundant. Moreover,
the law has never been tested. However, these facts do not diminish its
importance to the regulation of sexuality. Even before Section 28 became
law, numerous incidents of anti-gay and lesbian discrimination began to
appear, legitimated in the name of Section 28: teachers were suspended for
coming out at school, universities tried to ban lesbian and gay societies,
adult education programmes insisted that lesbian and gay courses change
their names or be dropped, public librarians described the policing of their
shelves by right-wing groups, local councils even banned the screening of
videos on 'Clause 28' on their premises, and in one major city the annual
Women's Festival was prevented from including any lesbian events by
Labour councillors who feared negative publicity. These and many other
examples,[4] then, illustrate that self-censorship and informal regulation,
produced by the fear of prosecution, as well as legal prohibition, were
direct consequences of Section 28.

Despite the apparent failure of Section 28 in terms of its legal ambiguities
and misplaced remit, its passage through Parliament was accompanied by
countless examples of discrimination and homophobia. The 'success' of
Section 28 can therefore be seen in terms of the legitimation of existing
homophobia and the government-sponsored incentive to put prejudice into
practice. However, even more significant was the impact of particular definitions of sexuality which occurred in the public debate over Section 28. The
public debate was framed within and structured by very specific discourses
of sexuality and it is to these discourses which I shall now turn.

The right to define

An important discourse emerging out of the Thatcher years has been that
of sexuality as an increasing threat. Sexual liberation, for example, figured
largely in the Thatcherite construction of the 1960s as a period of moral,
national and economic decline. Similarly, the more recent association of
AIDS with so-called sexual perversion and promiscuity has contributed to
the notion that sexuality, particularly homosexuality and lesbianism, are
threatening to the fabric of British society.

These fears of sexuality played an important role in the mobilization of the
Thatcherite redefinition of British society. For example, one of the cultural

successes of Thatcherism was its ability to cement together a supposedly natural relationship of the individual, the family and the nation. 'The family' was firmly situated at the centre of Thatcherite discourse and its vision of a healthy future.[5] This concept did not operate from rational or logical bases, given the small number of us whose living situation resembled the ideal; rather, it offered an appeal to the desire to belong, the need to feel included, to be one of the 'us' and not the 'them' of Thatcherism. 'The family' was constructed as the central institution mediating between the individual and the nation. Importantly, it was defined as the only legitimate place for sexuality to be expressed, in the hope that only legitimate sexualities will be expressed.

Media representations of the debate about Section 28 often drew upon narrative conventions to construct a story characterized by the opposition between the family and lesbian and gay sexuality. Typically, popular narratives are structured around a threat, a hero who vanquishes the threat, and the restoration of the status quo with the reassuring narrative closure. Looking at media representations of debates about Section 28 in terms of their use of narrative structures, it becomes clear how central the family was to the construction of insiders and outsiders in this debate. The family seen as under attack from outside threats has been a familiar concern in many forms of popular narrative.[6] Through the use of popular narrative conventions, lesbians and gay men were successfully constructed as threats within these media representations, particularly to children, who depended on the protection represented by the family. The government, in the conventional hero's role of protector of good and innocence, endorsed a new law to destroy the threat and restore the family to its rightful place at the heart of British society.

Underlying many of the media representations, then, was a familiar story of the innocent family, site of health, happiness and normality, which was under threat from the evil, deviant outsiders, lesbians and gay men, who signified the more general decline in moral standards. The government who, in contrast, represented traditional British values, had justifiably intervened to protect the sacred institution of the family and rescue it from the outside threat. Elements of this narrative construction of the family as under threat from lesbian and gays were to be found throughout the press coverage of the debate. Typical of such coverage was this leader entitled 'A Right For A Family':

> The rights of adult homosexuals to adopt, in private, the way of life they choose is not in question. The rights of the majority to uphold traditional family life and standards for themselves and for their children were being threatened. The progress of the government's action to safeguard these rights will be widely welcomed. (*Birmingham Evening Mail*, 10 March 1988, p. 6).

What was at stake in such representations was not only the use of narrative devices in the construction of desirable subjects and undesirable objects, but also the way in which this narrative masked a fundamental reversal. This reversal constructed the powerless group, lesbians and gays, as powerful, and thus legitimated the government's attack upon them. The institutions of heterosexuality, marriage and the nuclear family, with their privileges and power, on the other hand, were constructed as the powerless and persecuted majority. Thus the systematic discrimination of lesbians and gay men and their exclusion from so many parts of everyday life in Britain was made invisible. According to this construction it was families, rather than members of oppressed minorities, that needed to demand 'rights' in late 1980s Britain.

A second characteristic within public debates surrounding Section 28 was the discourse of homosexuality and lesbianism as 'a problem'. Clearly, this was not new; indeed, it has always been one of the main characteristics of dominant discourses of lesbianism and homosexuality. These forms of sexuality have long been seen to require explanation and theorization, while heterosexuality is accepted as a natural given. Within medical, legal and psychological discourses, homosexuality and lesbianism have been seen as the deviant other to the heterosexual norm.

However, there was a new and distinct way in which lesbians and gays were constructed as a problem: the demand for lesbian and gay rights characteristic of politics of the 1970s and 1980s was constructed as a bid for special and illegitimate *privilege*. The issue of lesbian and gay rights was thus represented as part of the problem which Section 28 needed to solve. Oppressed groups, such as black people and lesbians and gays, who had organized politically to challenge dominant discourses constructing them as deviants or outsiders, were being blamed for causing problems themselves. The claim to an identity as an oppressed group was constructed as a wish for special status and privileges.

Thus lesbians and gays were defined as the problem in a very specific way within this debate. By blaming the 'victims' or the oppressed group it was possible not only to deny the validity of their challenges to their oppression, but also to construct lesbians and gay men as a social group who had brought their problems upon themselves. Lesbians and gays are no longer criminals or sick people, but are pushy, demanding misfits who should keep themselves to themselves, and if they do not, they only have themselves to blame for the consequences. The following extract from the *Sun* exemplifies many of these constructions:

The Sun Speaks its Mind: 'When the Gays have to Shut Up'.

We live in a time of growing tolerance and understanding. Once homosexuals were reviled. Mere suspicion was enough to drive a man out of public life and polite society. The homosexual act was a crime punishable by a lengthy imprisonment. *The age of the witchhunt is gone forever.* We now believe that homosexuals cannot help being what they are. How they behave as adults in private is their own affair. But the danger is that the pendulum has swung too far the other way . . . Homosexuals no longer campaign merely for the right to be left alone or regarded merely as equals. *Many now regard themselves as superior.* They believe it is *they* who are normal, and the rest of society which is perverse. They want grants from local councils for meeting places. They want preference for jobs. Above all, some of them want the opportunity to go into schools and make known to children the homosexual way of life. *They are risking a terrible backlash.* The mass of people have no great sympathy or understanding of homosexuals. They want them to be left alone. But more important, they want homosexuals to leave *them* alone . . . That especially applies to their children. No one, in reason, can possibly blame the homosexual community for what happened to Stuart Gough,[7] any more than a reasonable woman would blame all heterosexual men for an act of rape or murder. But people are not always reasoning. Homosexuals have achieved equality. They have public understanding, and they have the law as protection. They would be wise to leave it at that. (The *Sun*, 10 February 1988, p. 6; emphasis in original).

This construction of lesbians and gays as having brought their problems upon themselves, of having themselves provoked a backlash, was not one that was restricted to the sensationalist pages of the popular tabloid press. Even amongst so-called progressives, such as in the liberal press, similar sentiments were expressed. Polly Toynbee, writing in the *Guardian* argues similarly: 'The tragedy for the gay movement is that it has nurtured within it the seeds of its own destruction' (14 January 1988, p. 13).

A third example of this construction of lesbians and gays as the powerful rather than the oppressed group was published in the *Sunday Telegraph*. In a manner reminiscent of anti-semitic rhetoric, in which Jews have been represented as plotting a take-over, an article entitled 'Is there a Homosexual Conspiracy?' investigated the claim that there might have been an organized bid for power by homosexuals in British society:

the changed intellectual climate has been created by a sustained propaganda campaign designed to portray homosexuality as thoroughly natural and normal. Some suspect that there is a 'gay' lobby which operates in a more or less cohesive way, though they are disinclined to regard it as a conspiracy . . . The advertising campaign to combat Aids is the one case which gives pause even to those reluctant to entertain conspiracy theories. (5 June 1988, p. 18).

The article then proceeds to illustrate the argument that this campaign successfully disassociated AIDS from homosexuality in a misleading way, and furthermore supported the idea that homosexuality was an acceptable alternative to heterosexuality. Thus 'the "gay" lobby won the battle, game set and match' (p. 18). This success is attributed to the fact that 'homosexuals are well established and have powerful influences behind the scenes' and that government is ignorant about 'how entrenched homosexuals were in the upper reaches of the medical establishment' (p. 18). The association of homosexuals with power and influence is thus discussed in the language of suspicion and anxiety. Portrayals of homosexuality as anything other than deviant are considered to be indicative of the selfish needs or self-promotion of 'the gay lobby'. The image of the predatory infiltrators is continued:

> 'Don't Die of Ignorance' was all very well . . . but there was another side to ignorance. It could so easily foster an attitude where young men felt they'd missed out if they hadn't done it. And, of course, homosexuals wanted that, because they needed a steady supply of young people with whom to engage in their activities. (*Sunday Telegraph*, 5 June 1988, p. 18).

This construction of homosexuals as having vampire-like needs parallels a popular image of drug-pushers who need fresh supplies of victims at regular intervals. Underlining the pre-existing link between homosexuality, drugs and AIDS, homosexuality is presented here as a threat to social stability and is associated with predatory and destructive tendencies.

Furthermore, the increased openness and availability of knowledge about sexuality promoted in conjunction with campaigns combatting AIDS is represented as threatening and provocative. The article finishes with a quotation from the writer Kingsley Amis:

> I have no feeling of hostility towards homosexuals . . . In fact you'll find a number of sympathetic portrayals of queers in my books . . . My own belief is that queers were better off when less was known about them. One of the great liberal fallacies is that hostility and prejudice come out of ignorance, but to explain what they do to each other does *not* make queers more attractive. There is a deep abhorrence which will never be reduced and which will, indeed, only be exacerbated by finding out more. By flaunting their activities, they will only fuel that abhorrence. (*Sunday Telegraph*, 5 June 1988, p. 18).

These press representations typify some of the ways in which lesbianism and homosexuality were constructed as the problem in the debates about Section 28. By demanding rights as an oppressed minority, by attempting to open up discussions about sexuality and by trying to challenge definitions of themselves as unacceptable or undesirable, lesbians and gay men were seen to be 'going too far' and thus 'asking for', and indeed 'deserving', any trouble which might come their way.

The reversals of power

The above constructions work by effecting a series of discursive reversals. First, the subject of the threat is reversed: rather than lesbians and gays being under attack from Section 28, conservative moralism and homophobia in society in general, it is the family which is under threat. The rhetoric of the threat to the family displaces the object to the position of subject: the object under attack from this legislation, lesbians and gay men, becomes the subject which threatens, and the family is constructed as an appealing and inclusive unit, under threat from the deviant outsiders.

Second, there is a reversal of who is sexually threatening to children in society. The widespread publicity given to the extent of child sexual abuse, as well as the still hidden amount of sexual violence against women, has reinforced the longstanding feminist claims about male violence. Heterosexual men are in fact the group in this society which has proved most threatening to children. Yet Section 28 was consistently legitimated by the claim that children need protection from lesbians and gay men who threaten them with corruption, if not implicit seduction. Indeed, Section 28 was seen by some as a response to the increased coverage of child sexual abuse following moral panics such as that aroused by the Cleveland incidents.[8]

Another reversal evident in these examples concerns the construction of lesbians and gay men as the problem. It is homophobia in society that forces many lesbians and gay men to lead secret double lives, to fear physical violence in public, to lose their jobs, or even to commit suicide, and yet the dominant construction is that of a self-inflicted problem. Lesbians and gay men are represented as having produced 'the problem' with which society has to deal and against which the government has to legislate on its behalf.

Finally, there is a reversal within these debates in terms of the construction of the family as a place of happiness, health and safety, rather than as an institution which for many may involve violence, abuse, exploitation, isolation and loneliness. 'Happy Families' are contrasted with lesbians and gay men: 'I feel sorry for homosexuals. I don't know why they are called gay. The one thing they're not, it's gay', claims Jill Knight in the *Birmingham Evening Mail* (10 March 1988). The image of family life as happy, healthy and harmonious is one which saturated the rhetoric of Thatcherism. In this context Section 28 could be read as an attempt to project the *internal* problems of the nuclear family on to *external* demons – lesbians and gay men.

But if 'the family' is indeed such a stable and harmonious institution, why is it necessary continually to reaffirm its authority through legislation such as Section 28? More specifically, why are families represented as under threat within this debate by using lesbians and gay men as the deviant other against which to define the norm? One argument is that the conventional family *is* under threat, but from internal, rather than external sources. In fact, some have argued that it is the family which has 'nurtured the seeds of its own destruction'.[9] The lived experience within families is seen to be fraught with ambivalence and contradiction, and thus contrasts sharply with the *image* of the family circulating in this culture. The inequalities and forms of exploitation within families produce dissatisfaction amongst women, who, for a whole variety of reasons, are becoming increasingly visible as they are more able to seek alternatives. Recent social trends figures show that divorce rates, the number of illegitimate children and the number of single-parent households in Britain are all rising (Walby, 1990, pp. 83–4). In addition, the extent of violence and sexual abuse within families has led many to agree with the feminist challenge to the myth of the family as a 'haven in a heartless world'.

However, given the centrality of the family to much Thatcherite rhetoric, in relation to education, consumerism, notions of nationhood and British respectability, and in terms of providing the pivotal link between the nation and the individual, the family needed to be maintained as a legitimate and successful institution. In this context, initiatives such as Section 28 could be seen as rather desperate attempts to preserve and help sustain the institution of the family in the face of its gradual collapse brought about by its own internal contradictions.

The terms of resistance

Despite the success of the supporters of Section 28 in establishing particular constructions of lesbians and gays as the threat to innocent and respectable family life in Britain, there were arguments against the legislation which achieved some visibility in the public debate. Three challenges to Section 28 surfaced repeatedly in the parliamentary debate and media representations covering this issue. These must also be considered part of the discursive field in which Section 28 can be understood. These arguments are particularly interesting indications of the kinds of commonsense frameworks and idioms through which sexuality in general, and lesbianism and homosexuality in particular, are popularly understood. Despite their limitations from a feminist perspective, it is important to take them seriously and evaluate their effectiveness in opposition to Section 28.

The 'born that way' argument

One of the most convincing challenges to legislating against the promotion of homosexuality was the 'born that way' argument. This draws on pathological models of sexuality which posit sexual identity as fixed in a person's biological make-up and therefore as unchangeable. This model of sexuality as an immutable biological fact, rather than as a form of identity which is constructed by social institutions and beliefs, has sustained a high degree of legitimacy despite being discredited by a wide variety of sources. None the less, this argument proved one of the most forceful commentaries on the illogic and absurdity of the proposed legislation. Claire Rayner, for example, joined together with other agony aunts from various publications, and produced a powerful challenge to Section 28 on these grounds:

> Permit me to offer the authors of the clause some information culled from an extensive study of published literature and a wide acquaintance with facts gathered from the work I have been doing for over 30 years with distressed and anxious people. That might be the basis for a little clear thinking. Firstly, homosexuality can't be 'promoted', using that word to mean encouraged or sold, which is its commonest meaning these days. *Homosexuality is like the colour of your skin or your eyes; an inborn part of you that cannot be altered.* You can't persuade people to be homosexual any more than you can persuade white people to become black. (*Birmingham Daily News*, 3 February 1988; emphasis added).

This argument was not only represented in the popular press but was also put forward by the gay press, demonstrating the weight of the biological model of sexuality within gay subcultures. In a letter to *The Independent*, the editors of the gay newspaper the *Pink Paper* state that

> like those who seek to 'promote' ignorance and prejudice, you have fallen into the trap of assuming that sexuality of whatever kind can somehow be taught. Genuine sexuality can be repressed, but false sexuality cannot be taught – as many thousands who have grown up lesbian or gay in spite of overwhelming odds would attest. Surely heterosexuality is not so fragile that it can be destroyed by the merest hint of any alternative. (*The Independent*, 12 January 1988).

This rejection of the possibility of imposing sexual identities on people if it is against their genuine feelings is based on a biologically essentialist model of sexuality which holds a continuing appeal within lesbian and gay communities. It is also a particularly effective model of sexuality with which to oppose a Bill banning the promotion of homosexuality, since it undermines the basic premiss of the legislation.

The problem with this argument, however, is that while it may have been an effective counter to the proposed legislation, it contains many conservative and untenable assumptions about the biological and fixed nature of sexuality. As I shall discuss later, feminists, amongst others, have argued for the importance of the view that sexuality is socially constructed and therefore transformable. The argument that sexuality is firmly rooted in biology or is inborn has been seen by feminists as a dangerous justification of patriarchal forms of sexuality, resulting in a pessimistic acceptance of male domination, female passivity and heterosexual 'normality'.

The 'Oscar Wilde' argument

The second argument against Section 28 to gain legitimacy, and around which a powerful and visible campaign was built, was the demand for freedom of artistic expression which was seen as under threat from the new law. This position saw 'great works' of art, literature and the theatre threatened by the possible banning of public funding to events and institutions seen to 'promote homosexuality'. Both works which related to homosexuality, such as Marlowe's *Edward II* or Shakespeare's sonnets, and those produced by well-known homosexuals, such as Oscar Wilde or David Hockney, were cited in these debates. Many argued that works of such 'greatness' should not disappear from our culture, simply because their producers were homosexual men.

The arts lobby, as it became known, led by well-known artists, actors and playwrights, provided a strong focus for the campaign against the proposed legislation. The public proclamation of the homosexuality of many famous people was part of a general attempt to demonstrate the existence of homosexuality within respected British institutions, thus challenging the notion that homosexuality is either something contemptible, or something which can be easily suppressed. Ian McKellen's public and proud declaration of his homosexuality, for example, was part of a more general realization of the importance of 'coming out' amongst those who had previously never seen the necessity of taking such a step. This challenge to Section 28 was strategically effective in that it highlighted the number of contributors to British culture who were already highly valued within conventional establishments, such as the theatre or literature, and who were thus difficult to dismiss and discredit. Since many of these 'masters' were a fundamental component of British cultural education, their exclusion from publicly funded bodies such as schools, museums and art galleries became increasingly unrealistic as more and more of them were associated with homosexuality.

This challenge to Section 28 also raises particular problems from a feminist perspective. The arguments about the freedom of artistic expression reduced the political problem of lesbian and gay oppression to liberal notions of individualism. In addition, many of these arguments reinforced the bourgeois and patriarchal values of 'the Great Masters of Art and Literature' which inform dominant notions of the universality and excellence of British high culture, a model which feminists and other radical critics have previously attempted to challenge. Notably, the 'great works' tended to be works by men and not by women. A final problem with the arts lobby challenge lay in its focus on the greatness of the art, rather than the question of sexual oppression. In other words, the argument seemed to be saying that if the work of art conformed sufficiently to the values of dominant culture, then the deviant sexuality of its author need not prevent the general public from appreciating its contribution to society.

The libertarian argument

The final argument, which achieved less success, but nevertheless recurred frequently within these debates, was that sexuality is a private matter and not something which the government has any right to legislate about. The notion that the government has 'no business in the bedroom' situates sexuality firmly within the discourse of individualism. This approach is associated particularly with MPs of the new right, such as Teresa Gorman. This challenge has been particularly useful in opposition to legislation such as the Alton Bill, where it was effective precisely because it undermined the right of men in Parliament to pass laws which regulate and control women's bodies. Similarly, the radical individualism of this position has, ironically, offered the space to defend the rights of lesbians and gays. This 'compatibility' might be accounted for by the use of discourses of individualism within lesbian and gay politics, as well as within right-wing initiatives.

However, the argument that sexuality should not be legislated about since it is a private matter contradicts the basic feminist claim that the 'personal is political' in an area where this slogan has perhaps had the greatest impact. Feminists have argued that issues such as sexual violence, sexual practice and sexual pleasure are all political questions relating to the power structures and ideologies in a patriarchal society. The radical libertarian argument also denies the extent to which the personal has already been constructed within particular power relations: opposing a piece of legislation will not keep politics out of the bedroom, they argue, since sexuality has already been subject to regulation within patriarchal relations.

These, then, were the main arguments against Section 28 which achieved any attention or credibility within the public debate. They provided important challenges to the dominant discourses discussed earlier and they offered a focus for the mobilization of resistance. They were formulated, in part, as a defensive strategy in relation to the terms of the proposed law. To deconstruct these three arguments and challenge the limits of the discourses of biological essentialism, artistic individualism and radical libertarianism, respectively, is not to deny the importance of their effectiveness. Indeed, the appeal of these particular arguments in the late 1980s must be taken into account (Franklin and Stacey, 1988), and strategic use of whatever arguments win public support was argued for by many campaigners against the Section. However, as outlined above, each of these challenges to Section 28 raises problems for a feminist analysis of sexual politics. In addition to the problems with these terms of opposition, what was particularly striking in the public context was the virtual absence of feminist challenges to Section 28. Where, then, was the feminist analysis of Section 28, and how should we explain the apparent invisibility of feminist challenges in this public debate?

Feminism: the structuring absence or the lingering presence?

Despite the fact that many feminists were heavily involved in the 'Stop the Clause' campaigns around the country, feminist perspectives on sexuality were not amongst the challenges to the introduction of Section 28 visible in the public debate. Given the impact of feminism on discourses of sexuality in the 1970s and 1980s, the absence of feminist challenges in the public debate about Section 28 was particularly disturbing.

Many feminists saw Section 28 as part of a broader attack on the achievements of feminism, as well as other movements of this period, such as gay liberation. Together with other legislation introduced during the Thatcher governments, Section 28 was considered a direct backlash against feminism. It was criticized for being a repressive piece of legislation which returned us to pre-feminist, if not to Victorian, values. While there is no doubt that Section 28 was a repressive piece of legislation in the context of the ground gained by feminism and gay liberation in the 1970s and 1980s, it did not, however, represent a straightforward backlash in the sense of returning to a pre-feminist sexual discourse, nor simply a return to 'Victorian values', as the popular refrain so frequently suggested. This understanding of Section 28 ignored the complexities of social change and the newness of many of the Thatcherite discourses.

Rather than a simple backlash against feminism, returning us to pre-existing discourses of sexuality, I want to argue that the public debate about Section 28 demonstrated a more complex reworking of and response to feminist sexual politics. Given the relative success of feminism in challenging many patriarchal discourses of sexuality, in conjunction with other influences Section 28 can be seen as an attempt to displace this impact of feminism. Thus, although feminist arguments remained marginal to the public debate, it can be argued that Section 28 was an implicit response to many feminist ideas and practices which had gained a certain foothold.

In this section, I shall investigate this argument through an analysis of

Section 28 in the context of particular feminist challenges to dominant discourses of sexuality. The first relevant feminist argument is that sexuality is not an individual and private question, but rather a social and political one, and the regulation of women's sexuality an important form of social and political control. Indeed, feminists have criticized the construction of sexuality as private and individual precisely because this has been seen to facilitate the maintenance of patriarchal power relations; once women began to recognize certain commonalities in the construction of their sexualities, the political nature of the power relations involved became clearer. This challenge to the notion that sexuality is a private, personal and individual matter had widespread impact, exposing previously hidden forms of violence and domination in sexual relationships, and encouraging women to redefine their sexuality on new terms.

The politicization of sexuality is an important factor in relation to Section 28. Clearly, all legislation about sexuality demonstrates its political status. But the formulation and discussion of Section 28 demonstrated an implicit acknowledgement of the political dimensions of sexuality in a very specific way. While it can be seen as the latest in a whole series of repressive laws concerning homosexuality throughout British history, Section 28 produced a distinctive conflict, fought on the terrain of the politics of sexuality established to a great extent by the feminist movement. Unlike previous legislation, which was fought on the basis of individual sexual acts being indecent or immoral, Section 28 was fought on the basis of the social reproduction of sexual identities and life styles through state institutions. The role of social and political life in reproducing sexual identities was central to arguments about whether particular publicly funded bodies could or could not, should or should not, promote homosexuality. Section 28 was fought over on a very different terrain from the battles over the kinds of sexual acts which are permissible in which private and public spaces which had characterized previous debates over regulatory legislation. It was thus, in part, a response to the redefinition of sexuality as politicized, an intervention which had been established, to a large extent, by feminists.

This leads directly to the second feminist argument about sexuality relevant to the debate surrounding Section 28, namely, that sexuality is socially, rather than biologically, determined. Feminists have consistently challenged the notion that sexuality is a biological phenomenon and that patriarchal definitions of female and male sexuality can be justified as natural. The denaturalization of sexuality has led feminists to criticize men's sexual domination and women's sexual passivity previously justified by references to so-called biological needs or dispositions. That sexuality has been socially constructed within patriarchal relations, then, has been a central assertion within feminist analyses of sexuality.

The perceived need for a law to prohibit the 'promotion of homosexuality' carries with it an assumption that homosexuality can indeed be promoted, and furthermore that we cannot rely on nature or biology to maintain the dominance or stability of heterosexuality. If homosexuality were the inborn defect of a few unfortunates, how could it be promoted in schools and by other publicly funded bodies? Similarly, if heterosexuality were a natural set of relations based in biology, rather than a compulsory social institution (Rich, 1980b), why would it be necessary to ensure its status and its continuity through legal regulation? The discussion around Section 28 offered a clear recognition that sexuality is socially produced; indeed, it identified social sites, such as education, the media and leisure activities, as playing a role in the reproduction of sexual identities.

Significantly, the argument that sexuality is socially constructed within dominant relations of patriarchal society was important for feminists in terms of offering the possibility for change: if sexuality is socially constructed then it can be socially reconstructed in new and different ways.[10] Social constructionism appealed to feminists, on the one hand, because it offered a way to undermine existing patriarchal discourses which attempted to justify and naturalize male sexual domination, and on the other hand, because it established the possibility that sexual identities were not fixed and immutable, but rather, to some extent, changeable. Rethinking sexual identities within these terms opened up the possibility of lesbian relationships for many women who had previously considered their heterosexuality a permanent fixture. As a result many women found the opportunity to explore their lesbianism within the women's movement, some for the first time, others in a more open way than their previous closeted existences had allowed.

Furthermore, one of the outcomes of many feminists' arguments and activities was indeed the promotion of lesbianism, in that feminists sought to challenge the heterosexism and homophobia which has meant that many women have denied their desires, hidden their feelings and lived in fear of discovery and exposure. Lesbian and gay liberation movements had similar aims in their reclamation and affirmation of previously despised sexual identities as something positive. Challenging the fears and anxieties produced within such a deeply homophobic society, gay liberation proclaimed the political importance of 'coming out' as lesbian or gay in an open and public way to families, colleagues and friends. One of the aims of this strategy was to encourage other people to overcome their internalized homophobia, which prevents so many from acting on or admitting to homosexual desires, and to feel confident in their chosen sexual identities. Thus the promotion of homosexuality was very much a part of feminist and gay liberationist strategies and was considered a political necessity in the context of a society which at best tolerated and at worst attempted to silence, suppress and indeed eradicate homosexuality and lesbian existence. Ironically, the introduction of Section 28 provided an example of homophobic legislation and foregrounded an enormous amount of anti-lesbian and gay feeling which demonstrated precisely why the promotion of homosexuality is necessary and politically important.

A further argument within feminist challenges to dominant sexual discourses relevant to the debates surrounding Section 28 was connected to the concept of choice and self-determination. Within the women's movement generally there has been an emphasis on self-empowerment and transformation as part of a broader collective political struggle. The process of women reclaiming control over various aspects of their lives was a powerful form of resistance to male domination. Sexuality, just as reproduction, household organizations, or personal appearance, was seen as something which had been organized by others and for others and the feminist challenge to this often took the form of reclaiming the right to control and define one's own body and sexuality.

The reconstruction of female sexuality within a framework of choice, however, is problematic for several reasons. Not only does this notion belong to a liberal tradition which assumes that people are individuals who can be free agents and exercise conscious rational control over their lives, uninhibited by broader structures and institutions, but it ignores the complexities in the formation of sexual identities. For example, many feminists have pointed to the unconscious as well as conscious forces at work in the development of desire and pleasure[11] which undermine any simple notion of sexual identity as something one can choose.

Nevertheless, problematic as this discourse of choice might be, it has been a powerful one within feminist politics for many years and has opened up the space for many women to rethink their sexual identities. The resulting flexibility of sexual identities has produced a destabilizing threat to patriarchal definitions of sexuality as fixed and confinable within heterosexual monogamy. The feminist challenge that sexuality should be a question of individual choice and can indeed be something within one's own personal control undermined the dominant notion that heterosexuality is an inevitable component of everyone's life and validated the exploration of alternative life styles. In the light of this shifting discourse about choice, Section 28 can be seen as an attempt to prevent further legitimation of alternatives to heterosexuality, marriage and the nuclear family which feminism had clearly begun to establish.

A final example of feminist challenges to patriarchal discourses relevant to understanding the Section 28 debate regards the family. Feminists have criticized the patriarchal nuclear family as one of the key sites of the reproduction of gender inequality (Millett, 1970; Barrett and McIntosh, 1982). The image of the family as a happy and healthy place, for example, had been undermined by feminist arguments demonstrating the extent of violence, exploitation and insecurity for women and children in many family situations (Kelly, 1988; Hamner and Maynard, 1987; Hamner,

Radford and Stanko, 1989). The reaffirmation of the family through legislation such as Section 28 could be seen as an attempt to displace these criticisms of the patriarchal nuclear family and re-establish its legitimacy and authority. The explicit reference to lesbian and gay households as 'pretended families' suggests not only the widespread anxiety from conservatives about the general breakdown of conventional family arrangements, but also the extent of the perceived threat posed by lesbian and gay households. Previously easily dismissible as the deviant minority, lesbians and gays are now perceived as posing such a threat to the family that legislation is necessary to prevent this take-over. To use a term such as 'pretended family' which includes lesbians and gays within the remit of the family, be it only a poor imitation, suggests a certain shift in the previously stable boundary between acceptable and unacceptable life styles. Furthermore, the problems existing within heterosexuality and marriage are thus displaced on to the threat from the outside posed by the 'pretended families' of lesbians and gay men.

Feminist challenges to dominant discourses of sexuality, then, have posed a substantial threat to patriarchal definitions of heterosexuality and the family. To some extent, feminists succeeded in politicizing sexuality, the domestic sphere and other areas previously deemed private and outside politics. The struggle to define the terms in the Section 28 debate can be seen as an attempt by the right to reclaim that territory from feminism. Sexuality has been increasingly defined as a social and political issue. If this were not the case then legislation such as Section 28 would have been defeated on the basis of its being an intrusion into people's private lives; this challenge, however, won relatively little support. Furthermore, Section 28 represented an implicit acknowledgement of the idea that homosexuality can indeed be promoted, and that sexual identities are not fixed and immutable, and thus presumably that sexuality is not secured in biology but is open to social influence.

Thus, although feminist discourses were noticeably absent from the public debate about Section 28, they can be seen in fact to provide the context for this particular piece of legislation. Indeed, the hysterical anxieties about sexuality which became increasingly evident during the passage of this legislation must be considered in the light of the successful impact of feminism and gay liberation on the redefinition of sexuality in the 1970s and 1980s. The introduction of Section 28, then, can be read as a sign of the impact of these movements and indeed of the instability of the patriarchal discourses of sexuality.

Initiatives from the right, such as Section 28, then, do not simply represent a return to social values of the 1950s or indeed the Victorian era, as the notion of a backlash against feminism, gay liberation and left politics suggests. Instead, it is important to understand the debate about Section 28 in the context of the contested meanings of sexuality. While it is crucial to recognize the explicit attacks on these political influences of the 1970s, it is equally important to highlight the complexities of the operations of power in relation to discourses of sexuality. What I have emphasized above is the extent to which Section 28 reworked existing feminist discourses of sexuality, rather than representing a complete departure from them. Section 28 was publicly debated on the terrain of sexuality partly established by feminism, where sexuality is recognized as political, socially produced and regulated, and changeable or open to influence.

Clause and effects

[D]iscourses are not once and for all subservient to power or raised up against it, any more than silences are. We must make allowance for the complex and unstable process whereby discourse can be both an instrument of and an effect of power, but also a hindrance, a stumbling block, a point of resistance and a starting point for an opposing strategy. (Foucault, 1978, pp. 100–1).

The introduction of Section 28 aimed to prevent further validation of lesbian and gay sexuality within publicly funded institutions. Its initiators clearly hoped to fuel existing homophobia in society and to quash any lingering notions of the acceptability of homosexuality and lesbianism. They hoped that, with a bit of encouragement, lesbians and gays would crawl back into the closet from whence they came and become suitably invisible once again.

However, as the above quotation suggests, discourses do not only regulate sexuality, they also produce opposing strategies. The actual effects of Section 28 could not have been more different from its initiators' intentions. The huge national and international challenge to Section 28 surprised even the most optimistic members of lesbian and gay communities. Throughout the country there were 'Stop the Clause' campaigns including demonstrations, benefits, rallies, concerts, meetings, publicity stunts, leafleting and public meetings. Never had there been such a proliferation of lesbian and gay activities simultaneously and nationwide. Unusually, it became very easy for people to find out about widely publicized lesbian and gay activities and social events. Ironically, lesbian and gay subcultural social activities thrived and romances were started in the context of the banning of 'the promotion of homosexuality'.

If invisibility is one of the specificities of lesbian and gay oppression, then Section 28 provided an excellent context for reversing this problem. Not for many years had there been such media coverage of homosexuality and lesbianism. Years of campaigning by feminist and gay activists had not produced the extent of public, high-profile debate about the rights and wrongs of homosexuality and lesbianism evident during the passage of this legislation. This increased visibility was not restricted to the time of the struggle over Section 28, but has continued to some extent within mainstream broadcasting. The television series *Out On Tuesday* (produced by Abseil Productions, a name derived from the lesbian campaigners against Section 28 who abseiled into the House of Lords during its final reading) was the first lesbian and gay weekly magazine programme in Britain. The recent screening of an adaptation of Jeanette Winterson's novel *Oranges Are Not The Only Fruit* at prime time on BBC 2, as well as programmes such as *Sticky Moments* and the inclusion of Simon Fanshawe, a gay comedian well known for his cabaret acts on sexual politics, in the BBC programme *That's Life*, have added to the increasing visibility of lesbians and gays on television.

As well as greater visibility in the media there was a consolidation, rather than the intended disintegration, of lesbian and gay communities and identities. The consolidation of sexual identities may seem problematic, naive or simply passé in these postmodern times, yet the continuing importance of establishing the possibility of lesbian and gay sexual expression, in a country where this possibility is still met with fear and loathing, cannot be underestimated. Part of this affirmation of collective lesbian and gay identities was the renewed urgency ascribed to the political significance of 'coming out' of the closet: famous people were encouraged to take a stand and recognize that sexuality was indeed a political, as well as a personal, issue. For example, Ian McKellen and Michael Cashman came out, led marches and were interviewed in the press. Coming out was not only about being visible and being proud, it was a deliberate strategy against Section 28: if enough culturally significant figures claimed a lesbian or gay identity, it would prove increasingly difficult for Section 28 to be implemented in that to withdraw public funding from *everything* which could be positively associated with homosexuality and lesbianism would prove virtually impossible.

The effects of the introduction of Section 28, then, contradicted its aims and produced an inadvertent promotion of homosexuality. Rather than silencing and marginalizing lesbians and gays, the introduction of Section 28 set in motion an unprecedented proliferation of activities which put homosexuality firmly on the agenda in Britain in 1988–9. The terms of the public debate may have been set by the right, but the widespread resistance to the Section and its implications brought about greater visibility, a strengthened lesbian and gay community and a politicized national and international network of lesbian and gay activists.

This understanding of Section 28 moves us away from the idea that power is simply monolithic and repressive. Instead, it emphasizes the ways in which sexual discourses are sites of struggle producing as well as controlling subjects. The regulation of sexuality in Thatcher's Britain cannot be understood purely in terms of repression and control: it has also been a time when the proliferation of sexual discourses has produced new social and sexual identities.[12] Foucault's work on the nineteenth century emphasizes this productive dimension of sexual discourses:

> There is no question that the appearance in nineteenth-century psychiatry, jurisprudence and literature of a whole series of discourses on the species and sub-species of homosexuality, inversion, pederasty, and 'psychic hermaphrodism' made possible a strong advance in the social controls into this area of 'perversity'; but it also made possible the formation of a 'reverse' discourse: homosexuality began to speak in its own behalf, to demand that its legitimacy or 'naturality' be acknowledged, often in the same vocabulary, using the same categories by which it was medically disqualified. (Foucault, 1978, p. 101).

Similarly, the construction of sexuality in Thatcher's Britain must be seen as a constant struggle, where the attempts to control and repress may produce the opposite effects. The challenge to Section 28 and the cultural and political activity which surrounded its opposition took place on an unanticipated scale. Had the initiators of the section had any idea of the extent of the response they would meet, they may have thought twice before proposing a piece of legislation to ban the promotion of homosexuality which achieved just the opposite.

Notes

This chapter is based on a paper, 'Clause and Effects: Clause 28 and Lesbian and Gay Representation', originally presented at a day school at The Watershed in Bristol in June 1988. A later version was presented to the Women's Studies Research Group, University of Lancaster in February 1989. I would like to thank those who commented on those earlier versions. Initially, this chapter was to be written jointly with Sarah Franklin, combining the arguments here with her analysis of other legislation (see Franklin, 1988); thus many of the ideas discussed in this chapter evolved from our joint discussions and I am grateful to her for inspiring and encouraging this piece. I would also like to thank Celia Lury, Sally Hickling and Richard Dyer for their useful comments on earlier drafts of this chapter, and especially Hilary Hinds for her rigorous commentary and enthusiasm throughout.

1 The connection between sexuality and the risk to public health and morality was not new: see, for example, the analysis of the regulation of prostitution in Victorian society (Walkowitz, 1980).
2 For a discussion of the links between Section 28 and other legislative initiatives during the Thatcher governments, see Franklin (1988).
3 Before this piece of legislation passed into law it was known as Clause 28; once on the statute book it became known as Section 28.

4 For an extensive discussion of the publishing practices of Manchester University Press during this period, see the Introduction in Shepherd and Wallis (1989).

5 For a more detailed discussion of the centrality of discourses of familialism to Thatcherism, see the second introduction to this volume.

6 See, for example, recent films such as *Fatal Attraction* (dir. Adrian Lyne, 1988) and *Someone to Watch Over Me* (dir. Ridley Scott, 1988), in which the threat to the nuclear family is of central narrative concern.

7 The murder of a young boy, Stuart Gough, by a gay man produced considerable negative coverage of homosexuality in the media at this time.

8 There were 545 cases of child sexual abuse referred to the county council in Cleveland between January 1987 and March 1988. The number of such referrals produced an unprecedented public controversy about this subject (see Campbell, 1988).

9 Richard Dyer discussed the internal contradictions within the nuclear family in relation to Section 28 at a *Marxism Today* conference in Birmingham, 19 March 1988.

10 There is, however, considerable debate between feminists about the possibility of reconstructing sexuality. The socialization model of sexuality assumes a more straightforward process of self-transformation than the psychoanalytic model (see Wilson (1981) and Rose (1986)).

11 For a discussion of the significance of the unconscious to a feminist analysis of sexuality, see Mitchell and Rose (1982), Rose (1986) and Sayers (1986).

12 Janet Newman has developed this argument in relation to sex education in Britain in the 1980s (Newman, 1990).

Bibliography

Althusser, L. (1969), *For Marx* (London: Allen Lane).

Alton, D. (1988), 'It is a modest measure', *Sunday Times*, 17 January, p. 65.

Amos, V., and Parmar, P. (1981), 'Resistances and responses: the experiences of black girls in Britain', in A. McRobbie and T. McCabe (eds), *Feminism for Girls: An Adventure* (London: Routledge & Kegan Paul), pp. 129–48.

Appleyard, C. (1988), 'Emma – the story Susan Hill thought she would never tell', *Daily Mirror*, 22 January, p. 5.

Arditti, R., Duelli-Klein, R., and Minden, S. (eds) (1984), *Test-Tube Women: What Future for Motherhood?* (London: Pandora).

Atkins, S. (1986), 'The Sex Discrimination Act, 1975: the end of a decade', *Feminist Review*, no. 24, pp. 57–71.

Balio, T. (ed.) (1976), *The American Film Industry* (Wisconsin: University of Wisconsin Press).

Banham, R. (1981), 'The throw-away aesthetic', in R. Banham (ed.) *Design By Choice* (London: Academy), pp. 89–94.

Barrett, M. (1980), *Women's Oppression Today: Problems in Marxist Feminist Analysis* (London: Verso).

Barrett, M. (1987), 'The concept of difference', *Feminist Review*, no. 26, pp. 29–42.

Barrett, M., and McIntosh, M. (1982), *The Anti-Social Family* (London: Verso).

Bart, P. (1989), 'Rape as a paradigm of sexism in society – victimization and its discontents', in R. D. Klein and D. L. Steinberg (eds), *Radical Voices* (Oxford: Pergamon), pp. 55–69.

Barthes, R. (1975), *S/Z* (London: Cape).

Batsleer, J. (1981), 'Pulp in the pink', *Spare Rib*, no. 109, pp. 52–5.

Baudrillard, J. (1983), *Simulations* (New York: Semiotext(e)).

Baudrillard, J. (1988), *Selected Writings*, (Cambridge: Polity Press).

Beard, W., and Nathanielsz, P. W. (eds) (1976), *Fetal Physiology and Medicine* (London: W. B. Saunders).

Beechey, V. (1987), *Unequal Work* (London: Verso).

Beechey, V. (1988), 'Rethinking the definition of work: gender and work', in J. Jenson, E. Hagen, and C. Reddy (eds), *Feminization of the Labour Force: Paradoxes and Promises* (Cambridge: Polity Press).

Benston, M. (1970), 'The political economy of housework', in Tanner (ed.), *Voices from Women's Liberation* (New York: Signet).

Betterton, R. (ed.) (1987), *Looking On: Images of Femininity in the Visual Arts and Media* (London and New York: Pandora).

Bilgorrie, L. *et al.* (1984), 'Writing with women', *Feminist Review*, no. 18, pp. 11–21.

Biskind, P. (1983), *Seeing is Believing* (London: Pluto Press).

Bland, L., Brunsdon, C., Hobson, D., and Winship, J. (1978), 'Women inside and outside the relations of production', in Women's Studies Group, Birmingham CCCS, *Women Take Issue* (London: Hutchinson).

Bleier, R. (1984), *Science and Gender: A Critique of Biology and Its Theories on Women* (New York: Pergamon).

Bleier, R. (ed.) (1986), *Feminist Approaches to Science* (New York: Pergamon).

Blumer, H. (1973), 'Fashion: from class differentiation to collective selection', in D. Midgeley and G. Willis (eds), *Fashion Marketing* (London: Allen & Unwin).

Boston Women's Health Collective (eds) (1973), *Our Bodies Ourselves* (New York: Simon & Schuster).

Bourdieu, P. (1980), 'The aristocracy of culture', *Media, Culture and Society*, vol. 2, no. 3, pp. 225–57.

Bowlby, R. (1985), *Just Looking: Consumer Culture in Dreiser, Gissing and Zola* (London: Methuen).

Bradford, B. T. (1980), *A Woman of Substance* (London: Granada).

Brennan, T. (ed.) (1989), *Between Feminism and Psychoanalysis* (London: Routledge).

Bridgewood, C. (1986), 'Family romances: the contemporary family saga', in J. Radford (ed.), *The Progress of Romance: The Politics of Popular Fiction* (London: Routledge & Kegan Paul), pp. 167–93.

British Medical Association (1988), *Philosophy and Practice of Medical Ethics* (London: British Medical Association).

Brod, H. (ed.) (1987), *The Making of Masculinities: The New Men's Studies* (Winchester, Mass.: Allen & Unwin).

Brown, P., and Jordanova, L. (1981), 'Oppressive dichotomies: the nature/culture debate', in Cambridge Women's Studies Group (eds), *Women in Society: Interdisciplinary Essays* (London: Virago), pp. 224–42.

Bruegel, I. (1989), 'Sex and race in the labour market', *Feminist Review*, no. 32. pp. 49–69.

Brunsdon, C. (1978), '"It is well known that by nature women are inclined to be rather personal"', in Women's Studies Group, Birmingham CCCS (eds), *Women Take Issue: Aspects of Women's Subordination* (London: Hutchinson).

Brunsdon, C. (1981), '*Crossroads*: notes on soap opera', *Screen*, vol. 22, no. 4, pp. 32–7.

Brunt, R. (1987), 'Thatcher uses her woman's touch', *Marxism Today*, June, pp. 22–4.

Bryan, B., Dadzie, S., and Scafe, S. (1985), *The Heart of the Race: Black Women's Lives in Britain* (London: Virago).

Bryce, L. (1989), *The Influential Woman: How to Achieve Success without Losing your Femininity* (London: Piatkus).

Budge, B. (1988), 'Joan Collins and the wilder side of women', in L. Gamman and M. Marshment (eds) *The Female Gaze* (London: The Women's Press), pp. 102–11.

Bunch, C. (1988), 'Making common cause: diversity and coalitions', in C. McEwan and S. O'Sullivan (eds) *Out The Other Side: Contemporary Lesbian Writing* (London: Virago), pp. 287–95.

Cameron, J. (1989), *The Competitive Woman: A Survival Guide For The Woman Who Aims to be Boss* (London: Mercury).

Campbell, A. (1984), *The Girls in the Gang* (Oxford: Basil Blackwell).

Campbell, B. (1984), *Wigan Pier Revisited: Poverty and Politics in the Eighties* (London: Virago).

Campbell, B. (1987), *The Iron Ladies: Why Do Women Vote Tory?* (London: Virago).

Campbell, B. (1988), *Unofficial Secrets: Child Sexual Abuse – the Cleveland Case* (London: Virago).

Canaan, J. E. (1990), 'Individualizing Americans: the making of American suburban middle class teenagers', PhD thesis, Department of Anthropology, University of Chicago.

Canaan, J. E., and Griffin, C. (forthcoming), 'Men's studies: part of the problem or part of the solution?', in J. Hearn and D. Morgan (eds) *Men, Masculinity and Social Theory* (London: Unwin Hyman).

Carby, H. (1982), 'White women listen! Black feminism and the boundaries of sisterhood', in CCCS, University of Birmingham, *The Empire Strikes Back: Race and Racism in 70s Britain* (London: Hutchinson), pp. 212–36.

Carter, E. (1984), 'Alice in consumer wonderland', in A. McRobbie and M. Nava (eds), *Gender and Generation* (Basingstoke: Macmillan), pp. 185–214.

Centre for Contemporary and Cultural Studies (CCCS), University of Birmingham (1982a), *Making Histories: Studies in History – Writing and Politics* (London: Hutchinson).

Centre for Contemporary and Cultural Studies (CCCS), University of Birmingham (1982b), *The Empire Strikes Back: Race and Racism in 70s Britain* (London: Hutchinson).

Chaney, D. (1983), 'The department store as a cultural form', *Theory, Culture and Society*, vol. 1, no. 3, pp. 21–31.

Chodorow, N. (1978), *The Reproduction of Mothering* (Berkeley: University of California Press).

Clarke, G. (1982), 'Defending ski-jumpers: a critique of theories of youth subcultures', stencilled paper no. 72, Centre for Contemporary and Cultural Studies, University of Birmingham.

Clarke, J., and Critcher, C. (1985), *The Devil Makes Work: Leisure in Capitalist Britain* (London: Macmillan).

Clarke, L. (1989), 'Abortion: a rights issue?', in R. Lee and D. Morgan (eds), *Birthrights: Law and Ethics at the Beginnings of Life* (London: Routledge), pp. 155–71.

Cliff, M. (1983), *Claiming an Identity They Taught Us To Despise* (Watertown, Mass.: Persephone Press).

Cockburn, C. (1983), *Brothers: Male Dominance and Technological Change* (London: Pluto Press).

Cockburn, C. (1985), *Machinery of Dominance: Women, Men and Technical Know-how* (London: Pluto Press).

Cohen, S. (1978), 'Breaking out, smashing up and the social context of aspiration', in B. Krisberg and J. Austin (eds), *The Children of Ishmael* (Palo Alto, Calif.: Mayfield), pp. 257–79.

Cole, J. B. (ed.) (1986), *All American Women: Lines that Divide, Ties that Bind* (New York: Macmillan).

Coleman, W. (1977), *Biology in the Nineteenth Century: Problems of Form, Function and Transformation* (Cambridge: Cambridge University Press).

Conran, S. (1975), *Superwoman* (London: Sedgwick & Jackson).

Corea, G. (1985), *The Mother-Machine: Reproductive Technologies from Artificial Insemination to Artificial Wombs* (New York: Harper & Row).

Corea, G., et al. (1985), *Man-Made Women: How New Reproductive Technologies Affect Women* (London: Hutchinson).

Corner, G.W. (1945), *Ourselves Unborn: An Embryologist's Essay on Man* (3rd printing) (London: Oxford University Press).

Corrigan, P. (1976), 'Doing nothing', in S. Hall and T. Jefferson (eds), *Resistance*

Through Rituals: Youth Subcultures in Postwar Britain (London: Hutchinson), pp. 103–5.

Coward, R. (1980), '"This novel changes lives": are women's novels feminist novels?', *Feminist Review*, no. 5, pp. 53–65.

Coward, R. (1984), *Female Desire: Women's Sexuality Today* (London: Paladin).

Coward, R., and WAVAW (1987), 'What is pornography? Two opposing feminist viewpoints' in R. Betterton (ed.), *Looking On: Images of Femininity in the Visual Arts and Media* (London and New York: Pandora).

Cowie, E. (1978), 'Woman as sign', *m/f*, no. 1, pp. 49–63.

Cowie, E. *et al.* (1981), 'Representation vs. communication', in Feminist Anthology Collective (ed.), *No Turning Back: Writings from the Women's Liberation Movement, 1975–80* (London: The Women's Press), pp. 238–46.

Coyle, A. (1983), *Redundant Women* (London: The Women's Press).

Coyle, A. (1985), 'Going private: the implications of privatisation for women's work', *Feminist Review*, no. 21, pp. 5–25.

Coyle, A. (1988), 'Continuity and change: women in paid work', in A. Coyle and L. Skinner (eds), *Women and Work: Positive Action for Change* (London: Macmillan), pp. 1–12.

Coyle, A. (1989), 'The limits of change', *Public Administration*, vol. 67, pp. 39–50.

Crowe, C. (1990), 'Whose mind over whose matter? Women, *in vitro* fertilisation and the development of scientific knowledge', in M. McNeil *et al.* (eds), *The New Reproductive Technologies* (London: Macmillan).

Curti, L. (1988), 'Genre and gender', *Cultural Studies*, vol. 2, no. 2, pp. 152–67.

Daily Mail (1988), 'Abortion baby took three hours to die', 8 February, p. 2.

Daily Mirror (1988), 'My abortion agony: MP Rosie reveals heartache over her unborn babies', 23 January, p. 1.

Daily Mirror (1988), 'Aborted baby's "3 hours to die"', 8 February, p. 5.

Daly, M. (1978), *Gyn/Ecology: The Metaethics of Radical Feminism* (London: The Women's Press).

Daly, M. (1984), *Pure Lust: Elemental Feminist Philosophy* (London: The Women's Press).

David, M. (1983), 'The New Right in the USA and Britain: a new anti-feminist moral economy', *Critical Social Policy*, vol. 2, no. 3, pp. 21–45.

Davidoff, H., and Hall, C. (1987), *Family Fortunes: Men and Women of the English Middle Class, 1780–1850* (London: Hutchinson).

Delaney, C. (1986), 'The meaning of paternity and the virgin birth debate', *Man*, vol. 21, pp. 494–513.

De Lauretis, T. (1989), *Technologies of Gender: Essays on Theory, Film and Fiction* (London: Macmillan).

De Man, P. (1979), *Allegories of Reading: Figural Language in Rousseau, Nietzsche, Rilke, and Proust* (New Haven, Conn.: Yale University Press).

Delmar, R. (1986), 'What is feminism?' in J. Mitchell and A. Oakley (eds), *What is Feminism?: A Re-examination* (New York: Pantheon).

Delphy, C. (1977), *The Main Enemy* (London: Women's Research and Resources Centre).

Delphy, C. (1984), *Close to Home: A Materialist Analysis of Women's Oppression* (London: Hutchinson).

Department of Health and Social Security (DHSS) (1987), *Human Fertilisation and Embryology: A Framework for Legislation* (London: HMSO), Cm. 259.

Derrida, J. (1981), *Writing and Difference* (London: Routledge & Kegan Paul).

Dex, S. (1985), *The Sexual Division of Work: Conceptual Revolutions in the Social Sciences* (Brighton: Wheatsheaf).

Diamond, I., and Quinby, L. (eds) (1988), *Feminism and Foucault: Reflections on Resistance* (Boston, Mass.: Northeastern University Press).

Doane, M. A. (1982), 'Film and the masquerade: theorizing the female spectator', *Screen*, vol. 23, nos 3 and 4, pp. 75–87.

Donnison, J. (1988), *Midwives and Medical Men: A History of the Struggle for the Control of Childbirth* (London: Historical Publications).

Dworkin, A. (1981), *Pornography: Men Possessing Women* (London: The Women's Press).

Dworkin, A. (1983), *Right Wing Women: The Politics of Domesticated Females* (London: The Women's Press).

Dyer, R. (1981), 'Stars as signs', in T. Bennett (ed.), *Popular Film and Television* (Milton Keynes: Open University Press).

Easlea, B. (1980), *Witch-hunting, Magic and the New Philosophy: An Introduction to Debates of the Scientific Revolution 1450–1750* (Brighton: Harvester).

Easlea, B. (1981), *Science and Sexual Oppression: Patriarchy's Confrontation with Women and Nature* (London: Weidenfeld & Nicolson).

Eccleshall, R. (1984), 'Ideologies in modern Britain', in R. Eccleshall *et al.*, *Political Ideologies* (London: Hutchinson), pp. 7–35.

Eccleshall, R., Geoghegan, V., Jay, R., and Wilford, R. (eds) (1984), *Political Ideologies* (London: Hutchinson).

Ehrenreich, B., and English, D. (1979), *For Her Own Good: 150 Years of the Experts' Advice to Women* (London: Pluto Press).

Elsaesser, T. (1973), 'Tales of sound and fury: observations on the family melodrama', *Monogram*, no. 4, pp. 2–15.

Elshtain, J. B. (1987), *Women and War* (New York: Basic Books).

EMAP (1988a), *Report and Accounts* (Leicester: EMAP).

EMAP (1988b), *Segment by Segment* (Leicester: EMAP).

Epstein, L. F. (1988), *Deceptive Distinctions: Sex, Gender and the Social Order* (New Haven, Conn.: Yale University Press).

Fausto-Sterling, A. (1985), *Myths of Gender: Biological Theories About Women and Men* (New York: Basic Books).

Ferguson, A. (1989), *Blood at the Root: Motherhood, Sexuality and Male Dominance* (London: Pandora).

Ferriman, A. (1988), 'Children's cancer ward shuts down', *Observer*, 24 January, p. 1.

Feuer, J. (1984), 'Melodrama, serial form and television today', *Screen*, vol. 25, no. 1, pp. 2–15.

Finch, J., and Groves, D. (eds) (1983), *A Labour of Love: Women, Work and Caring* (London: Routledge & Kegan Paul).

Findlay, A. L. R. (1984), *Reproduction and the Fetus* (London: Edward Arnold).

Firestone, S. (1974), *The Dialectic of Sex: The Case for Feminist Revolution* (New York: Morrow).

Fiske, J. (1987), *Television Culture* (London: Methuen).

Fitzsimons, C. (1988), 'Abortion case father raises campus baby', *Observer*, 17 January, p. 1.

Ford, N. M. (1988), *When Did I Begin? Conception of the Human Individual in History, Philosophy and Science* (Cambridge: Cambridge University Press).

Forty, A. (1986), *Objects of Desire: Design and Society 1750–1980* (London: Thames & Hudson).

Foucault, M. (1978), *The History of Sexuality, Vol. 1: An Introduction*, trans. R. Hurley (Harmondsworth: Penguin).

Franklin, S. (1988), 'Happy Families in Thatcherite Britain: an analysis of recent legislative initiatives', *Streit* (Journal of Feminist Perspectives on the Law, FRG), vol. 6, no. 3, pp. 109–13.

Franklin, S., and McNeil, M. (1988), 'Reproductive futures: recent literature and current feminist debates on reproductive technologies', *Feminist Studies*, vol. 14, no. 3, pp. 545–61.

Franklin, S., and Stacey, J. (1988), 'Dyketactics for difficult times: a review of the "Homosexuality, Which Homosexuality?" conference', *Feminist Review*, no. 29, pp. 136–51.

Fraser, N., and Nicholson, L. (1988), 'Social criticism without philosophy: an encounter between feminism and postmodernism', *Theory, Culture and Society*, vol. 5, nos 2 and 3, pp. 373–94.

Frith, S. (1983), *Sound Effects: The Sociology of Rock* (London: Constable).

Gaines, J. (1982), 'In the service of ideology: how Betty Grable's legs won the war', *Film Reader*, no. 5, pp. 47–59.

Gallagher, J. (1985), 'Fetal personhood and women's policy', in V. Sapiro (ed.), *Women, Biology and Public Policy* (Beverly Hills: Sage).

Gallop, J. (1982), *Feminism and Psychoanalysis: The Daughter's Seduction* (London: Macmillan).

Gamble, A. (1988), *The Free Economy and the Strong State: The Politics of Thatcherism* (London: Macmillan).

Game, A., and Pringle, R. (1984), *Gender at Work* (London: Pluto Press).

Gamman, L., and Marshment, M. (eds) (1988), *The Female Gaze: Women as Viewers of Popular Culture* (London: The Women's Press).

Gardener, A. (1986), 'Fashion retailing 1946–86', in P. Sparke (ed.), *Did Britain Make It?* (London: The Design Council).

Gardiner, J. (1983), 'Women, recession and the Tories', in S. Hall and M. Jacques (eds), *The Politics of Thatcherism* (London: Lawrence & Wishart), pp. 188–206.

Gilroy, P. (1987), *There Ain't No Black in the Union Jack: The Cultural Politics of Race and Nation* (London: Hutchinson).

Givanni, J. (1988), *Black and Asian Film/Video List* (London: British Film Institute of Education).

Gledhill, C. (ed.) (1987), *Home is Where the Heart Is: Studies in Melodrama and the Woman's Film* (London: British Film Institute).

Glomery, D. (1982), 'The movies become big business: public big business: public theatres and the chain-store strategy', in G. Kindem (ed.), *The American Movie Industry* (Carbondale and Edwardsville, Ill.: Southern Illinois University Press), pp. 104–16.

Goldstone, N. (1988), *Trading Up: One Woman's Story of Survival in the Wall Street Jungle* (London: Pan).

Gordon, D. (1976), 'Why the movie majors are major', in T. Balio (ed.), *The American Film Industry* (Wisconsin: University of Wisconsin Press).

Gordon, P. (1988), 'What is the new racism?', in P. Gordon and F. King (eds), *New Right New Racism* (Nottingham: Searchlight), pp. 1–12.

Gorman, T. (1988), 'Why I believe that David Alton must be stopped', *Daily Mail*, 20 January, p. 12.

Grice, E. (1988a), 'Look special: the abortion debate', *Sunday Times*, 17 January, p. 65.

Grice, E. (1988b), 'A matter of conscience', *Sunday Times*, 24 January, p. 131.

Griffin, C. (1985), *Typical Girls? Young Women from School to the Job Market* (London: Routledge & Kegan Paul).

Griffin, S. (1978), *Woman and Nature: The Roaring Inside Her* (New York: Harper & Row).

Guardian, The (1988), 'Mr Alton's Big Day' (leader column), 21 January, p. 14.

H.D. (1984), *Her* (London: Virago).

Hall, S. (1979), 'The great moving right show', *Marxism Today*, January.

Hall, S. (1988a), *The Hard Road to Renewal: Thatcherism and the Crisis of the Left* (London: Verso).

Hall, S. (1988b), 'New ethnicities', in *Black Film British Cinema*, Institute of Contemporary Arts Document 7, (London: ICA), pp. 27–30.

Hall, S. *et al.* (eds) (1980), *Culture, Media, Language* (London: Hutchinson).

Hall, S., Jacques, M. (eds) (1983), *The Politics of Thatcherism* (London: Lawrence & Wishart).

Hall, S., and Jefferson, T. (eds) (1976), *Resistance Through Rituals: Youth Subcultures in Postwar Britain* (London: Hutchinson).

Hall, S., Critcher, C., Jefferson, T., Clarke, J., and Roberts, B. (1978), *Policing the Crisis: Mugging, the State and Law and Order* (London: Macmillan).

Hamilton, R., and Barrett M. (eds) (1986), *The Politics of Diversity: Feminism, Marxism and Nationalism* (London: Verso).

Hanmer, J., and Maynard, M. (eds) (1987), *Women, Violence and Social Control* (London: Macmillan).

Hanmer, J., and Saunders, S. (1984), *Well-Founded Fear* (London: Hutchinson).

Hanmer, J., Radford, J., and Stanko, E. (eds) (1989), *Women, Policing and Male Violence* (London: Routledge).

Hansard, House of Commons. Abortion (Amendment) Bill, 22 January 1988. Order for Second Reading. Cols 1227–1296, pp. 631–65.

Haraway, D. (1985), 'A manifesto for cyborgs: science, technology and socialist feminism in the 1980s', *Socialist Review*, no. 80, pp. 65–107.

Haraway, D. (1988a), 'Situated knowledges: the science question in feminism and the privilege of partial perspective', *Feminist Studies*, vol.14, no.3, pp. 575–600.

Haraway, D. (1988b), 'The biopolitics of postmodern bodies: determinations of self in immune system discourse', *differences: a Journal of Feminist Cultural Studies*, vol. 1, no. 1, pp. 3–44.

Haraway, D. (1989), *Primate Visions: Gender, Race and Nature in the World of Modern Science* (London: Routledge).

Harding, S. (1986), *The Science Question in Feminism* (Milton Keynes: Open University Press).

Harris, R. (1989), 'Mrs. T's kitchen cabinet', *Observer*, 27 November, pp. 16, 26.

Hartley, J., Goulden, H., and O'Sullivan, T. (1985), *Making Sense of the Media: Introduction* (London: Comedia).

Haskell, M. (1973), *From Reverence to Rape* (Harmondsworth: Penguin).

Heath, S. (1982), *The Sexual Fix* (London: Macmillan).

Hebdige, D. (1979), *Subculture: The Meaning of Style* (London: Methuen).

Hebdige, D. (1981), 'Towards a cartography of taste', *Block*, no. 4 pp. 39–55.

Hebdige, D. (1987a), 'The impossible object: towards a sociology of the sublime', *New Formations*, no. 1, pp. 47–76.

Hebdige, D. (1987b), 'Digging for Britain: an excavation in seven parts', *The British Edge* (Boston, Mass.: Institute of Contemporary Arts).

Hebdige, D. (1988), *Hiding In The Light: On Images and Things* (London: Routledge).

Hencke, D. (1987), 'Alton faces moral dilemma', *Guardian*, 17 September, p. 6.
Herzog, C., and Gaines, J. (1985), 'Puffed sleeves before teatime: Joan Crawford, Adrian and women audiences', *Wide Angle*, vol. 6, no. 4, pp. 24–33.
Himmelweit, S. (1988), 'More than "A Woman's Right to Choose"?', *Feminist Review*, no. 29, pp. 38–56.
HMSO, (1989), *Human Fertilisation and Embryology Bill* (London: HMSO).
Hodgkinson, N. (1988), 'The brain: cut into controversy', *Sunday Times*, 17 April, p. A20.
Hoggart, R. (1958), *The Uses of Literacy* (Harmondsworth: Penguin).
Holloway, W. (1984), 'Gender difference and the production of subjectivity', in J. Henriques *et al.* (eds) *Changing The Subject* (London: Methuen), pp. 227–43.
hooks, bell (1982), *Ain't I a Woman? Black Women and Feminism* (London: Pluto Press).
hooks, bell (1984), *Feminist Theory: From Margin to Center* (Boston, Mass.: South End Press).
hooks, bell (1989), *Talking Back: Thinking Feminist, Thinking Black* (Boston, Mass.: South End Press).
Howatch, S. (1974), *Cashelmara* (London: Hamish Hamilton).
Hubbard, R., Henifin, M. S., and Fried, B. (eds) (1982), *Biological Woman: The Convenient Myth* (Cambridge, Mass.: Schenkman).
Huettig, M. (1976), 'The motion picture industry today', in T. Balio, *The American Film Industry* (Wisconsin: University of Wisconsin Press), pp. 228–55.
Human Life Educational Aids (1980), 'How you grew before birth' (Bournemouth: Human Life Educational Aids), wallchart distributed by LIFE.
Hustwitt, M. (1984), 'Rocker boy blues: the writing on pop', *Screen*, vol. 25, no. 3, pp. 89–98.
Huyssen, A. (1986), 'Mass culture as woman: modernism's other', in T. Modleski (ed.), *Studies in Entertainment: Critical Approaches to Mass Culture* (Bloomington and Indianapolis: Indiana University Press).

James, S., and Dalla Costa, M. (1973), *The Power of Women and The Subversion of the Community* (Bristol: Falling Wall Press).
Jameson, F. (1984), 'Postmodernism, or the cultural logic of late capitalism', *New Left Review* no. 146, pp. 55–92.
Jay, R. (1984), 'Nationalism', in R. Eccleshall *et al.*, *Political Ideologies* (London: Hutchinson), pp. 185–216.
Jelinek, E. C. (1980), *Women's Autobiography: Essays in Criticism* (Bloomington and Indianapolis: Indiana University Press).
Jelinek, E. C. (1980), 'Women's autobiography and the male tradition', in Jelinek, *op. cit.*, pp. 164–79.
Jessop, B., Bonnett, K., Bromley, S., and Ling, T. (1988), *Thatcherism* (Cambridge: Polity Press).
Johnson, M., and Everitt, B. (1988), *Essential Reproduction* (Oxford: Blackwell Scientific Publications).
Johnson, R. J. (1983), 'What is cultural studies anyway?', stencilled paper no. 74, Centre for Contemporary Cultural Studies, University of Birmingham.
Johnstone, C. (1975), 'Feminist politics and film history', *Screen*, vol. 16, no. 3, pp. 115–24.
Jordanova, L. (1980), 'Natural facts: a historical perspective on science and sexuality' in C. MacCormack and M. Strathern (eds), *Nature, Culture and Gender* (Cambridge: Cambridge University Press).
Jorgensen, D. (ed.) (1985), *Concepts of Conception: Procreation Ideologies in Papua New Guinea, Mankind*, vol. 14, (entire volume).

Joshi, H. (1987), *The Cash Opportunity Costs of Childbearing* (London: Centre for Economic Policy Research).
Juhasz, S. (1980), 'Towards a theory of form in a feminist autobiography', in E.C. Jelinek, *Women's Autobiography* (Bloomington and Indianapolis: Indiana University Press), pp. 163–97.

Kaplan, C. (1985), 'The feminist politics of literary theory', in L. Appignanesi (ed.) *Ideas From France: The Legacy of French Theory* (London: ICA), pp. 13–16.
Kaplan, E. A. (ed.) (1980), *Women in Film Noir* (London: British Film Institute).
Kaplan, E. A. (1980), 'The place of women in Fritz Lang's *Blue Gardenia*' in Kaplan, *Women in Film Noir* (London: BFI), pp. 83–90.
Kaplan, E. A. (1987), *Rocking Around The Clock: Music, Television, Postmodernism and Consumer Culture* (New York: Methuen).
Kaufman, M. (1987), 'The construction of masculinity and the triad of male violence', in M. Kaufman (ed.), *Beyond Patriarchy* (Toronto: Oxford University Press), pp. 1–29.
Keller, E. F. (1983), *A Feeling for the Organism: The Life and Work of Barbara McClintock* (San Francisco: W. H. Freeman).
Keller, E. F. (1985), *Reflections on Science and Gender* (New Haven, Conn.: Yale University Press).
Kelly, L. (1988), *Surviving Sexual Violence* (Cambridge: Polity Press).
Kennedy, M. (1988), 'Life and time of an Act', *Guardian*, 27 October, p. 24.
Kimmel, M. (ed.) (1987), *Changing Men: New Directions in Research on Men and Masculinity* (New York: Sage).
Kitzinger, S., and Lennart, N. (1986), *Being Born* (London: Dorling Kindersley).
Klein, R. (ed.) (1988), *Infertility: Women Speak Out About Their Experiences of Reproductive Medicine* (London: Pandora).
Koch, G. (1985), 'Why do women go to men's films?', in G. Ecker (ed.), *Feminist Aesthetics* (London: The Women's Press).
Koonz, C. (1987), *Mothers in the Fatherland: Women, the Family and Nazi Politics* (London: Methuen).
Kricorian, N. (1984), 'Kaleidoscope: Roland Barthes and Monique Wittig', unpublished paper.
Kroker, A., and Cook, D. (1986), *The Postmodern Scene: Excremental Culture and Hyper-Aesthetics* (New York: St Martin's Press).
Kuhn, A. (1982), *Women's Pictures: Feminism and Cinema* (London: Routledge & Kegan Paul).
Kuhn, A. (1984), 'Women's genres', *Screen*, vol. 25, no. 1, pp. 18–28.

Lacqueur, T. (1986), 'Orgasm, generation and the politics of reproductive biology', *representations* (special issue: 'Sexuality and the Social Body in the Nineteenth Century'), vol. 14, pp. 1–41.
Layton-Henry, Z., and Rich, P. B. (1986), *Race, Government and Politics in Britain* (London: Macmillan).
Leacock, E. (1981), *Myths of Male Dominance: Collected Articles on Women Cross-Culturally* (New York: Monthly Review Press).
Lerner, G. (1986), *The Creation of Patriarchy* (New York: Oxford University Press).
Lewis, P. (1978), *The Fifties* (London: Book Club Associates).
LIFE (n.d.), 'Abortion and Human Rights', pamphlet.
Lister, R. (1987), 'Future insecure: women and income maintenance under a third Tory term', *Feminist Review*, no. 27, pp. 9–17.

Loach, L. (1987), 'Can feminism survive a third term?', *Feminist Review*, no. 27, pp. 24–36.

Lorde, A. (1984), *Sister-Outsider: Essays and Speeches* (Trumansburg, NY: The Crossing Press).

Lorde, A. (1988), *A Burst of Light* (Trumansburg, NY: The Crossing Press).

Lovell, T. (1981), 'Ideology and *Coronation Street*', in R. Dyer (ed.), *Coronation Street* (London: British Film Institute).

Lowe, M., and Hubbard, R. (eds) (1983), *Women's Nature: Rationalizations of Inequality* (New York: Pergamon).

Lugones, M., and Spelman, E. V. (1983), 'Have we got a theory for you? Feminist theory, cultural imperialism and the demand for "The Woman's Voice"', *Women's Studies International Forum*, vol. 6, no. 6, pp. 573–82.

Lyotard, J. (1984), *The Postmodern Condition: A Report on Knowledge* (Minneapolis, Minn.: University of Minnesota Press).

Lyotard, J. (1986), *The Postmodern Condition: A Report on Knowledge*, trans. G. Bennington and B. Massumi, (Manchester: Manchester University Press).

Mac an Ghail, M. (1988), *Young, Gifted and Black* (Milton Keynes: Open University Press).

MacCormack, C. (1980), 'Nature, culture and gender: a critique', in C. MacCormack and M. Strathern (eds), *Nature, Culture and Gender* (Cambridge: Cambridge University Press).

McKie, R. (1988), 'Doctors plan to weed out sick embryos', *Observer*, 24 January, p. 11.

MacKinnon, C. (1979), *The Sexual Harassment of Working Women: A Case of Sex Discrimination* (New Haven, Conn.: Yale University Press).

MacKinnon, C. (1982), 'Feminism, Marxism, method and the state: an agenda for theory', *Signs*, vol. 7, no. 3, pp. 515–44.

Mackinnon, C. (1987), *Feminism Unmodified: Discourses of Life and Law* (Cambridge, Mass.: Harvard University Press).

MacKinnon, C. (1989), *Toward a Feminist Theory of the State*, (Cambridge, Mass.: Harvard University Press).

McLaren, A. (1984), *Reproductive Rituals* (London: Methuen).

McLaren, A. (1987), 'Can we diagnose genetic disease in pre-embryos?', *New Scientist*, 10 December.

McRobbie, A. (1980), 'Settling accounts with sub-cultures: a feminist critique', *Screen Education*, vol. 34, pp. 37–49.

McRobbie, A. (1981), 'Just like a *Jackie* story', in McRobbie and McCabe, op.cit., pp. 113–28.

McRobbie, A. (1987), 'Postmodernism and popular culture', *Annali*, vol. 28, no. 3, pp. 63–78.

McRobbie, A., and Garber, J. (1974), 'Girls and subcultures: an exploration', in S. Hall and T. Jefferson (eds) *Resistance Through Rituals: Youth Subcultures in Postwar Britain* (London: Hutchinson), pp. 209–22.

McRobbie, A., and Nava, M. (eds) (1984), *Gender and Generation* (London: Macmillan).

Marks, E., and de Courtivron, I. (eds) (1981), *New French Feminisms* (Brighton: Harvester).

Martin, E., (1987), *The Woman in the Body: A Cultural Analysis of Reproduction* (Boston, Mass.: Beacon Press).

Mason, K. (1989), 'Abortion and the law', in S. Mclean (ed.), *Legal Issues in Human Reproduction* (London: Gower), pp. 45–79.

Masterman, L. (1985), *Teaching the Media* (London: Comedia).

Mercer, K. (1988), 'Recoding narratives of race and nation', in *Black Film British Cinema*, Institute of Contemporary Arts Document 7 (London: ICA), pp. 4–14.

Merchant, C. (1980), *The Death of Nature: Women, Ecology and the Scientific Revolution* (New York: Harper & Row).

Merck, M. (1987), 'Pornography', in R. Betterton (ed.), *Looking On: Images of Femininity in the Visual Arts and Media* (London and New York: Pandora), pp. 151–61.

Mies, M. (1986), *Patriarchy and Accumulation on a World Scale: Women in the International Division of Labour* (London: Zed Books).

Mies, M. (1988), 'From the individual to the dividual: in the supermarket of "reproductive alternatives"', *Reproductive and Genetic Engineering*, vol. 1, no. 3, pp. 225–38.

Miller, W. (1978), 'Lower class culture as generating milieu of gang delinquency', in B. Krisberg and J. Austin (eds), *The Children of Ishmael* (Palo Alto, Calif.: Mayfield), pp. 139–55

Millett, K. (1969), *Sexual Politics* (London: Virago).

Millett, K. (1974), *Flying* (New York: Knopf).

Millett, K. (1977), *Sita*, (London: Virago).

Mitchell, J. (1975), *Psychoanalysis and Feminism* (Harmondsworth: Penguin).

Mitchell, J., and Oakley, A. (1986), *What is Feminism?* (Oxford: Basil Blackwell).

Mitchell, J., and Rose, J. (eds) (1982), *Feminine Sexuality: Jacques Lacan and the Ecole Freudienne* (London: Macmillan).

Mitter, S. (1986), *Common Fate, Common Bond: Women in the Global Economy* (London: Pluto Press).

Modleski, T. (1982), *Loving with a Vengeance: Mass-produced Fantasies for Women* (London: Methuen).

Modleski, T. (1986), 'Femininity as mas(s)querade: a feminist approach to mass culture', in C. McCabe (ed.), *High Theory/Low Culture* (Manchester: Manchester University Press).

Moi, T. (1985), *Sexual/Textual Politics* (London: Methuen).

Moore, D. (1989), *When a Woman Means Business* (London: Pavilion Books).

Moore, S. (1988), 'Getting a bit of the other: the pimps of postmodernism', in R. Chapman *et al.* (eds), *Male Order: Unwrapping Masculinity* (London: Lawrence & Wishart), pp. 165–92.

Moraga, C., and Anzaldua, G. (eds) (1981), *This Bridge Called My Back: Writings by Radical Women of Colour* (New York: Kitchen Table Press).

Mount, F. (1982), *The Subversive Family: An Alternative History of Love and Marriage* (London: Jonathan Cape).

Mulvey, L. (1975), 'Visual pleasure and narrative cinema', *Screen*, vol. 3, no. 16, pp. 6–18.

Mulvey, L. (1989), *Visual and Other Pleasures* (London: Macmillan).

Myers, K. (1986), *Understains: The Sense and Seduction of Advertising* (London: Comedia).

Neale, S. (1986), 'Melodrama and tears', *Screen*, vol. 27, no. 6, pp. 6–22.

Newman, J. (1990), 'Sex education and social change: perspectives on the 1960s', PhD thesis, Open University.

Nicholson, L. J. (ed.) (1990), *Feminism/Postmodernism* (London: Routledge).

Nilsson, L. (1965), 'The drama of life before birth', *Life*, 30 April (reprinted by *Time* Inc., 1980).

Nowell-Smith, G. (1977), 'Minelli and melodrama', *Screen*, vol. 18, no. 2, pp. 113–18.

Oakley, A. (1984), *The Captured Womb: A History of the Medical Care of Pregnant Women* (Oxford: Basil Blackwell).
O'Brien, M. (1981), *The Politics of Reproduction* (London: Routledge & Kegan Paul).
Ortner, S. (1974), 'Is female to male as nature is to culture?' in M. Rosaldo and L. Lamphere (eds), *Woman, Culture and Society* (Stanford, Calif.: Stanford University Press).
Ortner, B., and Whitehead, H. (eds) (1981), *Sexual Meanings: The Cultural Construction of Gender and Sexuality* (Cambridge: Cambridge University Press).
Orwell, G. (1937), *The Road to Wigan Pier* (London: Gollancz).
Owusu, K. (1986), *The Struggle for Black Arts in Britain* (London: Comedia).
Owusu, K. (ed.) (1988), *Storms of the Heart* (London: Camden Press).

Panorama (1987), 'Harming or Helping? – The New Abortion Bill', 16 December, BBC 1.
Parker, R., and Pollock, G. (1981), *Old Mistresses: Women, Art and Ideology* (London: Routledge & Kegan Paul).
Parmar, P. (1982), 'Gender, race and class: Asian women in resistance', in University of Birmingham, CCCS, *The Empire Strikes Back: Race and Racism in '70s Britain* (London: Hutchinson), pp. 236–76.
Parmar, P. (1988), 'Emergence 2', in K. Owusu (ed.) *Storms of the Heart* (London: Camden Press), pp.47–54.
Partington, A. (1989), 'The designer housewife in the 1950s', in J. Attfield and P. Kirkham (eds), *A View from the Interior: Feminism, Women and Design* (London: The Women's Press), pp. 206–14.
Pateman, C. (1988), *The Sexual Contract* (Cambridge: Polity Press).
Petchesky, R. (1984), *Abortion and Woman's Choice: The State, Sexuality and Reproductive Freedom* (Boston, Mass.: Northeastern University Press).
Petchesky, R. (1987), 'Foetal images: the power of visual culture in the politics of reproduction', in M. Stanworth (ed.), *Reproductive Technologies: Gender, Motherhood and Medicine* (Cambridge: Polity Press).
Phillips, A., and Taylor, B. (1980), 'Sex and skill: notes towards a feminist economics', *Feminist Review*, no. 6, pp. 79–83.
Phillips, E. (1987), 'Pushing back the tide: women in the public sector', *Feminist Review*, no. 27, pp. 17–23.
Phillips, M. (1988), 'A matter of life and death, as medical ethics go plunging down the slippery slope', *Guardian*, 22 April, p. 21.
Phizacklea, A. (1983), *One Way Ticket* (London: Routledge & Kegan Paul).
Phizacklea, A. (1988), 'Gender, racism and occupational segregation', in S. Walby (ed.) *Gender Segregation at Work* (Milton Keynes: Open University Press), pp. 43–55.
Phizacklea, A., and Miles, R. (1980), *Labour and Racism* (London: Routledge & Kegan Paul).
Pines, J. (1983), 'Editorial', *Art Rage*, no. 3/4, summer.
Polan, B. (1988), 'Handbag and rule', *Guardian*, 29 December, p. 27.
Pollock, G. (1977), 'What's wrong with images of women?' *Screen Education*, no. 24.
Press, A. (1989), 'Class and gender in the hegemonic process', *Media, Culture and Society*, vol. 11, pp. 229–51.

Radford, J. (ed.) (1986), *The Progress of Romance: The Politics of Popular Fiction* (London: Routledge & Kegan Paul).

Radway, J. A. (1987), *Reading the Romance: Women, Patriarchy and Popular Literature* (London: Verso).

Ramazanoglu, C. (1989), *Feminism and the Contradictions of Oppression* (London: Routledge).

Reiter, R. R. (ed.) (1975), *Toward an Anthropology of Women* (New York: Monthly Review Press).

Rich, A. (1977), *Of Woman Born: Motherhood as Experience and Institution* (London: Virago).

Rich, A. (1980a), *On Lies, Secrets and Silence: Selected Prose, 1966–1978* (London: Virago).

Rich, A. (1980b), 'Compulsory heterosexuality and lesbian existence', *Signs: Journal of Women in Culture and Society*, vol. 5, no. 4, pp. 631–60.

Ricoeur, P. (1981), *Hermeneutics and the Human Sciences*, ed. and trans. by J. B. Thompson (Cambridge: Cambridge University Press).

Ricoeur, P. (1986), *Lectures on Ideology and Utopia* (New York: Columbia University Press).

Riley, D. (1988), *Am I That Name?: Feminism and the Category of 'Women' in History* (London: Macmillan).

Roelofs, S. (1988), 'Clause 28', *Spare Rib*, no. 189, pp. 38–41.

Rosaldo, M. Z. (1974), 'Woman, culture and society: a theoretical overview', in M. Rosaldo and L. Lamphere (eds) *Woman, Culture and Society* (Stanford, Calif.: Stanford University Press), pp. 17–43.

Rose, J. (1983), 'Femininity and its discontents', *Feminist Review*, no. 14, pp. 5–22.

Rose, J. (1986), *Sexuality in the Field of Vision* (London: Verso).

Rose, J. (1988), 'Margaret Thatcher and Ruth Ellis', *New Formations*, no. 6, pp. 3–31.

Rose, H., and Rose, S. (1976), *The Radicalisation of Science: Ideology of/in the Natural Sciences* (London: Macmillan).

Rosenfeld, A. (1980), 'Pushed out into a hostile world', (postscript to Nilsson, op. cit., p. 18).

Rosenfelt, D., and Stacey, J. (1987), 'Second thoughts on the second wave', *Feminist Review*, no. 27, pp. 77–96.

Rothman, B. K. (1986), *The Tentative Pregnancy: Prenatal Diagnosis and the Future of Motherhood* (New York: Viking).

Rothman, B. K. (1989), *Recreating Motherhood: Ideology and Technology in a Patriarchal Society* (New York: W. W. Norton).

Rowbotham, S. (1981), 'The trouble with "Patriarchy"', in Feminist Anthropology Collective (ed.), *No Turning Back: Writings From the Women's Liberation Movement, 1975–1980* (London: The Women's Press), pp. 72–9.

Russell, D. E. H. (1984), *Rape in Marriage* (New York: Macmillan).

Sayers, J. (1986), *Sexual Contradictions: Psychology, Psychoanalysis, and Feminism* (London: Tavistock Publications).

Savage, W. (1987), 'Why there must be no erosion of the liberal abortion laws', *The Independent*, 28 October, p. 18.

Savage, W. (1988), 'We need more permissive laws', *Sunday Times*, 17 January, p. C5.

Schneider, D. (1978), *American Kinship: A Cultural Account* (Englewood Cliffs, NJ: Prentice-Hall).

Schwartz-Cowan, R. (1976), 'The "Industrial Revolution" in the home: household technology and social change in the 20th century', *Technology and Culture*, no. 19, pp. 1–23.

Scott, H. (1984), *Working Your Way To The Bottom: The Feminisation of Poverty* (London: Pandora).

Seabrook, J. (1985), *Landscapes of Poverty* (Oxford: Basil Blackwell).

Seabrook, J. (1988), *The Leisure Society* (Oxford: Basil Blackwell).

Seccombe, W. (1974), 'The housewife and her labour under capitalism', *New Left Review*, no. 83, pp. 3–24.

Segal, L. (1983), 'The heat in the kitchen', in S. Hall and M. Jacques (eds), *The Politics of Thatcherism* (London: Lawrence & Wishart), pp. 207–15.

Segal, L. (1988), 'Look back in anger: men in the fifties', in R. Chapman and J. Rutherford (eds) *Male Order: Unwrapping Masculinity* (London: Lawrence & Wishart), pp. 68–97.

Seidler, V. (1988), 'Fear and intimacy', in A. Metcalfe and M. Humphries (eds), *The Sexuality of Men* (London: Pluto Press), pp.150–80.

Sharratt, B. (1982), *Reading Relations: Structures of Literary Production: A Dialectical Text/Book* (Brighton: Harvester).

Shepherd, S., and Wallis, M. (eds) (1989), *Coming On Strong: Gay Politics and Culture* (London: Unwin Hyman).

Silverman, K. (1986), 'Fragments of a fashionable discourse', in T. Modleski (ed.), *Studies in Entertainment: Critical Approaches to Mass Culture* (Bloomington, Ind.: Indiana University Press), pp. 139–52.

Simms, M. (1974), 'Gynaecologists, contraception and abortion – from Birkett to Lane', *World Medicine*, 23 October, pp. 49–59.

Slater, D. (1987), 'On the wings of the sign: commodity, culture and social practice', *Media, Culture and Society*, vol. 9, pp. 457–80.

Smart, C. (1989), *Feminism and the Power of the Law* (London: Routledge).

Snell, M. W. *et al.* (1981), *Equal Pay and Opportunities*, Department of Employment Paper no. 21. (London: DoE).

Snow, C. P. (1959), *The Two Cultures and the Scientific Revolution* (Cambridge: Cambridge University Press).

Spallone, P. (1989), *Beyond Conception: The New Politics of Reproduction* (London: Macmillan).

Spallone, P., and Steinberg, D. L. (eds) (1987), *Made to Order: The Myth of Reproductive and Genetic Progress* (New York: Pergamon).

Spelman, E. V. (1990), *Inessential Woman: Problems of Exclusion in Feminist Thought* (London: The Women's Press).

Spivak, G. C. (1985), 'Strategies of vigilance', *Block*, no. 5, pp. 5–9.

Spivak, G. C. (1987), *In Other Worlds: Essays in Cultural Politics* (London: Methuen).

Stanworth, M. (ed.) (1987), *Reproductive Technologies: Gender, Motherhood and Medicine* (Cambridge: Polity Press).

Steedman, C. (1986), *Landscape For A Good Woman: A Story of Two Lives* (London: Virago).

Strathern, M. (1980), 'No Nature, No Culture', in C. MacCormack and M. Strathern (eds), *Nature, Culture and Gender* (Cambridge: Cambridge University Press).

ten Tusscher, T. (1986), 'Patriarchy, capitalism and the New Right', in J. Evans *et al.*, *Feminism and Political Theory* (London: Sage).

Thatcher, M. (1986), Speech to the Conservative Women's Conference, London, 4 June.

Thompson, E. P. (1961a & b), 'Review of Raymond Williams' *The Long Revolution*', *New Left Review*, May–June and July–August, pp. 24–33, 34–9.
Thompson, E. P. (1965), 'The peculiarities of the English', *Socialist Register*, pp. 311–62.
Thompson, E. P. (1968), *The Making of the English Working Class* (Harmondsworth: Penguin).
Thompson, E. P. (1978), *The Poverty of Theory and Other Essays* (London: Merlin Press).
Thorne, B., and Yalom, B. (eds) (1982), *Rethinking the Family: Some Feminist Questions* (New York: Longman).
Tolson, A. (1977), *The Limits of Masculinity* (London: Tavistock Publications).
Travis, A., and Kennedy, M. (1988), 'Alton to curb abortion wins with a 45 majority', *The Independent*, 23 January, p. 3.
Travis, A., and Veitch, A. (1987), 'Alton advised to compromise on Bill', *Guardian*, 26 September, p. 4.

Walby, S. (1986), *Patriarchy at Work: Patriarchal and Capitalist Relations in Employment* (Oxford: Polity Press).
Walby, S. (ed.), (1988), *Gender Segregation at Work* (Milton Keynes: Open University Press).
Walby, S. (1990), *Theorizing Patriarchy* (Oxford: Basil Blackwell).
Walker, A. (1984), *In Search Of Our Mother's Gardens: Womanist Prose* (London: The Women's Press).
Walkowitz, J. (1980), *Prostitution and Victorian Society: Women, Class and the State* (Cambridge: Cambridge University Press).
Ward, T. (1989), *Working the System: 12 Ways for Women to Achieve Career Breakthroughs* (London: Columbus Books).
Warner, M. (1985), *Monuments and Maidens: The Allegory of the Female Form* (London: Picador).
Warner, M. (1988), 'Viragos and Amazons', review of Antonia Fraser, *Boadicea's Chariot: The Warrior Queens*, *Observer*, 16 October, p. 43.
Watney, S. (1987), *Policing Desire: Pornography, Aids and the Media* (Minneapolis, Minn: University of Minnesota Press).
Weedon, C. (1987), *Feminist Practice and Poststructuralist Theory* (Oxford: Basil Blackwell).
Weeks, J. (1981), *Sex, Politics and Society: The Regulation of Sexuality Since 1880* (London: Longman).
Weeks, J. (1985), *Sexuality and Its Discontents: Meanings, Myths and Modern Sexualities* (London: Routledge & Kegan Paul).
Weiner, A. (1978), 'The reproductive model in Trobriand society', *Mankind*, vol. 11, no. 3, pp. 175–86.
Weiner, A. (1979), 'Trobriand kinship from another view: the reproductive power of women and men', *Man*, vol. 14, pp. 328–48.
Weiner, A. (1985), 'Oedipus and the ancestors', *American Ethnologist*, vol. 12, pp. 758–62.
Westwood, S., and Bhachu, P. (eds) (1988), *Enterprising Women: Ethnicity, Economy and Gender Relations* (London: Routledge & Kegan Paul).
Whitney, S. (1982), 'Antitrust policies and the motion picture industry', in G. Kinderm (ed.), *The American Movie Industry* (Carbondale and Edwardsville, Ill.: Southern Illinois University Press), pp. 161–204.
Williams, G. (1983), *Textbook of Criminal Law* (London: Stevens).
Williams, R. (1961), *Culture and Society, 1780–1950* (Harmondsworth: Penguin).

Williams, R. (1965), *The Long Revolution* (Harmondsworth: Penguin).
Williams, R. (1973), *The Country and the City* (London: Chatto & Windus).
Williams, R. (1974), *Television: Technology and Cultural Form* (London: Fontana).
Williams, R. (1976), *Keywords: A Vocabulary of Culture and Society* (London: Fontana).
Williams, R. (1980), *Problems in Materialism and Culture: Selected Essays* (London: New Left Review).
Williams, R. (1981), *Politics and Letters: Interviews with New Left Review* (London: Verso).
Williams, R. (1983), 'Culture and technology' in his *Towards 2000* (London: Chatto & Windus).
Williamson, J. (1978), *Decoding Advertisements: Ideology and Meaning in Advertising* (London: Marion Boyars).
Williamson, J. (1986a), *Consuming Passions: The Dynamics of Popular Culture* (London: Marion Boyars).
Williamson, J. (1986b), 'Woman is an island', in T. Modleski (ed.), *Studies in Entertainment* (Bloomington and Indianapolis: Indiana University Press), pp. 99–118.
Willis, P. E. (1977), *Learning to Labour: How Working Class Kids Get Working Class Jobs* (Aldershot: Saxon House).
Willis, P. E. (1978), *Profane Culture* (London: Routledge & Kegan Paul).
Willis, P., *et al.* (1988), *The Youth Review: Social Conditions of Young People in Wolverhampton* (Aldershot: Avebury).
Wilson, E. (1977), *Women and the Welfare State* (London: Methuen).
Wilson, E. (1981), 'Psychoanalysis: psychic law and order', *Feminist Review* no. 8, pp. 63–78.
Wilson, E. (1982), *Mirror Writing* (London: Virago).
Wilson, E. (1987), 'Thatcherism and women: after seven years', in R. Miliband *et al.* (eds), *Socialist Register*, pp. 199–235.
Winship, J. (1983), 'Femininity and women's magazines, in *The Changing Experiences of Women*, Unit 6, U221 (Milton Keynes: Open University Press).
Winship, J. (1987), *Inside Women's Magazines* (London: Pandora).
Winston, E. (1980), 'The autobiographer and her readers: from apology to affirmation', in E. C. Jelinek, *Women's Autobiography: Essays in Criticism* (Indiana: Indiana University Press) pp. 84–98.
Wittig, M. (1988), 'On the social contract', in D. Altman *et al.*, *Homosexuality, Which Homosexuality?* (London: Gay Men's Press).
Wolf, C. (1982), *The Quest for Christa T* (London: Virago).
Women's Studies Group, Birmingham Centre for Contemporary Cultural Studies (1978), *Women Take Issue* (London: Hutchinson).
Woodside, M. (1988), 'The woman abortionist', *National Abortion Campaign Newsletter*, vol. 5, pp. 3–4.
Worpole, K. (1983), *Dockers and Detectives* (London: Verso).
Worpole, K. (1984), *Reading by Numbers* (London: Comedia).

Zachery, R. B. (n.d.), 'The humanity of the fetus', LIFE pamphlet.

Notes on contributors

Joyce E. Canaan, who recently received a PhD from the Anthropology Department at the University of Chicago, is now a sociology lecturer at Birmingham Polytechnic. She spent two years as a visiting fellow at the Department of Cultural Studies, then worked with Paul Willis on a research project on youth. Her research interests include: gender and sexuality, youth, the ethnographic method, social and culture theories.

Sarah Franklin teaches women's studies and cultural anthropology at Lancaster University. Her research addresses the changing cultural construction of reproduction in the context of new reproductive technologies.

Wendy Fyfe did an MA at the Department of Cultural Studies in 1987/88. She is continuing to research the issue of abortion, focusing particularly on its socio-psychological dimensions.

Celia Lury was a member of the Women's Thesis Writing Group from 1984 while she was researching and lecturing at Wolverhampton Polytechnic. She now teaches women's studies and media/cultural studies in the Sociology Department at Lancaster University.

Maureen McNeil is lecturer at the Cultural Studies Department, University of Birmingham. Her publications include *Under the Banner of Science: Erasmus Darwin and His Age* (Manchester University Press, 1987) and, as editor, *Gender Expertise* (Free Association Books, 1987). Her current research and teaching interests revolve around gender relations, knowledge, work, science and technology, and popular culture.

Janet Newman works for the Women and Work Programme at Coventry Polytechnic. Her PhD thesis was completed with the support of the Women's Thesis Writers Group linked to the Department of Cultural Studies, University of Birmingham.

Angela Partington has studied at CCCS/Department of Cultural Studies since 1981, and completed her PhD (on working class femininity and consumerism) in 1990. She lectures in cultural studies on Art and Design degree courses at Bristol Polytechnic and Bath College of Higher Education. She has published a number of articles about the relationship between women and visual culture.

Helen Pleasance was an MA student at the Department of Cultural Studies 1987–88. Her article in this collection is based on the research undertaken for her MA dissertation. She is currently contemplating a career in teaching and further research on women and office work, and the singing careers of Tammy Wynette, Dolly Parton and Dusty Springfield.

Tess Randles while studying for her BA and MA degrees at the Department of Cultural Studies has taken a particular interest in women's politics. Tess's thesis takes up at length the subject of her chapter in this book. She is currently working at the Media Development Agency in Birmingham, and plans to move to Europe within the next few years.

Evelyn Reid has worked as a lecturer for Wolverhampton Polytechnic, the University of London and the Open University. She is particularly interested in women's issues, media and race, and has researched and published on those subjects. She is also a journalist.

Jackie Stacey teaches women's studies and media/cultural studies in the Department of Sociology, Lancaster University. She is also currently completing doctoral research on Hollywood stars and British women audiences in the 1940s and 1950s at the Department of Cultural Studies, Birmingham University. She has published articles in *Screen*, *Feminist Review* and elsewhere on feminism, film theory and sexuality.

Deborah Lynn Steinberg has co-edited, with Patricia Spallone, the book: *Made to Order: The Myth of Reproductive and Genetic Progress*. She holds both a BA and an MA in Women's Studies and is currently engaged in her doctoral research at the Department of Cultural Studies at the University of Birmingham.

Yvonne Tasker studied for an MPhil on feminist thrillers at the Department of Cultural Studies. She now teaches Film Studies at Sheffield Polytechnic and is currently working with Duncan Webster on *Muscular Myths*, a study of masculinity and popular culture.

Estella Tincknell completed the MA course at the Department of Cultural Studies, University of Birmingham, in 1988, having previously worked as a librarian. Since then she has taught media studies course at Birmingham University and Birmingham Polytechnic, and is at present working in Brussels.

Publications from the
Department of Cultural Studies at Birmingham

This book forms part of a new Cultural Studies Birmingham series published by HarperCollins, which replaces the former association between the Centre for Contemporary Cultural Studies and Hutchinson Education. At the same time the department will discontinue the former series of cheap stencilled papers offered by CCCS. Two newly edited volumes, concerned with women's studies and with youth cultures, will review and re-publish work in the series concerned with those areas. The rest of the series will be offered in bound volumes for libraries until the end of 1992, and will then cease to be available. A new series, desktop published and laser printed, will be offered by subscription. Subscribers will normally receive four papers a year, arriving simultaneously in the autumn and suitable for binding. These will represent work in the last year by undergraduates, postgraduates, staff and visiting speakers or associate/attached members. For details on these changes and a pamphlet please write to Publications, Department of Cultural Studies, Social Science Faculty, University of Birmingham, Birmingham B15 2TT (or phone 021–414–6060). Please note that the HarperCollins books should be obtained through booksellers in the usual way, not from the Department. We should be pleased, however, to hear of any difficulties you may have in obtaining publications in either format, and even more pleased to hear any reactions you may have to them.

For information on the following previously published CCCS books, contact the Department of Cultural Studies.

The Crisis of the British State
1890s–1920s
Centre for Contemporary Cultural Studies, University of Birmingham

Working Class Culture
Studies in history and theory
Edited by John Clarke, Chas Critcher and Richard Johnson

Making Histories
Essays on history-writing and politics
Centre for Contemporary Cultural Studies, University of Birmingham

Culture, Media, Language
Working papers in cultural studies 1972–79
Edited by Stuart Hall, Dorothy Hobson, Andrew Lowe and Paul Willis

The Empire Strikes Back
Race and racism in 70s Britain
Centre for Contemporary Cultural Studies, University of Birmingham

Education Limited
Schooling and Training and the New Right Since 1979
Cultural Studies Birmingham

Index

abortion
  as a legal issue 175
  as conflict of rights 185-6
  as murder 177, 178-80
  as violence 152, 171, 209
  Carver case 153-4
  consensual government position 212, 230
  consent 166
  criminalization 162, 170-1, 183-4
  cultural dimensions 148, 175
  Down's syndrome argument 199, 212
  eugenics issues 186-8
  impact of health service cuts 150
  'late' 177-80, 188
  legal 165-6
  legal definition ambiguities 169-70
  newspaper coverage 151, 154, 206-13
  notifications 166
  parameters 215
  post-abortion trauma 158, 181
  punishments 171-3
  social contexts 149, 169
  time limits 176, 218, 230
  victims 180-4
Abortion Act 1967 163, 165-7, 172, 173
abortion clinics 182
abortion legislation 17, 147, 154
  adversarial construction 184-5
  ambiguities 169-73
  early 161-2, 164
  feminist influences 188
  powers to define 164-5, 167-9, 173-4,
    188, 190
  separation concepts 164-5, 167, 169, 171,
    173, 194-5
  social framework 160-1
abortion rights 147-8, 214
  conflicts 185-6, 212-13, 215
  eugenics issues 186-7
  press coverage 211
  technicization 157
academic practice
  collective approaches 2

feminist issues emergence 2
academic theories
  influence of cultural studies 5
  influence on feminist thought 4
active citizenship 18, 38, 42
advertising 73
  banking services 73-5
  images and ideals of difference 71-2
  use of lifestyle fantasy 81
  use of pop music 77
AIDS
  government responses 234
  pathologization of homosexuality 285,
    286, 290
alienation 142
Althusserian framework, cultural analysis 8,
  131
Alton, D. 155, 158, 176, 177, 179, 182,
  185, 208
  use of expertise language 209-10
  use of feminist arguments 181, 182,
    188, 216
Alton Bill 16, 147-8, 150, 188, 215
  construction of conflicts of rights
    185-6
  feminist anti-Alton campaign 216-17
  influences of 218
  media representation 17, 206-13, 218
  moral climate context 157-9
  parliamentary debate influences 175-6
  parliamentary process 17, 175
  proposals 176-7, 208
anthropological analysis
  body images 138
  female subordination 3
  of science and culture 142
anti-nuclear movement 133
Archer, J. 234
arts lobby, against Section 28 294-5
authoritarianism 23, 35, 274
autobiography
  as literary form 97-8
  feminist criticisms of 100-1